The I Ching (Book of Changes)

ALSO AVAILABLE FROM BLOOMSBURY

Doing Philosophy Comparatively, Tim Connolly

The Bloomsbury Research Handbook of Chinese Philosophy and Gender, edited by Ann A. Pang-White

The Bloomsbury Research Handbook of Chinese Philosophy Methodologies, edited by Sor-hoon Tan

The Bloomsbury Research Handbook of Early Chinese Ethics and Political Philosophy, edited by Alexus McLeod

Understanding Asian Philosophy, Alexus McLeod

The I Ching (Book of Changes)

A Critical Translation of the Ancient Text

Geoffrey Redmond

Bloomsbury Academic
An imprint of Bloomsbury Publishing Plc

B L O O M S B U R Y
LONDON · OXFORD · NEW YORK · NEW DELHI · SYDNEY

Bloomsbury Academic

An imprint of Bloomsbury Publishing Plc

50 Bedford Square	1385 Broadway
London	New York
WC1B 3DP	NY 10018
UK	USA

www.bloomsbury.com

BLOOMSBURY and the Diana logo are trademarks of Bloomsbury Publishing Plc

First published 2017

British Library Cataloguing-in-Publication Data

A catalogue record for this book is available from the British Library.

ISBN:	HB:	978-1-4725-0524-8
	PB:	978-1-4725-1413-4
	ePDF:	978-1-4725-1271-0
	ePub:	978-1-4725-0594-1

Library of Congress Cataloging-in-Publication Data

Names: Redmond, Geoffrey, translator, editor.
Title: The I ching (Book of changes) : a critical translation of the ancient text / Geoffrey Redmond.
Other titles: Yi jing. English.
Description: New York : Bloomsbury Academic, [2017] | Includes bibliographical references and index.
Identifiers: LCCN 2016052129| ISBN 9781472505248 (hardback) | ISBN 9781472512710 (epdf)
Subjects: | BISAC: PHILOSOPHY / General.
Classification: LCC PL2478 .D675 2017 | DDC 299.5/1282–dc23 LC record available at https://lccn.loc.gov/2016052129

Cover design: Catherine Wood
Cover image © Illustrations and calligraphy by Mingmei Yip

Typeset by Fakenham Prepress Solutions, Fakenham, Norfolk NR21 8NN
Printed and bound in India

To find out more about our authors and books visit www.bloomsbury.com. Here you will find extracts, author interviews, details of forthcoming events and the option to sign up for our newsletters.

Most of all, for Mingmei, who has always been there for me during my seemingly endless journey to the Far Side, to translate one of the world's most enigmatic books in the world, and also for her profound knowledge of Chinese culture, both literary and popular.

And especially for twenty-five years of love and companionship.

*An excerpt from the oldest (c. 300 BCE) existing Zhouyi manuscript; the
original is on bamboo strips. For the anecdote upon which it is based, see
page 368. (All calligraphy and illustrations by Mingmei Yip)*

CONTENTS

Preface ix
Foreword xiii
Acknowledgments xxi
Quick Start Guide for the Ancient Book of Changes xxv

Part 1   Approaching one of the world's oldest books

1   Why another translation? 3

2   Making sense of divination 15

3   History and the intellectual context 23

4   The unique structure of the *Book of Changes* 43

5   Before the birth of the author: How the *Zhouyi* was composed 55

Part 2   The translation and commentaries

Part 3   The quest for philosophy in the *Zhouyi*

6   What kind of book is the *Book of Changes*? 329

7   Philosophy in the *Zhouyi* 353

Part 4 Practical and theoretical aspects

8   Reading by topic 383

9   How to consult the *I Ching* 385

10 The challenges of translating the *Zhouyi* 393

Bibliography 411
Index 417

PREFACE

Coming of age in the sixties, I was fascinated by what was still referred to as the "mysterious Orient," as well as Western occultism, itself somewhat beholden to Asian religious and philosophical ideas. At the same time I became attracted to Chinese art, particularly Song landscape and Shang and Zhou bronzes. Western interest in China and Japan began far earlier than the sixties. It started with the early Jesuit missionaries and European philosophers, notably Gottfried Leibniz and Voltaire, who knew about China only through the accounts of others.

The sudden rise of interest in Asian religion and philosophy in the sixties was partly due to media popularization, but also because the times were hungry for new ideas, particularly for philosophies that might offer something life-changing. Through my own engagement with Chinese culture this came true for me, though not entirely in ways I expected. I had limited opportunity to pursue this interest during the long years I was engaged in the ordeal of medical training, though I did find time to acquaint myself with the *Dao De Jing* in the translation of Gia-fu Feng and Jane English, a work that helped me through this difficult time. While my approach to science has always been strictly empirical, I found that Asian thought offered me something that Western science did not. It is not that I thought these philosophical traditions were somehow superior to science, rather, they addressed deep human concerns that the hard sciences by their nature cannot. For this reason I have always been impatient with the notion that science and spirituality are incompatible—humanity needs both.

I was particularly fascinated by divination, not as a means of predicting for myself but as an alternative mode of knowledge, one that many still find of value in their lives. Scientism rejects such as not empirically verifiable, but neither is the beauty of a painting verifiable, despite its enhancing life.

Neither my scientific studies nor my graduate study of renaissance and later literature spoke to me about the sort of knowledge-seeking that is the basis of divination and the esoteric more generally. It was the sixties counter-culture that prompted a fresh look at these matters, previously rejected as unworthy of serious attention. I have still not decided if the counter-cultural movement of the sixties was overall good or bad, but it did open minds to previously rejected knowledge. Much of this knowledge was deservedly rejected, but not all.

One result of my awakening to non-scientific ways of thought was fascination with the *Book of Changes*, variously called *I Ching*, *Yijing*, and *Zhouyi*. Impecunious in my student days, I deferred buying the omnipresent Wilhelm-Baynes translation, waiting for it to come out in paperback. It never did, so, once I was a resident, with the modest affluence of an actual salary, I made the financial commitment of buying the iconic hardcover volume. I found it difficult going. During my pre-medicine years as a graduate student of early English language philology I had often been frustrated by texts when I could not determine the provenance of their various components. Like those who avoid Chinese food because they want to know what they are eating, I need to know what I am reading. As presented by Wilhelm-Baynes, the text is best described as a *gemisch*, a Yiddish term used by biochemists to refer to a mixture of known and unknowable ingredients. Interspersed in this masterpiece of book design by the Bollingen Foundation/Princeton University Press are prolix commentaries of diverse authorship and date; and sprinkled within these are bits of the 3,000-year-old Western Zhou text, though mostly unrecognizable as translated. These commentaries intermingle more than 2,000 years of reflection on the classic, including the *Ten Wings*, composed centuries after the early text, and late Qing Confucians' interpretations as passed on to Wilhelm by his traditionally educated Chinese informant. As if these ingredients were not enough, Jungian psychology was then slipped in by the English translator, Cary F. Baynes.

I was at last able to make progress with the *Changes* when in 1997 I acquired the immensely learned version of Richard Rutt, which I began to read on a sunny afternoon in Paris at the Café de Flore, waiting for my wife to return from a meeting with a former Sorbonne classmate. I will not say I understood the *Book of Changes* on that afternoon but I had a sudden realization that with enough study the *Changes* might actually be understood. It took nearly twenty years from that moment to the translation you are now reading, but that is about average for translators of the *Changes*. Early on, I realized that understanding of this text is impossible without knowledge of the Chinese language of its long-ago era. I had long appreciated the aesthetic aspects of the Chinese writing system and so began a gradual study of the ancient written language, starting out by learning to write the name of my wife, Mingmei Yip 葉明媚, and going on from there.

How I have come to view this classic will be apparent in my translation. As I suspect is true for many translators of obscure ancient texts, the deep motivation for undertaking the translation was to be able to understand it for myself—though also to pass on the fruit of this immense labor to anyone similarly intrigued by one of the world's strangest classics.

My guiding principle in translating the *Zhouyi*, the ancient textual layer of the *I Ching*, is this: Since it must have made sense to those who composed it and to its early readers, it should be possible to translate it so that it makes sense to us. I believe that it should be mostly understandable to modern readers who have been given a little background about Western Zhou life. By this I mean that we should understand the meaning of most phrases, though the ways of thought will still often seem strange. In translation I have tried to avoid two extremes: making the text sound contemporary, which most existing translations do, or not adequately resolving obscurities.

There are many different ways to translate the *Book of Changes*; the result depends on one's assumptions about the nature of the work and the best way to present it. Although my translation is quite different from theirs, I need to acknowledge that I could not have translated at all without extensively consulting the work of several distinguished scholars of the *Zhouyi*: Richard Kunst, Richard Rutt, as already mentioned, and Edward Shaughnessy. Other versions I have consulted include the works of James Legge, Wilhelm and Baynes, Gregory Whincup, and Margaret Pearson, among others.

It has been said that literary Chinese is so difficult that you cannot understand it unless you already know what it means. Paradoxical as this may sound, there is some truth to it, because in ancient China the classics were never studied by themselves but always with teachers and written commentaries that transmitted earlier understanding of the works. Since such teachers are no longer among us, I have provided line-by-line commentaries to explain the ancient text as best I understand it.

Geoffrey Redmond
雷文德
New York City
January 2017

FOREWORD

This new translation of the *I Ching* by Geoffrey Redmond stands out among the many other translations of the 3,000-year-old classic in several important respects. First, it focuses on the original meanings, not the later ones overlaid with Confucian moralistic philosophy (and misogyny). For clarity I have referred to the work as the *I Ching*, not the newer pinyin spelling of *Yijing*. The term *Zhouyi*, refers to the earliest version of the *Changes* which does not include the centuries-later *Ten Wings*. The *Zhouyi* together with the *Ten Wings* constitutes the received version, the *I Ching*.

As Geoffrey Redmond acknowledges, the well-known Wilhelm-Baynes translation made the *Book of Changes* a world classic, and was an unexpected bestseller. In 1950 Derk Bodde called the Wilhelm-Baynes translation "the best available in the English-speaking world."[1] In the ensuing more than sixty years, much has changed. And yet, for most who start with the Wilhelm-Baynes translation, the *I Ching* is astoundingly confusing. Redmond indicates admiration for its literary qualities, but finds it has only limited fidelity to the early meanings.

Based on current scholarship, Geoffrey Redmond offers us a new translation that is substantially different from that of Wilhelm-Baynes. Textually speaking, Redmond's translation follows what has become standard among *Changes* scholars—focusing on "the book of oracles" rather than "the book of wisdom."[2] His translation is of the core texts, those originally associated with the sixty-four

---

[1] Derk Bodde, review of the Wilhelm-Baynes translation, *Journal of the American Oriental Society* 70 (4) (October–December 1950): 329.
[2] Although started in the mid-1970s with Edward J. Shaughnessy's and Richard Kunst's PhD dissertations, two recent translations are especially revealing in this trend of focusing on *I Ching* as a book of oracles. See Richard Rutt, *The Book of Changes (Zhouyi): A Bronze Age Document* (New York: Curzon, 1996), and

hexagrams. This allows the early meanings to reveal themselves as they were (as much as we can tell) without the more than two millennia of commentary that often altered the classic almost beyond recognition although, as the title "*Ten Wings*" implies, the commentarial materials were supposed to help the *I Ching* bird to fly. Unfortunately, they flew it too far away. Redmond began his study of the *Changes* years ago with the Wilhelm-Baynes version but tells us he could never quite grasp the *Changes* as a product of Chinese thought. His revelation came when he realized that it had been possible, beginning with the Doubting Antiquity movement of early twentieth century China, to reconstruct the early meanings.

While the work of the Doubting Antiquity philologists greatly stimulated his interest, he felt they were too often needlessly obscure. Thinking that if you do not find what you need in an existing translation you should do your own, he embarked on this undertaking. His principle is that if people of 3,000 years ago understood it, it should be possible to make it understandable today. Readers will have to judge for themselves, but in my estimation he has succeeded admirably. His approach to attaining clarity is not to use modern colloquialisms, but to translate each word precisely into standard English with due consideration of context. True, there is still much that is strange in his *Zhouyi*, but the strangeness is due to the very different way of life of the Western Zhou, not to eccentric translation.

In his chapter on the relation of *Zhouyi* to later Chinese philosophy, Redmond makes a major contribution to *I Ching* scholarship by showing how the Doubting Antiquity scholars went too far in claiming that the *Zhouyi* had no spirituality and no philosophy. As he demonstrates, the work contains what he terms "seeds" that blossomed in later Chinese philosophy. For example, he makes it clear that the *yin-yang* dichotomy was not present in the *Zhouyi* but that the dualism of the lines allowed imposition of the duality of *yin* and *yang*.

For Redmond, the purpose of this reorientation goes beyond reaffirming the *I Ching* as a text of the "Bronze Age of China."[3]

Margaret J. Pearson, *The Original I Ching: An Authentic Translation of the Book of Changes, Based on Recent Discoveries* (Tokyo: Tuttle, 2011).
[3] According to Richard Rutt, the "Bronze Age of China" refers to the Shang and the

By emphasizing *I Ching*'s close connections to a primitive agrarian setting, Redmond draws our attention to a way of life radically different from our own. In highlighting the challenges of Chinese life in the Bronze Age (particularly perpetual violence, constant threat of disease, and the frequent disruption of social order), Redmond helps us develop a better understanding of the *I Ching* as revealing the hopes and fears of a remote time.

Today, we may still appreciate the profundity of *I Ching* divination, especially its illumination of the complexity and fluidity of human existence. But we must also guard against our impulse of idealizing the *I Ching* as a panacea for our problems in the modern times. In Wilhelm-Baynes' translation we see this danger first hand. Carl Jung, in his foreword, insists that the "synchronicity" of the *I Ching* must be contrasted with the scientific "causality" of our technocratic society.[4]

To appreciate how Redmond's version is different, I need to explain the ways in which Wilhelm-Baynes muddle the classic. First, the *I Ching* is presented in three separate segments.[5] It begins with the sixty-four hexagrams, including the hexagram names, hexagram images, judgment statements, and line statements. Just as readers have begun to think of the *I Ching* as a "book of oracles" giving inquirers illuminating guidance to cope with the unknown and uncertainty, they come upon two philosophical essays: "Shuokua" (pinyin: Shuogua, Explanations of the Trigrams) and "Ta Chuan" (pinyin: Dazhuan, The Great Treatise). In these two essays, readers are asked to stop considering

---

Zhou dynasties (roughly from 1560 to 221 BCE). Although covering a broad period, Richard Rutt argues that it is beneficial to situate the *I Ching* in the *longue durée* of early China, to fully understand the subtlety of the *I Ching* text. Rutt pays special attention to late Shang and the Western Zhou period (roughly from 1000–771 BCE) when the core text of the *I Ching* was compiled.
[4]See *The I Ching or Book of Changes*, translated by Richard Wilhelm and rendered into English by Cary F. Baynes (Princeton: Princeton University Press, 1961), xxii–xxv.
[5]The Wilhelm-Baynes translation presents the *I Ching* text in three "books": Book One (The Text), Book Two (The Material), and Book Three (The Commentaries). Note that the Wilhelm-Baynes translation, originally in two volumes, was first published in 1950 by the Bollingen Foundation. Its second edition (in one volume) was published by Princeton University Press in 1961 and has been reprinted twenty-some times.

the hexagrams as oracles and turn their attention to their hidden meanings. Sharply different from the first part, the second part presents the hexagrams as metaphors for the constant changes in the universe and the incessant serendipity in the human world. As Richard J. Smith elegantly states, the hexagrams become symbols for "fathoming the cosmos and ordering the world."[6]

Just as the readers begin to develop a taste of the *I Ching* as a "book of wisdom" about cosmology and moral-metaphysics, they find the reappearance of the oracles in part three.[7] This time, the return of the oracles not only reaffirms the *I Ching* as a divination manual; it also introduces five additional commentaries: "Tuan" (Commentary to the Judgments), "Xiang" (Commentary to the Images), "Wenyan" (Words of the Text), "Xugua" (Hexagrams in Sequence) and "Zagua" (Hexagrams in Irregular Order). Blurring the line between text and commentary, materials from these five distinct appendices are inserted into each chapter as if they are part of the core text. What was already a complex text now becomes even more complicated and convoluted.

Why is the *I Ching* text so terse, incoherent, and repetitious? Why are the core text and the commentarial materials not clearly separated? Would the *I Ching* be more coherent if it was presented either as a "book of oracles" (the core text) or a "book of wisdom" (the commentarial materials)? Should Richard Wilhelm—the missionary-cum-scholar who translated the *I Ching* into German in the 1910s—be blamed for this messy arrangement of the *I Ching* text? Or should Cary F. Baynes—the American woman who rendered Wilhelm's German translation into English through the lens of Jungian psychology—be responsible for this jumbled text?

In fact, neither Wilhelm nor Baynes is culpable. From the time the *I Ching* was originally compiled, it has always been a composite text. As shown in the complex arrangement in the Wilhelm-Baynes

---

[6]"Fathoming the cosmos and ordering the world" is the title of Richard J. Smith's majestic account of the transformation of the *I Ching* from oracles to a multi-layered canonized text. For the symbolism of the hexagrams, see Smith, *Fathoming the Cosmos and Ordering the World: The Yijing (I-Ching or Classic of Changes) and Its Evolution in China* (Charlottesville and London: University of Virginia Press, 2008), 7–30.
[7]The terms "book of oracles" and "book of wisdom" are Wilhelm's. See Wilhelm-Baynes, *The I Ching*: xlix–lviii.

translation, there are three distinct layers of the *I Ching* text: the images of the sixty-four hexagrams, the hexagram and line statements, and a group of early commentarial materials collectively known as the *Ten Wings*.[8] For readers who focus on the first two layers, they consider the hexagrams as divinatory tools that help inquirers to find answers to their questions. For readers who focus on the *Ten Wings*, they see the hexagrams as graphic illustrations of early Chinese cosmology and moral-metaphysics, revealing a philosophical system that connects the natural and the human realms. While these two readings are different, they complement each other in highlighting the complexity and fluidity of human existence. Throughout imperial China, the *I Ching* was considered a Confucian classic precisely because it raised questions about the human condition. Knowledge of it was tested by the civil service examinations, and it was frequently quoted by literati officials in discussions with colleagues and even the emperor.

Even though, by and large, the Wilhelm-Baynes translation follows the Confucian interpretation of the classic, it is dated because of important new scholarship since its 1967 third edition. With advances in phonetic reconstructions of ancient Chinese and especially the discovery of excavated texts far closer to the original composition, our knowledge of the *I Ching* has been revolutionized. Redmond incorporates this new information into his translation. He also emphasizes how recent studies of *I Ching* commentaries demonstrate that there had never been a single universally accepted interpretation of the *I Ching* in imperial China. On the contrary, due to its multifarious nature, the *I Ching* was read from a wide variety of angles including astrology, cosmology, geomancy, mantic prognostication, medicine, moral philosophy, and self-help.[9] We now know that Wilhelm's predilection toward

---

[8]Since three of the seven commentaries ("Tuan," "Xiang," and "Dazhuan") are divided into two parts, the commentarial materials are known collectively as the *Ten Wings*: the ten supplemental writings that help the *I Ching* core text to "fly." For the significance of the *Ten Wings* in sealing the textual body of *I Ching*, see Geoffrey Redmond and Tze-ki Hon, *Teaching the I Ching (Book of Changes)* (Oxford: Oxford University Press, 2014), 140–57.
[9]For a succinct account of the different uses of the *I Ching*, see Richard J. Smith, *The I Ching: A Biography* (Princeton and Oxford: Princeton University Press), 17–123.

the moral-philosophical rendition of the *I Ching* was based on the views of the late Qing Dynasty.[10]

Secondly, recent archaeological discoveries show that the *I Ching* text was not completely stable and its transmission (even after its canonization) was a lot more circuitous than Wilhelm presented. Three archaeological findings are particularly noteworthy. One is the Wangjiatai bamboo-strip manuscript that gives us a glimpse of another divinatory text, the *Gui Zang*, which is believed to be older than the *I Ching*.[11] The other is the Shanghai Museum bamboo-strip manuscript that shows a different form of early *I Ching* text.[12] The last one is the Mawangdui silk manuscript that indicates that after the canonization of the *I Ching* in 136 BCE, there were still variant *I Ching* texts with somewhat different sequences of hexagrams and variants of the hexagram names.[13] Together, these archaeological discoveries challenge the conventional moral-philosophical interpretation of the *I Ching* on which Wilhelm based his translation. In particular, they caution us that the original *I Ching* might not put as much emphasis on hierarchy, patriarchy, and elitism as later commentators did.[14]

While Redmond focuses our attention on the historicity of the *I Ching*, he avoids excessive historicalization. Unlike some translators who stress the primitiveness of ancient China in order to show how greatly we (as modern people) have "progressed," Redmond reminds us that Chinese life in the Bronze Age, though often harsh, was not altogether bleak and hopeless. On the

---

[10] For a summary of the rise of the moral-philosophical interpretation of the *I Ching*, see Richard J. Smith, *Fathoming the Cosmos and Ordering the World*, 89–194; see also Redmond and Hon, *Teaching the I Ching*, 171–80.

[11] For the importance of the Wangjiatai manuscript, see Edward L. Shaughnessy, *Unearthing the Changes: Recently Discovered Manuscripts of the Yijing (I Ching) and Related Texts* (New York: Columbia University Press, 2014), 141–70.

[12] For the importance of the Shanghai Museum manuscript, see Shaughnessy, *Unearthing the Changes*, 37–60.

[13] For the importance of the Mawangdui manuscript, see Edward J. Shaughnessy, *I Ching (The Classic of Changes): The First English Translation of the Newly Discovered Second-Century B.C. Mawangdui Text* (New York: Ballantine Books, 1996), 1–29.

[14] For the significance of archaeological discoveries to our understanding of the complexity of the *I Ching* text, see Redmond and Hon, *Teaching the I Ching*, 93–139.

contrary, in a pre-Confucian and pre-imperial society, there was more equality in genders (e.g. the absence of the *yin-yang* dichotomy), more fluidity in movement (e.g. the constant joy as well as danger in climbing a mountain or crossing a river). For decision-making the *Zhouyi* was there as a guide, not only for earthly matters but also for alleviating anxieties about propitiating vengeful spirits.

Certainly life was tough in early China. In a farming community, one had to constantly work to make ends meet. In a sustenance economy, maintaining health was extremely difficult—all were constantly surrounded by sick animals, poisonous weeds, and tainted food. Nevertheless, Redmond demonstrates that the divinatory responses recorded in each *I Ching* hexagram—auspicious or inauspicious, hopeful or downtrodden, uplifting or depressing—we find both the constancy of change in human life and the human determination to make the best of it. Although these core ideas of the *I Ching* are usually presented in mundane circumstances (such as family reunion, hunting, marriage, making preparation for war, skinning animals), they led to the seemingly more profound philosophy of the *Ten Wings* and later commentaries. After all, the sixty-four hexagrams are thought to be records of seeking guidance from a deity or an ancestor's spirit to solve problems at hand. They are, in essence, concrete examples of someone creatively responding to the circumstances and earnestly looking for ways to make a better life.

In terms of fidelity to the original Chinese version, Redmond's translation clearly supersedes Wilhelm-Baynes' translation and is a major new chapter in the transmission of the *I Ching*. First and foremost, the confusing textual body of the *I Ching* is now given a more manageable form where the core text is presented by itself with the removal of millennia of encrustations that obscure the early meanings. This foregrounds the divinatory function, presenting it as it was first used in China, not as re-invented with Jungian psychology. As modern readers, we can draw on this fresh version to better appreciate the fluidity and complexity of human existence since the dawn of civilization.

Unlike the Wilhelm-Baynes version, Redmond's does not ask us to imagine an exotic "East" to critique a supposedly technocratic "West." Rather, it offers us an *I Ching* that is a "book of everyday life," used three thousand years ago and still today to look more deeply into the challenges of our daily lives. For casual reading, Wilhelm-Baynes is satisfactory, but for those who really want to know the *I Ching*, Redmond's translation with his extremely helpful commentaries is the place to begin.

Tze-ki Hon
Professor of History
State University of New York at Geneseo
March 28, 2016

ACKNOWLEDGMENTS

My editor, Colleen Coalter was enthusiastic about the project from the beginning, appreciating its challenges, and helping me stay inspired. Her suggestions resulted in a much better book, particularly adding philosophy to the analysis. She was also patient with a string of now resolved personal mishaps that slowed my progress at times.

Without the knowledge and encouragement of my good friend and collaborator, Hon Tze-ki, this book would not have come to pass. My many hours of discussion with him have always been both pleasurable and educational. I have also benefited from my membership of the Columbia Early China Seminar, now a part of the recently founded Tang Center at that university.

For everyone working on the *Zhouyi* the foundational works of Richard Kunst, Richard Rutt, Edward Shaughnessy, Richard J. Smith, Joseph Adler, and Gregory Whincup are essential. The work of independent scholar Bradford Hatcher provided me a provocative counterpoint to standard views.

Others with whom I have discussed matters related to early China, and/or whose books I have read and lectures attended include Sarah Allan, Constance Cook, Catherine Despeux, Li Feng, Norman Girardot, Paul Goldin, Marc Kalinowski, Ng On-cho, Michael Nylan, Edward Shaughnessy, Robin Yates, and many others.

Such facility as I have for working with difficult texts I owe especially to my teachers at the University of Virginia, where I studied early English textual criticism and philology with Lester Beaurline and Fredson Bowers, "doyen of the post-war" textual critics according to Eggert [106]. Robert Kellogg's encouragement of my youthful work on an extremely obscure Middle English text gave me confidence when I was finally able to return to literary study after my long years of medical training. At Riverdale School I was fortunate to be able to take a two-year course, invitation only, on the history of philosophy by William Williams. Setting aside his telling us that Asian philosophy was not worth studying—the general view among philosophers then and one I am sure he would not subscribe to now—he said something else that I have kept in mind ever since: one's personal opinions are of no interest to anyone else until you actually know something about your subject. As a result, I spent over twenty years studying the *Book of Changes* before daring to write about it. Finally, I would not know most of what I now know were it not for my many informal conversations with my fellow Riverdale student, Christopher Hobson, the smartest person I have ever met.

In memoriam
The unknown sinologist,
Richard Rutt (1925–2011)

I think of this distinguished scholar as The Unknown Sinologist because his ground-breaking work on the *Zhouyi* has yet to receive the attention it merits. This epithet is, of course borrowed from the sobriquet *le philosophe inconnu*, referring to Louis Claude de Saint-Martin (1743–1803; a mystical Catholic philosopher, about whom I know little more than his intriguing *nom de plume*. As with the *Zhouyi*, the unknown has always seemed more interesting to me than the known, hence my prolonged struggle to translate the ancient meanings of this 3000-year-old classic.

The first Western scholars of China who devoted themselves to this ancient work were a collection of fascinating eccentrics. In this group are included Rev. Canon McClatchie, who imagined the *Changes* was sexy. Also James Legge, laboring tirelessly to create the earliest accurate English versions of the Chinese classics, despite the disparagement of these works by his fellow missionaries who disdained the heathen Chinese classics as obstacles to conversion. And of course, Richard Wilhelm, a Jungian and missionary who boasted of never having converted a single Chinese. His collaborator, Cary F. Baynes was the first woman and the first American to work on the *I Ching*.

Father Rutt belongs in this illustrious company of genius-eccentrics. He learned of the *Book of Changes* from elderly men in rural Korea when he was an Anglican missionary there. He later returned to Britain and became a bishop. After the death of his wife he became a Roman Catholic priest in protest against the ordination of women in the Anglican communion. One need not agree with all his views to appreciate that he was an individualist— he was flexible enough on gender roles that he took up knitting as an avocation and wrote the definitive history of it.

Sadly, Rutt, whom I regard as one of the great China scholars of the past century, is rarely cited and few sinologists recognize his name when I mention it. I suspect this is because he spent most of his life as a churchman rather than an academic. For centuries, scholars in the West were priests or monks—Rutt was one of the last in this lineage. Perhaps because he was an outsider, he had a unique perspective on the *Zhouyi*, somewhat antagonistic, yet saying much that needed to be said. His critical approach brought the work to life for me, more than the hagiographic rhetoric of the book's uncritical admirers.

Regrettably, I never met the man and know him only through his invaluable book on the *Zhouyi* and his obituary. I invariably find myself in vigorous disagreement whenever I reread passages in his book, itself a mixture of pointed attacks and painstaking, meticulous scholarship. Yet every time I browse his work, as I do quite often, I always feel my understanding has grown. His ideas are always in my mind when I think about the *Zhouyi*. Rutt was a paradox and perhaps that is what one has to be to fully appreciate the ancient book.

QUICK START GUIDE
FOR THE ANCIENT
BOOK OF CHANGES

Despite its reign in the West during the sixties and seventies as a hippie scripture, the *Book of Changes* is far from being an easy read. It reveals itself more completely to those with some knowledge of its historical and literary background, hence the detailed supplementary material I have provided. While I believe this material will greatly enhance the experience of reading the *Changes,* some may want to dip into the text to get a taste of it first—this is what I would do. For eager readers, therefore, I have provided this quick start guide in the hope that it ameliorates the confusion that is often the first response to this 3,000-year-old classic.

Terminology

Most Anglophones know the book by its old Wade-Giles Romanization of *I Ching,* usually mispronounced "eye ching." Using the modern pinyin Romanization, standard in the People's Republic of China, it is spelled *Yijing,* and pronounced "eee jing." My translation is of the earliest portion of the book consisting of the sixty-four chapters, each comprising the titles or tags, the six-line diagrams and the judgment and line texts. This layer is referred to as the *Zhouyi,* or *Changes of the Zhou.* This version of the title refers back to the dynasty in which it was composed, the Western Zhou (1046–771 BCE). Centuries later a collection of commentaries was appended, the *Ten Wings.* These added philosophical and cosmological meanings were not present in the early portion. My translation is based on the ancient meanings, which were forgotten by the time of the *Ten Wings*—the actual characters were basically the same but many of their pronunciations and meanings had changed. (The exact form of the characters changed, but they had standard equivalents in newer scripts.)

The early text, which is what I have translated, consists of phrases used for divination; the notion of the *Changes* as a book of wisdom arose much later, though it has predominated ever since. With the flowering of evidential and critical scholarship in China's late nineteenth and early twentieth centuries, scholarly interest shifted toward textual accuracy and restoration of the early meanings. In my view, while restoring the ancient meaning, needless obscurities were introduced. The present translation is based on my belief that if the text could be understood 3,000 years ago it can be understood today. Understanding the *Zhouyi* still takes effort, but I have tried in this translation to ease the effort by increasing clarity while remaining true to the text. Mental stretching will always be needed to put oneself into the mind of any ancient culture, especially one of a different tradition to one's own. I have been studying the *Zhouyi* for more than two decades, and hope my labors have succeeded it making more accessible for my readers.

The basic history

The *Book of Changes* has had three major stages: The *Zhouyi*, already mentioned above, was composed about 3,000 years ago during the Western Zhou dynasty (1046–771 BCE) and was a plain divination manual based on the primitive conditions of the era. Several centuries later, possibly during the Spring and Autumn period (770–503 BCE) but certainly by the Warring States period (ca. 475–221 BCE) the text began to be read quite differently, as a work inculcating Confucian morality and philosophy. A progressively more elaborate metaphysics became associated with it in the Han Dynasty (202 BCE–220 CE). The metaphysical and cosmological meanings became canonical with the inclusion of the *Ten Wings* with the *Zhouyi* to form the *I Ching*. Most writings on the *Changes* do not distinguish between the ancient concrete meanings and the later metaphysical ones, thus obscuring the actual history of the classic. With the iconic Wilhelm-Baynes translation, with its extremely influential Foreword by Carl Jung, the *Changes* became a world classic, familiar in the obsolete English spelling of *I Ching*, at the price of obscuring its historical development.

The 3,000-year-old early meanings were forgotten by the time the *Changes* attained its status as a classic. Only the Doubting Antiquity movement, which began circa 1910, by making use of advances in philology was able to restore the early meanings. This movement was in part based on the desire to restore China's past by demythologizing it, but was also intended to discredit it as the basis for Chinese society and government, following the humiliations of the Opium Wars and discovery of Western advanced technology. Despite this bias, it is because of the textual research initiated by this movement that we can now come close to reading the *Zhouyi* as it was originally written. This also gives us the chance to observe the very beginnings of Chinese philosophy.

Structure and content

The *Zhouyi* consists of sixty-four chapters, each with four sections. These consist of: a tag or title; a six-line diagram or hexagram; a brief text referred to as the "judgment" or "hexagram text" that often includes all or part of the invocation: "Begin with an offering; favorable to divine." The remaining section consists of six "line texts," each nominally associated with one of the lines of the hexagram figure. It is likely these elements originated separately and were assigned to the hexagram lines by compilers, of whom we have no record. The texts and/or hexagrams were not intended as literature in an aesthetic sense, and certainly not as psychological guidance. The *Zhouyi* was simply a catalogue or compendium of reponses to divinatory inquiries. Unfortunately we have no records of the actual inquiries, nor of how the *Zhouyi* phrases were interpreted during actual divination, nor of the sociology of their use. The *Zhouyi* is really a sort of reference book. The various bits of text only occasionally form a sequential narrative, and then for only a few lines.

To select the appropriate diagram and text, a variety of random methods have been used. These include sorting of a bundle of fifty yarrow stalks, tossing three coins, other ways of counting to generate random numbers from one to six, and selection of beads from a pouch. These lines can be solid or broken (later *yang* or *yin*) and each can be fixed or changing. Each action is repeated six times to generate a complete hexagram. Usually only one line of text constitutes the response, but there are an immense variety of interpretive systems. Some of these are discussed in Part 4. Whatever method is used, the replies generated by the *Changes* are much more concise than those of such currently popular divination methods such as astrology or Tarot. It works to clarify a present situation, not to tell an entire life story.

Interpretation

The *I Ching* has been interpreted in two distinct ways, though these are often merged in actual practice. So far as we know, the earliest method was based only on the texts. This became the *yili* or meaning and principles method. Later, possibly by the Spring and Autumn Period, but certainly by the Warring States Period, *yin* and *yang* were added to the types of lines, and also to the positions of the lines within the hexagram. Two schools of divination arose, the *xiangshu* 象數 or images and numbers method, and the *yili* 義理, or meaning and principles method. [Nielsen: 303; Rutt: 45] Many commentaries on the *Changes*, including those of Wilhelm-Baynes, confuse these two methods by implying that the meanings are based on the texts, while they are more often based on trigram and line positions. We should not fault Wilhelm for this. His interpretations reflected the practice of his Chinese "honored teacher" Lao Nai-hsuan, who in turn understood the text as it was read by the literati of the late Qing Dynasty. Such distinctions are important for scholarly study, but not necessarily when the *I Ching* is used for divination or spiritual inspiration.

As a reconstruction of the ancient meanings, the present translation bases its readings entirely on the texts because there is no evidence for diagram-based interpretations in the Western Zhou. It is important to note that the early meanings may not be the "original" ones, nor are they the only "correct" ones. From a scholarly viewpoint, the meanings of any scriptural text have a history; believers, in contrast, tend to regard their texts as unchanging.

A message of encouragement

Since the *Zhouyi* is notoriously obscure, no one need feel discouraged if it seems baffling at first. With a little study the classic can yield many of its secrets; historical secrets, not necessarily the later mystical ones that have been much more written about. For me, the greatest reward of reading the *Zhouyi* is experiencing the ways of thought of a remote time. If the ancient work contains wisdom, it is what we can learn about ourselves from its glimpses into the early life of our species.

My translation is of the early text, without the later overlays that completely altered how it was read. I have tried to present it as accurately as possible in plain English. Rather than leaving readers on their own, I have provided concise explanations of the meaning of every line, as best can be determined three millennia later. In these explanations I have tried to avoid the extremes of leaving too much unexplained, or of overwhelming the text with many pages of notes.

Of the wisdom for which *I Ching* has been admired, not much is to be found in the Western Zhou text. If it is a self-help book, it is a self-help book for life as it was lived 3,000 years ago. For those interested in the *Changes* as a book of wisdom, Chapter 8 offers my thoughts on how the *Zhouyi* might have inspired the later philosophical and ethical ideas associated with it.

Starting out, it is best not to try the read the work straight through as one would read a novel or history book, because the order of the hexagrams and the texts associated with them is mostly arbitrary. A better way is to start reading by topic, as suggested in Part 4. For a quick first reading, I suggest hexagrams 1, 2, 11, 12, 63, and 64, which are some of the most interesting.

As a primary goal in this work is reconstruction of the early meanings, I have not designed the translation for contemporary divination, but it can be used for this purpose, though with some exercise of imagination.

PART ONE

Approaching one of the world's oldest books

1

Why another translation?

Confucius famously said, "Give me a few more years—if I have fifty more years to study the *Book of Changes*, then perhaps I, too, can avoid any great errors" (*Lunyu* 7.16, in Watson 2007: 50).

I am certainly no Confucius, my publisher will not give me fifty more years to complete this translation, and it is exceedingly unlikely that I will ever be without errors. Having acknowledged this, we have the advantage of knowing a lot more about the *Book of Changes* than Confucius could have. It was at least 200 years old when he lived. In fact it is doubtful he knew of it at all; the reference to the *Changes* in the famous quotation above is likely an editorial addition.

To explain the need for a new translation I need to clear up some of the many confusions that have grown around the *Book of Changes*. Most fundamentally, although it is often referred to as a single work, this is misleading. As originally proposed by my colleague and collaborator, Hon Tze-ki, it is useful to consider it as three distinctive works. First is the *Zhouyi*, the ancient text produced in the Western Zhou Dynasty of China's Bronze Age (1046–771 BCE) and the basis of my translation. Next is the *I Ching* (*Yijing*), consisting of the *Zhouyi* text to which were added the canonical *Ten Wings*. The date of these is uncertain, sometime in the late Warring States Period (403–221 BCE) or early Western Han Dynasty (206 BCE–24 CE). It is in the *Ten Wings*, particularly the 大傳 *Dazhuan* or *Great Commentary*, that we first find the cosmological and philosophical ideas that became associated with the classic. During most of Chinese history, this philosophy was assumed to be somehow latent in the early text, but modern scholarship has cast doubt on this. Finally, there is the modernized version now read in many different languages and cultures. I here refer to it by the older Wade-Giles Romanization, *I Ching*, usually mispronounced by Anglophones as *eye ching*. The correct pronunciation is more like *eee jing*, spelled *Yijing* in the modern pinyin Romanization.

Credit for recreating the classic for modern non-Chinese readers unquestionably goes to Richard Wilhelm (1873–1930), a Protestant missionary long resident in China who studied the *Changes* with the 'aid of his traditionally educated informant, Lao Nai-hsuan. It is particularly the Bollingen Foundation/Princeton University Press edition, with Wilhelm's German translation rendered into English by Cary F. Baynes, that made the work famous. Baynes was educated in psychology and was a follower of the Swiss psychiatrist Carl F. Jung. She knew German but not Chinese, though Richard's son, Helmut Wilhelm, also a sinologist, checked her translation, as did many others whom she acknowledges in her "Translator's Note." Though meticulously composed, the Wilhelm-Baynes translation, inevitably, was a product of its time. As Baynes admits:

> one very real compensation for my lack of Chinese [was] the access to its philosophy afforded me through my growing knowledge of the work of Jung. (Wilhelm Baynes: xli)

Thus from its entry into world literature, the *I Ching* was seen through the perspective of modern depth psychology, despite the fact that nothing like Jungian psychology existed in traditional China. Psychological interpretation of religion and spirituality has become so pervasive in modern culture as to usually pass unnoticed. The *I Ching* had been translated before, though never readably enough to attract more than specialist interest. The Wilhelm-Baynes version, with its Foreword by Carl Jung, benefited by appearing at a time when depth psychology, with its ideology of exploring the unconscious, provided a theoretical basis by means of which all sorts of seemingly non-rational mental phenomena— myth, fantasies, dreams, and the like—could be valued rather than dismissed.

This psychological mode of reading the *I Ching* is a creation of the modern West, though also influential in China. This mode is not wrong—it is the latest in a long succession of ways to under-stand the *Changes*. It is, however, not the way it was understood in traditional China. While justly admired for its literary qualities, the German-into-English of Wilhelm-Baynes has only occasional resemblance to the Western Zhou meanings. It is best thought of as an adaptation rather than a translation. Strongly in its favor, it extended the readership of this very ancient work exponentially. Its attractive presentation of many of the key ideas of Chinese philosophy has inspired many, including myself, to delve more deeply into them. Yet at the same time, its synchronic approach to the classic limits its suitability as a source for learning about Chinese intellectual history.

Of the many published and self-published translations, few have sinological or literary value. For those seriously interested in the classic, it is important to be aware that most books that purport to be the *Book of Changes* or *I Ching* are no such thing, not trans-lations at all but paraphrases, often quite loose, by believers or practitioners who feel that they have special insight into what the classic "really means," despite not being able to read any Chinese. On the one hand, the proliferation of such works demonstrates the interest engendered by the *Book of Changes*; on the other hand it makes it harder for would-be readers to recognize the wheat amidst the chaff. I discuss the nature of some of these pseudo-translations in the final chapter.

It has been said that one cannot understand a classical Chinese text unless one already knows what it means. This is only a slight exaggeration. Chinese literati studied the ancient texts under the tutelage of masters who had often specialized in a specific work, and who had themselves received transmission from earlier scholars. Since such traditions now survive only incompletely, we are to an extent starting over. This allows a fresh look, but also calls for remaining conscious of the many uncertainties involved. I have noted some of these in my commentaries.

Given the polymorphic nature of the *Book of Changes*, there are many ways to read it so that any interpretation or translation can be criticized from a viewpoint different from that of the translator. While I have often departed from the readings of even my most learned predecessors, I make no claim that my rendering is inher-ently better, only that it embodies a different vision of the *Zhouyi*. I feel that some of my predecessors have not sufficiently escaped the influence of the early twentieth-century "Doubting Antiquity Movement School" (*vide infra*) in its fondness for obscure, often unsupported emendations. I offer my version as an alternative, based on my guiding principle that since the *Zhouyi* was understandable to the readers of 3,000 years ago, a translation should make it understandable to readers of today. My version is a new incarnation of the ancient classic and likely not the last. I think of incarnation in the Buddhist fashion as each life having continuity with previous ones, but presenting a fresh opportunity to go beyond what was done in the past.

An all too common problem with Chinese to English translations, even scholarly ones, is imprecision—they do not consistently translate Chinese words with the same English word. This is particularly confusing with prognostic terms, given that the connection between the rest of the line text and whether the prognosis is auspicious or ominous are frequently unclear. My own view is that the reason for reading an ancient text is to learn how people thought in that remote era. This requires translating the special vocabulary of the text consistently rather than turning it into a contemporary English book.

A new paradigm arises: The Doubting Antiquity Movement and its followers

My translation is intended as a reconstruction of the early meanings of the *Book of Changes* at the time of its origin, the Western Zhou Dynasty (c. 1046–771 BCE). China was still in the Bronze Age— though so accomplished in using this alloy as to have created some of the most beautiful objects in the history of art. I am not the first to have translated with this objective; indeed, this is becoming standard among Western scholars. The principal translators of this school, if I may call it such, are Richard Kunst, Richard Rutt, and Edward Shaughnessy, all of whom have produced versions that shed great light on the early meanings of the *Zhouyi*.

The notion of restoring the early meanings originated with the already mentioned Doubting Antiquity Movement (疑古派 *Yigupai*) of early twentieth century China, although there were a few in the Song Dynasty who questioned the received readings. The philologists of the Doubting Antiquity Movement were traditionally educated Chinese of great erudition who applied text-critical methodology to reconstruct what the text meant when it was actually composed. Theirs was not entirely neutral scholarship however, but had the underlying agenda of discrediting the pre-Qin Dynasty ancient classics as the basis for Chinese education, government, and society. This was part of an overall re-evaluation of Chinese culture by some of its literati, who considered China to be backward in comparison to the West, in large part due to the superiority of Western technology as demonstrated in the Opium Wars of the mid-nineteenth century. The school was started by Hu Shi 胡適 (1891–1962) and continued by Gu Jiegang 顧頡剛 (1893–1980), its best-known advocate, and several others. Perhaps the most influential later Chinese follower of this approach was Gao Heng 高亨 (1900–86). In the West, the highly esteemed Arthur Waley (1889–1966) published an article, still influential today, that set what seems to me an unfortunate precedent for fanciful emendations, though he never fulfilled his promise to translate the full text (Waley: 121–42).The most complete exposition of the critical approach in English is that of the late Father Richard Rutt, whose work has greatly influenced my own.

These scholars employed a demythologizing approach that revolutionized our understanding of the *Zhouyi*, although has not been universally accepted. Because the reconstructed early *Zhouyi* is clearly a divination manual, not a book of wisdom, many aficionados of the classic have resisted its findings, though without much objective evidence to support their case. For me, though some of the reconstructed meanings are unappealing, evidence for them is persuasive and they transform what seems a swamp of peculiar phrases, overly-elaborate cosmology, and meaningless numerology into a text that makes historical sense.

The Doubting Antiquity approach, however, though greatly enhancing understanding of the *Changes,* is not, in my opinion, the final word, due to its discrediting agenda and to a now outmoded tendency for imaginative, but unsupported, emendations. Gao Heng, despite his brilliance, was one of those whose far-fetched emendations needlessly increased the obscurity of the text, yet he remains influential. Most of the early translators, notably Richard Wilhelm, erred in the opposite direction—making the text clearer, but at the cost of faithfulness. Wilhelm's rendering was long unquestioned because until recently translators could work very freely, given the paucity of Westerners who could read the ancient language. Despite these animadversions, all these scholars made enormous and indispensable contributions to our understanding of the classic.

However one retrospectively criticizes the Doubting Antiquity Movement and its successors, they led the way for a total reassessment of the *I Ching*. They were basically correct in their belief that education solely in the ancient classics was not suitable for governing a twentieth-century country. Their goal was a constructive one, to maintain Chinese culture by helping to adapt to new circumstances. Rather than simply condemning the *I Ching*, they created a new way to conceive it. The influence of their work is now scholarly rather than political. Because this movement played an indispensable role in the development of critical analysis of the ancient texts, their influence on American sinology continues to be substantial. My own translation would not have been possible without their work. Indeed, at the risk of seeming presumptuous, I consider myself to belong to the Doubting Antiquity tradition, though with the difference that I prefer to select the most straightforward meanings for difficult terms rather than seeking out obscure ones. I also consider the classics still invaluable for modern China, and indeed, the rest of the modern world. While translating, I have imagined myself to be in dialogue with the scholars of the Doubting Antiquity tradition, hence I have very frequently referred to the work of Kunst, Rutt, and Shaughnessy, whom I regard as being in that lineage, broadly considered. I have of course considered other important English translations, especially those of Richard John Lynn and Greg Whincup.

The early twentieth-century agenda of discrediting the classics as the basis for Chinese government and society is now moot, given the vast political changes that have since occurred. This opens the door for translation that is mainly determined by one's beliefs about the nature of the text. Scholarship is blossoming in China as well. Largely suppressed under Mao, the classics are now experiencing something of a revival, both scholarly and popular, stemming from national pride and a desire to reconnect with traditional culture.

Study of the *Changes* must now consider the recently excavated manuscripts, particularly those of the Shanghai Museum and Mawangdui, published with transcriptions and English translation

(Shaughnessy 1996, 2014). Despite numerous variants, mostly homophone substitutions, these texts closely resemble the received one while at the same time shedding new light on it. Accordingly, I have collated my translation with the Shanghai Museum and Mawangdui versions in Shaughnessy's transcriptions. When I have substituted their reading I note this in the commentary. For the most part however, I have stayed with the received text when there has been no clear reason to change it.

Work on the excavated manuscripts is still at an early stage and there are advances in phonetic reconstruction that have not yet been applied to study of the *Zhouyi*. Thus there is potential for further advances in our understanding of the *Zhouyi*.

Dispelling the obscurity of the *Zhouyi*

So difficult is the *Book of Changes* that scholars have tended to avoid it and those who do admit interest in it have often been viewed with suspicion. I discussed this stuffy attitude in some detail in my previous work (Redmond and Hon 2014: 1–18).This suspicion is partly due to its association with its faddishness during the counter-cultural movement of the 1960s and 1970s. Another is that many in the modern world, even if they do not admit it, are uncomfortable with the supernatural and try to avoid anything related to it. Still another factor is that some textual scholars are understandably uncomfortable with texts whose meanings seem almost impossible to pin down. Philology is about precision and when accuracy is hard to establish, many scholars tend to stay away.

A more fruitful approach, I suggest, is to confront the obscurity directly so as to determine what is causing it. In my view much of the confusion is due to approaching the text with the wrong expectations. The *Zhouyi* is not a narrative and was never intended to be read in linear, consecutive order. It is made up of fragments collected from unknown informants and organized to fit the hexagram structure. Confusion is greatly reduced once it is recognized that the fundamental unit of meaning in the *Zhouyi* is not the chapter, nor paragraph (of which there are none), nor even the line, but the phrase. Phrases within the judgments or numbered lines are only sometimes related to each other. Nor, with a few brief exceptions, is there any narrative development. This inevitably creates difficulties for contemporary readers as we are conditioned from a very early age to expect coherent stories.

Here are some possible reasons for the *Zhouyi*'s obscurity:

First, the text might be highly corrupt, surviving only as unconnected fragments, like the Greek poetry of Sappho or the philosophy of Parmenides. To the extent that this is a factor, it is probably a minor one. From the excavated manuscripts we have learned that the text was highly conserved, suggesting that the received text is quite close to what was originally composed. The fragmentary nature of the text is almost certainly its original form. If manuscript misadventures play a role it is a minor one.

Many early texts were essentially mnemonics or notes. The meanings of the text would have been supplemented by orally transmitted material passed from teacher or master to student. This is hardly unique to the Chinese classics. For example, it is true of many difficult Buddhist texts as well, notably the *Heart Sutra*. Some of the orally transmitted explanations have been set in writing, but a large portion must inevitably have been lost. This master-to-student mode of teaching was still prevalent at the end of the imperial system, but in the case of the *I Ching*, what was transmitted was not the Western Zhou meanings but the much later Confucianized ones. Oral teachings by their nature tend to present the material as timeless, rather than as historically conditioned.

A further source of mystification is the very thing that made the *Changes* unique—the hexagrams. These serve to give the appearance of precise organization to what otherwise were random and often unrelated fragments. The texts are not meaningless, rather they are mostly simple, down-to-earth statements without hidden meanings. Given the profundity attributed to the *Zhouyi*, it was the task of later exegetes to uncover—actually mostly invent—its deep meanings, assumed to be present considering the work's sagely origins. The textual basis of the meanings that became attributed to the ancient texts is by no means self-evident; readers have been struggling ever since to connect the Confucian interpretations with the Western Zhou text. Even the *Ten Wings*, supposedly clarifying the meanings, are mostly about matters not present in the Western Zhou text. As a result, the *Zhouyi* can be better understood without relying on the *Wings* or other later commentaries.

With texts that can be regarded as occult or esoteric, there is a tendency for the meanings attributed to them to become progressively more elaborate and convoluted over time, increasing their seeming obscurity. We see this in some sections of the *Ten Wings*, with lists of symbolic associations, and in the work of later commentators such as Shao Yong 邵雍 (1011–77), whose mystical interpretations of the trigrams and hexagrams became so elaborate that even his friends found them baffling. Of course, there might be as yet unrevealed secrets in the text or hexagram figures, but I leave this possibility to those who enjoy such speculations.

The reconstruction of early meanings replaces the abstruse philosophy attributed to the classic with the difficulty of understanding an historically remote way of life, different in many ways even from Confucius's time. However, as I hope my translation will demonstrate, once we release ourselves from the need to discover profound secrets in the *Book of Changes* and read it in the language and context of Western Zhou civilization, most meanings became clear. Many of the folkways, notably human sacrifice, will forever remain strange, but this is the strangeness of the human species, not the text.

Opening a 3,000-year-old book

So different is the *Changes* from the other Chinese classics that even learned sinologists often confess to difficulty comprehending it. The best advice I can give anyone starting to read the *Zhouyi* is to give up one's assumptions about what constitutes a book. Most translations of the *I Ching*, while replacing the Chinese with English, leave it up to the reader to figure out what it means.

In the hope of sparing my readers from the anguish I at times endured in grappling with this elusive text, I have provided commentary explaining nearly every line as best I can, based on the presumed early meanings. I also point out some of the irresolvable ambiguities to give a better sense of the multiple ways the text could have been read. This strikes me as the only truthful way to do this, because the *Zhouyi* works by what might be termed fuzzy logic—it is suggestive rather than specific. In starting to read the *Changes*, it is best to accept that many passages will seem strange, even bizarre, at first. With further reading most passages become clear as one gets a feel for how its imagery works. Still, a few passages will always resist attempts at explanation. Accordingly, I have tried to point out when my translations are merely speculations. Indeed, I suspect that a few phrases were not understandable even 3,000 years ago. Frustration can be minimized by recognizing that, like many divinatory texts, the *Zhouyi* works by stimulating thinking rather than by directly conveying information.

In reading the *Book of Changes*, and therefore in translating it, it should be kept in mind that there are two fundamentally different ways it can be read. Most readers, both past and present, have been enthusiasts or aficionados for whom it is a form of spiritual practice, either for divination or as a source of wisdom. Some practitioners attain a deep scholarly knowledge of it as well. Many develop a deeply affectionate bond with the book. They may use it daily for divination, or they expend countless hours trying to find a hidden pattern in hexagram arrays, or they may re-read it frequently as some do with the Bible.

While I appreciate much of the philosophy that has been attributed to the *I Ching*, particularly that of the *Dazhuan,* or *Great Commentary*, to me what is most interesting about the classic is the Western Zhou layer and the glimpse it provides of human consciousness at an early stage, during the slow transition from orality to literacy, arguably the most important event in the existence of *homo sapiens*. (Although the earliest extant evidence of Chinese writing, the Wu Ding oracle bone inscriptions, preceded the *Zhouyi* by several centuries, the development of the expressive capacity of written language was very gradual.) Recovery of the early meanings requires a critical, scholarly approach that tries as much as possible to let the words have the meanings they do and remains untroubled when the text is not as one would like it to be.

Within a page or two of starting, the reader of the *Changes* will be confronted with a paradox. He or she is holding a book that has been held in immense esteem for thousands of years by one of the world's most admired cultures. Yet the immediate impression is of a jumble of phrases ranging from incoherent to bizarre. Only courtesy restrains one from calling it nonsense. If one decides to persevere—as I have for more than two decades—one will encounter a text unlike any other he or she has read. Continuing to read, neither plot nor thematic development is apparent. An early Western scholar mistook it for a dictionary, and he was more correct than has been acknowledged. The *Book of Changes* is indeed a reference work, but of a sort that is no longer standard— a compendium of phrases for responding to divinatory inquiries. So important were divination manuals in early China that this was one of the few categories of books not ordered to be burned by Qinshi Huangdi the notorious first emperor of the Qin Dynasty, perhaps best known for the terracotta army that that still guards his tomb.

Even if we allow for the vastly different problems of our long-ago ancestors, we are still challenged as we try to understand a text composed in a very different way from even the oldest Western classics that we are likely to have encountered: Homer, Plato, the Greek dramatists, etc. Much more like the *Zhouyi* are fragmentary texts, such as Heraclitus, Sappho, and occult texts such as those used for divination or other magical procedures. We need to bear in mind that the criterion for inclusion in magical texts was their presumed efficacy, not clarity. They were generally attributed to a mythical figure such as Hermes Trismegistus in the West or Fu Xi in China. With occult or esoteric matters it is never self-evident why a particular divinatory system, or spell or incantation, was considered efficacious. We must prepare ourselves to engage with a mentality almost impossibly remote from our own, keeping in mind that such works held meaning for some smart people long ago, and ponder why such texts meant so much to so many in the remote—and even not so remote—past.

2

Making sense of divination

Divination has been widely practiced at all times and in all cultures. Attitudes tend to be split between skepticism and belief, with relatively little middle ground. In the modern world it tends to be assumed without any actual familiarity that divination was only practiced by the ignorant. With recent recognition that scholarship should study the broad range of human phenomena, not just the "high culture," study of divination has become less marginalized.

The frequent claim that the *Book of Changes* was not a divination manual, but a book of wisdom is not historically correct. Hence to appreciate the work in any of its incarnations, it is necessary to begin with an unbiased look at divination—a human activity practiced in all cultures, in all eras. Despite the dominance of the scientific worldview, taking into account population growth it can be safely said that divination is practiced by more people now than ever before. Despite frequent efforts to suppress its practice by governments, religious authorities and, more recently, scientific establishments, the mantric arts continue to thrive.

The universality of divination

That so many ancient writings about divination survive indicates how important it was to the ancients. What is thought to be the earliest reference to divination is a Sumerian cuneiform text from late in the third millennium BCE (Barton 1994: 11). The earliest of the Chinese oracle bones, which are records of divination, date from about 1200 BCE (Keightley 1985) and have been extensively written about and studied in both Chinese and English. Critical scholarship on divination also began quite early, with Cicero's wide-ranging *De Divinatione* (44 BCE) plausibly being the first comprehensive and skeptical assessment.

A broad modern conception of divination, that goes beyond dismissing it as mere fortune-telling, recognizes it is a multiplicity of methods for seeking knowledge that is not attainable by normal means. A useful definition is that of Ulla Susanne Koch:

> [...] a practical means of obtaining otherwise inaccessible information ... . The kind of knowledge involved can pertain to the future, the present, or the past; the source can be ... gods, ancestors, spirits, or there may be no personal interlocutor as such; the privileged knowledge can be obtained by various means, ranging from such quiet pursuits as studying the sky ... or even violent in the form of possession and ecstasy. Divination can involve elaborate rituals performed by specialists or it can be part of daily life accessible to Everyman. (2010: 44)

Whether divination provides real knowledge, or how it might do so, is less obvious than usually thought. Divination certainly affects the mind of the inquirer. While it can be done simply out of curiosity, it can benefit by providing fresh ways of looking at a situation. It can allay anxiety—or increase it. At times it has been thought to reveal the will of the gods, at others to be an intrusion on God's omniscience. It can inform about the nature of the cosmos, the state of the dead, the presence of curses, and more. Without excluding consideration of these functions, our main purpose in the present work is to yield insights into the minds of people from some of the earliest written records of human concerns.

Divination systems, in providing prognostications, must have implicit notions on the nature of human existence within the cosmos. Like other systems such as astrology, the *I Ching* developed into a means for philosophical inspiration and ethical cultivation, conceived in Chinese thought as living in accord with the *Dao* or Way of Heaven. Whether divination "really works," or how it might do so, is less obvious than usually thought. Accuracy of prediction is not easily assessed because criteria for accuracy are difficult to define. Seemingly erroneous readings tend to be explained away as incorrect interpretations. What divination does do is create a narrative about the inquirer's life, giving significance to events that may otherwise seem random. Thus it gives an individual a sense of his or her life as part of the overall pattern of the cosmos. On a psychological level, the great antiquity of some divination methods still practiced, such as astrology and *I Ching*, demonstrates continuity of modern consciousness with the beginnings of human self-awareness.

With respect to astrology, the philosophical sense of divination is well summarized by Mircea Eliade:

> [...] the horoscope reveals to you a new dignity: it shows how intimately you are related to the entire universe ... Besides, this cosmic predetermination of your existence constitutes a mystery: it means that the universe moves according to a pre-established plan; that human life and history follow a pattern and advance progressively toward a goal. (1976: 61)

In the present work I treat divination as a cultural phenomenon, rather than as debased science. While many questions posed in divination may now be better answered by science, such as when rainfall will occur, the cause of a disease, or even the gender of a fetus (the subject of a famous, but mistaken, oracle bone inscription), there are many other sorts of questions that science cannot address and so remain in the provenance of religion and spirituality, of which divination can be considered an aspect. Psychotherapy has more in common with divination than its practitioners would care to admit. The basis of Freud's famous method was, after all, dream interpretation.

There have been attempts to find a scientific basis for divination, such as associating *yin* and *yang* with negative and positive in electricity. Astrology has postulated unknown forces by which the planets affect humans. Such theories distract from serious study of divination because none stand up to scrutiny. Two approaches seem more useful to me. First is the historical study of divination, as in the present work. The second is investigation of how it functions in the lives of people who use it, which I have addressed in an earlier work (Redmond and Hon 2014: 19–36). Popular treatments are often too general to be of serious interest but a few, such as that of Barretta (2009), give a vivid sense of the role divination plays in the lives of actual believers. A fascinating personal account of contemporary Asian divination is that by the late Tiziano Terzani, an Italian journalist long resident in Asia (1997).

It is curious that divination, including the *I Ching*, was orthodox in traditional cultures yet counter-cultural in the modern West. Its appeal is well described by Bernadette Brady, a prominent astrologer, in a discussion of the relation of astrology to modern science. Summarizing the views of Patrick Curry, she writes:

> astrology is a form of enchantment, a way in which humanity encounters mystery, awe, and wonder ... it was necessary for astrology to be marginalized by science in order for it to maintain this position ... any success gained by astrology in becoming creditable in the view of science would be at the price of its soul. (70f.)

This well expresses the nostalgia for the enchanted world that is common in our time and is, no doubt, a major reason for contemporary interest in the *I Ching*. Nostalgia was also part of its allure in traditional China for those who, like Confucius, longed for the supposed virtue of the long-past era of King Wen and the Duke of Zhou. Thus the *I Ching* was in a sense counter-cultural in that its association with an idealized antiquity could serve to criticize the present. The modern nostalgia for the enchanted world is to some degree fallacious—the *Zhouyi* depicts an era when all were in constant terror of supernatural entities who required human sacrifice to be propitiated, and of pervasive warfare without notions of peace or compassion.

Curry's opinion illustrates another set of assumptions that impede serious consideration of divination—that divination, like other "superstitions" is in a zero-sum contest with science for the contemporary mind. In actuality, all sorts of spiritual beliefs can be held simultaneously with scientific ones. Here Curry inadvertently accepts the narrative he resists—that religion and magic will entirely be replaced by science. In this view, those who continue to adhere to religious modes of understanding are stuck in a primitive way of thought. Furthermore, religion and magic are harmful as they inhibit the progress of the rationality needed to solve human problems. In contrast, no less a rationalist than Ludwig Wittgenstein was more open-minded, declaring that we cannot understand early beliefs and practices if we regard them as simply mistaken. This brings us back to my basic point that what is important about the study of divination is not whether it "works" or not, but its place in the lives of those who used it. While divination has long been excluded from academic philosophy, many practitioners of divination hold advanced degrees and write with considerable learning and intelligence. One psychic who advertises online was a professor at Yale. This does not mean that divination is "true," whatever that might imply, but it does establish that it cannot be dismissed as the product of ignorance.

Divination is related to philosophy in another way—it must be based, if only implicitly, on a cosmology, a mental model of the universe. The earliest divinatory method is probably the assumption that there exists another realm, one inhabited by supernatural beings who can know things that we do not. These beings might be deceased ancestors, gods (Apollo for Delphi, for example), or spirits, who might be angelic or malevolent. Christian heresiology denounced divination but did not question its reality. Rather, it forbade it, claiming that the information came from diabolic spirits intent on causing harm to the practitioner and to the Christian faithful generally. A deeper reason is probably that divination provided access to transcendent reality outside the church's control. That even the most draconian repression has never succeeded in eliminating divination suggests how much it is valued by those who resort to it.

Divination and psychology

Insecurity is an obvious reason for divination, but this is not in itself a criticism as behaviors to alleviate anxiety are universal. It is also obvious that many diviners are fraudsters who prey on their clients. Divination can be a powerful means of manipulation. In the past when diviners served as advisors to the powerful, they must have acted in their own interest—failure to please the client could prove fatal. In my experience many contemporary diviners—astrologers and Tarot readers, for example—are honest and sincere, though this does not ensure that they always give sound advice. Nor should we assume that clients credulously accept whatever they are told by diviners.

While the ability to perform divination is sometimes presented as a rare psychic or spiritual ability possessed by only a few, it is actually quite common, as is the ability to pray or perform rituals. People who feel they have an ability typically want to use it, whether it is driving a car, playing a musical instrument, speaking a foreign language—or even channeling the dead. In this sense, divination is carried out for personal satisfaction beyond any specific practical need. Most astrologers or *I Ching* readers, for example, do it for themselves and family and friends, not for income.

There are several useful ways to think about divination that are more productive than condemnation on religious or scientistic grounds. Since the last century, the predominant explanation of divination has shifted from supernatural and cosmological to psychological. This was established as the new paradigm by Carl Jung who redefined the ancient Chinese classic, and divination generally, as tools for exploring the unconscious mind.

Jung explained the *I Ching* with his famous concept of "synchronicity" or "meaningful coincidence." Synchronicity can be viewed as correlative cosmology in modern garb in that it finds associations between mental and external events. The notion has become part of contemporary culture, despite being subjected to stringent criticism, both by psychologists and scientists. It is suspect for them because the notion of "meaningful coincidence" or "non-causal" connection, while not explicitly supernatural, does not close the door to it. In his writings Jung seems to vacillate on this issue, perhaps wanting to have it both ways. Indeed, Jung's archetypal psychology does seem to embody a fundamental modern ambivalence about the supernatural, although, unlike Patrick Curry, he does not propose a necessary conflict with science. Indeed, Jung's work can be seen as providing a corrective to scientistic views in showing that the supernatural is embedded in human consciousness.

From the somewhat different perspective of cognitive science, it is almost impossible for the human mind to conceive events as random. Divination uses randomness to create seeming order. (Some phenomena used in divination are not truly random, such as the positions of heavenly bodies at the time of birth, but they function this way because they are not based on choice.) Seeking causes of events is of obvious benefit in helping one control them. Divination activates the mind's often unconscious processing of apparent randomness into pattern, but this processing is not perfect. Thus mental patterns often include irrational elements, such as vengeful ancestors or spirits or conspiracy theories. Many contemporary practitioners of divination, to sustain credibility, tend to avoid referring directly to anything supernatural. This is not dishonest—psychic mechanisms, though never convincingly established in scientific experiment, are not necessarily supernatural (regarding psi generally, see Blackmore 1996, 2004).

The simplest psychological explanation of divination is that it is intuition, that is, rapid processing of clues that is not fully conscious. On this account, the diviner senses things about the inquirer that are then attributed to a hexagram line text, an array of cards, planet locations on a birth chart, or a special ability, such as channeling. Because we are all vulnerable to the same afflictions, it is often easy for the diviner to guess the inquirer's concerns. In the Western Zhou common concerns included pleasing the powerful, avoiding blame, correct military tactics, sacrifice, safe traveling, and avoiding bandits. All these are life or death matters, in contrast to modern divinatory queries, which most often involve romance, career decisions, and the like. Those are rare in the *Zhouyi* because for arranged marriages mutual attraction was not necessarily a factor, though partner suitability was. Career was more determined by birth than choice.

Much of what happens in divination can be explained as "cold reading." In this technique, which lends itself to outright deception, broad statements are put forth by the diviner, who then develops them based on the inquirer's response. Statements such as, "You are under a great deal of stress right now," or, "You've had a loss," are so open-ended as to almost always attain an affirmative response from anyone. In the Western Zhou, the equivalents might be, "You will be meeting a powerful person," or "Your servants might run away." Skeptics often dismiss all divination as cold reading, but it seems to me excessively reductionist. I think we can understand the experience of divination better if we allow it to keep some of its mystery.

Intuition is a common explanation for correct divinations, but this faculty is itself mysterious. It is usually explained as very rapid, not fully conscious mental processing of subliminal clues. In contrast, psychic explanations imply direct, non-sensory communication between minds. Extensive research has failed to

convincingly demonstrate paranormal capacities, though many
individuals believe they have had such experiences. (For a skeptical
account see Blackmore 2004: 288–303 *et passim*.)Yet direct,
non-sensory communication between minds, while unproven, does
not inherently require the existence of anything supernatural, and
could be due to an as yet undiscovered physical interaction. While
anecdotes of psychism abound, almost invariably these are third
person accounts that require suspension of disbelief. So we are left
where we began—divination and the supernatural are common
modes of human experience, partly but perhaps not entirely
explainable by psychology. Love of mystery and belief in unseen
realms seem to be hard-wired into the human brain. (Science also
has its unseen realms—neither subatomic particles nor black holes
can be perceived through the senses.)

Regarding the *Changes* and divination generally, the dominant
paradigm of reducing these to psychology has the appeal of
bypassing all these uncertainties. As Jung himself, while clearly
advocating the *I Ching* as a tool for self-discovery, by means of the
non-causal principle of synchronicity, declared:

> I have no answer to the multitude of problems that arise
> when we seek to harmonize the oracle of the *I Ching* with our
> accepted scientific canons ... nothing "occult" is to be inferred.
> My position in these matters is pragmatic ... (1949: xxxiiif.)

This leaves open the question of why, in the present day, many
turn to divination instead of, or in addition to, more conventional
sources of advice such as psychotherapy. One reason may be that
it is easier and cheaper. But beyond this, there is something about
divining that satisfies human needs. It holds the allure of adding
something unknown to one's life.

I like to let Jung have the last word:

> The less one thinks about the theory of the *I Ching*, the more
> soundly one sleeps. (1949: xxxix)

This is true not only because of supernatural fears but also
philological ones. Obsessing over possible meanings of ancient
words is not necessarily conducive to easy sleep.

3

History and the intellectual context

The date of the *Zhouyi*

The most basic fact about anything historical is its date. This is not only important in itself, it allows us to explore context, as well as what preceded and followed it. History is about development. When studying ancient times, even approximate dating is still helpful for many purposes. While we do know that the *Zhouyi* is very old, its composition can only be fixed within a range of centuries. Needham once termed the dating of the *Zhouyi*, "one of the most disputed of sinological questions," and it remains disputed today (1956: 306). Given that the received text was almost certainly developed over many years, and contains much that had previously been transmitted orally, a single date is not to be expected.

According to myth, Fu Xi, nominally c. 12,000 BCE, was inspired to invent the trigrams by numbers or figures that he saw on the shell of a turtle. The addition of the judgment and line texts were apocryphally attributed to King Wen and/or the Duke of Zhou, which would approximately date the origin of these texts to c. 1046, the time of the Shang to Zhou dynastic transition. This date was widely accepted in traditional China but recent scholarship finds no evidence of a role for these culture heroes and has moved up the estimated date of composition.

Rutt, who does not accept the tradition about King Wen and the Duke of Zhou, summarizes what we know about dating as follows:

> It is not unreasonable to conclude that the book as we now have it comes from later Western Zhou times, possibly the last quarter of the ninth century (825–800 BC); but the material in it may well reflect an oral history going back three to five centuries or more. (33)

He further notes that quotations in the divination anecdotes of the *Zuozhuan*, (which he dates as late fourth or early third century BCE), differ minimally from the received text, suggesting that the text was relatively fixed by this time. The earliest excavated manuscript of the *Zhouyi*, that owned by the Shanghai Museum, is reliably dated to c. 300 BCE. Though there are many varia, most are non-substantative, confirming that the text was mostly stable by that time. It is similar with the Mawangdui silk manuscript, found in a tomb sealed in 168 CE. This also has variants, notably a different ordering of the hexagrams and different tags for thirty-three of the sixty-four hexagrams. Yet the variants are not such as to radically alter our understanding of the *Changes*.

Shaughnessy (1999: 295f.) has proposed a somewhat less ancient date, close to the end of the Western Zhou (771 BCE). While these estimates vary over a range of nearly three centuries, it remains that the *Zhouyi* is very ancient and was transmitted with relative consistency. Whatever date is accepted for the *Zhouyi* it, along with the Hebrew Bible, remains one of the two oldest texts in continuous use. (There are older texts from Mesopotamia and Egypt but these have not been in continuous use.)

Stephen Field takes an alternative approach and accepts the traditional view that the line texts were authored by the Duke of Zhou (2015: 16 *et passim*). His commentaries attempt to connect many of the lines to events at the beginning of the Zhou Dynasty. This is in accord with a revisionist tendency that wants to maintain the traditional beliefs about the *I Ching*. I regard this as providing a useful counterbalance to Doubting Antiquity but feel that, just as we should not arbitrarily discard traditional accounts, neither should we accept them without evidence. Field is a distinguished sinologist and scholar of divination so I suspect his translation is akin to a thought experiment—working out what the line texts would mean if they really were composed by the Duke of Zhou. To my knowledge there is no evidence for this culture hero's role other than a tradition that arose centuries after his lifetime. Nonetheless, given all the uncertainties about this mysterious text, I believe there is room for translations that, like Field's, employ alternate assumptions, so long as they are stated forthrightly.

The physical nature of ancient Chinese texts

Some idea of the physical basis of ancient Chinese texts helps to appreciate the problems faced by paleographers (specialists in ancient writing) in restoring the archaeological remnants to readable form. Bound books of the sort that fill our shelves did not exist in ancient China. Books were either bamboo strips or silk; characters were brushed on (see frontispiece). Bamboo was most widely used. Fewer silk manuscripts have survived, perhaps because silk is more perishable. Important examples of the latter are the Mawangdui *Changes* and the so-called *Chu Silk Manuscript*, which date to approximately 300 BCE (Barnard). For the received text as read from the Han Dynasty onward, we have no early manuscript version.

Virtually all early manuscripts have lacunae. Additionally, the order of textual elements is often uncertain because the leather thongs that bound the bamboo strips disintegrated long ago, leaving the strips scattered out of their original order. (For the fascinating story of the reconstruction of the order of the Shanghai Museum bamboo manuscript based on the breakage patterns of the strips, see Shaughnessy [2014: 47–66].) Silk manuscripts are more perishable but have the advantage of preserving the order of the text. All manuscripts were chirographic until the rise of woodblock printing, which is better suited to Chinese characters than movable type. The earliest known printed book, many centuries later than any *Changes* manuscript, is the British Museum's famous *Diamond Sutra*, dated 868 CE. With the invention of printing the Chinese classics attained wider dissemination and hence inspired many commentaries.

All of the manuscripts of the *Zhouyi* are written in ancient forms of the Chinese scripts. Except for facsimile versions, nearly all of which are published in China, all printed versions use *Kaishu* (standard traditional characters which came into use gradually, beginning in the late Han Dynasty) or *Jiantizi* (simplified characters). Most modern printed editions of ancient manuscripts are actually transcriptions of the bamboo strip, oracle bone, bronze or other early scripts. For the most part, the transcription of ancient scripts into contemporary ones is straightforward for those with the necessary paleographic knowledge. However, what we read now looks quite different from the early originals.

The (dis)organization of early Chinese texts

Modern books, other than some that are deliberately *avant garde*, are organized upon clear principles. Novels are narratives; although there may be flashbacks, the story unfolds in a coherent way. Non-fiction is organized by chapters, each of which has a specific topic. Dictionaries and encyclopedias are alphabetical. Early Chinese texts follow none of these principles. They are compilations of material from diverse, unspecified sources. While they may have a unifying theme—answers to divinatory queries in the case of the *Zhouyi*—the ordering of material within the text often seems random. The *Lunyu* (usually translated as *The Analects of Confucius*) for example, is an assembly of anecdotes without clear thematic organization but unified by the presence of Confucius and his disciples. The *Zhuangzi* (which takes its name from its philosopher author), like the *Lunyu*, has a generally consistent philosophical outlook, yet treatment of specific topics extends for at most a few paragraphs and thematically related anecdotes are not necessarily placed together. Other early texts similarly are not thematically organized. Familiar examples are the *Dao De Jing* (*The Classic of the Way and Virtue*), the *Zhuangzi*, the *Lunyu*, and the *Zuozhuan* (supposedly a commentary on the *Spring and Autumn Annals*). All have some degree of unity with respect to ideas, style, rhetorical patterns, voice, and so on, but lack the coherently organized structure we expect from books. Thus early editors thought differently from later ones. They seem to have envisioned their role as getting all the material safely into written form, rather than imposing systematic organization. And, to give them their due, at a time when few copies of texts existed and writing materials were scarce, their priority had to be preservation of the material entrusted to them.

With early Chinese literature we can see a progression toward greater thematic organization, although collections of anecdotes continue to be created. (I use the term literature to refer to any writing other than mere record-keeping, not in the modern sense that limits it to poetry, fiction, drama, and essays.) The *Spring and Autumn Annals*, a bare listing of events during the 241 years from 722 to 481 BCE has only a few events recorded for each year, many of which are executions, with the criteria for including specific events being unclear. The work can be likened to a random collection of newspaper headlines without any articles below them. In the *Zuozhuan*, nominally a commentary on the *Spring and Autumn Annals* but probably composed centuries later, we have complete anecdotes. Still later, the Grand Historian, Sima Qian (d. 86 BCE) assembled material from diverse sources, put them together into chronological narratives and provided his own commentary.

In this evolutionary scheme of Chinese writing, the *Zhouyi* belongs almost at the earliest stage. Only the Shang oracle bone inscriptions are more limited in their expression. The earliest of these inscriptions were made c. 1200 BCE and consist of brief divinatory inquiries, sometimes with a few words recording the outcome. These writings are of great historical (and aesthetic) interest but do not attain literary status. In the *Zhouyi*, unlike the oracle bone inscriptions, phrases are assembled into larger units, made possible by use of bamboo and silk instead of bone, but are still extremely terse.

It is hard to escape the conclusion that earlier writers simply did not have the expressive concepts that were available to later ones. Either the vocabulary and concepts did not yet exist, or the mental effort to write more details was simply too great. (If the latter seems implausible, remember how hard it was to write a paper of just a few sentences in elementary school.) I do not believe these early writers were holding back or lazy; rather, their culture had simply not developed the means to express much that later could be done with ease. This is a significant factor accounting for the laconic nature of the *Zhouyi*, and also for its suggestive rather than precise mode of expression.

What comes across as lack of organization in ancient texts makes them less easily readable than later ones. At first they can seem a confusing jumble. We wonder why they include what they do and wish they would tell us more. Once we let go of many of our expectations of what a book should be and take the text on its own terms, we can make sense of books like the *Zhouyi* and even enjoy the reading of them. This enjoyment is not the complete absorption into a flow state that many novels and some non-fiction provide, but the excitement of mental travel to a remote place, not only far away in space and time but, most important, having a different mode of human consciousness.

Personally, I am unfazed by the somewhat haphazard organization of the old classics, partly from long familiarity with them and partly because I have the peculiar habit of opening scholarly books at random until I find a particularly interesting or provocative passage. I do eventually read the whole book, or most of it, but in my own order. I am not recommending this peculiar way of reading, but simply pointing out that books can be read in non-linear fashion. I suspect that many skip around when studying, based on unconscious shifts in attention or mental energy. Indeed, when using the Internet, cognitive random walks are the rule rather than the exception. When we recognize the variability of attention, the lack of linearity in these old texts should seem less strange.

The first great transition: From oral to written

The earliest texts we have contain much that I refer to as transcribed oral material, that is material that originally was orally transmitted and later put into writing. The foundational texts of many civilizations are of this sort. Examples are the Homeric epics, the *Book of Songs* of China, the *Ramayana*, and the Gospels. What we know of the words of Socrates, Confucius, Shakyamuni Buddha, and even Jesus were written down by others, in some cases centuries later. (The oxymoronic term "oral literature" is best avoided, but a good substitute has yet to be proposed.) For both translators and readers of early texts, being aware of the distinctive features of originally oral material, as contrasted with purely chirographic or printed texts, helps resolve some of their seeming strangeness. (The distinction is not absolute, because even today characteristically oral elements are frequently incorporated into written texts.)

In what follows I have made much use of Walter Ong's notions of orality and literacy, and those of Eric Havelock, the latter based on the very different Homeric epics. Their scholarship guided me in being aware of the problems unique to oral transmission and in recognizing transcribed oral material in the *Zhouyi*. Walter Ong holds that underlying the specific characteristics of oral material is the need to compensate for the limitations of memory. Thus stock phrases are commonly used and are often put to use to serve multiple purposes. Referring to the work of Havelock, Ong points out that:

> an oral culture demands that knowledge be processed in more or less formulary style and that it be constantly recycled orally— otherwise it simply vanishes for good ... (Ong and Farrell 2002: 432)

Furthermore:

> An oral culture does not *put* its knowledge *into* mnemonic patterns: it *thinks* its knowledge in mnemonic patterns ... It does not add formulaic patterns to its thinking. Its thinking consists in such patterns. Clichés constitute its thought. (Ong 2002: 480)

And:

> Homeric Greeks valued clichés because ... the entire oral noetic world or thought world relied upon the formulaic constitution of thought. In an oral culture, knowledge, once acquired, had to be constantly repeated or would be lost; fixed formulaic thought patterns were essential for wisdom and effective administration. (1982: 23)

From this latter observation we can start to appreciate why a book filled with repetitions of standard phrases could come to be respected as a book of wisdom—it records in permanent form the key phrases used to express thought.

There are many set phrases in the *Zhouyi*, of which the most obvious are the opening four words, *Yuan, Heng, Li, Zhen*, in the

Western Zhou a simple invocation, but later read as an itemization of Confucian moral principles. Set phrases can seem to make sense almost anywhere. In written material repetitions or clichés can be annoying, but in oral material they serve to orient the listeners by expressing a familiar theme. The pervasiveness of set phrases is a major reason why the *Zhouyi* seems peculiar to us. Because, as Ong stresses, oral cultures were always pressing against the limitations of memory, it was more efficient to employ set phrases that could be adapted to fit many situations than to constantly create new ones. Someone had to invent the formulaic phrases of course, but then they became akin to memes, perpetuating themselves by a process akin to natural selection. Their use was not without controversy—Eric Havelock suggests that Plato's famous exclusion of poets from his *Republic* was because they relied on the use of set phrases, rather than the newly invented analytic prose that he felt was superior.

Set phrases are incorporated into texts by the process of *bricolage* in the sense employed by Claude Levi-Strauss to describe myth—making use of whatever materials are at hand to serve a communicative purpose. *Bricolage* results in a certain monotony of ideas and some degree of imprecision but at the same time it shows, by this very repetition, the obsessions of the culture that produced them. And it makes for efficiency in communication, hence the pervasiveness of clichés in all languages.

Ong states that:

> [...] abstractly sequential, classificatory, explanatory examination of phenomena or of stated truths is impossible without writing and reading. (Ong 2002: 8)

These literary elements are also lacking in the *Zhouyi*, persuasive evidence in my view that it was created by assembling oral fragments, the sheer quantity of which made complete memorization rare, if possible at all. Unique to the *Zhouyi* is the innovative way invented to organize the oral material—use of the hexagrams as templates. Joseph Needham termed this a "stupendous filing system." Unlike an alphabetical filing system, the contents were organized to be accessed by a random method—which is exactly what the yarrow sticks or coins were suited for, making the structure ideal for divinatory use. What the diagrams accomplished, other than providing a visual enhancement for the *I Ching* was to provide a framework for rendering the collected material into written form without altering its original fragmentary nature. This mode of organization ensures frustration when trying to read the *Zhouyi* in linear sequence as one would a narrative text. When used as originally intended—to locate responses to divinatory inquiries— the *Zhouyi* is highly efficient. The experience is further enhanced by the aura of mystery created by the diagrams.

Organizing the text by using the hexagrams as templates was an inspired invention—perhaps even a "disruptive technology"—in that it gradually replaced the more expensive and time-consuming pyromancy. As a technology, the hexagrams were a great success; they are still in use 3,000 years later. As technology advanced from printed books to computer screens the hexagrams were easily assimilated. On the other hand, they are a limited invention, with no application other than divination and metaphysical speculation.

A few variants on the *I Ching* arose, using modifications of the hexagrams. For example the *Tai Xuan Jing,* or *Canon of Supreme Mystery,* used four-line figures with two types of broken lines (Nylan 1993) but these *I Ching* derivatives never supplanted the Western Zhou invention.

Building on Ong's point about the limitations of orality, we can recognize that the diagrams provide a system of access that permits transcribed oral material to be easily located. Many of the line texts must have been diviners' oral prognostications, but no diviner could have remembered all of them. Nor would a randomly ordered listing of hundreds of divinatory responses be useful; a method for picking particular ones would be necessary. To be credible as divination, the method must not seem like conscious choice on the part of inquirer or diviner, but a mysterious special ability. Shamans, channelers, psychics, to give a few examples, present their pronouncements as obtained from another realm or an alternative form of consciousness.

Some *I Ching* practitioners, past and present, open the book and browse to find something inspirational for a current problem, just as some do with the Bible, or Shakespeare, or other similar repositories of wisdom. I do this myself at times, particularly with the *Dazhuan,* the *Dao De Jing,* and the *Lunyu.* This is not quite the same as bibliomancy, in which a passage is selected at random.

The hexagram system bears a certain resemblance to the Roman *ars memorativa,* in which things to be remembered are mentally placed on a spatial array. Astrology is another example of this sort of mental mapping; character traits and life events are assigned to astronomical bodies and their positions. In a sense the *Changes* is similar, placing prognostications on a spatial array. Although the technique is traditionally attributed to a story about the poet Simonides of Ceos, the method is clearly pre-literate in that it is a means of compensating for the limitations of memory. (The first extended consideration of this important aspect of early consciousness is the justly renowned 1996 monograph by Frances Yates.)

In oral cultures, the manner of recitation is particularly important. As stated by the New Testament textual scholar Werner Kelber:

> As was well known by most ancient cultures, living words, especially those uttered by charismatic speakers, are the carriers of power and being.
> [...]
> If Jesus was a charismatic speaker, he risked his message on the oral medium and did not speak with a conscious regard for literary retention. (2002: 481)

Kelber makes the important point that hearing a charismatic figure is quite a different experience from reading his words. Applying this insight to the *Zhouyi* reminds us that phrases that may seem banal now would have been more moving when sonorously voiced by a charismatic diviner. Virtually any prognostication would have emotional impact because it would concern the inquirer's vital interests. Yet, particularly in a culture that was only partially literate, the written word would have been regarded with awe. The mythical attribution to Fu Xi and the Zhou culture heroes would have augmented the prestige of the prognostication.

Ong makes another observation pertinent to that of Kelber and helpful in understanding the *Zhouyi:*

> in a culture that lives on clichés [set phrases], almost everything that is said for purposes of deliberation or reflection, or speculation is known to everyone already.

The implication is that because the material is familiar to most listeners, it is the vigor of the delivery, rather than the content, that makes recitation interesting. This is true of most political speeches today as well as those given at ceremonial occasions such as graduation. In such it is the importance of the speaker that matters, not the content.

The *Zhouyi* was composed at the intersection of orality and literacy, making the distinction somewhat hazy. A divination would be delivered vocally, but using a text that in turn consisted mainly of transcribed oral material. The unique feature of the *Changes*, its mysterious-seeming diagrams—intentionally or not—provided visual stimulation that may have compensated for a less than intense auditory presence. By its nature, divination is a rhetorical process and must employ methods of persuasion, often including visual aids. The hexagrams have a numinous quality akin to yantras, mandalas, astrological charts, and other sorts of mystical or sacred diagrams. Though any meaning found in the hexagrams is the creation of the user, they serve to give an enigmatic authority to the *Book of Changes*, an authority that it holds to the present day.

Kelber does not discuss the different sort of charisma possessed by texts, whether manuscript or printed. Texts such as the Bible or Quran can be extremely moving to believers. We cannot recreate the experience of listening to Jesus or Mohammed, but we have powerful substitutes. The *I Ching* in book form was charismatic in China. Traditionally it was kept wrapped in silk and it was considered improper to put another book on top of it. For many modern *I Ching* admirers the simple but elegant gray and yellow Wilhelm-Baynes volume has a special aura. This is true even for me, despite my approach to the *Changes* being very different.

As suggested above, it is not the *Zhouyi* texts by themselves that fascinate but their combination with the hexagrams. Together they signified the possibility that the nature of the cosmos, and our lives within it, could be explained if one fully understood the diagrams. Thus the loss of charisma with the transcription of the oral phrases into writing is compensated by the addition of the hexagrams. Without these the *Zhouyi* would simply be a collage of phrases, many already largely familiar to people of the Western Zhou. By a phrase's location in relation to the diagram it seems to have a unique place within the cosmos. This provides a reassurance that one's life events are part of a larger pattern. The Western Zhou text

makes no such abstract claim, but it would have been implicit in the use of the classic. In the later *Dazhuan* or *Great Commentary*, the claim is explicit:
The *Changes* is a paradigm of Heaven and Earth ...

And, in a phrase repeated in Chinese writings down to the present:
Looking up we use it ... to observe the configurations of Heaven, and looking down, we use it to examine the patterns of earth. (1: 4; Lynn 51)

Of course there are ways of making texts charismatic other than diagrams or illustrations. Buddhist sutras serve more as devotional objects than as books to be read. In New York's Chinatown is a small Buddhist temple that proudly displays a copy of the extremely lengthy *Hua Yen* sutra written by a monk with his own blood. It was locked securely in a thick glass case—not to be read but to display the power of the Dharma as revealed in this extreme devotional act. While not the same as actually hearing the Buddha speak the Dharma, it tells of its extreme inspirational power.

In printed books, spiritual authority often derives from its supposed origin as the words of a religious founder. With the *Book of Changes* the authority figures were not deities but Fu Xi, a kind of trans-human, and the fully human King Wen and the Duke of Zhou, whose roles as authors of the judgment and line texts are now considered to be mythical. This helps bridge the oral-written gap but makes the texts the special knowledge of sagely figures.

While Kelber argues that oral language is the most democratic form (21), Ong points out that what is useful is not nostalgia for the supposedly more authentic non-literate phase of civilization, but keeping in mind as we read that the material originally held attention *because* of its oral presentation. This would be particularly true of divination or any other magical or ritual use of language—both are mainly oral, even today, despite the Internet. (The question of the relation between Internet transmission and orality I will leave to others.) Thus in reading the ancient texts, it is useful to imagine the intonation and setting that to a great degree were responsible for their authority. Phrases from the *Zhouyi* would have seemed particularly profound if resonantly recited by a revered adept. Even now, divinations are mainly provided orally, the foibles of memory contributing to their perceived accuracy.

The second great transition: Axialization and the Confucianization of the *Zhouyi*

The most helpful heuristic I have found for characterizing the differences between the mind of the *Zhouyi* and that of the later *I Ching* is the concept of axialization. This term is an expansion of the notion of the axial age, the contribution of the German psychiatrist and philosopher Karl Jaspers (1883–1969), although similar ideas had been expressed by others. The basic concept is that for unknown reasons, reflective thought arose spontaneously in several cultures at about the same time in history, without those cultures having any direct contact with each other.

As a powerful synthesizing concept this has attracted controversy, although I feel the critiques suggest modification, not rejection, of Jasper's basic idea. The objections to the axial age concept are basically twofold. First, that the religious and philosophical ideas that arose in the several cultures were not identical; and second, that the "axial age" did not occur at exactly the same time in all cases. I grant these objections and use the concept in the more limited sense of describing a pivotal transformation in human consciousness that occurred in many—but not all—cultures at different times and in very different ways. In this formulation the "axial age" is modified to "axialization," a kind of cultural change that occurred at various points in history, not only c. 500 BCE. In what follows, I refer to those thinkers who initiated the new ideas as "axial" and those who followed them as "post-axial," although these are not hard categories.

Confucius is perhaps the earliest axial thinker in China, followed by Laozi, Zhuangzi, Xunzi, and Mengzi, to name some of the best known. The *Ten Wings* of the *I Ching* also have axial characteristics, though inconsistently. These often inject ideas not evident in the *Zhouyi*, such as this from the *Daxiang, Greater Commentary on the Diagrams*, referred to as The Image in Wilhelm-Baynes, for hexagram 42:

Wind and Thunder: *Yi.*
A prince thus sees good and follows it,
Has faults and corrects them. (Rutt 387)

The *Zhouyi* text for this hexagram contains no reference to a prince
or upright person, or to self-improvement. The interpretation is
attributed to the trigram positions rather than the line texts, though
how wind over thunder becomes a reference to virtue is obscure.
What is post-axial in this excerpt is the notion of self-examination;
recognizing one's faults and striving to correct them, a central
theme in Confucius and post-axial Chinese texts generally. While
there are many references to the behavior of princes and nobles
in the *Zhouyi*, none suggest any concept of moral insight or
self-improvement. These are distinctive axial ideas.

Among the axial thinkers outside China were Shakyamuni
Buddha, the Hebrew prophets, Socrates, Plato, and Aristotle.
Significantly, only Plato and Aristotle actually wrote the works
attributed to them. Axialization seems to have first appeared
around the dawn of literacy, though there are other theories as
to why it occurred at a particular point in cultural development.
There is also controversy about which early figures were part of
the axial age. For the present discussion it is Confucius (551–479
BCE) on whom I will focus. This is because it was mainly Confucian
ideology that produced the axial transformation of the pre-axial
Zhouyi to the post-axial *I Ching*. Although, contrary to myth,
Confucius himself had nothing to do with the writing or editing
of the *I Ching*, the ethical, philosophical, and cosmological ideas
added to it are those conventionally referred to as "Confucianism."

The basic components of axialization are divided into six aspects
by Charles Taylor (30–46). With some additions and modification
of my own these are:

1   Transcendence or going beyond the visible natural
    and human worlds. This often means an alternative
    reality apparent only to a few individuals with special
    insight. Shamanism and some other divination methods
    foreshadowed the notion of transcendent reality.

2   Social, ethical, and philosophical criticism based on
    transcendent ideas. Taylor's examples are the Hebrew
    prophets.

3 "Second order thinking" in which concepts used to describe the cosmos—heaven, earth, and humanity in the Chinese formulation—are subjected to critical analysis.

4 Globality (not the same as globalization as an economic term)—the belief that ideas apply not only to one's own culture but to all of humanity. Proselytizing derives from this aspect of axial thought.

5 Disembedding—being able to somewhat separate one's thinking from that of one's culture. In pre-axial cultures religion was an integral part of personal and social life not a separate one, and beliefs were neither chosen, nor questioned. With axialization, religion and spirituality become distinct areas of life and to some degree a matter of choice. This permitted the diversity that has been characteristic of religious life ever since.

6 Religion expands beyond "feeding the gods," that is, making offerings to them to obtain prosperity. The pre-axial gods were not necessarily predisposed to benefiting humans and had to be bribed. Under axiality, gods or God were benevolent, but judged humans on the morality of their behavior. However, pre-axial beliefs persisted to varying degrees, as we see in present-day Chinese funeral rituals.

Karen Armstrong summed up axialization in a more direct way:

> The Axial sages were not interested in providing their disciples with a little edifying uplift ... Their objective was to create an entirely different kind of human being. (123)

This is something of an over-statement. Like the Hebrew prophets, the "axial sages" would have considered themselves as restoring the proper way for humanity, not creating a new form. Armstrong is correct in that axiality initiated new concepts of how humans should live, but typically, as with Confucius and Laozi, new ideals were presented as those of a mythical high antiquity.

Confucius's thought was axial in nature, though it is sometimes argued that it lacked a notion of transcendence because his ideal was a life fully lived in society. However, Confucius's authority was the Way of Heaven, a clearly transcendent notion, though not mystical. He was highly critical of the society of his day that had fallen away from the ritually correct and simpler society of high antiquity. He never doubted that his moral principles were universal. For him ritual was not embedded but a special area of life that required conscious compliance. The proper motive for proper behavior was not personal benefit but living in accord with the Way of Heaven. In contrast, the *Zhouyi* is clearly pre-axial. There is no notion at all of transcendence, no reflection on ideals, people were embedded in society and lacked any perspective from which to criticize it. Thus the *Zhouyi* was pre-axial, but with the addition of the *Ten Wings* to become the *I Ching* it became axialized. In a passage already quoted in part:

> The *Changes* is a paradigm of Heaven and Earth ... Thus we understand the reasons underlying what is hidden and what is clear. We trace things back to their origins then turn back to their ends. Thus we understand the axiom of life and death. (I: 4; Lynn 51)

Here the nature of reality is analyzed; there is nothing like this in the Western Zhou text, which contains no mention of metaphysical or abstract ethical ideas, no social criticism (regrettably, human sacrifice and warfare were routine), and no explicit metaphysical theorizing.

In translating, I have consciously used the notion of pre-axiality as an aid for my choice of meanings. I do not believe that I forced this onto the text but rather used it as a guide for consistency with the characteristics of ancient ways of thought. In my view, some of the other translations purporting to be of the Western Zhou meanings, though not the main ones I have cited, have been anachronistic in allowing ethical and philosophical abstractions to creep in. The notion of axiality helps one avoid such errors.

At the same time we must keep in mind that the pre-axial *Zhouyi* did become the post-axial *I Ching*. How this happened is a question of great importance in Chinese intellectual history but it has not been sufficiently studied, in no small part because suitable sources are very limited. My tentative suggestions as to how the *Zhouyi* may have foreshadowed some of the ethical and philosophical ideas later attached to it are presented in Chapter Seven, which follows the translation.

Dialogue and the rhetoric of ancient thought

In the West, philosophy and divination often overlapped until the general rise of skepticism in the eighteenth-century Enlightenment. Both Socrates and Confucius had some faith in divination, without it being prominent in their teachings. This does not mean that everyone was a believer. Jonathan Swift, in 1708 under the *nom de plume* of "Isaac Bickerstaff Esq.," wrote a famous series of satires discrediting a prominent astrologer, John Partridge. Yet many philosophers from the axial age on, including Plato, Aristotle, Confucius and Augustine assumed that divination could be a valid way of learning truth, at least in some circumstances. Similarly, in China, many of the most influential philosophers, including not only Confucius but also Wang Bi, Cheng Yi, Zhu Xi, and Shao Yong were known for their commentaries on the *I Ching*. Not that efficacy was unquestioned; even Confucius was quoted as saying that when he divined he was correct only 70 percent of the time. At the same time, there have always been skeptics, such as the Confucian philosopher Xunzi (310–220 BCE) and the Roman orator Cicero (106–43 BCE).

Many of the earliest philosophical records are in the form of questions and answers. Discussion, or argument, was the only way philosophy could be done prior to writing. This is why early writings such as the Socratic dialogues, the Confucian *Analects*, and the Buddhist *Questions of King Milinda* (c. 100 BCE) are in dialogue form. Dialogue is still intrinsic to education and scholarly exchange, but with the major difference that participants can also draw on an immense quantity of material in printed or electronic form. Though our resources are greater, the methods of teaching and learning have some continuity with those of Socrates and Confucius—they still involve debate, then and now quite often acrimonious.

Walter Ong emphasizes that pre-literate conversation was "agonistic," by which he means that each tried to get the upper hand on his (usually) opponent (478). Ong rather quaintly attributes this change to "co-education." My experience of medical training and practice demonstrates that agonistic interaction is still with us. This seems to be less extreme in sinology than the sciences, or perhaps the one-upmanship is more subtle. The basic point here is that intellectual exchange inherently involves parties contesting with each other, whether cordially or not. This is apparent in the *Lunyu*, in which Confucius frequently admonishes his followers, sometimes insultingly. In a famous example, when asked about death, he replied, "You don't yet understand life, how can you understand death." There is rhetorical cunning involved here—by combining insult with evasion the Master implies he knows about death without having to actually say anything about it.

Preservation of the rhetoric of orality in spiritual texts is not confined to those of ancient China. The Theravada Buddhist suttas, presumably the oldest Buddhist texts, contain deliberate indications that the material was originally oral, particularly the famous opening expression, "This is what I heard at one time ..." This phrase serves to orient the listener or reader to the sutta's supposedly being a transcription of a talk delivered by the Buddha himself at a particular place and time, though the time is indefinite. We are told that even though the Buddha is not present, we will hear (or read) his words and be brought back to a time when the sacred was still present in the world.

There are elements of question and answer in these texts but their structure is mostly master speaks and followers listen. The questions are generally rhetorical, usually from close companions of the Buddha. Though sharing the characteristics of transcribed oral material, the Buddhist suttas (and sutras) are quite different in character from either the *Zhouyi* or the *Lunyu*.

Divination, like philosophical discourse, is inherently dialogic. A question is asked and a response is given. We have no record of how the *Zhouyi* was actually used for divination in the Western Zhou, but it must usually have involved discussion between diviner and client. In later times, inquirers would dialogue with the text as a self-cultivation practice, but the *I Ching* was itself personified as a sage. Thus even in solitary consultation the process was imagined as a dialogue.

The *Zuozhuan* contains the earliest descriptions of *I Ching* divinations, although how much they are related to actual events is impossible to determine. In one anecdote Lady Wu Jiang is under house arrest for her part in a conspiracy (Rutt: 187f.). Her inter-action with the diviner is agonistic in that she directly challenges the prognostication and clearly wins the argument, even though it was by criticizing her own character. By foreseeing, correctly, that she will never be released from house arrest and admitting that her troubles are due to her own actions, she demonstrates moral stature. Here, as often with *Lunyu*, the purpose of the dialogue is not defeating an opponent but ethical clarification or improvement. While we do not find this sort of dialogue in the text of the *Zhouyi*, it is useful to try to imagine the rest of the dialogue of which the phrase is a part.

Textual exegesis has occasionally been likened to divination. Henderson in his study of Chinese exegesis argues convincingly, based on some early Chinese texts, that "divination and textual commentary are ... interwoven in several intricate ways" (1999: 85). To modern readers however, philosophical and divinatory texts seem radically different. This is in part because expectations tend to filter out discordant elements of a text, including references to divination, which most still think has no place in serious philosophy. Setting this bias aside we can see that divinatory dialogues have a remarkable similarity of rhetorical structure with philosophical ones, though they differ in content. In both, ideas are put out and argued over. Both involve fundamental life issues. Verbal exchange of ideas recreates pre-literate modes of cognition. With *I Ching* readings the selected text is not entirely sufficient in itself, hence the need for discussion. Agonistic interaction occurs not only in teaching, but also in doctor-patient discussions, religious devotional activities, such as the Catholic sacrament of confession and even prayer as well as many other activities that involve oral exchange. Though these may at first seem non-argumentative, consider that teachers are constantly correcting students, doctors advising patients to give up unhealthy behaviors, ministers exhorting their parishioners to give up sin, and so on. Thus divinatory interactions involve a very basic and ancient mode of behavior.

4

The unique structure of the *Book of Changes*

In the preceding sections I have discussed the nature of early texts, how they were composed, and how to read them. Now I will go on to show how these principles can be applied to the *Zhouyi*, both to locate it in the history of human consciousness and to explain how it can now be understood 3,000 years later.

The *Changes* has a structure like no other book, a cause both of its fascination and of its difficulty. To make sense out of it, one needs to understand its structure, a fusion of four kinds of components. These are the titles or tags, the hexagram figures, the judgment or hexagram texts, and line texts. The term "hexagram" has two referents. First and most specifically, it refers to the six-line diagram associated with each of the sixty-four units that make up the *Zhouyi*. Because the hexagram is the first and most distinctive aspect of each chapter, by synecdoche an entire chapter group of four elements is often referred as the "hexagram." Although strictly speaking "hexagram" should designate only the six-line diagram, I have followed the usual convention in English and also used the word to refer to the entire four element unit, though at times to avoid ambiguity I have used the term "chapter" instead.

The tags

These are the words, or pairs of words, that appear at the top of most printed versions and seem because of their position to be the titles of each chapter. Rutt argues, in my opinion correctly, that most of these words are not strictly titles because they do not necessarily indicate the subject of the associated lines, rather they are labels for ease of reference. This is based on several lines of evidence. First, while some line texts incorporate the tag character, most do not. Second, in many cases the tag bears little or no relation to the themes of the line texts of the same chapter. Later commentators contrived ways of reading the tags, diagrams, and lines to make them seem related to each other, but these are mostly forced. The most important evidence of the often arbitrary nature of the tags is that in the Mawangdui silk manuscript, thirty-three of the sixty-four tags are different from those of the received versions (Shaughnessy 1996: 16f.).

The Wilhelm-Baynes translations of the tags are often poetic, but at the cost of accuracy. They tend to be based on later methods of interpreting the trigram components of the hexagrams. Other English translations of the tags vary greatly—to add to the potential confusion, there is no standard system of translating them. Hacker provides a table, though not up to date, that lists variant translations (1993: 42–63). In the present translation I have been as literal as possible and avoided altering the meanings to seem to relate to the judgment and line texts of their chapter. I believe that the *Zhouyi* is much clearer if one accepts that texts grouped together do not necessarily have thematic unity, because one can then simply accept the literal meanings. In the translation I have provided the Wilhelm-Baynes renderings in parentheses, since these are the most familiar to English-language readers.

The hexagram figures or diagrams

The famous six-line diagrams are the most distinctive feature of the *Book of Changes*. (The term "hexagram" is a Western invention; the Chinese word for the diagrams is 卦 *gua*, which can refer both to trigrams and hexagrams.) Without the figures, the *Zhouyi* would be just another strange old text. The origin of the figures is uncertain. One theory is that the hexagrams originally represented numbers used in the divination process. This is plausible, given that the numbers one, two, three, and four are written 一, 二 , 三, and 四; this last having originally been written as four horizontal lines. Some Chinese Neolithic pottery is decorated with linear figures but none form trigrams or hexagrams. Another suggestion is that the hexagrams derived from a simple divination system using single lines, with solid being auspicious, and broken inauspicious. This seems the most plausible to me, first because yes-no is the simplest form of divination and still in use with coin tosses, and second because it is consistent with a simple system that expanded over time. Many divination systems gradually increase in complexity in order to provide richer responses, and in the hope of improving accuracy. Unfortunately, we have no extant materials that show intermediate stages between the simple linear figures and the hexagrams.

At some point another variable—fixed versus changing—was added to the broken-solid duality so that each line could have four possible values. Changing lines switched to their opposite so that the first hexagram obtained could generate a second one. Alternatively, the changing line was considered to be the answer to the query. The four possible line types came to be associated with the numbers 6, 7, 8, and 9. This seems not to have been the earliest number association. Changing lines were "old," that is, yin or yang reaching its peak and about to change into its opposite. As yin was even and yang odd, changing yin was 6 and changing yang was 9; that is to say, they were at the two extremes of the sequence.

Despite the eventual predominance of numerological/geometric interpretation during the Western Han, we have no indication of such a system in the Western Zhou. It was in the Han that use of the trigrams and hexagrams lines had become the major way of interpretation, termed the *xiangshu,* or images and numbers school in contrast with the more text-based meaning and pattern school, *yili.* Regarding the early meanings of the *Zhouyi* we have only the texts as evidence. Hence in the present work I do not cover the many ideas about the diagrams that are only attested much later, preferring not to add to the many fanciful beliefs about them. I must also admit that while I appreciate the aesthetics of the hexagrams and their arrays, I personally find the texts of greater interest.

Many readers have sought meaning in the ordering of the hexagrams. Here the Mawangdui manuscript is of particular interest because the hexagram order follows a different principle to that of the received version. The sequence is, however, based on a consistent scheme. (For discussions of trigram and hexagram patterns see Chung Wu: xxxiii–lx; Hacker 1993: 31–130 *et passim*; Rutt: 87–118.) A subculture of *I Ching* aficionados has concerned itself with discovering the true order of the hexagrams but to me this seems somewhat akin to seeking occult meanings in the proportions of the Great Pyramid. For a very elaborate instance of reading mathematical patterns into the hexagrams, see R. S. Cook.

Why six lines?

The final configuration consisting of six lines was probably not arbitrary, but based on cognitive factors. I conclude this because the number of elements in many different divination systems is of similar magnitude. The Chinese calendar worked on a system of sixty days and years. Pre-modern astrology had seven planets (the sun and moon were considered planets) plus twelve zodiac signs and twelve houses, for a total of thirty-one elements. Runes work by a system of twenty-four pebbles with symbols. Tarot has seventy-eight cards. It seems that the mind can most comfortably grasp elements in this range of between thirty and eighty elements. Mathematically these numbers are all of similar magnitude. With respect to the *I Ching*, diagrams of five or seven would have been cognitively suitable but would have removed the vertical symmetry that is visually pleasing as well as the convenient division into two figures of three lines each. Four or eight lines would have given too few or too many possibilities respectively. There are also physical constraints. With runes, more pebbles would have been unwieldy, as would a larger number of Tarot cards.

Systems with elements in the magnitude of those discussed seem to be enough to be responsive to any inquiry; proponents of the various systems believe they can represent all possibilities. Should answers prove inadequate, all systems have means for generating more information. Thus the *I Ching* has moving lines, Tarot has spreads of varying numbers of cards, and astrology can calculate innumerable aspects—angles between any two or more elements. Now with computers, asteroid positions can be added to the mix. The possibilities are unlimited but, like language itself, all systems of divination developed from a limited number of primary elements or building blocks.

The texts

How the hexagrams became associated with the texts is another of the many mysteries that surround the *Book of Changes*. It seems virtually certain that the invention of four types of lines and their grouping into arrays of six elements was separate from the collecting of phrases that make up the texts. One reason for my conclusion is that the cognitive style of working with geometry is quite different from that of working with texts. (If this seems questionable, consider how many textual scholars are geometricians, and vice versa.) The diagrams were likely created based on the visual and geometric possibilities for expanding the two original types of lines. At some point the idea arose to associate the lines with specific prognostic texts. Completing the compilation would require 450 texts (64 judgment texts plus 386 line texts). No single individual could have known 450 prognostic phrases. (The amazing feats of memory attributed to reciters of epics were possible because the material formed coherent narratives, which are far easier to remember than random phrases. Furthermore, their recitations varied considerably.) To simply make up this many phrases would strain anyone's imagination and would lack any basis of authority. Thus the only plausible hypothesis is that officials went around collecting phrases from people thought to have some special knowledge. These may have included diviners, wu-shamans and shamanesses, herbalists, and perhaps non-literate people such as farmers, often assumed by the high-born to have special knowledge. Given the importance of divination for royal authority, a king may have decreed development of an official system, or others may have had the idea, but it seems almost certain that such a project would have required official sponsorship. How it was decided which phrase should go with a specific line is uncertain. Certain patterns can be discerned but this is a subject for another time.

The judgments

These are the brief texts that follow the figures in the received text. There is no consistent English term for this textual element. I follow Wilhelm-Baynes, who entitle each "The Judgment." The other common English term is "Hexagram text." Both are misleading. "Hexagram text" implies an explanation of the diagram or a summary of the line texts of the chapter. The judgments do neither of these—in most cases, they have no clear relation to the hexagram or to the line texts. Later, when the *Zhouyi* became the *I Ching*, it was assumed that the judgments explained the hexagram figures and summed up the prognoses of the line text, but this was based on the Confucians changing the meanings.

The judgments are separate divinatory phrases, somewhat different in character from the line texts and thus likely to have come from different sources. This would also account for why they were separated from the line texts. Possibly the line text positions were all filled but it was desired to add material from another source. There are some phrases found in both kinds of lines, but for the most part they do not overlap. The judgments are often more detailed than the line texts, but sometimes are only a few characters, as with the first hexagram, *Qian*. An example of an extended judgment is that of *Kun*.

Citation conventions

In referring to hexagram lines, the modern convention is to give the hexagram number, then a colon, then the line number. In this system, judgments are designated as 0 and the line texts as 1 through 6. Thus the third line of hexagram 18 would be designated as 18.3. The first two hexagrams have seven lines, designated as 1.7 and 2.7.

This numbering system does not appear in the received or excavated texts but is a Western innovation created for scholarly citation. Sometimes an additional number is provided indicating the specific phrase within a line text. I have not done this, since the division into phrases is not always clear. Instead, in the English I have placed each phrase on a separate line so that references to first, second, third phrase, etc. are clear. The Chinese text has no phrase separations and so I have not added them. I have added punctuation to the Chinese to agree with the English.

As already noted, judgments have two kinds of components. The first of these makes up the entirety of *Qian* 1.0 元亨利貞 *yuan, heng, li, zhen*. This is an invocation. Sometimes other stock phrases appear. The other kind of phrase consists of substantive material more closely resembling the line texts. An example is 2.0, which contains the same invocation as 1.0, though with intercalated words, and other material regarding several matters, including sacrifice and travel.

I have translated the judgment of *Qian*, as "Begin with an offering for favorable divination." In some hexagrams all of the four characters appear, while in others none of them do. The character 亨 *heng*, meaning to offer/receive occurs most often and is clearly the key word, indicating that making a ritual offering to initiate the divination is beneficial. I strongly suspect that to begin every actual divination, the entire four character phrase would have been recited. If so, when incomplete or omitted from the written text it would be assumed.

Most translators have taken this four-character phrase as a favorable prognostication, seemingly ignoring the fact that in many instances the same line includes unfavorable prognoses. However, once *yuan, heng, li, zhen* is recognized as simply the standard invocation, it is clearly neutral as to whether the appended divination will be auspicious or not.

Legge's translation of 1.0, "Great and originating, penetrating, advantageous, correct and firm," is based on the later Confucian moralistic reading. While it seems simply to be a list of virtues, in ritual context it likely was intended to help one attain these virtues. The simple wish for good luck had evolved into a wish to improve one's character.

With the possible exception of 2.1, which refers to sacrifice of a mare, the nature of the offering referred to in the formula is not stated. Likely offerings varied depending on circumstances. It seems unlikely that blood sacrifice would have been practiced for frequent, routine divinations. Later, use of the *Changes* was often preceded by a token offering in the form of burning incense.

The line texts

Following the judgment, except for hexagrams 1 and 2, all the diagrams are followed by a series of six texts, each associated with a specific line. The lines are numbered 1 to 6 from bottom to top. (Hexagrams 1 and 2 have six lines but an extra line text, designated as 1.7 and 2.7.) Each line also has another number indicating whether it is *yin*, designated by 6, or *yang*, designated by 9. I have omitted these numbers in the translation as they are self-evident from the type of line and simply add visual clutter.

The line texts vary grammatically; some are short phrases, others are several sentences. The subject matter is not always consistent within a line. These texts vary in interest. Some are merely set phrases, while others are substantive and give us glimpses into Western Zhou daily life and its difficulties.

Some scholars find a consistent syntax in the line texts. Rutt describes their structure as composed of up to four elements: oracle, indication, prognostic, and observation. He notes that many lines do not have all four elements and some have none (131). Field proposes a slightly different scheme of omen, counsel, and fortune and separates these in his translation, which appears in tabular form (59–62). These schemes are reasonable approximations but I have not used either because I feel they give a mistaken impression that the texts have a more regular structure than is the case. Also, if the compilers were not completely consistent in assembling the material, I do not feel the translator should presume to alter what they did. To the extent there is a recurring pattern I see it more broadly as a statement of the situation, a prognosis, such as beneficial or ominous, and sometimes a recommendation for action, such as making an offering.

The phrase as the unit of meaning

A common confusion that arises when trying to read the *Zhouyi* is trying to relate different phrases in a line, or in the chapter as a whole, to each other. Though a normal expectation when reading most literature, this does not apply to the *Zhouyi*, for which the unit of meaning is not the chapter, nor entire line text, nor the sentence, but the phrase. Put bluntly, the *Zhouyi* is a collection of scraps. Thus a line of text often assembles phrases without evident thematic relationship. To make matters even more confusing, ancient Chinese was unpunctuated, as was much of later classical Chinese. An important—and often difficult—part of translating, even into modern Chinese, is supplying punctuation to clarify the grammatical relation of the words to each other. Dangling modifiers abound. Sometimes the same character can function as a noun or a verb. Particularly vexing is deciding if a noun is the object of the preceding verb, or the subject of the following one. Chinese has helping words for this but they themselves are not always clear. In contrast to Western languages, pronouns in Chinese have no gender, verbs no tenses, and nouns no inflections. Furthermore, Chinese is only incompletely phonetic. Recognizing the meaning of a character does not ensure one will know how it is pronounced. Despite all this, Chinese are quite able to communicate with each other and created one of the world's great literary and philosophical traditions.

Although the characters look intimidating, knowledge of the stroke order rules for writing them quickly helps make them recognizable and will rapidly bring rewards in reading bilingual versions, such as this one. The *Zhouyi* is best read phrase by phrase, not as an ongoing narrative. This means one cannot attain the relaxed flow state one does when reading a novel or a newspaper article.

There are many instances in which phrases about unrelated matters are combined in a line text. Here is an example:

21.5 Biting dried meat, gets yellow metal. Divination harsh. There will be no blame.

The yellow metal is probably an arrowhead, presumably found in the dried meat, making this an auspicious sign. But then the prognosis is harsh, paradoxically followed by reassurance there will be no blame. The latter phrase might be a spell to banish the unfavorable prognosis, otherwise the combination of good and bad prognoses makes no sense. Here, as often, it seems some phrases were inserted at random, characteristic of oral material that depends on memory. Translations add punctuation, which can make the texts clearer, but care is required to avoid inadvertently altering the meanings.

In my view: *sense should be discovered in the Zhouyi, not added to it.* Thus I have not changed word meanings to make the lines read better. However, some lines have quite different meanings depending on how they are punctuated. Often the basis for placement of phrases is not self-evident. Let us look at two examples. First:

8.5 Appearing together for the king to employ to drive out game from three directions.
Misses the birds and animals in front.
The people of the region are not admonished. Auspicious.

This line text is a coherent anecdote from early Chinese life: a group is assembled to aid the king in his hunt. He misses the game, but those involved are not scolded or punished. There is no real doubt about the division into phrases.

But then consider the following:

9.6 Now rains, now stops.
This place still holds potency.
The wife's divination is harsh.
Moon nearly full; for the cultivated person a long journey is ominous.

Each phrase, with the possible exception of the second one, can be understood by itself, but they do not have any self-evident relationship to each other. Perhaps the rain has some relation to the potency of the location. Together with the third phrase these may have some reference to the wife's fertility but we cannot even guess what this might be. The wife receives an inauspicious divination, but is this related to her fertility, or to the journey—will her husband fail to return? Does the phase of the moon refer to her fertility or to her husband's journey? Perhaps diviners did not know either, but read the line to fit the inquiry.

Here, as throughout my translation, I have used punctuation and line breaks to divide the judgment and line texts into phrases. These parsings are my additions, though I have tried not to go beyond what is implicit in the text. As best I can, I have arranged them so as to bring out meanings, but resisted the temptation to add relationships between phrases that are not apparent in the Chinese original. This seems appropriate for a divination text, as ambiguity would allow the diviner latitude in interpretation. To be fair to the compilers, given that they had to work with a collection of randomly chosen phrases, they made the best they could with the material they had. To give an analogy, putting the phrases together into an organized book would have been comparable to taking documents out of a paper shredder and trying to make sense of them. It is true that the hexagrams provided locations to place the phrases, but as to how the compilers decided where to put each phrase there is no evidence.

Commentaries

The *Ten Wings*, which are integral parts of the *I Ching*, are the only commentaries that are part of the canonical received version. Many editions of the *Changes*, both Chinese and English, include commentarial material that varies considerably in extent and quality. Regrettably, the source of the commentary is often not specified and worse, it can be difficult to tell what is text and what is commentary. This is particularly true of the Wilhelm-Baynes version, termed by Joseph Needham, "a sinological maze" belonging to "the Department of Utter Confusion." S. J. Marshal has provided an invaluable map of this maze, but it is unlikely that most readers will want to take the trouble to seek it out (151–4).

With the important exceptions of the translations of Kunst and Rutt, and those of Shaughnessy on the excavated texts, most base their commentaries on the much later Confucianized meanings. Often they present the Confucianized meanings as the only ones and in so doing, while they seem to enrich the meanings with their commentaries, they also impoverish the classic by depriving it of its history. Many commentaries, both early and modern, paraphrase rather than explain difficult passages, limiting their usefulness. Others provide learned commentaries for some text portions but say nothing about others.

The commentaries I have provided with the present translation have the simple purpose of trying to make each line understandable, in line with my assumption that since it was understandable 3,000 years ago, it can be understandable today. I have tried to explain obscure words and phrases and admitted when I cannot be confident in some specific readings. Rather than offer my preferred choices of meanings as definitive, I often point out at least some of the plausible alternative meanings. Except when absolutely essential for clarity, I have avoided adding words not in the original, with the exception of helping words such as articles and pronouns. I am sure I have made mistakes despite my best efforts, but I have felt it more useful to express my opinions on difficult passages than to simply pass over them.

I have separated my commentaries from the translation so that they will not interrupt the flow of reading the actual text. They provide several sorts of information. First, they give historical and cultural background for lines that shed light on early Chinese life or have broad human interest. For key concepts I have provided more extended explanations. Finally, I have provided glosses on words of particular significance. These are particularly intended for readers with some knowledge of Chinese, but should also be clear to others with interest in the fine points of textual interpretation. In some cases I have felt the need to justify translating a word or phrase differently than other translators. Usually this is because I have a slightly different concept of the nature of the classic. As I make no claim to infallibility, I feel I should disclose my reasoning about some of the difficult portions.

5

Before the birth of the author: How the *Zhouyi* was composed

It was fashionable not long ago to write of the "death of the author," though mainly in reference to modern literature. I have reversed this notion to explain that there was no author for the *Zhouyi* and many other early texts, as they are compilations with no identifiable authors and no conception of authorship. We tend to take for granted that a book is created by an author or authors who create or direct its content. This reasonable assumption is actually one of the many sources of confusion when encountering the *Book of Changes*. Hence it is important to consider how early texts came to be.

Just as the *Zhouyi* does not meet many of our expectations for a book, it does not meet our expectations about authors. There were no identifiable individuals who consciously created a text imbued with their own style, point of view, and quirks. The romantic notion of the unappreciated genius with a unique message for humanity must be set aside, as must the mythical image of the sage-hermit meditating in the mountains, occasionally speaking profound words which were recorded by devoted students. Instead, early texts were assembled from sources long lost to us—which is why I refer to compilers rather than authors or editors. A compiler simply puts together material and may or may not play a role in selecting and organizing it. An editor shapes the text to varying degrees with the intent of correcting or improving it. Editing complicates analysis of ancient texts as it is often impossible to distinguish the earliest material from that added by editors long afterwards. We know that many of the Chinese classics were modified over time, but there is no textual evidence of this in the *Zhouyi*. The work is too complex and heterogeneous to have been the work of a single person, but as to whether it was put together by a small group working together or by multiple compilers and editors over years or even centuries, we have no evidence. Nor do we have any record at all of the sources that were used. A few lines are similar to passages in the *Shijing*, indicating common sources, but even whether these were oral or written cannot be determined.

In the absence of actual historical records the best we can do is make reasonable inferences about the processes that created the *Book of Changes* in both its received and excavated versions. Phrases were collected, as noted previously. Compilers somehow made decisions as to which of the collected material should be transcribed into the written manuscript. It is plausible that they or others combined the short phrases to create the judgment and line texts.

The next important step would have been to assign each line of text to a numbered line position within a hexagram. Contrary to later exegetical tradition, thematic connections between lines in the same hexagram are limited. There are some distinct patterns of organization that recur, though only in a few hexagrams. Perhaps most common is to have line texts within a hexagram share a common character. Sometimes it is also the tag. Another pattern is anatomic progression from the feet upwards, for example number 31 咸 *Xian* Sensation,which describes random-seeming sensations in different body areas, a common sort of omen. Often, as with 31.4 some lines do not fit the overall pattern. Possibly there was not enough text and so phrases were inserted to fill the gap. This is known to be common in recited oral material. One can speculate that this preference for ascending organization was the specialty of a specific compiler, with others having different specialties. Another example of bottom to top progression is number 52 艮 *Gen* Splitting, about butchering an animal.

It is best not to imagine that it is possible to identify groups of hexagrams that were assembled by the same compiler. The various individuals who collected the phrases, made decisions about where to place them, and served as scribes must have exerted great effort and believed that what they were doing was important—and likely they were also motivated by the threat of punishment if they failed to please the powerful figures in charge of the project. Yet there is no sign of literary creativity in the work—it seems intended simply as a catalogue of divinatory responses. There are no explicit over-riding themes, as we expect from literary texts. The *Zhouyi* is more akin to a technical manual, which is the supposed reason it escaped destruction in the notorious Qin Dynasty (221 to 206 BCE) book burning.

We do find recurring subjects, even obsessions, but not the imprint of an authorial personality. As I demonstrate in Chapter 7 however, close reading of the *Zhouyi* can reveal themes, not so much hidden as not conscious, because the means of expressing them had not yet developed.

Later ancient texts, such as the *Dao De Jing,* though they are also compilations, have clearly identifiable themes and styles of expression. With Laozi, though he is almost certainly mythical, we have a sense of a personality behind the words. Even more vivid is the personality of Zhuangzi, an historical person but not the author of all the material attributed to him in his corpus. The *Lunyu*, though not itself written by Confucius, gives a very vivid sense of the character and style of the man. The putative authors of the *Ten Wings* also express distinctive ideas, but in a more imper-sonal way.

Collection of folk material persists in China. Mao sent soldiers around the countryside to collect the thoughts of the common people. While this was based on Marxist ideology, the notion that the common people have a sort of honest wisdom that the upper classes have lost, and the practice of collecting such material long antedates Marxism. The *Shijing* or *Book of Songs* was created by this sort of collection but for a book of song lyrics, criteria for inclusion are relatively straightforward. With the *Zhouyi*, the basic principle was divinatory use, a much more nebulous category than poetry. Many of the phrases are obvious choices—proverbs, omens, incantations, and prognostic terms. Yet for some others, it is not clear how they would be applied for divination—for example some referring to specific historical events, as 35.0:

Bestowed upon Marquis Kang were numerous horses.
They became abundant, mated three times a day.

This is a mini-narrative, describing the Marquis as having a benefactor and being skilled in animal husbandry, and perhaps himself as sexually potent as a stallion. Yet, it is not clear how this phrase constitutes advice and it has no prognostic term, although the theme of fecundity is obviously auspicious. As with nearly all the lines, one can find a way to read it as a divinatory response, in this case to exert oneself to father children, or that diligent application to one's work can multiply one's wealth. Perhaps the phrase was inserted to flatter the Marquis, or had a prestigious source. We can make guesses, but cannot be certain of why these lines were incorporated into the *Zhouyi*.

What may seem meaningless to a modern reader—sights such as piglets, sounds such as birdcalls, sensations such as bodily twitches, all these would have been immediately recognized as omens by everyone in the Western Zhou. But what would readers think of Marquis Kang's horses or the bridesmaid's sleeves (54.5), or a melon wrapped in leaves (44.5)? All we can do is speculate. Perhaps some phrases were heard by the compilers in situations that seemed significant. We know that chance meetings were considered omens, so perhaps bits of overheard conversations by strangers would have been included. Some sources may have been particularly charismatic so that any utterance of theirs would have been assumed to have meaning, however obscure. Such thinking is commonplace today. For example, banal words spoken by a cult leader are often considered significant by disciples. To give a literary example, lines of Ezra Pound's *Cantos*, though seemingly gibberish, are thought to have meaning because of the genius of the poet (however despicable his character). The same is true of works by Shakespeare and many other authors.

It is likely that many of the sources were professional diviners (possibly the true "oldest profession"), or "cunning" women or men, but probably not all. They need not have been literate. Some may have been court officials, others may have been farmers or soldiers. The prognoses, such as "ominous," or "beneficial to ford the great river," were probably standard expressions that might be affixed by the compilers—who may not have been the ones who collected the phrases. Not infrequently the prognoses do not seem to fit the rest of the line text. Perhaps they were sometimes simply placed to fill in lacunae, as is usual in performances of oral material.

It is obvious that the diagrams must have existed before the line texts became associated with them, yet it is likely that some of the textual material was quite ancient and widely familiar. By this hypothesis, once the diagrams were set at six lines, some textual material would have been ready to hand or would have been collected and inserted to fill the line positions. It seems almost certain that much of the divinatory material circulated orally during the Shang. There might even have been earlier written collections of them that were drawn upon to create the *Zhouyi*.

In concluding this discussion of the composition of the *Zhouyi*, I point to the admonitions of the Tang Dynasty Confucian scholar Han Yu (769–824) who "would frequently reprove earlier commentators for having attempted to impose a spurious order and consistency on ... mutually contradictory parts of the canon" (Henderson 1991: 208).

It would have been better if Han Yu's advice had been more often followed by *I Ching* commentators, all too many of whom essentially rewrote the text to their own specifications. This tendency to improve on the actual *I Ching* was not unknown in traditional China and persists to the present day in such New Age works as the *I Ching for Lovers*, the *Toltec I Ching*, and the pop psychology of Carol Anthony and Hanna Moog. I have done my best to translate the *Zhouyi* rather than create a new one.

PART TWO

The translation and commentaries

Part One

1. 乾 *Qian* Heaven (The Creative)

The Judgment:

1.0 Begin with an offering; beneficial to divine.
元亨利貞.

1.1 Hidden dragon, do not act.
初九潛龍勿用.

1.2 The dragon is seen in the field.
It is favorable to see the powerful person.
九二見龍在田. 利見大人.

1.3 The upright person strives energetically all day long.
Vigilant day and night, thus averting blame.
九三君子終日乾乾. 夕惕若厲. 无咎.

1.4 Sudden leap into the whirlpool.
Blame averted.
九四或躍在淵. 无咎.

1.5 The dragon soaring in heaven. Favorable to see the important person.
九五飛龍在天. 利見大人.

1.6 Overbearing dragon will have remorse.
上九亢龍有悔.

1.7 There appears a flight of dragons without heads. Auspicious.
用九見羣龍无首, 吉.

1. Commentary 乾 *Qian* Heaven

Qian originally meant dry. This fits with the lines all being *yang* because dryness is one of the correlates of *yang*, actually the earliest one. However, the word *yang* does not appear in the *Zhouyi*, nor is there anything related to dryness in the text associated with this hexagram. The usual translations of *Qian*, such as heaven, or strong action, are based on its later cosmological associations. Hacker provides a table listing variant English translations of hexagram titles, with a useful itemization of his criteria for selecting the most suitable version (1993: 42–63). As with many of the hexagram tags, a single English word cannot capture the multiple associations of *Qian*.

In Mawangdui the tag of this hexagram is 鍵 *Jian,* a near homophone, meaning latch pin (Shaughnessy 1998: 38f., 287). One can speculate, though without any actual evidence, that the *Jian* variant came earlier and was later changed to the homophone *Qian* to fit the later cosmological meaning of this hexagram. I have kept the standard translation as heaven since the line texts are clearly cosmological, unlike most of the other *Zhouyi* texts.

The first four words of the *Zhouyi*

The phrase *Yuan, Heng, Li, Zhen* opens the *Zhouyi* and was known to all educated Chinese. It would have been as familiar to Confucians as the first words of *Genesis,* "In the beginning God created heaven and earth ..." are to Jews and Christians, though the meanings are in no way similar.

In the *Zhouyi* this phrase is an invocation or introduction to the act of divination. It proclaims, presumably to supernatural beings such as ancestors, though the recipients of the sacrifices were never specified, that their aid is being sought. Perhaps the intended recipients of such messages would have been self-evident to Western Zhou Chinese. They are not so to us. The second two characters indicate that carrying out divination will be beneficial. This phrase is ambiguous as to whether it means, "It will be of benefit to carry out divination," or "The divination will be favorable." Such ambiguity is common in the *Zhouyi* and readers could construe it either way.

The first character, *yuan*, could mean "begin" or "great." Given that this word does begin the divination, I have generally chosen, "begin." Also, given how often divination was carried out, it seems unlikely that routine ones would require a major offering every time. Indeed, the *Zhouyi* refers several times to small offerings.

Kunst (200–11) notes that the term *zhen* is also frequent in oracle bone inscriptions. There "beneficial" does not mean that the prognostication will necessarily be favorable, but rather that it would be prudent to divine for advice about the matter at hand. After all, an unfavorable divination result might still benefit the inquirer by warning about difficulties ahead.

Heng, or "offering given (and received)," is the key character in the judgments, appearing a total of forty-six times in forty-four different hexagrams, indicating the necessity of making an offering for the divination to be efficacious. However, in many cases the formula is partial or abbreviated, with not all four characters being included. Another variation is intercalation of other characters within the invocatory phrase. With rare exceptions, the nature of the offering is not specified. This is in contrast with the oracle bone inscriptions, which are often quite specific regarding the animal to be sacrificed.

Later, perhaps in the Spring and Autumn Period, *yuan, heng, li, zhen* came to refer to virtues. Since this was the era in which Confucius lived we know that ethical philosophy was developing at that time. There is also explicit moral discussion related to the *Changes* in the *Zuozhuan*, notably in the famous anecdote of Lady Mu Jiang. While this text is nominally a commentary on the *Annals of the Spring and Autumn,* the date it reached its current form may have been much later.

Here are some examples of translations of these four words as virtues:

Wilhelm-Baynes (4): sublime success, furthering through perseverance.
Lynn (130): Fundamentality, prevalence, fitness and constancy.
Rutt (187): Goodness ... excellence ... right ... kingpin of activity.
(As spoken by Lady Mu Jiang in the *Zuozhuan.*)

In translating this phrase, as is often the case with Chinese ethical writings, it is hard to identify specific English equivalents for these rather vague terms. Rutt's version seems most direct to me— the phrase is a general statement implicitly commending being virtuous. When these words are attributed to Lady Mu Jiang, they are meant as self-criticism—that she lacks these virtues. This is the earliest textual witness to moralistic reading of the *Changes.*

In Western Zhou usage, *zhen* clearly meant something like "determine" or "ask." Etymology is thought to be from the character for *ding,* a ritual cauldron and *bu,* to divine, a zodiograph for cracks on oracle bones (Boltz: 33, 54, 183). Thus its early meaning was clearly, "to make a determination by divination."

If one takes the later meaning of *zhen* as "correct" in the sense of behaving properly (Kunst: 205), then the evolution of the term seems straightforward: "determine what is correct by divination" could come to refer to "correctness" of behavior as a virtue, especially as the *Zhouyi* came to be regarded as a guide to morally proper behavior. Once this character was associated with a virtue, other virtues could be assigned to the remaining three characters. *Yuan* as grand could easily refer to being exemplary in virtue, etc. This etymology is clearly retrospective; that is, the virtue meanings were added later, by editors intent on finding Confucian meanings in the early classics.

The *Qian* dragon sequence

The first and second hexagrams, *Qian* and *Kun*, are the only ones referring to dragons. In *Qian*, all lines except 1.3 refer to these potent symbolic creatures. The reference to dragons in *Kun* 2.6 is enigmatic—it has no evident relationship to the other lines. Since dragon images are found on Western Zhou artworks, it is odd that we do not find more of them in the *Zhouyi*. Also striking about the *Qian* line texts is that they have a more definite thematic organization than we find in most of the other hexagrams. These attributes have led some scholars to speculate that the *Qian* line texts are later additions from a time when the work was developing cosmological meanings. This is plausible, although the substantial similarity of the lines in the Mawangdui and Fuyang manuscripts (these lines are damaged in the Shanghai Museum bamboo strips) indicate that any such addition must have been quite early. No other hexagram has such explicit cosmology in its texts. *Kun*, despite its later representing pure *yin*, lacks any clear thematic pattern in its line texts, nor does its mention of a mare have any *yin* association.

The *Qian* dragon imagery can be read in two distinct ways. As expressed by Wilhelm-Baynes:

> The dragon is a symbol of the electrically charged, dynamic, arousing force that manifests itself in the thunderstorm. In winter this energy withdraws into the earth; it the early summer it becomes active again.

Setting aside Wilhelm's reference to electrical charge, one of many attempts to find modern science in the *Changes*, we can see the dragon is a symbol of energy, at times latent, as in winter, at other times active, as in summer. In this reading the texts refer to seasons, but also more generally to the energies that may be active or only potential in the situation divined about, but which need to be taken into account in deciding one's own actions. When the forces are hidden, one had best to wait rather than undertake any direct actions. This is a common life situation. A modern variant is, "Don't do anything until you have to." This applies to many areas of life: medicine, in which treatment decisions are postponed, warfare, in which one must await accurate intelligence, business etc. Timing of actions has always been a Chinese preoccupation, as embodied in the concept of the sage whose essential ability is perceiving incipience, seeing patterns in events before they become apparent to ordinary people.

Later, when the dragon is in the field or sky, one is able to sense the very powerful forces acting upon one. This also corresponds to the agricultural year—little work in the winter, intense work in spring summer and fall. Energy here is subjective energy, not that of modern physics.

The other way to read the dragon imagery in *Qian* is astrological, or as a reference to seasonal movements of asterisms (star groupings). While the divinatory component of astrology is now dismissed as a pseudoscience, we should not ignore the fact that it has always involved accurate observation and calculation of the position of stars and planets. Though there was always some skepticism, large numbers of people have always assumed that the stars affected destiny. Shaughnessy noted in his dissertation that the baffling reference to "dragons without heads" appearing in the sky as an auspicious sign actually refers to the position of an asterism (1983: 268–87). Pankenier provides an extensive treatment of dragon asterisms in the *Zhouyi* and other early texts (2013: 38–80).

1.2 Now the dragon is visible, a decision can be made because the forces affecting one are apparent. As often in life, the next step is a meeting with a powerful person. Such meetings were best held when the powerful person, who might have the power of life and death, was in a good mood.

1.3 The meaning of the repeated 乾乾 *Qian Qian* seems unrelated to the same character of the tag. Although this line lacks direct reference to dragons it is related to the theme of activity. I have translated this word as "energetically" to emphasize the association of the all *yang* hexagram with energy, despite it being unlikely to have had direct *yang* associations in the Western Zhou. Rutt prefers "active," because he feels it important to avoid implications such as "work ethic" or "diligence" and the like (292). Perhaps that is so, but hard work has always been necessary for most of humanity. This phrase also seems to be a seed of later ethical concepts.

One of the most famous phrases in Wilhelm-Baynes' iconic English version is 无咎 *wu jiu*. It is translated by Wilhelm-Baynes as "no blame." This cannot be an abstract ethical pronouncement by an impersonal narrator because we do not find such in the *Zhouyi*. In his English phrase it seems to mean getting away with something. When it refers to human sacrifices, "no blame" seems particularly bizarre to modern readers. Properly understood this phrase is not so much an ethical judgment, as a verbal spell or incantation to avert blame. This is important in any society, but in a hierarchical one where irascible superiors with absolute power could hand out harsh punishments on a whim, avoiding blame was vital for survival. To give but one historical example, when a newly enthroned emperor in the Han Dynasty was told that one of his friends' vulgar manner of speech detracted from his own prestige, he had the friend executed.

Many Anglophone readers are puzzled by the phrase *wu jiu*, because it often follows phrases that do not suggest blame at all, or that seem highly blameworthy, such as sacrificing captives. Considering the phrase as a spell or incantation seems to me to solve the problem—it would be especially important with just those actions that are potentially blameworthy. This hypothesis is consistent with the later oracle bone inscriptions that tend to be charms intended to bring about a desired outcome, rather than predictions. Consistent with this I have translated the phrase as "blame averted" or "there will be no blame."

1.4 Here it must be the dragon that leaps into the whirlpool. Omission of the subject is usual in Chinese grammar, inference from context being assumed. Dragons in later Chinese art are regularly depicted among turbulent waves. These could also have been covert sexual references because dragons are *yang* and whirlpools represent intense *yin* energy. The divinatory meaning of this line is clearer than many, referring to jumping into an intensely chaotic situation, yet managing to avoid blame. In divination, it would mean that the inquirer is in a tumultuous situation, but will come out safely.

1.5 This completes the upward movement of the dragon from underground upwards.

1.6 The usual translations are similar to Wilhelm-Baynes' "Arrogant dragon will have cause to repent." This, however, makes no sense as humility is not an attribute one associates with dragons. Hence it is more plausibly an omen that a dragon high in the sky portends regret, or more specifically, when read astrologically it means that when the dragon asterism (the second of the Chinese Zodiac) is in the second lunar mansion, there will be regret.

1.7 As discussed above, this refers to asterism positions and so is a seasonal reference. For further discussion on dragon imagery, see 2.7 and related commentary.

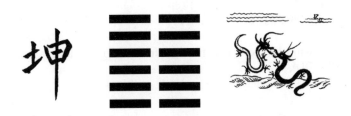

2. 坤 *Kun* Earth (The Receptive)

The Judgment:

2.0 Begin the offering, beneficial if a female horse, for the divination.
The upright person has somewhere to go. At first lost, he obtains a master. Auspicious.
In the west and south one obtains companions.
In the northeast one loses companions.
Safe. Divination auspicious.
元亨, 利牝馬之. 君子有攸往. 先迷後得.
主利. 西南得朋. 東北喪朋. 安貞吉.

2.1 Tread on frost, soon ice will come.
初六履霜, 堅冰至.

2.2 Straight, square, great, not usual. Nothing not beneficial.
六二直方大, 不習无不利.

2.3 Holding in the mouth a jade tablet.
Can divine, perhaps in attending to the king's affairs.
Though nothing accomplished, it has an end.
六三含章. 可貞, 或從王事. 无成有終.

2.4 Tying in a sack avoids blame, but there is no praise.
六四括囊, 无咎无譽.

2.5 Yellow skirt; begins auspiciously.
六五黃裳; 元吉.

2.6 Dragons battle in the wilderness. Their blood is black and yellow.
上六龍戰于野. 其血玄黃.

2.7 Using all sixes: Beneficial divination for the long term.
用六利永貞

2. Commentary 坤 *Kun* Earth

Kun in the Wilhelm-Baynes translation means "earth" or "receptivity." The latter is likely based on the earth being receptive to planted seeds. In the Mawangdui version, this is hexagram 33 *Chuan*, River or Flow (Shaughnessy 1985: 103, 302f.). It has been suggested that flow here is a reference to female genitalia, complementary to the supposed phallic implication of the Mawangdui tag for number 1, which is *Jian* (for *Qian*) as "latch pin." Despite my belief that there are likely many sexual references in the *Zhouyi* that are no longer recognizable, this one seems implausible to me, simply because there is little other genital symbolism. Sometimes a latch pin is just a latch pin. For the extreme speculations that have been advanced regarding *Kun* and possible variants, see Rutt (295–6) and Bernardino (201f.).

2.0 The judgment text of Kun is the longest in the *Zhouyi*. The reference to a female horse has been interpreted in diverse ways. If one accepts the early meaning of 亨 *heng* as offering in the sense of a sacrificial offering to an ancestor or deity, then the text ties together as a narrative in which sacrifice of a mare will ensure that it will be favorable to go somewhere. Rutt alludes to this possible meaning of sacrifice but does not choose it for his translation. This being a recommendation for sacrifice seems to me almost inescapable, although a possible alternative is the mare being served by a stallion for reproduction. In any case, nothing in the text states that compliance or submission is specifically the female role, despite later being interpreted in this way. Indeed, other than the reference to a female horse there is no gender reference at all.

The reference to service to a king suggests that the journey is part of official duties. As always with the *Zhouyi*, one can propose other meanings that are consistent with the wording: for example, that going somewhere will be favorable if one is taken by a mare, presumably pulling a cart as horses were not yet ridden in the time of the Western Zhou. We should not assume in reading the *Zhouyi* that only one possible meaning is correct. It is almost certain that different readers or diviners understood the same phrases differently. Indeed, ambiguity is essential to the process of divination.

The adolescent prodigy Wang Bi (226–49) took the mare as a reference to female docility or compliance (Lynn: 142f.). This reading has no basis in the actual text because, as I have emphasized, *yin* was not correlated with the feminine until centuries later. Given the ambiguity of the Zhouyi, it was easy for Wang Bi and many other commentators to add this reading to serve the frequently misogynistic agenda of Confucian and other later commentators. This later interpretation tells us nothing about attitudes toward women at the time of the composition of the *Zhouyi*.

The text does hint that this is a time to be receptive and follow the lead of others. The term *junzi*, orignally meant "prince," but later came to mean a cultivated or virtuous person. While it does not specify gender, there is no doubt that *junzi* almost always refers to a male. So here it is almost certainly a man who is being counseled to act submissively. In a strictly hierarchical society, and even in our own, there are many occasions when it is advisable to yield to authority.

That attaining a master or lord was desirable may seem strange to a modern reader who values independence. However, in a feudal society, if early China can be so termed, being without a master was dangerous, as one would be without protection. Identity was to a great degree dependent on belonging to a group, usually based on family.

I have translated the third and fourth phrases as "west and south" and "east and north," rather than "southwest and northeast" as the prime directions were particularly important. Directionality was a preoccupation in early cultures. Many divinations indicate that good or bad fortune depends on the direction of the activity. Divination about traveling often indicates safe and dangerous directions. Given the dangers of traveling in that remote era, selection of route would have occasioned considerable anxiety.

I have translated 安 *an* as "safe," rather than "peace," because it is doubtful whether peace was a conscious value in early China, considering that war was one of the great affairs of state. Instead it seems to have been taken as a matter of course that states would wage almost constant war upon one another.

2.1 That *Kun* follows *Qian* was regarded as significant because after *yang* reaches its maximum, *yin* begins to rise, as the coming of frost and ice indicates the coming of winter, the *yin* season. Keeping in mind that in the Mawangdui version Kun does not follow the first hexagram (not *Qian* but *Jian*), but is number 33 *Chuang* or *Flow*, the placement of *Kun* as number 2 cannot be taken for granted as the original one. If could be that as the *Changes* came to be read as cosmological, this arrangement was made to accord with the cosmology. Or it could simply be that there was more than one organizing pattern for the hexagrams.

2.2 This is one of several lines in the *Zhouyi* that seem to have overt, though vague, ethical content. "Straight, square, great, not usual," would seem to be inborn character traits. The phrase does make sense if these are meant as personal qualities, although they could refer to a road, mountain, or other geographical feature. Rutt suggests they refer to the proper surveying of a field (294).

2.3 The first phrase is somewhat obscure. In imperial China, courtiers held an object in front of their mouths so that their breath would not touch the emperor. Whether such a custom existed so early is not known. Alternatively, this could refer to placing a piece of jade in the mouth of a corpse to prepare for burial. In any case the jade object does have something to do with honoring or respecting the king, perhaps when reporting a divination result to him.

2.4 This line seems straightforward: if you tie something in a sack it will be held securely and you will avoid blame, but since this is normal practice it will not win praise. For divination it means that keeping things secure will prevent blame, but not attain praise. Rutt suggests, plausibly, that what is tied in the sack is grain, making this a reference to the harvest (295).

2.5 The yellow lower garment likely had ritual significance, the meaning of which is now lost, though speculative theories abound. The divinatory meaning would have been clear: obeying ritual requirements will get one off to a good start.

2.6 A striking, but obscure, image. An unusual feature of this line is that it involves mythical creatures, while most *Zhouyi* imagery is based on nature and daily life. Dragons are not necessarily represented as fighting in Chinese culture, being symbolic of positive energy. The meaning of black (or dark) and yellow blood is also obscure, although yellow, as in the previous line, is an indication of auspiciousness. It has also been suggested that the colors referred to are not black and yellow but reddish brown (Pankenier 2013: 54f. n.26).

Wang Bi's commentary suggests that black is *yang*/heaven and yellow *yin*/earth. The problem with this is that the usual association is *yang* equals bright and *yin* equals dark. Pankenier suggests that the fighting dragons refer to a time of year when there are two dragon asterisms visible on the same night, one after twilight; the other before dawn, and so could symbolize *yin* and *yang* struggling to overcome each other in late winter/early spring (2013: 54). This is attractive, but the lack of evidence for *yin-yang* cosmology in the Western Zhou makes it doubtful as the early meaning. It is of course plausible that lines like this one, which seem to use imagery unlike the rest of the text, are later additions. Yet another theory is that the dragons are imagined as having sexual intercourse and that the two colors of blood refer to semen and menstrual blood (Lynn: 149f.; Rutt: 296). All that can be concluded is that this is an instance of the fecundity of the *Changes* in generating peculiar theories.

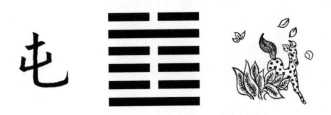

3. 屯 *Tun* Gathering
(Difficulty at the Beginning)

The Judgment:

Begin with an offering; beneficial to divine.
Not useful if having to go somewhere
Beneficial to enfeoff lords.
元亨;利贞. 勿用有攸往. 利建侯.

The Line Texts:

3.1 A boulder hinders. Beneficial to divine about a home.
Beneficial to enfeoff lords.
初九磐桓. 利居貞. 利建侯.

3.2 They seem to struggle, seem to falter—driving the team of horses.
Not bandits invading, but a wedding.
The chaste young woman does not give her word. In ten years then gives her word
[OR The young woman's divination: not pregnant. Ten years becomes pregnant.]
六二屯如邅如 — 乘馬班如. 匪寇婚媾. 女子貞不字.十年乃字.

3.3 Immediately a deer, alone without caution approaches into the midst of the forest.
The upright person soon gives up—going on would be shameful.
即鹿無虞, 惟入于林中. 君子幾不如舍—往吝.

3.4 Horse carts ranked for the proposed wedding.
Going is auspicious; nothing not beneficial.
六四乘馬班如求婚媾. 往吉. 无不利.

3.5 Collecting their fatty meat.
For minor matters divination auspicious; for major ones, ominous.
九五屯其膏. 小貞吉; 大貞凶.

3.6 Horse carts ranked.
Weeping, tears of blood flowing unceasingly.
上六乘馬班如. 泣, 血漣如

3. Commentary 屯 *Tun* Gathering

Wilhelm-Baynes translation of the title, "Difficulty at the Beginning," is based on the first phrase of the judgment text and imaginative reconstruction of the character's etymology as a pictograph showing a blade of grass struggling to break through the surface of the soil.

However, in lines 3.2 and 3.5, *tun* clearly means gathering or assembling, not initial difficulty. Furthermore 3.4 and 3.6 also refer to gathering of horse carts. Indeed, to the extent that there is a unifying theme in the line texts, it is about assembling for an important occasion such as a wedding or granting of noble rank.

3.0 I have used the somewhat obsolete term "enfeoff" to designate a practice no longer in existence—the grant of land and, usually, a title of nobility, in return for military or other service. Generally, larger grants of land meant higher titles. Wealth, until the rise of trade, was mainly in the form of land; taxes were paid in rice. Furthermore, this land supported the men who served the lord as workers and soldiers, so bestowal of land also allowed the nobleman to furnish soldiers to the ruler—though they could as easily be used for rebelling against him. Grants of land also served, not always successfully, to placate the powerful. This meant feeding a monster—in all feudal societies, powerful lords were a persistent threat to the rule, and often became *de facto* rulers.

3.1 The second phrase repeats that of the judgment. Since it fits better with divination about a home, this is likely the correct placement and the inclusion in the judgment a scribal error (dittography). In any case, such errors do not significantly affect the meaning.

"Not useful if having far to go," seems odd in English. However, the meaning is clear enough—traveling to a distant destination is not useful under the circumstances divined about. The *Zhouyi* has many such references to anxiety regarding travel.

3.2 Though 乘馬 *cheng ma* together can mean mounting or riding a horse, it is generally thought that horses were not ridden until the Spring and Autumn Period. Hence the meaning is likely riding in a horse cart. This line refers to the custom of mock bride stealing. This was a ritualized re-enactment of an older custom in which men from another village would attack and abduct young women to serve as their brides. Later such weddings were actually pre-arranged.

While this is the most likely reading, 匪 *fei* can also mean bandits or brigands and 媾 *gou* sexual intercourse, so it could refer to abduction and rape by brigands. One cannot help but wonder if it was read both ways, sometimes as a wedding ritual, others as a salacious episode.

Later commentators from Wang Bi, to Richard Wilhelm's late Qing-educated informant, Lao Nai-hsuan, took 貞 *zhen* as a reference to a woman maintaining her chastity for ten years until she is ready to marry; that is, giving her word *zi* 字 (Lynn: 154; Wilhelm-Baynes: 17f.). However, *zi* can mean "word" or "conceive." Using the former, it would suggest that the woman had some ability to make her own decision regarding marriage (Redmond and Hon 2014: 84). If one takes the latter, it means that she marries but does not become pregnant until ten years. In such a case a diviner saying that she would eventually become pregnant would benefit the woman—those who did not attain pregnancy soon after marriage were often harshly treated. Another possible meaning, not noted elsewhere, would be that the woman was a child bride and not able to consummate the marriage until she is ten years older. Ambiguity of this sort is frustrating, particularly here, because we would like to know what the passage is telling us about early Chinese marriage customs.

In pre-modern times, children were the only source of support for most elderly parents. As human reproduction is always uncertain divination was frequently sought regarding when a woman would conceive, whether gestation would proceed safely, and whether the child would be a boy or a girl. An oracle bone inscription in the Museum of the Institute of History and Philology in Taipei, now much quoted, predicts the queen will give birth next week to a boy, only to later state, "Disaster, it's a girl." A mother might be blamed if she gave birth to a girl. That it is the male sperm that determines the sex of a child and that at least 10 percent of infertility is due to male factors were, of course, unknown.

3.3 For a deer to approach without fear would be an anomaly; hence this is an omen. Given that the event is abnormal, the deer will perhaps not be killed, since doing so might be inauspicious. There is no evidence of compassion for animals in the *Zhouyi*, though there are hints of it later in the *Lunyu* and Mencius. Sparing the animal would be related to supernatural concerns, not compassion.

I have translated 虞 *yu* as "fear," but an alternative early meaning is gamekeeper—either way the animal's approach is abnormal. For 無 some editions read the simplified equivalent 无 but this makes no difference in sound or meaning.

3.4 媾 *gou*, translated discretely by Wilhelm-Baynes as "union," seems to refer here to remarriage but can mean "sexual intercourse." As I have commented elsewhere, the paucity of references to sexuality in the *Zhouyi* is surprising, as they are common in the 詩經 *Shijing* (*Book of Songs*) and the 楚辭 *Chu Ci* (*Songs of the South*).

3.5 The reason fat is avoided now is also the reason it was valued in earlier times—its high caloric content. When food supply was uncertain and many suffered from inadequate nutrition, high caloric foods were of greatest value. Even in the West, high fat content was integral to gourmet cooking until recent decades. When animals were sacrificed in ancient China, the meat was distributed according to social rank. Fat might be a reward for soldiers and others in attendance.

Kunst comments that *xiong* 凶 is "the most inauspicious prognostication used in the Yi text" (190f.). Given the uncertainty as to which matters are minor and which major, this prognostication cannot but be correct. It does offer actual advice, however, specifically to focus on less important matters for the time being. Thus room is left for optimism, something that characterizes Chinese culture from very early, despite the harshness of Bronze Age life—the risk of mass starvation with a bad harvest, bandit attacks, and arbitrary infliction of punishments. Thus, although 凶 *xiong* ominous appears fifty-seven times, 吉 *ji* auspicious appears 142 times. Of course, favorable prognostications are good for business for diviners.

3.6 The horse carts here may be ranked for a burial. Expressing grief appropriately in a prescribed manner has always been a preoccupation in China. Proper mourning is essential to the ordering of society. As expressed by Confucius, "Tend carefully to death rites, and pay reverence to those long departed, and the people will in the end be rich in virtue" (*Lunyu* 1.9; Watson: 17).

For an innovative alternative translation I am indebted to Mingmei Yip who proposes that it refers to a bride abduction. The woman resists for ten years and weeps tears of blood, but after ten years she accepts her situation. Several well-known anecdotes of the Han describe women bitter over being sent to marry a barbarian who eventually come to appreciate their wealth and comfort.

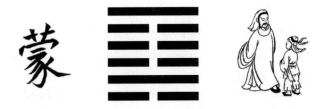

4. 蒙 *Meng* Neophytes (Youthful Folly)

The Judgment:

4.0 Make offering. Not I who asks the neophytes; the neophytes ask me.
The initial yarrow divination informs, but to repeat it several times shows disrespect.
When disrespected, then it does not inform.
Beneficial to divine.
亨. 匪我求童蒙; 童蒙求我.
初筮告, 再三瀆. 瀆則不告. 利貞.

The Line Texts:

4.1 In teaching neophytes, it is beneficial to use physical punishment.
Use scolding to restrain, in order to lead to remorse, before.
初六發蒙, 利用刑人. 用說桎梏. 以往吝.

4.2 To bundle up neophytes is auspicious.
To receive a wife is auspicious.
The son is capable of managing the household.
九二包蒙吉. 納婦吉. 子克家.

4.3 Do not use to obtain a woman, upon seeing a conscripted metal worker.
Not having bowed, nothing will go towards benefit.
六三勿用取女. 見金夫, 不有躬, 无攸利.

4.4 Beset upon by neophytes. Regret.
六四困蒙. 吝.

4.5 A young neophyte. Auspicious.
六五童蒙.吉.

4.6 Beat the neophytes.
Not beneficial to attack bandits; beneficial to resist bandits.
上九擊蒙. 不利為寇, 利禦寇.

4. Commentary 蒙 *Meng* Neophytes

In translating this hexagram, I have generally followed the reading
of Wilhelm-Baynes, making it about children or youth. I have translated the tag as "neophytes" which has the advantage of also meaning
sprouts. This seems a better fit than "immaturity," a psychological
concept almost certainly absent in the Western Zhou.

Kunst, Rutt, and Minford (528) translate the tag and other
occurrences of 蒙 *meng* as "dodder." This is derived from a
suggestion by Arthur Waley (1933) that the character refers to
a parasitic plant that grows on bushes (130f.) While the British
scholar does quote a single obscure source for this usage of the
character, to me his reasoning is entirely unpersuasive:

> It was not I who sought the stripling dodder; the stripling dodder
> sought me is clearly a spell for averting the evil consequences of
> tampering with the holy plant. (131)

This is a clear instance of the tendency inspired by the Doubting
Antiquity movement to substitute far-fetched meanings for received
ones that are quite clear. That a plant seeks someone is self-evidently
absurd, particularly as the sacredness of parasitic plants is not
attested in any Chinese text, at least of which I am aware. This
is doubly unfortunate because as translated by Wilhelm-Baynes,
Meng is one of the most easily understood hexagrams. Although
Waley was one of the greatest translators of Chinese and Japanese
texts into English, he was not an infallible one, having a penchant
for replacing obvious meanings with obscure ones.

4.0 Here three of the four characters of the invocation are present although embedded within other phrases. It is possible that in practice these four words began every *Zhouyi* divination, but were sometimes omitted from the written text. This is consistent with what is known about texts based on oral material. The character 亨*heng*, offering, seems to be the key one in this phrase, as the offering would have been essential. The questioning referred to can be read either as students asking a teacher or as an inquiry addressed to the *Zhouyi*. (To divine about the same question repeatedly would almost certainly generate contradictory prognostications, hence the need to discourage this.) Nonetheless, divinations tend to be done repeatedly over the same question, presumably in the hope of greater clarity and accuracy, or a better prognosis.

We do not know where inquirers in the Western Zhou believed the answers to their requests for divination to have come from. It seems to have been taken for granted that the classic would give valid answers. Oracle bone divination is assumed to have been addressed to ancestors or spirits, although not all scholars accept this hypothesis. So it is plausible that the *Zhouyi* was similarly regarded. If this surmise is correct, this passage could refer to repeated questioning of ancestors, who according to Chinese belief, were more irascible after death than before. At some point, the *I Ching* became regarded as a sage in itself, as it still is in the minds of many of its practitioners.

4.1 Physical punishment of young children, often harsh, has been routine in most of the world until quite recently. Supposedly the character for father 父 *fu* represents the belts with which the father disciplines his children. Although this etymology is likely fanciful, it illustrates an assumption about the role of paternal figures in child-raising.

A child or student speaking out would not seem to merit punishment, but teaching in traditional China did not follow the modern way of students asking questions; rather, students listened silently, or recited what they had memorized. The relationship between teacher and student was rigidly hierarchical. While memorization is now out of fashion as uncreative, we should keep in mind that China's mode of education has maintained its literary culture essentially intact for more than two millennia.

Harsh punishment of children unfortunately continues to be usual in much of the world. (Modern research on child development suggests that physical punishment of children results in worse behavior. This is not surprising—fear disrupts attention.)

Rutt translates line 1 as being about punishment, presumably of criminals rather than children, as does Shaughnessy (2014: 73; 1996: 62f.).

4.2 My translation that this means bundling up a child, presumably against cold, is at best a guess, perhaps because I would like to find some evidence of nurturing behavior in the classic.

4.3 Has been interpreted as advising a man not to marry a woman who sees a "man of bronze" or "man of gold" and loses her self-control. In modern slang it would mean one should avoid a woman who is a gold-digger. The text refers only to seeing this man, not to any behavior on the part of the woman, so this usual translation seems to me to miss the nature of this line. Nor do we find much in the way of this sort of character description of women, or of men, in the *Zhouyi*. Such seemingly obvious attributes as greed, selfishness, and laziness, do not appear in the ancient text. Since 夫 *fu* can mean a man of low rank, a commoner, this is likely an omen—seeing a man doing forced labor is a sign that it is not auspicious to choose a wife. (*Mea culpa*: I got this wrong in my prior translation in Redmond and Hon [2014: 84].) I have translated the second phrase to state that not bowing will keep one from advancing, undoubtedly true in pre-modern China but whether this is really the early meaning is no more than a guess.

4.5 In context, it is likely that seeing a young person was an omen.

4.6 This line has a clear divinatory meaning—in this situation, one should not attack but defend.

5. 需 *Xu* Waiting (Waiting; Nourishment)

The Judgment:

5.0 Holding captives.
Honorable offering for auspicious divination.
Beneficial to cross the wide river.
有孚. 光亨貞吉. 利涉大川.

The Line Texts:

5.1 Waiting at the outskirts to sacrifice to heaven.
Beneficial to use what is lasting to avert blame.
初九需于郊. 利用恆无咎.

5.2 Waiting on sand.
With a few words it ends auspiciously.
九二需于沙. 小有言. 終吉。

5.3 Waiting on the mud results in bandits arriving.
九三需于泥致寇至.

5.4 Getting wet with the blood [of the sacrifice].
Coming out from the pit.
六四需于血. 出自穴.

5.5 Waiting for food and wine.
Divination auspicious.
九五需于酒. 貞吉.

5.6 Go out from the pit.
Uninvited, several guests arrive.
Respecting them ends auspiciously.
上六入于穴. 不速之, 客三人來. 敬之終吉.

5. Commentary 需 *Xu* Waiting

需 *Xu* can be translated either as waiting or getting wet, both being universal life situations. Getting wet better fits several of the line texts and is supported by the Mawangdui manuscript, which has a different tag character, thought to be a homophone for "moist" (Shaughnessy 1997). "Getting wet" also accords with the top element of the graph, the radical, which means rain. In the line texts I have departed from my usual principle and translated it both ways, based on context.

5.0 This is the first hexagram in which the phrase 有孚 *you fu* appears. I have translated it throughout as holding captives. Often, as here, this is considered auspicious—for the sacrificers, not the captives, of course. Blood sacrifice was near-universal in the ancient world, particularly to propitiate ancestors or spirits. In the received version this was translated as trust or sincerity; the demonstration by the Doubting Antiquity philologists that the early meaning was captives to be sacrificed was of central importance in their transformation of traditional readings of the classic. While it has been suggested that this practice was abolished in the Zhou, archaeological evidence refutes this, although the practice gradually diminished.

Confucianism dealt with blood sacrifice by averting their attention. The Master frequently expressed admiration for the "ancient rites" without reference to their essential component being killing. There is one exception in which he defends the practice to a disciple by stating, "you care about the sheep. I care about the ritual" (*Lunyu* 3.17; Watson 28). Mencius also refers to the smearing of the sacrificed animal's blood as the validation event of the rite, despite his admonition elsewhere to stay away from the kitchen, lest the miseries of animals being butchered spoil one's appetite.

What are we to make of this unpleasant discovery about the supposedly morally pristine *Book of Changes*? First, we must accept that China's very ancient times were far from idyllic. Second, references to human sacrifice remind us that all cultures find excuses for gratuitous violence. In the West, the execution of Socrates, the witchcraft and heresy burnings, and many other state-sanctioned murders are considered by some to be equivalent to human sacrifice. Characteristic of human sacrifice is that the victims are innocent but the killing is supposed to benefit society. A familiar example is the sacrifice of Iphigenia to placate Artemis and enable the Greeks to sail to attack the Trojans.

5.1 Kunst (249) and Rutt (298) take this line to refer to a specific ritual, but since nothing is known about what this might have been, I have left it simply as "sacrifice."

5.3 Perhaps robbers would hide near mud as it would make it harder for their victims to run away.

5.4 While Wilhelm-Baynes translated this line as advice for getting out of a dangerous situation, this must originally have referred to sacrifice. Blood flow was essential to the efficacy of the sacrifice, as was the celebrants' smearing on themselves. Attitudes toward blood and other bodily fluids were quite different from modern ones, urine being commonly used as a medicine, for example.

5.5 Wine and food were either for a feast or an offering, or both.

5.6 *San* could mean three or simply several, as Chinese uses numbers to indicate approximate quantities. The best-known instance is the ten thousand things, used in the *Dao De Jing* to mean "myriad," as in the famous line "The 1 became 2, the 2 became 3 and the 3 became the 10,000 things."

6. 訟 *Song* Dispute (Conflict)

The Judgment:

6.0 Holding captives.
Obstruction, be cautious—auspicious in the middle but ends ominously.
Beneficial to see the important person.
Not favorable to cross the great river.
有孚. 窒惕—中吉, 終凶. 利見大人. 不利涉大川.

6.1 Do not persist for the long term with the matter.
With a few words it ends auspiciously.
初六不永所事. 小有言終吉.

6.2 Not successful in the dispute.
Returns, but from his town three hundred families had fled.
There was no mistake.
九二不克訟. 歸, 而逋其邑人三百戶. 无眚.

6.3 Dining with friends of ancient virtue.
Divination—harsh in the end.
Auspicious sometimes to follow the king's affairs, for which there is no completion.
六三食舊德. 貞—厲終. 吉或從王事无成.

6.4 Not successful in the dispute.
Reply quickly to the decree.
Change to be safe.
Divination auspicious.
九四不克訟. 復即命. 渝安. 貞吉.

6.5 Disputation begins auspiciously.
九五訟元吉.

6.6 Disputation begins auspiciously.
It happened that given a big leather belt, on the same day three
times it was taken away.
九五訟元吉.上九或錫之鞶帶, 終朝三褫之.

6. Commentary 訟 *Song* Dispute

The components of the character 訟 are those for "speak" and
"state," consistent with it meaning a verbal dispute, especially a
legal proceeding. Litigation might be a better translation but I have
avoided it because of its connotation of a modern complex court
case.

6.0 Kunst and Rutt translate the first phrase as the captives laughing
nervously, taking laughing captives to be a favorable omen (Rutt:
298f.). Given the *Zhouyi*'s obsession with sacrifice of captives this
is plausible, but speculative. Of interest, phrases that include 有孚
you fu "holding captives" though they often refer to the terror
of the captives, usually do not directly mention the killing itself.
Rather than a prediction, the phrase seems to be an incantation to
bring about a favorable situation. *Da ren* 大人 or important person
often contrasts with 小人 *xiao ren*, meaning small or petty person,
that is, one of low character.

6.1 This is repeated from 5.2 and in context perhaps suggests the
dispute can be settled auspiciously with only a few words. The
next phrase suggests that the dispute can be resolved without
litigation.

6.2 Some read this as about someone taxing his fief of three
hundred households to pay a court judgment (Rutt: 299). "No
mistake" seems contrary to the other phrases of this text.

6.6 Belts were symbols of rank, as still seen in contemporary Chinese images of warrior gods. This line may well refer to a particular historical event. Absolute power makes rulers capricious.

7. 師 *Shi* Troops (The Army)

The Judgment:

7.0 Divination for the family's head person is auspicious. Nothing blameworthy.
貞丈人吉—无咎.

7.1 The troops go out in accord with the regulations.
Not good! Ominously not good!
初六師出以律. 否臧! 凶臧!

7.2 To situate troops in the center is auspicious and averts blame.
The king three times confers rank.
九二在師中吉无咎. 王三錫命.

7.3 Some troops will be carried as corpses, ominous.
六三師或輿尸. 凶.

7.4 Ranking troops on the left averts blame.
六四師左次无咎.

7.5 Fields with birds and beasts.
Beneficial to seize captives to question. Blame averted.
The eldest son commands the troops.
The younger son carts the corpse. Divination ominous.
六五田有禽. 利執言. 无咎. 長子帥師. 弟子輿尸. 貞凶.

7.6 The ruler has decreed founding a family lineage.
Petty people are not to be made use of.
上六大君有命開國承家. 小人勿用.

7. Commentary 師 *Shi* Troops

I have translated as troops rather than army because the texts are about organizing soldiers, not about the army as an overall entity. This emphasis on proper position recurs frequently in the *Zhouyi* and in the case of soldiers being readied for battle is obviously vital for victory.

The general meaning of this hexagram is clear—it is about military organization and royal actions, presumably on the battlefield. It notes that the fate of troops in different positions (center and left) may be different. Corpses will be carried off the field in carts—a disaster but inevitable after a battle. It is unclear if the corpses referred to are the inquirer's own soldiers or those of the enemy. This chapter is more coherent than most, most lines being connected to military matters, including 7.6, as fiefdoms were a way of rewarding military success—and perhaps helping to prevent a successful commander attempting a coup against the ruler.

7.0 I have translated *ren* as "people" as the term in Chinese is gender neutral and there were some famous women generals in early times, notably Fu Hao (婦好 died c. 1200 BCE), the wife of King Wu Ding (武丁 reigned c. 1250–1192 BCE), famous from the oracle bone inscriptions. While the term usually refers to men, I see no reason to add gender when not in the original.

7.1 The phrase 以律 *yi liu* is translated by Kunst and Rutt, but not Shaughnessy as pitch pipes. This is plausible, as music was used to spur troops on to battle, but there is no evidence for this conjecture and the emphasis on positionality in the *Zhouyi* text favors this phrase referring to proper ordering of troops.

Fou zang 否臧 is often translated as "not good" but *zang* can also mean slaves, who served in armies, perhaps more in the Shang, but in the Western Zhou as well (Sawyer 2013: 271, 379 n.882). It might also mean that no enemy soldiers were captured to serve as slaves. As captives were clearly auspicious, lack of captives would be an unfavorable outcome.

7.2 The first phrase could also mean that for the soldiers it is auspicious to be located in the center, or that this is best for attaining victory. Ming 命 here is somewhat ambiguous. It could mean giving orders but also granting life in the sense of sparing people. In the context of organizing the troops, conferring command seems most plausible.

7.3 Rutt and Kunst note the tradition, recorded in the 楚辭; *Chu Ci* (*Songs of the South*) that King Wu's corpse, or perhaps his spirit tablet, was carried into the battle of Mu, the final defeat of Shang by Zhou. They suggest that 7.3 and 7.5 may be referring to this event (Rutt: 300; Kunst glosses 7.5.4). This suggestion is interesting but not consistent with the ominous prognosis. Any battle would result in dead bodies being carted from the field of action.

7.4 Whincup (1996: 43) notes that the left is the side of retreat, thus interpreting the phrase as indicating that in this situation, retreat is acceptable. This is plausible but the phrase may simply mean that in the specific battle, it would be advantageous to position troops on the left.

7.5 The first phrase might be a hunt to celebrate after a victory, as Rutt suggests (300). Alternatively, it might mean that the soldiers have to forage for their food and can find abundant game in a nearby field. If the younger brother accompanies the dead, it must be to honor someone of importance. Legends depicting dead leaders carried into battle are not unheard of, the best known in the West being that of El Cid of Spain.

7.6 *Guo* 國 is here somewhat ambiguous as to the size of the entity founded. It could be a territory, a country or a dynasty. Rutt takes this to be a reference to the founding of the Western Zhou (300). If so, petty people might be those of Shang who did not accept their new rulers. Alternatively, it might be a proviso that no low born be enfeoffed.

8. 比 *Bi* Joining
(Holding Together; Union)

The Judgment:

8.0 Auspicious original divination by yarrow.
Begin long-term divination, nothing unpeaceful coming from either direction.
A conscripted laborer, ominous.
原筮. 元永貞无不寧方來後. 夫凶.

The Line Texts:

8.1 When holding prisoners, joining them together will avert blame.
Holding prisoners and overflowing pottery jars.
In the end will come another auspicious omen.
初六有孚比之, 无咎. 有孚盈缶. 終來有它吉.

8.2 Join oneself with those inside.
Divination auspicious.
六二比之自內, 貞吉.

8.3 Joining with foreigners.
六三比之匪人.

8.4 Outsiders join us. Divination auspicious.
六四外比之. 貞吉.

8.5 Appearing together for the king to employ to drive out game
from three directions.
Misses the birds and animals in front.
The people of the region are not admonished. Auspicious.
九五顯比王用三驅. 失前禽. 邑人不誡. 吉.

8.6 Joining them without a chief, ominous.
上六比之无首, 凶.

8. Commentary 比 *Bi* Joining

This is one of several hexagrams in which the tag character is
repeated in each line text. That this stylistic trait is found in only
a few of the hexagrams is consistent with the hypothesis that there
were multiple compilers who used different modes of organizing
the text fragments. Another characteristic of these line texts is
that they seem to lend themselves more directly to divinations than
many of the others.

8.0 Zhen 筮 is an interesting character, one of relatively few that
seem to have a clear etymology. On top is the bamboo radical,
perhaps referring to writing on bamboo strips; underneath is *wu*,
shaman, suggesting its connection with divination. An alternative
meaning for this might be that the initial divination by yarrow
is auspicious. This character appears only one other time in the
Zhouyi, in 4.0, as part of an admonition against divining about the
same inquiry repeatedly. We know nothing of the actual method
of using yarrow to select hexagrams or line texts, or even if this
was the original method of *Zhouyi* divination. There are frequent
references to divination by yarrow in oracle bone inscriptions,
but these precede the *Zhouyi* by at least two centuries. Given
the variety of divination methods attested in later writings, it is
virtually certain that there were many in use in the Western Zhou
(Redmond and Hon 2014: 19–36).

Fu 夫 is usually a phase marker, but can refer to persons of
all sorts of social status, including conscripted laborers. In 4.3
seeing such a person is clearly a bad omen, as is the likely meaning
here.

8.1 *Fou* 缶 could also be an earthenware percussion instrument. This was a very ancient mourning practice. There is an anecdote in the *Zhuangzi* in which the nominal author is admonished for banging on a pottery jar following his wife's death. This was a symbol of returning to earth, perhaps originally to alert spirits to the sacrifice about to be offered to them.

8.2 *Nei* 內 within could refer to any enclosure, particularly to the women's section of the house.

8.3 *Feiren* 匪人 could also mean brigands or criminals, but given the inside/outside contrast here, foreigners seems a better fit. Kunst points out that literally this means something like "non-persons," one of many Chinese terms disparaging those considered foreign. Since China proper did not exist prior to the Qin, notions of foreignness differed from later ones.

8.5 One example of many in which the prognosis has an unclear relation to the preceding text. It does not fit with the rest of the text. Here the king misses the game animals in front but the people of the region have not been scolded. Yet it ends with 吉 good fortune, perhaps because the hunt is successful after that, or because the beaters escaped blame.

   Implicit here is the importance of hunting for the king to demonstrate his prowess. Rutt retells an anecdote related by Gao Heng in which a king tries three times to hit a bird with his arrow. Blaming a local for scaring the bird away, the king is about to have him executed but his aide successfully pleads for him to spare the man. Whether true or not it shows the absolute power of the king and his eagerness to execute those who annoy him, however trivial the offense. In another episode, a local chieftain is executed for being late to a meeting, though this was presumably a pretext for getting rid of a potential threat (Rutt: 301). These examples of the consequences of offending royalty illustrate the extreme importance of avoiding blame.

8.6 People joining together independently would be a threat to those in power. Rutt refers to Gao Heng's reading this as advising the king and getting one's head cut off for it (301). This was always a possible consequence of giving frank advice. However, this reading seems to me another instance of the Doubting Antiquity movement's adversarial attitude toward the ancient text. This emendation is hardly necessary as the cruelty of the era is regularly apparent in the *Zhouyi*.

9. 小畜 *Xiao Chu* Small Livestock (Taming Power of the Small)

The Judgment:

9.0 Make offering.
Dense clouds but no rain from our western outskirts.
亨. 密雲不雨自我西郊.

9.1 Returning along the road, what blame? Auspicious.
初九復自道, 何其咎. 吉.

9.2 Lead back. Auspicious.
九二牽復. 吉.

9.3 Like the cart scolding the wheel, husband and wife quarrel.
九三輿說輻, 夫妻反目.

9.4 Holding captives for blood sacrifice. They leave, shaking with terror as they go out. Nothing blameworthy.
六四有孚血. 去惕出. 无咎.

9.5 Holding captives twisted together.
Wealthy because of their neighborhood.
九五有孚攣如. 富以其鄰.

9.6 Now rains, now stops.
This place still holds potency.
The wife's divination is harsh.
Moon nearly full; for the cultivated person a long journey is ominous.
上九既雨既. 處尚德載. 婦貞厲. 月幾望; 君子征凶.

9. Commentary 小畜 *Xiao Chu*
Small Livestock

Wilhelm-Baynes' title is clearly too abstract for the Western Zhou. Small livestock is literal and fits well with the society's agricultural nature. However, the only other references to anything agricultural here are in 9.0, 9.2 and 9.6.

9.0 Rain was a matter of life and death for agricultural societies. Hence the phrase "clouds but no rain" indicates a situation where something important does not come as expected. In the oracle bones, divination about whether it will rain is common. It could also be a reference to sexual intercourse without ejaculation, an expression of male anxiety about potency and fertility.

9.2 This means leading an animal and is the only line that directly refers to livestock.

9.3 This sounds like a proverb, that spouses quarreling is like the cart contending with the wheel. It is interesting because it shows that wives were not as invariably obedient to their husbands as later Confucian orthodoxy prescribed.

9.4 This line seems clear enough. Kunst (257), Rutt (232), and Field (2015: 86f.) translate it as bloody castration of a horse or goat, presumably to make the phrase a reference to agriculture. However, since prisoners are being held and 有孚 *you fu* seems only to refer to humans, it seems more probable that the phrase is about the sacrifice of prisoners. That blame was avoided would suggest that the manner of the sacrificial ritual was correct. Sacrifice done improperly could annoy the spirit entities it was intended to propitiate. As elsewhere, there is no suggestion of any compassion for the victims.

9.5 Rutt suggests that a negation was lost, so that it should mean "not wealthy because of their neighbors." Either seems possible as rich neighbors might bring overall prosperity or appropriate the wealth of those less fortunate. The divinatory meaning would be that being around rich people would bring opportunities for profit.

The term translated as neighbors 鄰 *lin* referred to a five family organizational unit in the Zhou. Government has always intruded into domestic life in China.

9.6 Kunst (256f.) and Rutt (232) translate the second phrase as being about planting seeds. *De* 德 might refer to their potency to grow into crops.

In the final phrase, it is specifically the high born or upright who are in peril. Early Chinese astrology regarded the position of the moon, rather than its degree of fullness, as affecting good and bad fortune (Pankenier: 492–4). Here the moon reference seems to be simply a time marker. In passing, it should be noted that the still prevalent Western association of a full moon with insanity ("lunacy") has been completely refuted by scientific studies.

10. 履 *Lu* Treading (Treading)

The Judgment:

10. 0 Treading on the tiger's tail, the person is not bitten.
Make offering.
履虎尾, 不咥人. 亨.

The Line Texts:

10.1 In plain silk, treading onward.
There will be no blame.
初九素, 履往. 无咎.

10.2 Treading on the road; it is smooth and flat.
For the confined person the divination is auspicious.
九二履道坦坦; 幽人貞吉.

10.3 The one-eyed can see; the lame can tread.
Treading on the tiger's tail, it gnaws the person, ominous.
A soldier serves a great lord.
六三眇能視; 跛能履. 履虎尾, 咥人, 凶. 武人為于大君。

10.4 Treading on a tiger's tail, terrified, terrified—but ends auspiciously.
九四履虎尾, 愬愬—終吉.

10.5 Resolutely treading.
Divination harsh.
九五夬履. 貞厲.

10.6 Observing, treading, examining are propitious. Their turning back is an auspicious beginning.
上九視履考祥. 其旋元吉.

10. Commentary 履 *Lu* Treading

Lu means walking or treading, the latter better fitting the act of stepping on a tiger's tail. The hexagram lines are about the risks of treading—walking or traveling by foot. The character for this, 履 *lu* "treading" occurs in each line text.

This is one of my favorite hexagrams, not only because it is unusually lucid but especially because the image of treading on a tiger's tail is so memorable. This image must be a proverbial one, though with variations as in the different line texts.

The lines describe different results of stepping on the tiger's tail, but without evident progression in accord with the line position. One is not bitten in the judgment, then is bitten in 10.3, but seems to escape the situation in 10.4.

Perhaps the offering is in gratitude for not being bitten by the tiger, but more likely *heng* by itself stands for the full four-character invocation as in 1.0. Heng appears in only seven of the line texts, but thirty-nine of the judgment texts. Several of the line texts address the anxiety evoked by any sort of journey, even a local one. Meeting with a tiger or brigands while traveling have been common tropes in later Chinese literature.

10.1 This line text is rather bland but in divination it would be easily read as meaning that just walking along minding one's business will not incur blame. The Mawangdui manuscript has 錯 *cuo* meaning mistaken, instead of "plain silk." Both fit well enough, but like many of the other variants in excavated texts, these do not change our fundamental understanding of the *Zhouyi*.

10.2 As I have emphasized, based on study of oracle bone inscriptions it is clear that many apparent divinations are actually incantations intended to help bring about the desired outcome. The first phrase about the road being wide and smooth may be of this sort, a stock phrase for well-wishing someone embarking on a journey, just as we say "Have a safe trip."

You ren 幽人, which I have translated as "confined person," can mean "prisoner" but also a secluded person or hermit. Whether the seclusion is voluntary or not, the inquirer's outlook is favorable. The phrase also appears in 54.2.

10.3 This might be a proverb saying that despite limitations people can still function. More likely, it is an expression for an anomalous situation in which miraculous cures occur.

The second phrase returns to the treading-on-a-tiger theme. In this line it is proclaimed ominous, a masterpiece of understatement. For divination, stepping on the tiger would be similar to the English language situation of "stirring up a hornets' nest."

10.5 This line seems to advise that walking in an overly confident manner can attract disaster.

10.6 A warning to be cautious when traveling on foot. It recommends first observing, then walking, then checking an omen only to be told to turn back.

11. 泰 *Tai* Great (Peace)

The Judgment:

11.0 The petty depart; the great arrive. Auspicious, make offering.
小往; 大來. 吉亨.

The Line Texts:

11.1 Pulling up white (cogon) grass by the roots to bundle for their campaign, auspicious.
拔茅茹以其彙,吉.

11.2 Wrap in gourds to use to cross the He River, not far off.
Leaving behind friends, who will be lost.
Obtain honors by acting properly.
包荒用馮河不遐. 遺—朋亡. 得尚于中行.

11.3 Nothing level without hills.
No going without returning.
Divination: hardship, but nothing blameworthy.
Do not pity their captives.
With the meal will have good fortune.
无平不陂. 无往不復.艱貞无咎. 勿恤其孚.于食有福.

11.4 Fluttering, fluttering.
Not wealthy because of their neighbors.
Not on guard with the captives.
六四翩翩. 不富以其鄰.不戒以孚.

11.5 King Di Yi bestows his younger sister/cousin in marriage.
For happiness, greatly auspicious.
六五帝乙歸妹. 以祉元吉.

11.6 The city wall collapses into the moat.
Do not use the army; one's own city declares the order.
Divination—regret.
上六城復于隍. 勿用師;自邑告命. 貞—吝.

11. Commentary 泰 *Tai* Great

Wilhelm-Baynes' translation as "peace" is problematic because, as I
have already pointed out, there is no evidence for a concept of peace as
a desirable state in the Western Zhou; rather, warfare was considered
normal. Rutt makes a similar point (303). Rutt and Shaughnessy
translate as "great" and "greatness," respectively, which somewhat
fits with 11.1, but is not a general theme of the texts.

11.0 "The great arrive; the petty depart," refers to those who
occupy government positions. The competence and probity of
officials has always been a major preoccupation of Chinese thought
and continues in the anti-corruption campaign of the current
president, Xi Jinping. Corrupt officials are dangerous to honest
ones because they fear that the righteous will expose them.

Good and bad government was considered cyclical in Chinese
political theory. Sometimes the country will be run by the virtuous,
at others by the cunning and dishonest. The virtuous regimes are
usually ascribed to the remote past, notably the time of King Wen
and the Duke of Zhou, though no such idea appears in the *Zhouyi*
text itself.

This cyclic notion is expressed in the *Lunyu*:

When the Way prevails in the world, [the exemplar of the way]
appears; when the Way is lacking, he retires. (*Lunyu* 8.13,
Watson 55f.)

11.1 Cogon grass was used to thatch roofs and to wrap offerings.
This phrase is a reference to making offerings, but a more specific

procedure than implied by the recurrent 亨 *heng*. The same phrase appears in 12.1. Since hexagram 12 is the inversion of hexagram 11, it is conceivable that they were composed together. However, in Mawangdui, with hexagrams ordered by a different principle, 11 and 12 are 34 and 2 respectively.

A remote possibility is that 茅 *mao* (cogon grass) actually referred to yarrow for *Zhouyi* divination. However, the Chinese word for yarrow does not appear in the *Zhouyi*, though it does in oracle bone inscriptions and other early divination texts. Further against the possibility that 茅 *mao* referred to plant stalk divination is the lack of any reference to divination methodology elsewhere in the *Zhouyi*. Hexagram selection techniques are, however, mentioned in the *Zuozhuan* and the *Ten Wings*. The yarrow stick method most widely used since the Song Dynasty was a reconstruction by Zhu Xi (1130–1200), whose method is rather onerous. We have no record of earlier methods.

11.2 Rutt (304) notes that crossing the He (which may or may not be the Yellow River) is compared to grappling with a tiger in Ode 195.6. That the river is turbulent might be why gourds would be needed for flotation. The second phrase makes this an image for moving on and leaving friends behind, a common trope in later Chinese poetry and particularly poignant in an era when travel was arduous. The final phrase might simply be a set phrase, or may mean that the travel is for an official appointment that will bring honor.

11.3 This line, uncharacteristically for the *Zhouyi*, raises the possibility that some might sympathize with the captives about to be sacrificed. This reminds us that we should not imagine that everyone in ancient times was heartless. However, it is hard to make this into a wider indication of early Chinese feelings regarding human sacrifice. Rutt translates this phrase as:

> Be not anxious: there may be captives at the feast. Good Luck (234).

Which seems to mean that it would not be a real feast without human sacrifices. As with so many variant translations of the *Zhouyi*, this cannot be refuted, but neither can it be proven to be the early meaning. My personal feeling is that this is one of those instances in which Rutt's unrelievedly grim reconstruction of the *Changes* goes too far. The Western Zhou was a cruel era, but surely sometimes pity arose.

11.4 Regarding wealth and neighborhood, this is the negation of 8.5. It may be a continuation of the practice, pervasive in the oracle bone inscriptions of making an inquiry by stating the question in both positive and negative ways.

In the Shang, as in China today, neighborhoods were usually made up of families who worked in the same trade such as bronze casting, ceramic firing, etc. While it is tempting to regard the influence of neighborhood as based on "networking," it is more likely that geomancy—the antecedent of *feng shui*—is what is referred to.

11.4 The redoubled word *pian pian* can mean dancing, usually elegant dancing by males. The dancing might be part of the festivities referred to in 11.3 and 11.6. Alternatively, Rutt suggests that the fluttering is that of birds, hence an omen (304).

11.5 The first phrase recurs in 54.5, also about a royal wedding in which the bride is upstaged by a bridesmaid.

11.6 This line does not seem related to the others of this hexagram.

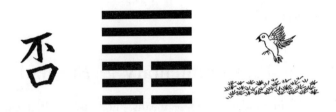

12. 否 *Fou* Bad (Standstill; Stagnation)

The Judgment:

12.0 Say no to brigands; they have no benefit for upright people.
Divination—the great depart; the petty arrive.
否之匪; 不利君子. 貞—大往小來.

The Line Texts:

12.1 Uprooting white (cogon) grass by the roots.
Divination auspicious, make offering.
初六拔茅茹以其彙. 貞吉, 亨.

12.2 Wrap for presentation.
For petty people, auspicious; for great people, not.
Make offering.
六二包承. 小人吉; 大人否. 亨.

12.3 Wrapped savory meat.
六三包羞.

12.4 Has been a decree. There will be no blame.
Cultivated field with orioles—prosperity.
九四有命. 无咎. 疇離—祉。

12.5 Refusing the bad, for the important person, auspicious.
They flee! They flee!
Tie to a thick white mulberry.
休否大人吉其亡其亡 繫于苞桑

12.6 Inclined to bad.
First bad; after, happy.
上九傾否. 先否後喜.

12. Commentary 否 *Fou* Bad

Fou 否 in modern Chinese means "no." By itself it can be an interrogative, but this is not usual in the *Zhouyi*. As the tag for this hexagram, *Fou* has been translated as obstruction, standstill, or simply bad. In the Mawangdui version, the character is 婦 *Fu*, meaning wife, a near-homophone (Shaughnessy 1997: 41f., 288). Since this is a poor fit for most of the lines, I have followed the received version. Some lines of Mawangdui can be read as about marriage or a wife, but for the others, especially 12.5 "wife" is a poor fit. Another argument against the tag meaning wife is the tendency of pre-modern Chinese texts to limit references to women. Certainly, women are mentioned in the *Zhouyi*, but infrequently.

This hexagram is the inversion of the preceding one, 11. Its constituent trigrams are also heaven and earth, but with the former on top. This was later interpreted as heaven and earth moving apart, an unfavorable situation. The judgments also contrast with the great arriving in 11, but departing in 12, to be replaced by the petty.

12.0 One of the many sources of frustration in translating the *Zhouyi* is the character *fei* 匪, which can mean either negation/not, or bandit/brigand. This character is often found in *Zhouyi* phrases about weddings which also include the character meaning woman or wife. Which meaning one chooses for *fei* will drastically alter the meaning of the phrase. In this case *fei* is followed by *ren*, "person" 匪人 so here it would seem to mean a brigand.

12.1 and 12.2. The mention of cogon grass and wrapping parallels 11.1 and 11.2.

12.3 Probably meat for a sacrificial offering. It would have been eaten after the ritual; the deceased always generously left their food for the living.

12.4 Here the divinatory structure is clear. The first line phrase indicates an event, while the following one gives the prognostic—no blame is involved. The next phrase gives a natural observation—a field with birds—while the final phrase interprets this as an omen: there will be prosperity.

Regarding the second phrase, oriole is an uncommon meaning but is attested in the earliest Chinese dictionary, the *Shuowen*. The phrase is a straightforward omen, the bird indicating that the field will be fecund. Although orioles may be unfavorable as omens (Rutt: 306; Bernardo: 205) in this context they are favorable. Wilhelm-Baynes translate 祉 *zhi* as blessing, an example of a perhaps inadvertent injection of Christian language. Such a concept is anachronistic for the Western Zhou.

12.5 The first phrase states that it is good to stand up to the bad elements. Perhaps the next phrase means that the bad run away when there is a righteous person in charge. Tying to a tree could mean that the bad ones are captured and bound. More likely, it was a procedure to avert bad luck, akin to a practice still popular in temples in Japan. One's fortune is provided on a slip of paper; if unfavorable it is tied to a tree in the temple grounds so that it remains there instead of accompanying its recipient.

12.6 Perhaps a proverb stating that a bad person is happier when he or she reforms. Such direct ethical admonitions are rare in the *Zhouyi*.

13. 同人 *Tong Ren* Assembling (Fellowship with Men)

The Judgment:

13.0 Assembling in the wilderness, making offering.
Beneficial to cross the great river.
Beneficial for the upright person to divine.
同人于野,亨. 利涉大川. 利君子貞.

The Line Texts:

13.1 Assembling at the gate; there will be no blame.
初九同人于門; 无咎.

13.2 Assembling at the ancestral temple, regretfully.
六二同人于宗, 吝.

13.3 The forces ambush from the thicket.
They climb the high hill, but for three passings of Jupiter, not achieved.
九三伏戎于莽. 升其高陵, 三歲不興.

13.4 War chariots at their city wall attack but unable to overcome.
Auspicious.
九四乘其墉弗克攻. 吉.

3.5 Assembled, they first wail, then laugh.
Great armies happen upon each other.
九五同人, 先號咷而後笑. 大師克相遇。

13.6 Assembling at the outskirts to sacrifice to heaven.
Nothing to regret.
上九同人于郊. 无悔.

13. Commentary 同人 *Tong ren* Assembling

Wilhelm-Baynes' title as fellowship with men misses the tone—much of this text is about assembling for military purposes. It is not about friendship or peace. As before, I have avoided specifying gender in translating the genderless *ren*.

The texts in this hexagram are relatively coherent. Gathering is translated by Rutt as "mustering," and does in this chapter usually refer to soldiers. However, mustering is a formal process of getting soldiers into position and the lines refer to more general forms of bringing soldiers together.

13.0 This is another example of how the judgment text includes three of the initial four words of the classic. The first word, *yuan* 元, is omitted—it is the least important word of the phrase. The other three words are in order, but with other words intercalated. The reason for these variations in the invocatory phrase is unknown, most likely scribal whim.

While *junzi* here probably refers to a sovereign, or someone of high rank leading the army, I have translated it as "upright person," as a reminder that high rank was assumed to correlate with good character, a claim common throughout cultures, though fallacious in all.

13.2 The reason for shame and regret is not apparent. Perhaps assembling at the ancestral temple was to atone for an error of some sort.

13.3 Jupiter was the "year star" because its passage across the sky took one year. In the absence of the light pollution that is pervasive in modern urban life, the phenomena of the night sky would be apparent to everyone and seasonal changes would be general knowledge.

It is hard to imagine that an attack on an enemy's hill position would last for three years, so more likely there was a siege, or repeated attacks over a long duration. Failure to capture a fortified position would have been a common military situation; this line might be a fragmentary record of an actual campaign.

13.5 First wail, then laugh, recurs in reverse order in 56.6, suggesting a set phrase that could be used either way to indicate a sudden change in how one's situation is perceived. The phrase refers to prisoners about to be sacrificed in 43.0, 45.1, and in other line texts. In context it seems to indicate intense emotion, usually negative.

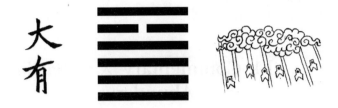

14. 大有 *Da You* Abundance
(Possession in Great Measure)

The Judgment:

14.0 Start with an offering.
元亨.

The Line Texts:

14.1 Cannot cross, catastrophe.
Bandits are punished for this difficulty.
Thus nothing blameworthy.
初九无交, 害. 匪咎艱. 則无咎.

14.2 A large cart used for transporting, having somewhere to go.
Nothing blameworthy.
九二大車以載, 有攸往. 无咎.

14.3 A duke can employ an offering to the Son of Heaven, but petty
people must not.
九三公用亨于天子, 小人弗克.

14.4 The brigands are powerful, but there will be no blame.
九四匪其彭, 无咎.

14.5 Fainting captives handed over, terrified. Auspicious.
六五厥孚交如威如.吉.

14.6 It is the way of things that heaven helps the lucky. Nothing not beneficial.
上九自天祐之吉. 无不利.

14. Commentary 大有 *Da You* Abundance

Da You literally means "great having"; that is possessing a lot, or abundance. Wilhelm-Baynes' "possession in great measure" is appealingly mysterious but not quite clear. There is nothing specifically about abundance in the texts, though avoiding bandits, the large cart, the duke's offering, and heaven helping the lucky can be related to the tag.

14.1 This is a highly ambiguous line. I take the first phrase as a set phrase to the effect that if catastrophe is coming it cannot be averted. This is similar to Kunst's reading as interpretation of a bird flight omen (267). Then brigands take the blame and are punished. This manages to make sense of a confusing passage, something other translators seem to have struggled to do. If 匪 *fei* is taken as "not" as most have done, then the phrase becomes "not blamed for the difficulty." *Jiao* 交 can also be translated as sexual intercourse, which would make the phrase, "There is no harm in copulating." This spices up the text, but it is hard to be certain if this was an intentional *double entendre*.

14.3 This alludes to the advantages of wealth and power. It is most likely a proverb, meaning that rich people can curry favor, but ordinary people cannot. There is nothing remotely like social criticism in the *Zhouyi*, although it is abundant in later classics, such as the *Lunyu*, *Dao De Jing* and *Zhuangzi*.

14.4 As elsewhere I have chosen to translate 匪 *fei* as bandits when this gives a clear narrative meaning to a phrase. Fear of bandits was pervasive during most of Chinese history. *Peng* 彭 can also refer to a kind of sacrifice (as translated by Kunst and Rutt) or a city in the ancient region of Chu.

14.5 That the captives were terrified would have been taken as confirming the power of the captors, presumably the Western Zhou rulers. The extreme suffering of the victim likely enhanced the efficacy of the sacrifice. Mutilation was often part of the procedure and execution methods were gruesome.

14.6 A proverb, though my translation is somewhat free. Like the earlier proverb about dukes, this expresses a down-to-earth realism. In a feudal state one's life was mainly determined by the status one was born into, a matter of luck.

15. 謙 *Qian* Humble (Modesty)

The Judgment:

15.0 The offerings of the high-born have been completed.
亨君子有終.

The Line Texts:

15.1 The humblest and the high-born alike must wade to cross a wide river. Auspicious.
初六謙謙君子用涉大川.吉.

15.2 The humble bird calls.
Divination auspicious.
六二鳴謙. 吉。

15.3 By laboring humbly, the high-born person has an auspicious outcome.
九三勞謙, 君子有終吉.

15.4 Nothing that is not beneficial about showing humility.
六四无不利撝謙.

15.5 Not wealthy on account of his neighbors.
Beneficial to invade with a military expedition.
Nothing not beneficial.
六五不富以其鄰. 利用侵伐. 无不利.

15.6 A modest bird calls.
Beneficial to set soldiers marching on a campaign against the capital city.
上六鳴謙. 利用行師征邑國.

15. Commentary 謙 *Qian* Humble

The usual translations of 謙 *qian* are "modesty" and "humility." However, given the limited description of character traits in the *Zhouyi*, I take *qian* as referring to behaving humbly; that is, as a description of social status or behavior, not as an abstract virtue. In a hierarchical society, acting humble in the presence of those of higher rank would have been essential for survival.

Kunst translates the tag character as Rat and Rutt does so more precisely as the Great Grey Hamster—not the pet but a large and voracious rodent [309f.]. If this is correct, then the lines become a series of omens based on animal sightings or behavior. The Mawangdui manuscript has *qian* 嗛 meaning modesty, but also animal jaws. The Shanghai Museum manuscript *qian* has a different character (not available in standard fonts), which Shaughnessy translates as "modesty" (84). I regard the rodent translation as another example of the Doubting Antiquity Movement's preference for rendering the classic as obscure as possible. Translation of the tag character as Rat seems to have a debunking motive, because this is one of the most explicitly moralizing chapters in the entire *Zhouyi*.

15.0 High-born person seems better here than "upright person," as carrying out ritual was important for rulers and nobles.

15.1 My rendering makes the line into a proverb—some things must be done by the high-born as well as the humble.

15.2 Also an edifying proverb. Even mere birds can provide guidance. In this and other line texts of this hexagram are hints of something like egalitarianism, not negating rank, but suggesting that all are subject to human limits.

15.3 This line is akin to 15.1. Even the high-born should work hard with a humble attitude. Confucianism also extolled humility, though not all Confucians have displayed this quality. While Confucius speaks in an authoritative voice in the *Lunyu*, much of what he says does display humility.

15.5 "Not wealthy on account of one's neighbors" also occurs in 11.4, indicating that it is a set phrase. It might have to do with what we call networking, or geomancy, or perhaps that the neighbors are stealing, likely a common situation.

15.6 The bird-call indicates that the outlook for the military action will be favorable. In ancient Greece also, military decisions were made on the basis of divination.

16. 豫 *Yu* Preparation (Enthusiasm)

The Judgment:

16.0 Beneficial to enfeoff a lord.
Set the army marching.
利建侯. 行師.

The Line Texts:

16.1 A bird calls. Prepare—ominous.
初六鳴. 豫凶.

16.2 Stuck at rocks, but not all day.
Divination auspicious.
六二介于石, 終日. 貞吉.

16.3 Open eyes to prepare. Regret—tardiness will bring regret.
六三盱豫. 悔—遲有悔.

16.4 From preparation, great things are acquired. Do not doubt this.
Friends, why not gather together quickly?.
九四由豫, 大有得, 勿疑. 朋盍簪.

16.5 Divination: sickness long-lasting, but not fatal.
六五貞: 疾恆, 不死.

16.6 Murky. Preparation accomplishes change.
Nothing blameworthy.
上六冥. 豫成有渝. 无咎.

16. Commentary 豫 *Yu* Preparation

The great variety of proposed translations for this tag, *Yu* 豫, provides a good example of the imagination exercised by translators of the *Changes*. Suggestions have included enthusiasm, contentment, joy, weariness, and elephant. The latter is that of Kunst based on a *Shuowen* definition and followed by Rutt (310). Given that the line texts generally do not suggest joy or contentment, preparation seems the best fit—divination, after all, is about being prepared.

In the Shanghai Museum manuscript the tag is 余 and in Mawangdui it is 餘; both translated by Shaughnessy as "excess" (2014: 86 n.1). Lynn translates the tag as "contentment," but then puts it in a rather colorful phrase that does not seem consistent with the style of the Western Zhou text:

> If one allows one's contentment to sing out here, there will be misfortune. (236)

16.0 As already noted, enfeoffment, establishing nobles by a grant of land, was the main way that a king could reward and retain the loyalty of those who had helped him. The term I have used to translate comes from medieval England.

16.1 Kunst and Rutt amend 鳴 *ming* to "elephant." Given the frequency of bird-call omens in the *Zhouyi*, I have stayed with the received translation. Most bird-call omens in the *Zhouyi*, unlike this one, seem favorable (15.2, 15.6, 61.2).

16.2 Presumably this refers to rocky terrain that delays the progress of troops.

16.4 Translations of the last phrase, *peng he zan* 朋盍簪, have varied considerably. Mine is the mainstream. Kunst and Rutt take

朋 *peng* to mean "cowrie shells," which were strung together for use as money. Wilhelm-Baynes translates this as hair-clasp. Literally the final character refers to a hairpin, which Wilhelm-Baynes explain as a metaphor for gathering together. That the phrase is about friends gathering seems most likely to me given the frequency in the *Zhouyi* of references to people gathering together.

16.5 Such a specific medical prognosis is unusual for the *Zhouyi*. It states the illness is chronic but will not be fatal. There are many medical conditions to which this might apply. How physicians of the time could provide such a precise prognosis is unclear but some would likely have some intuitive sense of disease and its outcome from long experience. Despite this, many divinations regarding disease must have been inaccurate.

16.6 This is a difficult line to make sense of. It might refer back to the previous line—preparations had been made for the death of the ill person, then changed when it was realized that death was not imminent. This makes sense of the lines but is no more than my guess.

17. 隨 *Sui* Pursuing (Following)

The Judgment:

17.0 Begin with an offering, beneficial to divine.
There will be no blame.
元亨利貞. 无咎.

The Line Texts:

17.1 The officials have changed their minds.
Divination auspicious.
Go out, engage, attain meritorious accomplishment.
初九官有渝. 貞吉. 出門, 交,有功.

17.2 Tying up the youths; letting slip the men.
六二係小子; 失丈夫.

17.3 Tying up the men; letting skip the young.
Pursue—obtain what is sought.
Beneficial divination for a home.
六三係丈夫; 失小子. 隨有求得。利居貞.

17.4 Pursue to have a capture.
Divination ominous.
Holding captives on the road for sacrifice, how could there be blame?
九四隨有獲. 貞凶. 有孚在道以明, 何咎.

17.5 Sacrificing captives is praiseworthy, auspicious.
九五孚于嘉, 吉.

17.6 Capture and tie them, then secure them with cords for the king to use as an offering on the west mountain.
上六拘係之, 乃從維之王用亨于西山.

17. Commentary 隨 *Sui* Pursuing

Most of the lines in this hexagram concern captives and their sacrifice. The tag could refer to pursuing people to take them captive, as in 17.4. The texts are both unpleasant and uninteresting, merely adding some more references to human sacrifice.

17.0 The judgment is a standard invocation.

17.1 We are not told how the officials changed their mind, but it was beneficial for the inquirer.

17.2 and 17.3 In the first case, the older captives are released, in the next, the younger ones. This suggests that some sort of principles existed for choosing sacrificial victims, but what these were is never directly stated.
   The remaining line texts repeat the theme of human sacrifice.

18. 蠱 *Gu* Sickness from Sexual Excess (Work on What Has Been Spoiled; Decay)

The Judgment:

18.0 Supreme offering for success,
Auspicious for crossing the wide river.
Before starting, three days.
After starting, three days.
蠱元亨，利涉大川．先甲，三日．後甲，三日．

The Line Texts:

18.1 Undoing illness from the father.
If he has a son, then the father is not culpable.
There is difficulty, but all ends well.
初六幹父之蠱．有子，考无咎，厲終吉．

18.2 Undoing illness caused by the mother, one must not be too strict.
九二幹母之蠱，不可貞．

18.3 In undoing illness caused by the father, there will be regrets, but no culpability.
九三幹父之蠱，小有悔，无大咎．

18.4 Be generous and indulgent toward illness caused by the father because excessive zeal would bring shame.
六四裕父之蠱往見吝．

18.5 For undoing illness caused by the father, one will be praised.
六五幹父之蠱，用譽.

18.6 Instead of serving kings and lords, one seeks self-respect in following one's own affairs.
上九不事王侯，高尚其事.

18. Commentary 蠱 *Gu* Sickness from Sexual Excess

The character 蠱 *gu* has multiple meanings, mostly ominous. That selected by Wilhelm-Baynes, "work on what has been spoiled," is based on the structure of the character. The bottom element means "bowl," while the top means worms or insects. Thus the image is of a bowl of spoiled food infested with vermin. This must have been an extremely common sight in a world without refrigeration or insecticides. This sort of etymology by breaking down characters into their constituents has always been extremely popular in China, but is frequently historically inaccurate. Furthermore, dissecting characters is a quite different mode of interpretation than considering actual usage of the word. Here, however, the etymology is entirely plausible.

The Mawangdui text (Shaughnessy 1997: 68–9; 295) uses a different character meaning "branch" for *Gu* (not available in standard fonts), and clearly a homophone substitution for the received version character.

The tag character is repeated in five of the six lines, so it is clearly the basic subject of the chapter. The exception is the final line, which is unrelated to any of the themes in the other lines. The line texts associated with the *gu* hexagram are of particular interest for what they tell us about the anxieties of traditional China. I have interpreted *gu* as "disease due to excessive sexual activity," a definite meaning of the word. This is specifically mentioned as a diagnosis in the *Zuozhuan*, as translated by Rutt:

> Men who often women woo
> Suffer a disease called gu,
> It is not demons, is not gluttony:
> This weakness is brought on by lechery. (191)

There are many mentions in later Chinese literature of disease brought on by excessive sexual activity. Only males seem to sustain this disease, not their partners. According to modern medical research, more frequent sexual activity, though it may be tiring, is associated with better health. For a more detailed discussion of Chinese attitudes toward sexuality and health, from the *Zuozhuan* onward, see Leo (2011: 165–76 *et passim*).

18.0 The judgment text seems to present a positive prognosis in contrast to the line texts, which indicate difficulties, though these can be overcome with careful control of one's behavior. The character *jia* 甲 is the first of the so-called "ten heavenly stems" of the Chinese dating system. It could mean beginning, as I have translated, or an indication of which dates would be favorable based on the Chinese sixty-day calendrical cycle. Hemerology, that is, the determination of favorable and unfavorable days, was and is pervasive in Chinese divination (see Kalinowski). Oddly, while the *Zhouyi* often gives a prognosis, whether auspicious or catastrophic, it is rarely specific about exact times or dates. Even if the judgment is interpreted as providing guidance regarding timing, it has no evident relationship to the line texts. Cyclic date specifications are generally days for specific sacrifices to be performed. (For further details on basis of sacrificial dates, see Rutt [312f.]. For an introduction to the complexities of the sexagenary cycle, see Wilkinson [2013: 496–502].) Three seems to be a common number, for example, three years in 29.6, three days in 36.1, three foxes in 40.2, and three people in 41.3. For other examples, see 47.1, 49.3, 53.5, 55.6, 57.4, 63.3, and 64.4. In context, three can mean several, but with reference to sacrifices it must have been exact. No doubt three held numerological significance, but lucky and unlucky numbers vary over time and place. Currently, due to the worldwide influence of Cantonese culture, four is unlucky because it is a homophone for "death," while eight is auspicious because *ba*, eight, sounds somewhat like *fa (cai)*, "to become rich" (for a concise discussion of Chinese numerology, see Wilkinson [2013: 485–8]). Marshal suggests that *gu* refers to an ancestral curse—this is not entirely different from the effects of parental sexual malfeasance on the offspring (Marshall: 128f.) Likely it had all these meanings in various contexts.

Lines one to five share similar tone and subject matter, suggesting illness or another toxic situation related to the father or mother that needs to be counteracted. As usual with the *Zhouyi*, the lines are allusive rather than explicit, but the general message of the first five lines is clear. One is faced with a potentially blameworthy situation, but if matters are handled judiciously, the difficulties can be minimized. Action is required, but should not be extreme. The most obvious connection between the line texts is that all are about family relationships, presumably in relation to reproduction since the terms are not man and woman, but father and mother. This makes it plausible that the illness has something to do with sexual activity on the part of the parents—the inquirer seems to be the offspring of the parents referred to. There is no suggestion in the text as to what sort of sexual impropriety might be affecting the offspring. Presumably it was excessive frequency. There was no concept of perversions or paraphilias as in modern theories of sexuality.

Later Confucian exegesis tended to hide indelicacies by reading them as moralistic lessons. Hence the sexual meaning of *gu* was ignored. This suppression of sexual, or simply romantic, content is even more evident in Confucian interpretation of the *Book of Songs* (*Shijing*), in which love poems became expressions of the admiration of the official for his superior.

Gu had other unpleasant associations that were probably as much in the minds of readers as the sexual ones. Spoiled food infested by worms has already been mentioned—it was believed they were somehow born from the food. For the many who barely had enough to eat, spoiled food would have meant hunger and economic loss. This reminds us that for most in the Bronze Age, simple matters such as preventing spoilage of food were a constant struggle.

Gu also referred to a particularly evil method of poisoning. Several venomous animals were placed in a vessel together. These included snakes, scorpions, spiders, and centipedes. The last one left alive was considered to have concentrated the venom and was ground up and served to the victim concealed in food. *Gu* poisoning, if it occurred at all, must have been rare. The greatest harm associated with poisoning was probably not in actual use, but false accusations. Like accusations of witchcraft, these were impossible to defend against. Anxiety about health is always present in human life, and was all the more so when there was no knowledge of the actual etiology of disease, whose cause was often attributed to poison or curses, both of which are invisible and impossible to prove or refute. Although detection of poisoning was difficult until it was too late, a variety of bizarre antidotes were recommended, such as ingesting a different venomous animal to counteract the one used to prepare the poison.

For other views on the meaning of *gu*, see Kunst (1985: 274f.), whose rendition of 18.4 refers to a "bathing father" and Rutt (1996: 241, 312f.) who translated *gu* as "mildew," based on the much later *Zuozhuan*.

In later China, pseudo-physiological theories of disease reached great complexity, partially—but not completely—supplanting supernatural etiology. These theories, making use of *yin yang* and *wu xing* metaphysics, were already evident in the 黃帝內經素問 *Huang Di Nei Jing Su Wen* (*Yellow Emperor's Inner Classic of Medicine*) (for a recent translation see Kong). The date of this compilation is controversial; current scholarship assigns a Western Han origin to it, though with inclusion of Warring States material (Unschuld 2003: 1–7).

18.1 If a man has had a son, his improprieties are forgiven. The responsibility to have sons was central in Chinese culture from ancient times. Several translations of this line refer to the father as being deceased.

18.2 This line indicates that the illness could come from the mother instead of the father. However, whatever the mother has done, one should not be too hard on her for it. This might be because of the natural affection one has for one's mother, or because women are entitled to more indulgence. Wang Bi, one of the most influential interpreters of the *Changes* gave a rather prejudicial tone to this passage. As translated by Lynn:

> The nature of woman is such that she is incapable of perfect rectitude, so it is appropriate to suppress one's own hardness and strength here ... (1994: 251)

This is one of many misogynistic *I Ching* readings by Wang Bi. His readings seem not to have been universally accepted since Legge's and Wilhelm's translations, both based on informants who were traditionally educated Chinese literati, simply render the line as suggesting not to be too severe on one's mother. Considering that the father is mentioned more frequently regarding *gu*, there is no indicating of greater blame for the mother in the Western Zhou text.

18.4 In Chinese this line is ambiguous as to whether what would be shameful was being too indulgent or too harsh. To be consistent with the other lines, it most likely means that harshness would be shameful. Such ambiguity would have given diviners much latitude in what they told their clients.

18.5 According to this line, one will be praised for correcting what the father did wrong. Such filial piety was laudable in ancient China. Writing much later, Confucius famously said, "In our district … a father covers up for his son; a son covers up for his father. There's honesty in that, too" (Watson 2007: 91).

18.6 This line text has no evident relation to the previous five. It could be read as indicating that after overcoming the family difficulties, one should focus on attaining higher goals for oneself. However, the issue of serving a superior versus serving oneself is not mentioned elsewhere in the chapter, so such a meaning seems to be an effort at harmonization of texts that are unrelated.

19. 臨 *Lin* Wailing (Approach)

The Judgment:

19.0 Begin with an offering, beneficial to divine.
Until the eighth month will be ominous.
元亨, 利貞. 至于八月有凶.

The Line Texts:

19.1 Salty tears and wailing.
Divination: auspicious
初九咸臨. 貞吉

19.2 Salty tears and wailing. Auspicious—nothing not beneficial.
九二咸臨. 吉无不利.

19.3 Willingly wailing.
Nowhere beneficial.
Now sorrowful; there will be no blame.
六三甘臨. 无攸利. 既憂之; 无咎

19.4 Extreme wailing.
There will be no blame.
六四至臨. 无咎.

19.5 Controlled wailing—proper for the great master. Auspicious.
六五知臨—大君之宜. 吉.

19.6 Loyally lamenting. Auspicious. There will be no blame.
上六敦臨. 吉. 无咎.

19. Commentary 臨 *Lin* Wailing

Lin 臨 has two quite different meanings. In ancient times it meant wailing or keening as mourning practices (Kunst: 276f., 242; Rutt: 314). In Mawangdui the tag is a homophone 林, *lin* meaning "forest," as it is in the Fuyang version (Shaughnessy 1997: 108f.; 2014: 236). The commonness and simplicity of 林 is consistent with it being a scribal substitution.

19.0 An unremarkable invocation.

    The line texts are simply variations on the theme of wailing.

    Initially puzzling in this hexagram are the lines that refer to wailing, then declare it as auspicious—19.1, 19.2, 19.5, and 19.6. Field explains this (as do Kunst and Rutt), as the lines being about proper attention to the dead. After a phase in which the deceased's spirit wanders and is a danger to the living:

    Once the spirit resides in the tablet and mourning ceases, the prognostication is a positive one: no harm will come (2015: 117).

    Here the harm would be from the ancestors' restless spirit. People feared the dead almost more than the living.

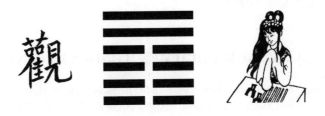

20. 觀 *Guan* Observing
(Contemplation; View)

The Judgment:

20.0 Perform ablutions, but do not sacrifice the captives with big heads.
盥, 而不薦有孚顒若.

The Line Texts:

20.1 Observing children.
For the petty people there will be no blame.
The upright people will have regret.
初六童觀. 小人无咎. 君子吝.

20.2 Peeking to observe.
Beneficial for a woman to divine.
六二闚觀. 利女貞.

20.3 Observing our lives going forward and retreating.
六三觀我生, 進退.

20.4 Observing the country's glory.
Beneficial to be guests of the king.
六四觀國之光. 利用賓于王.

20.5 Observing our lives.
Upright people will not be blamed.
九五觀我生. 君子无咎.

20.6 Observing their lives, upright people will not be blamed.
上九觀其生, 君子无咎.

20. Commentary 觀 *Guan* Observing

Guan 觀 means "observe." Much later, after the spread of Mahayana Buddhism into China, it became the first syllable of the name of the Bodhisattva Guanyin 觀音 (Sanskrit *Avalokitesvara*), s/he who observes the sounds of the world. In Buddhist terms it connotes observing with a wide perspective. In this *Zhouyi* hexagram it refers to simple observation of ordinary events, unfortunately including human sacrifice.

20.0 The sentence is confusing—Kunst and Rutt disagree as to whether it means to sacrifice the captives or to not sacrifice them. In either case, the text demonstrates that the physique of captives was important in decisions as to when to sacrifice them. (This phrase could also refer to captives who are tall, rather than ones with big heads.) Suitability of victims was important throughout the ancient world—one who was defective or deformed might be an affront to the spirits. Apart from this line, the *Zhouyi* does not have much to say about how victims were selected, other than their being captives. This is in contrast to oracle bone inscriptions and also the *Baoshan*, a divination text found in the Tomb of Shao Tuo, who was buried in 316 BCE, translated and analyzed by Constance Cook (2006: 6, 47 *et passim*). In this later, less cryptic text the nature of the victims to be sacrificed is specified in detail, for example strips 207–8 recommend sacrifice of male pigs, a white dog, and wine and food (Cook 2006: 168f.).

20.1 Children's movements would have been omens. The theme of petty people ascendant over the high-born or upright became especially prominent in the *Lunyu*, *Dao De Jing* and other later philosophical and ethical texts. This theme that the unworthy are chosen for government posts remains pertinent today.

20.2 Peeking to observe likely refers to women being required to remain behind a wall or screen, but it is uncertain to what degree this repressive custom existed in the Western Zhou. I have translated the second phrase to state that a woman performs the divination, but the divination might have been *about* a woman, rather than *by* her.

20.3 This could also refer to watching as a sacrificial victim paces back and forth. I prefer the more reflective meaning despite my reservations about direct philosophical expressions in the *Zhouyi*.

A line in the much later *Dao De Jing* indicates that in early times the roles of guest and host were precisely defined. When a guest of a king, one must be particularly alert not to be displeasing. Rutt raises the possibility that the guests might be sacrifices, but this seems to be no more than an instance of his preoccupation with this practice (315).

20.5/20.6 This is a proverb expressed in two forms to emphasize that it applies both to oneself and others. This seems to be encouragement that even the high-born should scrutinize their behavior. As paraphrased by Wilhelm-Baynes:

> A man in an authoritative position to whom others look up must always be ready for self-examination. (85)

Proverbs are perhaps the earliest way of expressing wisdom. Later, self-examination became central to Chinese ethical thought, perhaps reaching its culmination in the philosophy of Zhu Xi, often said to be the second most influential Chinese philosopher after Confucius. Written nearly 2,000 years later, here is his more sophisticated statement of the same idea:

> In all matters, examine into the right and wrong. Supposing you did something today; if you yourself are comfortable with it and have no doubts about it, it was the right thing to do. (Gardner 1990: 183)

While one must be cautious not to read too much into the Western Zhou texts, they do seem to recommend something akin to self-examination.

21. 噬嗑 *Shi ke* Biting and Chewing (Biting Through)

The Judgment:

21.0 Make offering, beneficial to go to law.
亨利用獄.

The Line Texts:

21.1 Shoes in the fetters; the feet disappear.
There will be no blame.
初九履校滅, 趾.无咎.

21.2 Biting the flesh, the nose disappears.
There will be no blame.
六二噬膚滅鼻. 无咎.

21.3 Bites the soft dried meat; gets poisoned.
Slight remorse, but there will be no blame.
六三噬腊肉; 遇毒. 小吝, 无咎.

21.4 Biting dried meat, obtains a bronze arrowhead.
Beneficial in difficulty—divination auspicious.
九四噬乾胏, 得金矢. 利艱. 貞吉.

21.5 Biting dried meat, gets yellow metal. Divination harsh. There will be no blame.
六五噬乾肉, 得黃金. 貞厲. 无咎.

21.6 Carrying on his shoulders a cangue, the ears disappear. Ominous.

上九何校滅耳. 凶.

21. Commentary 噬嗑 *Shi Ke* Biting and Chewing

The first character of the tag is repeated in lines 21.2, 21.3, 21.4, and 21.5. While the most obvious meaning is the literal one, biting and chewing, *shi ke* might also refer to the flesh damage inflicted by the torture devices of 21.0 and 21.6. This is perhaps the most unpleasant of all the hexagrams, its violence being particularly graphic. Even Wilhelm-Baynes could not find a way to soften it.

21.0 This phrase is rather incongruous. While it states that legal proceedings will be beneficial, 21.1, 21.2, and 21.6 refer to the mutilating punishments that could be inflicted as their result. While tattooing and amputation were abolished in the Western Han, cruel physical punishment persisted throughout imperial China's history and revived during the Cultural Revolution under Mao and the so-called Gang of Four.

21.1 Treading 履 *lu*, is also the name of hexagram 10. That the feet are gone might refer to them being hidden in the device, but if it was tight enough to block blood flow, the feet would have been severely injured or destroyed. Completely cutting them off was a standard punishment. What happened to people rendered footless is unclear. Many must have died from infection. Those who survived would not have been able to walk, except perhaps a very short distance with crutches and so would be entirely dependent on others. The prevalence of such punishments is also unclear. Zhuangzi states that if a man has no feet he need not worry about shoes. This strikingly insensitive one-liner suggests he had perhaps never seen anyone with this mutilation. One hopes it was rare.

Wu jiu 无咎, there will be no blame, seems particularly incongruous as used in this hexagram. Destroying feet or biting off a nose hardly seem blameless. However, this formula appears in conjunction with acts of sanctioned violence in many other *Zhouyi* passages. That it was stated so frequently in such instances suggests some sense that the act was wrong, or at least a need to defend it as just. Nowhere in the *Zhouyi* do we find any direct criticism of state violence. Mutilating punishments were not abolished until nearly a millennium later by order of Emperor Wen (202–157 BCE) of the Western Han. This did not stop state torture, however. It needs to be pointed out that gruesome public methods of execution were also practiced in the West until quite recently (the guillotine was last used in 1977) and continue to be inflicted in many parts of the world. A further possibility is that the phrase is an interpretation of an omen: that witnessing this punishment will not indicate bad luck for the inquirer. The frequent placement of the "no blame" phrase in such contexts is surely not random.

21.2 Perhaps "biting flesh" refers to the knife cutting off the nose.

21.3 With sacrifice, the fresh meat of the animal offered to the spirits was distributed among those present. This was in accord with social rank; the highest getting the choicest cuts. Here however, the meat is dried, this being an essential means of preventing spoilage in an era without refrigeration. It is not clear how one would know the meat was poisoned, so perhaps this referred to its being rotten. Divinatory meaning would then mean getting into a situation that seems all right but actually is toxic.

Poisoning was greatly feared because it was not usually detectable. As discussed in connection with hexagram 18, perhaps more common were wrong attributions of natural deaths to poisoning. This often led to accusations against completely innocent persons, akin to allegations of witchcraft and curses, all of which could lead to execution. The veracity of such accusations was determined, of course, by divination. Thus diviners might have the power of life and death. They were at high risk themselves, should their divinations be erroneous or offensive to those in power.

21.4 and 21.5 Finding an arrowhead in meat is plausible, as this is how game would have been killed. It would normally be significant as a favorable omen, though seemingly not in 21.5. Bronze arrowheads would have had considerable value, because bronze along with jade was one of the main forms of portable wealth.

Qian 乾, is the tag of the first hexagram but here has its usual early meaning of dry, transliterated as *gan*. This character appears in these lines in the Mawangdui silk manuscript, although there it is not the tag of the first hexagram. Later, dry was one of the main correlations of *yang*, but there is no suggestion of metaphysical meaning here.

21.6 This refers to a common but cruel punishment inflicted in China until the early twentieth century. It consists of heavy boards, together weighing over 30 pounds, placed around the neck and fastened together. Apart from public shaming, this prevented the unfortunate bearer from feeding himself and so could be fatal for those who had no one to help them. These highly visible punishments were less likely to be applied to women, presumably because putting them on display was disruptive.

As elsewhere in the *Zhouyi*, the line order is approximately anatomical with the base line referring to feet and the top line to neck and ears. That the prognosis here is ominous is not surprising, but it is odd that 21.1, which also refers to mutilation, has a neutral prognosis. This suggests that the prognoses refer to seeing the convicts as omens, not to the inquirer being subjected to the various miseries described. It is usual with omens that the divinatory meaning does not accord with its affective content. For example, in the numerous apocryphal works with titles such as *The Duke of Zhou's Manual of Dream Interpretation,* a bad dream is a good sign while a seeming good dream is unfavorable. Perhaps this serves to increase obscurity so as to require an expert in oneiromancy.

22. 賁 *Bi* Adornment (Grace)

The Judgment:

22.0 Make offering. Slight benefit for going somewhere.
亨. 小利有攸往.

The Line Texts:

22.1 Adorns his feet, abandons his cart and goes on foot.
初九賁其趾. 舍車而徒.

22.2 Adorns his beard.
六二賁其須.

22.3 Adorned glistening-like.
Long-term auspicious divination.
九三賁如濡如. 永貞吉.

22.4 Adorned in white, a white-plumed horse.
Not bandits invading, but a wedding.
六四賁如皤如白馬翰如. 匪寇婚媾.

22.5 To adorn the hillside garden with bundles of silk, so few so few.
Regrettable but ends auspiciously.
六五賁于丘園束帛戔戔吝.終吉.

22.6 White adornment, there will be no blame.
上九白賁, 无咎.

22. Commentary 賁 *Bi* Adornment

Wilhelm-Baynes translate this word as "grace." Adornment clearly fits the texts better—they are about self-adornment, presumably for a festival. Rutt is almost certainly correct in suggesting that the festival is a wedding—these are frequently referred to in the *Zhouyi*. Not only are weddings perhaps the most important of all rituals of daily life, along with funerals they would have been occasions for which divination was particularly important.

Grace is a specifically Christian concept, though so infused in world culture that it is often not recognized as such. The notion of being redeemed by an external power has no counterpart in early China. Wilhelm was a Protestant missionary and so would naturally have been given to the use of Christian language, despite his expressed lack of interest in converting Chinese. Interpretation of Chinese classical texts in terms of Christian concepts goes back to the figurist movement of the Jesuit missionaries in China, notably Matteo Ricci (1552–1610) and Joachim Bouvet (1656–1730). Figurism was an attempt to finesse the great gap between Christian doctrine and Chinese religions with the hope, largely unfulfilled, of facilitating conversion. As a result of the so-called "rites controversy" this conception was eventually outlawed by the Catholic Church.

As the *Changes* has lent itself to appropriation by all sorts of spiritual and philosophical systems, so it has at times with Christianity. This is part of the value of the work but such adaptations should not be confused with the early Chinese meanings. Historically-based scholarship must consciously avoid this sort of cultural anachronism. The reconstructed Western Zhou meanings, as in the present translation, do not lend themselves to Christian readings.

22.1 This could be a proverb to the effect that when at home, foot transportation is sufficient, or a gesture of humility for a special occasion.

22.4 The first phrase is difficult to render exactly. The final phrase is another reference to the practice of sham bride stealing at a wedding, a frequent theme in the *Zhouyi*, perhaps being the custom of the source culture. *Fei*, though here meaning "not," was perhaps written as 匪 also meaning bandits, to emphasize the mock abduction themes.

22.5 This admonishes against being too stingy with decoration, presumably for the wedding.

22.6 This seems to contradict the previous line by implying that the decoration is suitable. It might also be a proverb warning against excess, lest it create jealousy. It could even refer to bringing lavish items, while pretending they are modest.

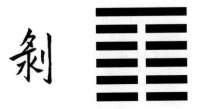

23. 剝 *Bo* Flaying (Splitting Apart)

The Judgment:

23.0 Not beneficial for going somewhere.
不利有攸往.

The Line Texts:

23.1 Flaying a ewe from the foot.
Set aside the ominous divination.
初六剝牀以足. 蔑貞凶.

23.2 Flaying a ewe to determine.
Set aside the ominous divination.
六二剝牀以辨. 蔑貞凶.

23.3 Flaying is without blame.
六三剝之无咎.

23.4 Flaying a ewe's skin. Ominous.
六四剝牀以膚. 凶.

23.5 A string of fishes to favor the palace ladies.
Nothing not beneficial.
六五貫魚宮人寵. 无不利.

23.6 Rich fruits go uneaten.
The upright person gets a cart.
A petty person is stripped of his house.
上九碩果不食. 君子得輿. 小人剝廬.

23. Commentary 剥 *Bo* Flaying

Bo 剥 contains the knife radical and clearly means flaying. Wilhem-Baynes translate *bo* as "splitting apart," and Lynn as "peeling." Neither is wrong on the face of it, but both are euphemistic. Confucian propriety resulted in violence being treated euphemistically, if at all—not a bad thing but clearly not the practice of the *Zhouyi* compilers. To fit with the tag, I have followed Kunst and Rutt in replacing 牀 *chuang* as referring to the legs of a bed with the near-homophone substitution of 牂 *zang* meaning ewe, consistent with the contexts of the lines (23.1, 23.2, 23.3, and 23.4) in which it appears (Kunst: 284f.; Rutt: 246, 317).

23.0 A set phrase prognostication, not related to the line texts.

23.1 Skinning of animals would have been an almost daily sight in early agricultural societies. Subsistence farmers could not afford to waste anything; animal skins would be a valuable by-product of raising animals for meat. While exotic animal skins were a means of conspicuous display of wealth, as they are now, common animal skins would have been used for multiple purposes, not only warmth but also military armor. Additionally, there was a shamanistic element in which wearing the skin of a particular animal was thought to confer the symbolic traits of the species.

The reference to starting at the foot suggests there might once have been bodily progression in the subsequent lines, but this is not carried out. The relation of the prognostic meanings to the act of flaying or skinning an animal are not self-evident. Given that in the third line skinning does not incur blame, there is no indication that the earlier ominous prognoses were related to the animal having been killed. It is plausible that the common activity of skinning an animal could be auspicious or inauspicious depending on which body area it is started at. This is suggested by the oracle bone inscriptions in which the details of the color of the animal and direction of the sacrificial act are crucial to its efficacy. Despite there being no overt expression of concern about cruelty, it is probably significant that so many of the omens mentioned in the *Zhouyi* are violent or emotionally intense sightings.

23.5 As early as Wang Bi's commentary the fish were taken as referring to the palace ladies. Supposedly the elegantly dressed concubines resemble the flashing scales of fish. Rutt notes that Gao Heng took the dried fish strung together as an analogy for palace ladies lined up in a prescribed order (317). Because fish symbolize abundance (裕 *yu* abundance, is a homonym for 鱼 *yu*, fish), the analogy of their streaming in might refer to there being many palace ladies, or a hint at fertility. The line can be taken as a disparagement of women but need not be.

23.6 A common factor in all the line texts is reference to food: ewe, fish, fruit. The last phrase may have been placed in this hexagram because it shares the character for flaying/stripping with the first four. Its first phrase is a metaphor, perhaps deliberately concealing its meaning of talent being unused. The paradigmatic example is Confucius, who was himself a disappointed office-seeker. However, the next phrase seems discordant as the upright person is rewarded with a cart, while the petty person is deprived of his house. In the context of the aristocratic society of the time, it is tempting to see these phrases as implied social criticism—the rich get more and the poor lose what they have. While the *I Ching* lacks the explicit social criticism of later texts such as the *Lunyu*, *Laozi*, and *Zhuangzi*, it is plausible that some phrases were intended as disguised complaints. Given the compiled nature of the text it is possible that what was originally social criticism was not recognized as such when incorporated into the *Changes*.

24. 復 *Fu* Return (Return; The Turning Point)

The Judgment:

24.0 Make offering.
Coming and going there will be no infirmity.
Friends arrive.
There will be no blame.
They turn back on their way and in seven days return.
Beneficial if having to go somewhere.
亨. 出入无疾. 朋來. 无咎; 反復其道七日來復. 利有攸往.

The Line Texts:

24.1 Not far away, returns.
There is neither respect nor regret.
Begins auspiciously.
初九不遠, 復. 无祗悔. 元吉.

24.2 Resting before returning is auspicious.
六二休復吉.

24.3 Repeatedly returning is harsh, but there will be no blame.
六三頻復厲, 无咎.

24.4 In the middle, walking back alone.
六四中,行獨復.

24.5 Encouraged to return—there will be no regret.
六五敦復—无悔.

24.6 Getting lost while returning, ominous.
There will be a disaster unforeseen.
Marching the troops ends with a great rout.
For their country's ruler, ominous.
For ten years, not capable of a military expedition.
上六迷復, 凶. 有災眚. 用行師終有大敗. 以其國君, 凶. 至于十年,
不克征.

24. Commentary 復 *Fu* Return

The tag occurs in all six line texts. According to the *Grand Ricci*
dictionary, in the Zhou this character could also mean calling the
soul of a dead person. I have not seen this in any translation but it
seems possible, given that necromancy was a method of divination.
However, "return" fits well with the line texts. Return, whether of
objects lent or lost, household members, or oneself, is frequently
the subject of line texts.

24.0 This text is a collection of predictions about returns.
The phrase, "Coming and going there will be no infirmity," or
variants of it is still in use 3,000 years later on Chinese lucky
posters and coins. The modern posters are typically printed on red
paper with gold characters. One adorns my own front door.
   Dao 道, along with *yin* and *yang* is the most famous concept
in Chinese philosophy. In the *Zhouyi* however, it has its original
meaning of path, road, or way, here and in its other appearances
(9.1, 10.2, 17.4, and 24.0).
   The phrase "seven days" is often translated as week, but the
early Chinese "week" was ten days. The numbers associated with
going and returning in the *Zhouyi* are often three or seven, perhaps
meaning several. While the lunar month of twenty-eight days and
solar year of 365 ¼ days are natural quantities, the seven-day week
and thirty or thirty-one day month are not.

24.1 This can also be rendered, "Far away, does not return." It has been translated both ways so a diviner could have chosen either meaning, ambiguity being the lifeblood of divination.

24.2 This phrase suggesting a rest before returning is interesting because the *Zhouyi* does not have much to say about basic human well-being. In the modern world we take for granted the need for resting and refreshing ourselves, but given that slavery and conscript labor were pervasive in the ancient world, most lives would have had little leisure.

24.3 Rutt (318) quotes Gao Heng 高亨 as saying that the phrase refers to "the frown of consternation that comes on the face of one startled to find himself on such a brink [of water.]" Gao (Heng 1900–86), although one of the most famous and influential of China's twentieth century critical philologists, was given to this sort of fanciful emendation of even the most straightforward passages. His proposed reading of this line is inconsistent with the nature of the *Zhouyi*, which provides only set phrases to describe behavior related to emotion. This does not mean that people were any less emotional than later in history, rather that written language to describe such behaviors as facial expression and tone of voice had not yet developed.

24.6 It is unclear which side wins the battle, reminiscent of the famous tale of King Croesus, who was told by his diviner that if he attacked, a great empire would be destroyed. He attacked, but it was his own empire that was destroyed.

25. 无妄 *Wu Wang* Unexpected
(Innocence; The Unexpected)

The Judgment:

25.0 Begin with an offering, beneficial to divine.
Those not upright will lack vision.
Not beneficial if having to go somewhere
元亨, 利貞. 其匪正有眚. 不利有攸往.

The Line Texts:

25.1 Unexpectedly, going is auspicious.
初九无妄, 往吉.

25.2 No tilling; no reaping.
No clearing; no cultivation.
Then beneficial if having to go someplace.
六二不耕穫. 不菑畬. 則利有攸往.

25.3 Unexpectedly, calamity. Their tied up ox—someone walked
by and took it. Disaster for the country person.
六三无妄之災 — 或繫之牛行人之得. 邑人之災.

25.4 Can divine; there will be no blame.
九四可貞; 无咎.

25.5 Unexpectedly ill; does not need medicine, happily.
九五. 无妄之疾; 勿藥, 有喜.

25.6 Unexpectedly walks into error.
Not beneficial if having to go somewhere.
上九无妄行有眚.无攸利.

25. Commentary 无妄 *Wu Wang* Unexpected

The title is translated by Wilhelm-Baynes as "Unexpected" but tends to have implications of something unfavorable. The Mawangdui manuscript has a different title, 无孟 *Wumeng*, translated by Shaughnessy as "Pestilence,"(50f., 291) following Waley (131f.). Waley's line of reasoning is based on the reference to a cow or bull in 25.3, which he takes to be an animal to be sacrificed to drive out disease. Waley assumed, as did Chinese literati, that the lines within a chapter are thematically related, but clearly this is not always the case. The more common reading, with seems quite straightforward to me, is simply a tied-up cow, no doubt an everyday sight.

A theme of this chapter is the reign of the unexpected; that is, the misfortunes that can occur despite careful planning. These are negative prognostications because the misfortunes are not preventable. An important term here is 眚 *shen,* which can imply failure of vision. This reminds us that the purpose of divination was to enable one to foresee what is not yet fully apparent, that is: to recognize incipience.

Despite modern dismissal of divination as irrational, it was an essential method for preparing for future possibilities. Since, despite the admonition in 4.0, multiple divinations were often performed, they would indicate different possible outcomes of a situation. We should not assume that divination always led to poor decisions. A comparable situation today is financial forecasting. It is clear that markets cannot be predicted, yet investment decisions are usually based on the advice of experts.

25.0 This judgment consists of two set phrases and the more interesting proverb to the effect that those not of low character do not fully see the world as it is. This would seem to be a moral statement, seeing the world as it is presumably implying recognizing the proper way to behave. One senses here a foreshadowing of the Confucian assumption that moral knowledge is factual.

25.2 The first two phrases are a proverb, meaning that if one does not lay the groundwork, one will not attain one's goals. The agricultural reference expresses the fundamental rhythm of life in the ancient world. If the first three phrases are combined, the meaning seems to be that if one cannot farm, one had best travel, perhaps to find a better living.

25.3 This seems to be about someone's ox being stolen but the word order leaves it unclear.
 Loss of a water buffalo is still an economic catastrophe in much of rural Asia.

25.5 It is curious that the *Zhouyi* contains relatively few references to disease, as divination was the main means of diagnosis in the ancient world. This would make it seem likely that other methods were used for this purpose. The *Baoshan* records many divinations regarding disease and treatment. The cause of Shao Tuo's disease—in whose tomb the text was found—is not diagnosable in modern terms by the limited description in the text, but was assumed to be transgression against unknown spirits. Cook points out that travel inevitably involved trespassing on regions ruled by irascible spirits who might inflict disease in retaliation. The only means of learning about spirits is, by necessity, some form of divination.
 In 25.6 as with 25.0 I have translated 眚 *sheng* as implying poor vision; in the sense of not seeing a situation clearly, based on its literal meaning as cataracts or other physical vision impairment.

26. 大畜 *Da Xu* Large Livestock
(The Taming Power of the Great)

The Judgment:

26.0 Beneficial to divine. Not eating at home is auspicious.
Beneficial to ford the great river.
利貞. 不家食吉. 利涉大川.

The Line Texts:

26.1 Harsh—beneficial to stop.
初九有厲—利已.

26.2 The cart's base loses its axle holders.
九二輿說輹.

26.3 A fine steed in pursuit, beneficial.
When in difficulty, divine.
Speak out: guard and protect the cart!
Beneficial if having to go somewhere.
九三良馬逐, 利. 艱, 貞. 曰: 閑輿衛. 利有攸往.

26.4 Bull-calf in its pen; horns held by a board.
Greatly auspicious.
六四童牛之牿. 元吉.

26.5 Castrated boar's tusk, auspicious.
六五豶豕之牙,吉.

26.6 Where the heavenly crossroads for making offering?
上九何天之衢亨.

26. Commentary 大畜 *Da Xu*
Large Livestock

Da Xu 大畜 literally means "large livestock" and is consistent with several references to farm animals in the line texts. Wilhelm-Baynes' translation as "taming power of the great" is not based on the Western Zhou texts, but on trigram positions. In this hexagram, the mountain trigram, also termed "keeping still," is above the trigram for heaven. Thus it is interpreted as the mountain taming heaven. This is not very clear as a cosmological conception—given that heaven symbolized the cosmic order, why would it need to be tamed?

The texts of this hexagram are mostly references to common sights in a farming society: calves, pigs, a broken cart. These could simply be observations of daily life, but more likely are included because they function as omens—seemingly unremarkable sights holding hidden meanings. This was equally true in the classical world of Greece and Rome. In the latter, augury, that is divination by bird flock patterns, was essential for political decisions. Cicero was an augur, despite his skepticism regarding divination as concluded in his detailed analysis in *De Divinatione*.

26.0 Why it would be auspicious not to eat at home is not stated. This could simply mean that it is favorable to eat away from home, or that at this moment, eating at home would be unlucky. The only way to make sense of this is to regard it as an instance of the early Chinese belief that the place where actions are performed affects one's luck. It is an example of the belief that even the simplest actions could have hidden consequences.

26.1 This is a straightforward divinatory admonition. Rutt notes that many Chinese scholars followed Wen Yiduo 聞一多 (1899–1946) in emending the last word so that the phrase means "beneficial to sacrifice" (249, 319). There is, however, no support for this speculation in the text. There are enough references to sacrifice in the *Zhouyi* that we do not need another one.

26.2 A cart stopped because its axle brackets were broken would have seemed inauspicious, but the meanings assigned to omens are often idiosyncratic. An idea common to many cultures is that a minor accident may be a good thing because it substitutes for one that would have been much worse.

26.3 In this case, the fine steed is likely an omen, though also an inspiring sight. A contemporary Chinese proverb tells us, "When the horse arrives, success follows." Thus I have placed 利 *li* beneficial, as part of this phrase rather than the following one.

26.4 A bull with undamaged horns would have been a desirable sacrifice, so a board was placed across the horns to prevent them from being broken. This is a suitable place to point out the immense depletion of resources resulting from the practice of sacrifice.

26.5 A castrated boar would have had much smaller tusks than an intact one. Perhaps such a tusk was a lucky amulet, as rabbit's feet once were in America. If not castrated, boars develop an unpleasant odor known as "boar taint," which renders their meat unpalatable. Though modern urbanites are likely to regard castration without analgesia as cruel, communities that depended on farming for their survival have to be matter-of-fact about such practices.

26.6 This is a reference to a location in the night sky, the crossroads of heaven being an asterism consisting of the four stars in Scorpio that mark the intersection of celestial equator and ecliptic. It is often translated as finding the way of heaven for oneself. Rutt, who was an Episcopal missionary, translated it as, "Receiving heaven's grace" (249).

27. 頤 *Yi* Lower Jaw (Corners of the Mouth; Providing Nourishment)

The Judgment:

27.0 Divination auspicious according to observation of the jaw.
One's own mouth asking if it is full.
貞吉觀頤. 自求口實.

The Line Texts:

27.1 Leave at home your numinous tortoise.
Observe my drooping jaw, ominous.
初九舍爾靈龜. 觀我朵頤, 凶.

27.2 Twitching jaw.
Brushing fabric for a burial mound.
Jaw: going on an expedition, ominous.
六二顛頤. 拂經于丘. 頤征, 凶.

27.3 Stroking the jaw—ominous divination.
For ten years, do not put to use. Nothing is beneficial.
六三拂頤—貞凶. 十年勿用. 无攸利.

27.4 Twitching jaw, auspicious.
Tiger stares—glaring, glaring.
Craving—chasing chasing.
There will be no blame.
六四顛頤, 吉. 虎視 — 眈眈. 其欲, 逐逐. 无咎.

27.5 Brushing silk. For a home, the divination is auspicious.
Should not ford the great river.
六五拂經. 居貞吉. 不可涉大川.

27.6 According to the jawbone, harsh.
Auspiciously beneficial to ford cross the great river.
上九由頤, 厲. 吉利涉大川.

27. Commentary 頤 *Yi* Lower Jaw

The tag designates the mandible, that is the lower bone of the jaw (Schuessler 1987: 732 n.16). The character for jawbone occurs in all lines but 27.5. I have translated as jaw, rather than jawbone, as the latter in English has the implication of haranguing not present in the Chinese. This is one of the rare hexagram figures that, like hexagram 50 *Deng* (cauldron), can be imagined to resemble what it designates. The upper and lower lines suggest an open mouth and the broken lines in between may be imagined to be teeth, as Rutt suggests (320). Plausibly, the tag and texts for this hexagram were together because of the resemblance of the hexagram to open jaws. Unfortunately for those learning to write in Chinese, only a tiny minority of the characters are at all pictographic. Some use imagined pictorial resemblances to use as mnemonics but these have nothing to do with the actual origin of the characters.

So pervasive were omens in ancient China that one hesitates to state that anything visible could not have been an omen. In context, a kind of physiognomy based on facial movements rather than dental condition seems more likely as bodily movements, voluntary and involuntary, were a pervasive means of divination. This is part of the pre-scientific enchantment of the world, in which virtually everything has a supernatural meaning.

Because the texts of this chapter, with their recurrent references to jaws or jawbones, seem particularly obscure, even nonsensical, they help us recognize how different from modern times was the *imaginaire* of the Chinese Bronze Age. The obscurity of the texts diminishes once they are recognized as a compilation of prognostications based on jaw movements, presumably human. Rutt translates the tag as "molars," speculating that the opened jaws revealed the condition of the teeth, which supposedly would have had mantric significance (250). Jaw movements would seem more likely as the basis of divination. It should be noted that divination by the face is based on physical features, not the emotion expressed. Though early Chinese writing contains relatively few descriptions of emotion, this of course does not mean that emotions were not felt.

Lines 27.3 and 27.6 may refer to use of a jawbone as a divinatory device. Use of bone objects as divinatory substrates is further suggested by the reference to the divinatory (or spirit) turtle. In many early texts reference is made to divination by tortoise and milfoil, but the *Zhouyi* rarely mentions the former. The tortoise mention is also puzzling as the method we know of, the oracle bones, was extremely elaborate, requiring a heated poker being pressed against the shell to cause cracks. Plastromancy was mostly for royal divination and would be too difficult and expensive for routine inquiries. How turtle shells or one may have been used as divinatory objects without crack-making we do not know.

In enchanted worlds, any object or event could be a communication from the spiritual world. While it might be hard to decipher the message correctly, the meaning was there. New Age writings often present the enchanted world as richer than our secular one, but fail to recognize the extreme anxiety regarding the often malign powers of supernatural beings in ancient times. Ordinary events taken as omens would be frequent triggers of anxiety and the risk of offending spirits was omnipresent. Life in an enchanted world is now almost impossible to conceive. It has been relegated to the realm of entertainment in which being scared can be fun. It was not fun in the Western Zhou. Later in China collections of strange or supernatural tales were published, perhaps the most famous was the Qing dynasty collection of Yuan Mei (Santangelo). This collection has a tongue-in-cheek quality reminiscent of the writings of Charles Fort. However, in the Bronze Age such stories were almost certainly taken as factual.

27.0 My translation makes the second phrase into a proverb meaning not recognizing the obvious.

27.1 This line seems to advise not using one's tortoise for divination, but look at someone's jawbone instead. Choice of divinatory method would have been a decision of great moment, though often multiple methods were used, a tacit admission of the uncertain reliability of divination.

27.2 *Jing* 經 here is the same character translated as "classic" in the titles of *I Ching*, *Shijing*, etc. The same phrase recurs in 27.5. In the *Zhouyi* texts *jing* does not mean classic. Since it contains the silk radical, it most likely refers here to preparing silk as a grave good. The word *jing* can also mean suicide; hanging with a silk scarf was a means for women to commit suicide, though not attested so early as far as I am aware. It is conceivable that this is the implication of *jing* here, given the reference to a grave. Finally, the word also referred to menstruation in the phrase 月經 *yue jing*, now read as "monthly classic," but originally would have been "monthly fabric," the cloth used to absorb menstrual blood. References to intimate aspects of femininity are, however, almost totally lacking in Chinese texts.

27.3 While the underlying theme of the *Book of Changes* is that situations change rapidly, in this case the prognostication is particularly unfavorable as the situation will last for ten years. Such long time frames are unusual in the *Zhouyi*.

27.4 The tiger-like staring is a phrase still in use today, indicating extreme lust or greed. It is not clear whether this line is a warning about being stared at in this fashion, or that seeing someone gaze like a tiger is a favorable omen. Such appearances of oral set phrases in the *Zhouyi* that are still in use 3,000 years later testifies to the extreme longevity of some oral material. It also suggests the possibility that some of the phrases may have been in use for centuries before being recorded in the written classic. Accordingly a single date for the composition of the *Changes* is misleading because it clearly contains much older material. While it is tempting to try to reconstruct dates for different portions of the text, they are at best guesswork and best avoided.

27.5 "Brushing fabric" here may refer to women's domestic activities, hence a good omen for a home.

The final phrase is anti-parallel to the final phrase of 27.6, a common structure in the *Zhouyi* that can be traced back to the

Shang oracle bone inscriptions, in which queries were often in the form of paired opposites such as, "tomorrow it will rain," "tomorrow it will not rain."

27.6 Here the jawbone seems to be that of an animal, somehow used for divination. Archaeology has discovered large bone workshops in the Yin ruins near Anyang. Their physical strength and ubiquity made them useful for practical, decorative, and ritual purposes.

28. 大過 *Da Guo* Big Mistake (Preponderance of the Great)

The Judgment:

28.0 The ridgepole sags.
Beneficial if having somewhere to go. Make offering.
棟撓. 利有攸往. 亨.

The Line Texts:

28.1 For mats use white grass.
Nothing blameworthy.
初六藉用茅. 无咎.

28.2 From a withered poplar come forth sprouts.
An old man gets his daughter married.
Nothing that is not favorable.
九二枯楊生稊. 老夫得其女妻. 无不利.

28.3 The ridgepole sags, ominous.
九三棟橈, 凶.

28.4 The ridgepole bends upward, auspicious.
Will have other regrets.
九四棟隆,吉. 有它吝.

28.5 A withered poplar brings forth blossoms.
An old woman gets herself a gentry husband.
Not blameworthy; not praiseworthy.
九五枯楊生華. 老婦得其士夫. 无咎; 无譽.

28.6 Mistakenly drowns while wading.
Ominous, but not blameworthy.
上六過涉滅頂. 凶, 无咎.

28. Commentary 大過 *Da Guo*
Big Mistake

This tag contrasts with the tag of number 62, "Small Mistake."
Both tags are simple divinatory responses but have no content
specifying the nature of the mistakes. They bear no evident
relationship to the line texts of their hexagrams. Wilhelm's translation of the tag is based on the hexagram figure in which the center
consists of four firm or *yang* lines, interpreted as meaning strength.

28.0 The ridgepole is the beam under the peak of the roof that
supports the entire structure, similar to the keystone of an arch. As
a critical part of a building it would have had magical significance.
The various ways the ridgepole is bent seem to be significant as
omens, not as indications of loss of structural integrity. Making an
offering might be part of preparations for a journey.

28.1 *Mao* 茅 literally is cogon grass but I have translated simply as
"white grass." This plant was used to wrap sacrificial offerings. It
is also referred to in 11.1 and 12.1. It grows prolifically and is now
considered a weed. It probably would have been also useful as floor
covering because of its easy availability and thickness. Rushes were
used for floor covering in the medieval West as well. The reference
here is about ritual use.

28.2 The first phrase seems to be a proverb, expressing the renewal
of nature.
    The second phrase has a symbolic meaning of renewal. Though
usually translated as "an old man gets a young wife," the man

getting his daughter married fits the theme of renewal better. It also draws attention to the traditional Chinese attitude that an unmarried daughter is a burden. In fact, feeding and clothing children were significant expenses for the common people and so marrying off a daughter would have been a relief for poor families. Cultural factors that restricted much economically productive labor to men were obviously a factor here. However, we should not imagine that there were never affectional ties between daughters and other family members. The *Zhouyi* contains little mention of emotions but this does not mean they were not felt. As in the *Lunyu* of Confucius, Chinese writings tended to speak of obligations rather than affection.

28.3/28.4 These explain how bends in ridgepoles were to be interpreted as omens. In 28.4 we have what is now called a mixed message. Diviners can easily fill in the blanks as to what is auspicious and what will be regretted.

28.5 *Shi* 士 is an important term for social status but can have multiple meanings. Later it came to mean the class of men who were educated, but not of noble rank, who sought government office. Confucius was of the *shi* class. It also, however, can mean a military officer, or simply a bachelor. In analogy to contemporary society, it referred to the middle class—people whose livelihood is based on education and ability, rather than family status. For detailed discussion of the social structure of early China see Hsu (1965).

The old tree producing flowers suggests that this marriage would be fertile. Depending on the age at which a woman would be considered 老婦 *lao fu* that is, old, this is plausible. In an era of child marriages, when life expectancy for women was the mid-twenties, women might be considered old before they were thirty.

28.6 "Ominous but without blame," need not be contradictory—something bad has happened, but the inquirer will not be blamed. Line six was usually read as referring to self-sacrifice, which was not blameworthy according to Chinese ethics. Indeed, the official sacrificing his life for the sake of principle was a common Confucian theme. In many stories, courtiers were executed for properly admonishing the ruler. Despite these exemplary tales, other documentary sources indicate that as in all governments, sycophants outnumber martyrs. This line might also refer to the practice of widows drowning themselves by wading into a river with stones tied to them. To the extent this actually happened, it may often have been to escape the deceased husbands' oppressive family. On the other hand, in later writings there were many salacious anecdotes about widows' licentious behavior, so such self-immolation could not have been common. For later stories of extreme self-denial for the sake of obligations, see Knapp.

29. 習坎 *Xi Kan* Numerous Pitfalls (Abysmal)

The Judgment:

29.0 Holding captives tied together; their hearts are the offering.
They walk with dignity.
有孚維; 心亨. 行有尚.

The Line Texts:

29.1 Repeated pitfalls. Entering into a pit or a cave. Ominous.
初六習坎. 入于坎窞. 凶.

29.2 The pit holds peril. Seek small gain.
九二坎有險. 求小得.

29.3 Coming to pit after pit.
Risky now to rest one's head.
Do not enter into a pit or cave.
六三來之坎坎. 險且枕. 入于坎窞勿用.

29.4 Wine in a *zun* bronze vessel and a two-handled *gui*.
Use a narrow-necked earthenware jar so one can receive at the window.
Ends without blame.
六四樽酒簋貳. 用缶納約, 自牖. 終无咎.

29.5 The pit not filled, only now levelled.
Nothing blameworthy.
九五坎不盈, 衹既平. 无咎.

29.6 Tie using braided cords.
Lay them crowded together in a bramble bush.
For three years cannot find, ominous.
上六係用徽纆. 寘于叢棘. 三歲不得, 凶.

29. Commentary 習坎 *Xi Kan*
Numerous Pitfalls

The first character of the title means repeated or numerous. The second character of the title 坎 *kan* has nearly always been translated as "pit." Among the uses of pits were disposition of rubbish, holding prisoners, and burial. Even in the Western Zhou it must have been a metaphor to refer to repeated obstacles or dangers, as it does in current English. Wilhelm-Baynes' translation as "abysmal" also makes the pits metaphorical but is misleading because in current English, "abysmal" usually means "terrible," rather than "deep."

Except for the recurring imagery of deep pits as hazards, this is not a particularly coherent hexagram. Most likely it was composed by combining separate fragments referring to pits. Pits are dangerous only if unnoticed so the divinatory meaning would be an unanticipated hazard.

Possibly pits were involved in sacrifice since that is the other main theme of the chapter—the wine vessel was likely used to make offerings.

29.0 The gruesome details of human sacrifice are suppressed not only in most classical texts but in modern scholarly ones as well. Bodily disruption was inflicted both in sacrifices and executions. The character for heart, *xin* 心 is plausibly said to be a pictograph of the heart and great vessels so whoever invented it obviously had knowledge of the appearance of this organ. The motif of going to one's death with dignity is common in Confucian hagiography. In the *Zhouyi*, except in this line, the victims are described as fearful rather than brave.

29.4 This line text seems somewhat garbled but refers to gathering food and drink.

29.5 Both Kunst and Rutt translate 祇既平 as the earth god being satisfied, apparently based on Waley. Though this is a plausible guess, the *Zhouyi* in its frequent advice to make offerings does not generally specify the entity to whom the offering is intended. There is no overt reference to an earth god in the *Zhouyi*.

29.6 Putting prisoners in a bramble bush is yet a further indication of the cruelty of the era. The final phrase about not being found does not seem to refer to the prisoners, unless it refers to their escaping.

Who or what cannot be found is unspecified. The much later Fuyang version begins with a phrase that is a fragment of what I have translated as, "For three years it is not possible. Ominous." The rest is entirely different, reading, as translated by Shaughnessy:

Divining about clearing: it will not clear; divining about hunting; you will not obtain anything; beneficial to the middle ... (2014: 251)

These variants are consistent with the current view that there was not one *Changes*, but a variety of *Changes*-type manuscripts. Some are fragmentary due to poor preservation but others add details not in the received version. The latter tendency is apparent in the still later Guoshan manuscript (Cook 2006).

30. 離 *Li* Oreole (The Clinging; Fire)

The Judgment:

30.0 Beneficial to divine; make offering. For breeding cows, auspicious.

利貞, 亨. 畜牝牛, 吉.

The Line Texts:

30.1 Treading unevenly, nevertheless respectfully, is not blameworthy.

初九履錯, 然敬之无咎.

30.2 Yellow oreole—greatly auspicious.

六二黃離, 元吉.

30.3 An oreole at sunset.
Not by drumming on an earthenware jar, but with a song.
Thus, those of great old age make lamentation.
Ominous.

九三日昃之離. 不鼓缶, 而歌. 則大耋之嗟. 凶.

30.4 Happening suddenly—like a fire, like death, like abandonment.

九四突如其來—如焚如, 死如, 棄如.

30.5 Weeping a flood of tears, as if grief-stricken, as if despairing.
Auspicious.

六五出涕沱, 若戚嗟若. 吉.

30.6 The king entering into a military expedition is praiseworthy.
Chops off heads, having captured the detestable rebels.
There will be no blame.
上九王用出征有嘉. 折首獲匪其醜. 无咎.

30. Commentary 離 *Li* Oreole

I have followed Rutt and used "oreole," which makes some sense
for lines 30.2 and 30.3, while alternatives such as "attach" do
not make sense for any of the line texts. The original suggestion
was that of Gao Heng, who based it on oreole references in some
of the lyrics in the *Book of Songs*, translated as "yellow oreole"
(322f.). Lines 30.2 and 30.3 are clearly bird omens, which are quite
frequent in the *Zhouyi*.

Wilhelm-Baynes' translate the tag as "fire," based on the
hexagram, which is the doubled trigram *Li*, fire in the correlative
system. However, there is no evidence that the names for the
trigrams existed in the Western Zhou, nor is there any reference to
fire in the line texts. Although in the modern world fire tends to
be thought of as destructive, according to the *Book of Documents*
(*Shangshu*) fire was one of the six treasures of life, the others being:
water, metals, wood, earth, and grains. This reminds us that for
most of human history, fire was the only means of heat, cooking,
and illumination, as well as firing ceramics and casting bronzes.

Mawangdui has *Luo*, a character not available in standard
fonts, translated by Shaughnessy as "net" (134f., 312). He translates the received tag as "Fastening" (2014: 252).

The texts associated with this hexagram are heterogeneous.
Only by creative exegesis can the lines be made to have any
thematic relationship. The imagery is quite concrete.

30.0 The specification of a female bovine suggests that breeding
here refers to putting the cow with a bull for impregnation. Thus it
is practical advice for agricultural management. Wilhelm-Baynes'
interpretation is that the cow represents docility and acceptance
of one's lot. In the *Zhouyi*, however, animals are almost always
omens, not symbols of personality traits. The tiger and leopard of
49.5 and 49.6 being exceptions.

30.1 履 *lu* treading is also the name of hexagram 10. This line provides advice on comportment. Ritually correct body position and movements in the presence of someone more powerful were extremely important, as perceived disrespect could prompt summary execution.

30.2 This is clearly an omen. Rutt, whose translation I have borrowed, shows convincingly that this refers to a specific species of oriole frequently mentioned in the *Shijing*, the *Book of Songs*.

In later China, yellow was the color associated with death. One term for the realm beyond death was the "yellow springs." However, yellow had many other associations, including use for imperial robes.

30.3 The image of the setting sun is an obvious allusion to death. In a famous episode, Zhuangzi is found beating on a pot after the death of his wife. An acquaintance remonstrates with him about this seeming disrespect, but Zhuangzi explains that everyone comes from earth and returns to it. Beating on a pot seems to have been an early way of expressing grief, which Zhuangzi contrasted with the elaborate rituals of his own time.

Shaughnessy notes that 耊 *die,* old age in the received text, is in the Mawangdui version written as 絰, also pronounced *die,* a scarf worn for mourning(134f., 313 n.7). This is a case in which the different characters are phonetically identical, yet both make equal sense. The prognosis of "ominous" is consistent because the earlier phrases are about death.

30.4 Wilhelm-Baynes' wording is elegant and plausible:

Its coming is sudden;
It flames up, dies down, is thrown away. (121)

Wang Bi interpreted this phrase as referring to light and dark, that is *yin* and *yang,* giving way to each other. However, like most of the cosmological interpretations, it is more a riff on the early text than actually contained in it. The allure of the *yin-yang* cosmology is that it can be applied to almost anything—gender, the cycle of day and night, dry and moist—and to any of the ups and downs of human life. The *yin-yang* concept has spread everywhere and does seem to help people make sense of events. It was not present in the *Zhouyi* but the diagrams made up of two kinds of lines seemed ready-made for representation of this duality.

30.5 This sort of line text almost makes the translator weep a flood of tears trying to figure out how despair can have an auspicious prognostication attached to it. It often seems that the prognoses are added at random. However, like so many of the puzzling phrases in the *Zhouyi*, this can make sense if seeing the crying person is an omen, though with an unusually paradoxical meaning. Conceivably, it may be an instance of one's potential misfortune being inflicted on someone else.

30.6 "Headsman" is the English term for those who carried out executions by beheading. Macabre as it sounds, the skill of these individuals was judged by the crowd attending public executions, a single stroke being considered merciful. In England, being beheaded rather than hanged was the "privilege" of nobility; often the offense was political. Beheading was the standard means of sacrificing captives in ancient China as attested by the thousands of skeletons of headless victims in the Anyang area and elsewhere.

Part Two

咸

31. 咸 *Xian* Sensation
(Influence, Wooing)

The Judgment:

31.0 Make offering. Beneficial to divine.
For choosing a woman, auspicious.
亨, 利貞. 取女, 吉.

The Line Texts:

31.1 Sensation in one's big toe.
初六咸其拇.

31.2 Sensation in one's calf, ominous.
For a home, auspicious.
六二咸其腓, 凶. 居吉.

31.3 Sensation in one's thigh. Grasping it while following. Going, regretted.
九三咸其股. 執其隨. 往吝.

31.4 Divination auspicious. Regret passes away.
Coming and going, back and forth. Friends follow in your longing.
九四貞吉. 悔亡. 憧憧往來. 朋從爾思.

31.5 Sensation in one's back. There will be no regret.
九五咸其脢. 无悔.

31.6 Sensations in one's jaws, cheeks, tongue.
上六咸其輔, 頰, 舌.

31. Commentary 咸 *Xian* Sensation

The division of the Zhouyi into two parts is an old one, though the reason for placing the division between hexagrams 30 and 31 is unclear. It has no thematic significance.

Although the tag 咸 *Xian,* has multiple possible translations, sensation fits well in all its occurrences. Shaughnessy points to convincing philological evidence for the tag character meaning feelings or sensations (1997: 309 n.1). The line texts of this hexagram are clearly about bodily sensations as omens, giving this hexagram a high degree of consistency. A few expressions that were originally based on bodily sensations being omens are still in use in the modern West: gut instinct, feeling in my bones, or the old notion that elderly people with arthritis can tell it will rain by how their joints feel.

Kunst and Rutt take the tag character as about mutilation, Kunst as "cut off" (300f.) and Rutt as "chopping" (324, 254); possibly butchering of an animal or the mutilation of a human sacrifice victim, a practice for which there is abundant archaeological evidence. Sensation is clearly a better fit both graphically and phonetically. While Rutt regarded Waley as, "perhaps over-enthusiastic about finding proverbs in *Zhouyi*," the counter-charge would be that Rutt was over-enthusiastic about finding sacrifice and mutilation. Not every reference to the body is about violence.

31.0 The woman to be chosen might be a wife, a concubine (secondary wife with legal status), or a servant. *Qu* 取, which I have translated as choosing, could also mean capturing or taking.

This uncertainty results in this phrase not being useful in assessing the degree of female autonomy in Western Zhou China. I selected choosing *qu* as open in meaning—the man making a choice does not necessarily mean that the woman cannot refuse. Significantly, the *Zhouyi* does not contain a parallel passage to the effect of, "favorable to take a husband." Even under the best of circumstances, a young woman's life choices were mostly made by her family. Powerful men, however, could force women, even if already married to someone else, to become their wives or concubines. Unlucky women served as spoils of war. The situation was similar throughout the ancient world and, regrettably, still exists in many non-Western societies.

As all but 31.4 refer to sensations in parts of the body in ascending order, this is one of the most systematic hexagrams, seemingly a guide to interpreting the location of bodily sensations as omens. The assignment of prognostics to body parts would have served as a mnemonic, something like *ars memorativa*, but simpler and requiring no literacy (Yates 1996; Spence 1985).

31.1 While the judgment text refers to a woman, the line texts have no gender specific reference; presumably bodily sensations would serve as omens for both men and women. Plausibly women had systems of their own, but there is no written record of these.

31.3. This might mean holding onto the thigh where the sensation is being felt, or that following or pursuing will bring regret, perhaps because of pain in the leg. For the next phrase my translation is an approximation.

31.4 The final word, 思 *si,* seems to refer to thoughts or longing. This is problematic as there are few references to mental states in the *Zhouyi,* although references to emotion are much more common in the approximately contemporaneous *Shijing.* Given the frequency of longing as a theme in poetry, especially that of China, it is tempting to regard the final phrases as borrowed from a song.

31.5 A simple omen.

31.6 This completes the bottom to top ordering of the omens.

32. 恆 *Heng* Enduring (Duration)

The Judgment:

32.0 Nothing blameworthy. Beneficial to make offering.
Beneficial to go somewhere.
无咎. 利贞. 利有攸往.

The Line Texts:

32.1 Deepening, enduring, ominous divination.
There is nothing beneficial.
初六浚恆, 贞凶. 无攸利.

32.2 Regret passes away.
九二悔亡.

32.3 Not endless, their obligation.
Perhaps receiving shame.
Divination: Stingy.
九三不恆, 其德. 或承之羞. 贞吝.

32.4 The fields are without game to hunt.
九四田无禽.

32.5 Long-lasting is their effectiveness.
Divination for a married woman is auspicious; for a husband, ominous.
六五恒其德. 贞妇人吉; 夫子, 凶.

32.6 Trembling that endures is ominous.
上六振恆凶.

32. Commentary 恆 *Heng* Enduring

Heng 恆 here refers to persisting over a long period of time, not to a character trait. *De* or virtue 德 appears in 32.3, but most likely refers to the kind of obligations that were fundamental to social cohesion in feudal-like societies. Having obligations implies a sense of responsibility, but here again we find statements about behavior rather than abstract virtues. This separates the Western Zhou meanings from the later Confucian readings. Still, in notions of obligation we find a seed of later philosophical theorizing.

32.0 The judgment text consists simply of routine prognostications, without any clue as to what circumstances they apply to. Of course in an actual divination the inquiry would make this clear.

32.1 This is quite vague but refers to a bad situation getting worse. This is a routine divinatory response as everyone has situations in their life that get worse.

32.3 *De* 德, familiar as the second word of the title of the *Dao De Jing*, is notoriously difficult to translate. At first it meant virtue in the sense of innate power or efficacy, later it also meant virtue as a moral quality. As noted above, it seems to have had the early meaning of obligations incurred by receiving favor. Mutual obligation is important in all societies but in early societies was so on a personal basis. For example, the king would grant land and in return be owed military service. This pattern is essential for the functioning of all societies—the government provides police protection, builds infrastructure and provides many other services; in return we owe taxes and sometimes military services.

The cause of the shame is unstated, but frequent shaming is unavoidable in a society with detailed and arbitrary rules for personal conduct. While the vocabulary of emotion in the *Zhouyi* is quite limited, shame is the affective state most frequently referred to. A once common Western critique of Chinese ethics was that morality was based on shame rather than guilt, that is, on fear of social disapproval rather than an inner sense of right and wrong. While it is true that the *Zhouyi* frequently mentions blame and shame but has nothing to say about self-criticism, this cannot be taken as evidence that what we call guilt did not exist. An open-minded reading of the *Lunyu* will quickly dispel this misconception. Moral self-examination has been a major theme in Chinese philosophy from Confucius and *Laozi* onward. Oddly, this can also be translated as: receiving delicacies.

32.4 This could imply without birds and beasts, but in early civilization the main interest in wild creatures was for hunting.

32.5 An odd domestic situation here implying a story. Unfortunately, as usual in this work, we are deprived of details.

32.6 Persistent trembling might be a medical observation based on experience, as even shamanistic healers must have learned from. It could be a sign of Parkinson's disease, for example. It might also be another bodily omen; indeed, there would have been no concept differentiating omens from symptoms.

33. 遯 *Dun* Piglet (Retreat)

The Judgment:

33.0 Make small offering, beneficial to divine.
亨小, 利貞.

The Line Texts:

33.1 Piglet's tail.
Harsh, do not use if having to go somewhere.
初六遯尾. 厲, 勿用有攸往.

33.2 To grasp it, use yellow ox's hide. Nothing can succeed in getting it off.
六二執之用黃牛之革. 莫之勝說.

33.3 Bound up piglet.
Will have harsh illness.
For raising livestock and male and female servants, auspicious.
九三係遯. 有疾厲. 畜臣妾, 吉.

33.4 A good piglet, for the upright person, auspicious.
For the petty person, not.
九四好遯, 君子, 吉. 小人, 否.

33.5 Excellent piglet. Divination auspicious.
九五嘉遯. 貞吉.

33.6 A fat piglet. Nothing not beneficial.
上九肥遯. 无不利。

33. Commentary 遯 *Dun* Piglet

Dun 遯 literally means flee or escape but the emendation of Gao
Heng, to *tun* piglet has been widely accepted (Field 2015: 156f.).
The tag character differs in the main excavated manuscripts.
In the Shanghai Museum bamboo slips, it is an obsolete graph
also pronounced *dun* and also containing the pig radical 豕 *shi*
as a component. Fuyang has 椽 *chuan*, meaning rafter or beam.
Mawangdui has 恆 *heng*, constancy, or long lasting. All of these
variants save the last share the pig component. This suggests either
that the early meaning was "pig," or was misread as pig. In general,
the less abstract meaning is likely to be the earliest but withdrawal
is a very basic concept, especially given the frequency of combat in
the Western Zhou. These variants suggest that the *Changes* circulated in slightly different versions, though the similarities between
versions are far more numerous than the differences.

Piglet fits all the line texts, where they are clearly omens. The
piglets are to be butchered, but the divinatory significance is
not their possible use for sacrifice, but simply to seeing them. If
anything, seeing a piglet would have given rise to thoughts of how
tasty it would be when cooked, not to concern for the animal. The
modern dissociation between a live animal and meat does not exist
in agricultural societies.

33.0 An alternative way to translate the judgment is, "Make
offering, small benefit to divine." There is no basis for concluding
which is correct—it could have been read either way in the Western
Zhou. This is another case in which the diviner would have
discretion in interpreting the line.

33.1 The reference to the tail rather than the entire pig is puzzling.
The meaning of "harsh," is a typical omen in the sense that there
is no intuitive connection between the omen and its meaning. Of
course, there might have been such an association 3,000 years ago
but then we might expect a few hints as to the connection.

33.3 This suggests that seeing a piglet bound up augurs a difficult illness, but for whom is not stated. We assume that divinatory responses refer to the person making the inquiry but this is not necessarily the case. One might ask about oneself but receive a reply about a family member, or even one's village or country. The conjunction of phrases forecasting both a harsh illness and favorable breeding of farm animals and servants seems peculiar to say the least. However, such combinations are so common in the *Zhouyi* that we should not be surprised by every such instance. The compilers evidently did not find anything odd about this, and the same may have been true in actual divinations—both good and bad news might be given in the same reading. There is also a frequent pattern in *Zhouyi* texts of giving disparate implications of the divination for different categories, as with husband and wife in 32.5. The seeming equation of breeding animals and human servants similarly should not be taken to conclude that servants were regarded simply as breeding stock. Early agricultural societies may not always have used special, politer, language for human as opposed to animal reproduction.

The *Zhouyi* does not tell us whether omens tended to have fixed meanings—a bound piglet portending success in animal breeding, for example, or whether they were spur of the moment on the part of the diviner.

33.6 Fat animals are a sign of abundance and so are positive omens in many cultures.

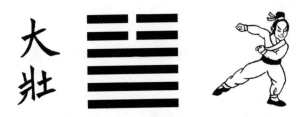

34. 大壯 *Da Zhuan* Great Strength
(The Power of the Great)

The Judgment:

34.0 Beneficial to divine.
利貞.

The Line Texts:

34.1 Strong feet for a military expedition. Ominous regarding captives.
初九壯于趾征. 凶孚.

34.2 Divination auspicious.
九二貞吉.

34.3 The petty person uses strength; the cultivated person uses deception.
Divination harsh.
A ram getting his horns entangled in a fence wearies his horns.
九三小人用壯; 君子用罔. 貞厲. 羝羊觸藩羸其角.

34.4 Divination auspicious—regrets will go away.
Fence breaks, [the ram] is not weak.
Strength like a big cart's undercarriage.
九四貞吉—悔亡. 藩決不羸, 壯于大輿之輹.

34.5 Losing the ram in Yi.
No regret.
六五喪羊于易. 无悔.

34.6 Like a ram getting its horns caught, it cannot pull back,
cannot go forward.
There is nothing beneficial.
Difficult, then auspicious.
上六羝羊觸藩. 不能退. 不能遂.

34. Commentary 大壯 *Da Zhuang*
Great Strength

Da Zhuang 大壯 means great strength or force. This hexagram
has more unity than most with 34.3, 34.4, 34.5, and 34.6 having
a degree of narrative structure. The ram who has gotten his horns
stuck in a fence is presented as an analogy for cleverness being
better than brute strength. The ram is at first stuck, then breaks the
fence and gets free, but only after being unable to move forward
or back for a period of time. The upright person who succeeds by
cunning is the model to be followed, not the ram.

In a clear example of a scribal substitution which is both
phonetic and semantic, Mawangdui has 泰 *tai* instead of 大 *da*.
Shaughnessy translates it as "great" in this context (1996: 88f.) *Tai*
is also the tag for hexagram 11 in the received version, but not in
the equivalent Mawangdui hexagram, which is 34.

Kunst and Rutt, following Gao Heng, translate *zhuang* as injury
rather than strength (Rutt: 326f.) Like many of the great Chinese
philologist's proposed emendations, this one seems gratuitous.
Claims of homophone substitutions cannot by their nature be
proven wrong, but my principle has been to avoid emending when
the received meaning makes sense, as it does here. This is not to
disparage the more far-fetched suggestions of learned philologists
such as Waley and Gao Heng. Not infrequently they are right and
their proposals are always stimulating. Textual criticism must
always be mindful of the risk of lapsing into rigidity. With texts
of the antiquity and terseness of the *Zhouyi* no suggestion can be
dismissed out of hand.

34.0 A routine invocation. Why some judgment texts simply repeat stock phrases, and others have substantive content more like line statements, is unclear. It could be that different compilers had different stylistic preferences. Some may have deliberately grouped phrases that shared key characters. Others may have seen their task as simply getting all the material put together—organizing the text bits to fit the six line templates may have been the sole principle guiding the work.

As a thought experiment, consider having a container filled with hundreds of bits of bamboo, each with a phrase brushed on, often in variant characters, and having to organize them into a book. Or think of what it would be like to take the *Changes* as we have it now and try to reorganize the phrases into thematic order. Frustrated as we are trying to figure out what the compilers have left us, we should remain thankful for their work, done when writing was still new. Just restoring the damaged strips of the Shanghai Museum *Zhouyi* and trying to determine their original order took China's greatest experts several years, though the parlous condition of the manuscript was a major factor.

34.1 Strong feet are obviously important for marching. If my punctuation is correct, this is the only instance in the *Zhouyi* in which it is dangerous to hold captives; usually doing so is highly auspicious, (though only for the captors). Alternatively, it could be that the military expedition carried out to take captives is hazardous.

34.3 As I have translated, the phrase states that the refined (or unscrupulous) accomplish their goals not with force, but with cunning. This is clearly a proverb and applies to politics everywhere. Confucian texts tend to recommend virtue rather than cunning, but here the *Zhouyi* is realistic about official life. The *shi* class of educated professionals did not exist as such in the Western Zhou. Most high officials were relatives of the king. Blood ties did not obviate cunning or treachery. The idea of meritocracy, so prominent in Chinese political theory, did not yet exist.

The last phrase of this line is a proverb about pointless effort. It reprises the idea that brute strength is not as effective as cleverness. A ram getting his horns caught in a fence is a proverb still in use today, another interesting example of the extreme persistence of oral material.

34.4 Eventually the ram does break the fence and free his horns, showing his great strength. The last phrase is uncertain. Some have translated it as the ram attacking the cart. Since this makes no sense I have rendered it as a comparison of a cart's sturdiness to a ram's physique.

34.5 *Yi* here is generally taken to be a place name, not "easy" nor "change," as it means in the title of the classic. Alternatively, it could mean, "To lose a sheep on the way is easy." If so, the shepherd escapes blame.

34.6 "The ram's horns are entangled," is a proverb referring to the common situation in which one is stuck with no evident way out. However, the final phrase indicates that after this difficulty, things will become favorable, perhaps referring back to 34.4.

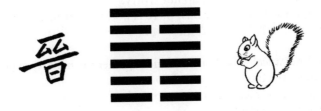

35. 晉 *Jin* Advance (Progress)

The Judgment:

35.0 Bestowed upon Marquis Kang were numerous horses.
They became abundant, mated three times a day.
康侯用錫馬蕃. 庶, 晝日三接.

The Line Texts:

35.1 If advance, will annihilate.
Divination auspicious.
Ensnare captives in abundance.
There will be no blame.
初六晉如, 摧如. 貞吉. 罔孚裕. 无咎.

35.2 If advance, then sorrow.
Divination auspicious.
Receive now good fortune from the king's mother.
六二晉如, 愁如. 貞吉. 受茲介福于其王母.

35.3 The common people approve.
Regret is gone.
六三眾允. 悔亡.

35.4 Advancing like a squirrel.
Divination harsh.
九四晉如鼫鼠. 貞厲.

35.5 Regret is gone.
About losing or gaining, do not worry.
Going forward is auspicious; there is nothing not beneficial.
六五悔亡. 失得勿恤. 往吉无; 不利.

35.6 "Advance!" Use horns to hold together the military expedition
to attack the city.
Harshness auspicious, not blameworthy.
Divination: regret.
上九晉! 其角維用伐邑. 厲吉, 无咎. 貞吝.

35. Commentary 晉 *Jin* Advance

Jin 晉 means advance and is included in lines 35.1, 35.2, 35.4,
and 35.6. Wilhelm-Baynes translate it as "progress," but this is
misleading with its implication of the modern concept of progress
as social and technological improvement. This, the Whig theory of
history, is contrary to the views of the early Chinese philosophers
including Confucius and *Laozi*, who considered that their time
had declined from the ideal society of high antiquity. Medieval
Christianity held a similarly negative idea of history as movement
away from the truth of revelation.

This hexagram shares some verbal elements with the preceding
one, suggesting either that compilers often grouped textual elements
simply because they shared words or phrases. Alternatively, adjacent
hexagrams could have been compiled by the same individuals, thus
displaying their stylistic preferences.

35.0 Because of the ambiguity of early Chinese, this could also
mean that the horses were conferred by Marquis Kang on someone
else. Gifts have always been very important in China—and other
cultures as well—to establish the mutual obligations that hold
societies together. Given that money was not widely used, grants
of valuables: livestock, land, ritual bronzes, ornamental clothing,
were the main forms of exchangeable wealth.

35.2 The "good fortune from the king's mother" is most likely a
reference to a specific historical event in which she bestowed benefits
upon an individual whose identity cannot now be determined.

35.3 That there should be concern for the welfare of the common people is expressed in Confucian and Daoist philosophy but is largely unmentioned in the *Zhouyi*, this line being an exception. It does suggest however that government may not have been entirely indifferent to their plight. That later mythology of the Western Zhou made it a paragon of good government tells us little about actual conditions.

35.4 Rutt points out that 鼫鼠 *shi shu* has been variously translated as "flying squirrel," "mole cricket," or "vole mouse." Ancient proper nouns such as names of species of plants and animals, town names, and the like are notoriously hard to translate with certainty. Mole crickets are omens of good luck or rain in some African and South American cultures. Whatever species is being referred to here, it is clearly an omen. That it is harsh presumably is because advance would be dangerous in the situation divined about. Squirrels are timid so perhaps this means to advance in an anxious situation. However, human traits that have been applied to animals vary between cultures. This line contrasts with 35.5 in which advancing is auspicious. As pointed out elsewhere, this is not a contradiction because the diviner would have obtained one or the other of these prognoses.

35.5 The second phrase expresses the wisdom, similar to that of the much later *Dao De Jing*, of being detached from gain and loss. However, it may simply be a prognostication to the effect that one need not worry about loss or gain because advancing is favorable.

35.6 "Advance!" is a military command to move forward to engage the enemy.

The remaining phrases are somewhat contradictory, seeming to advocate harshness against the enemy but warning that it will later be regretted. This is certainly a plausible scenario—one attains victory by ruthlessness, then regrets the misery resulting. Such sensitivity is largely lacking in the *Zhouyi* so it is, unfortunately, more plausible that the victors regret the destruction because their spoils are less. Such speculation, however, goes beyond the text.

36. 明夷 *Ming Yi* Calling Pheasant (Darkening of the Light)

The Judgment:

36.0 Divination beneficial if in difficulty.
利艱貞.

The Line Texts:

36.1 Calling pheasant in flight, swooping down on its wings.
The upright person walks for three days without eating.
Has someplace to go—his master has spoken.
初九明夷于飛, 垂其翼. 君子于行三日不食.
有攸往—主人有言.

36.2 Calling pheasant.
Wounded in the left thigh.
Use to geld a robust horse, auspicious.
六二明夷. 夷于左股. 用拯馬壯, 吉.

36.3 Calling pheasant during the king's southern winter hunt.
Gain their great leader.
Cannot divine about illness.
九三明夷于南狩. 得其大首. 不可疾貞。

36.4 Enters into the left flank, snaring the calling pheasant's heart.
Through the gate into the courtyard.
六四入于左腹, 獲明夷之心.于出門庭.

36.5 Jizi's calling pheasant—a beneficial divination.
六五箕子之明夷—利貞.

36.6 Not bright, but dim.
First rises toward the heavens, afterwards to the earth.
上六不明晦. 初登于天, 後入于地.

36. Commentary 明夷 *Ming Yi* Calling Pheasant

The Wilhelm-Baynes translation as "Darkening of the Light," is poetic, but clearly incorrect. It is derived from the structure of the hexagram, in which the earth trigram is above that for heaven, hence earth is obscuring the light of heaven (Rutt: 378). This cannot have been the early meaning because, as emphasized previously, there is no evidence for trigram correlations before the *Zuozhuan* and *Ten Wings*.

The modern consensus following the work of Li Jingchi and Gao Heng, is that *ming* in this hexagram does not have its usual meaning of bright but refers to a pheasant. Kunst (310f.), Rutt (259, 328–30), and Shaughnessy (2014: 258) all accept this and I have followed it also as it fits well with the *Zhouyi*'s predilection for bird call omens. The *Shijing* also refers frequently to birds, but seemingly as symbols rather than as omens.

The tag is repeated in all of the lines except the judgment. There is nothing surprising about this as scholarly consensus is that the judgments were composed separately from the line texts. There is similar repetition in the Mawangdui and Fuyang manuscripts, both excavated from tombs of the Western Han, indicating that these are intrinsic parts of the text.

Whincup translates the tag as, "Bright Pheasant," and explicates this image:

> The bright pheasant represents a brilliant minister, who remonstrates with his unworthy ruler … (125)

The pheasant as a symbol of the virtuous official is the invention of later exegetes; it is questionable if it had this meaning in the Western

Zhou. The worthy official remonstrating with his unworthy ruler is a central motif in Confucian writings. The Confucian officials believed they were best qualified to conduct government affairs. However as, members of the *shi*, or educated professional class, they had no actual power, except that of moral suasion. Hence the recurrent image of the virtuous official attempting to improve the morals of his ruler. As always, those in power often failed to appreciate being admonished. This idea of telling the ruler how to improve himself was often read into the Confucian classics but there is no evidence for this idea until the Spring and Autumn Era, when Confucius lived. The *Shijing* and *Chunqiu* began to be read as works of moral instruction, but there is little basis for this in their literal meanings.

36.0 The divination is favorable for those encountering difficulties. This is a typical sort of phrase used in "cold reading," a euphemism for fake psychic readings. Such phrases are usually on target since everyone alive has difficulties of one sort or another. (My experience suggests that many, but by no means all, who do readings with *I Ching*, *Tarot*, or astrology are sincere. I discuss the nature of divination in detail elsewhere. Redmond and Hon 2014: 19–36).

36.1 The meanings here are quite clear. The swooping pheasant is a good omen and the upright person obeys his master's summons. So eager is he to obey that he does not take time to eat during the three days it takes him to arrive. This theme is best known in the myth of Yu the Great who worked tirelessly on flood control; for thirteen years he never visited his family, even when passing by his home. From such stories we learn that work-life balance was problematic even in the Bronze Age. Examples of extreme virtue at the expense of oneself or family are common in early literature, such as Confucian tales of filial piety (Knapp 2005) and the Indian Buddhist Jataka tales.

36.2 Rutt and Shaughnessy (2014: 258) translate this phrase as the pheasant "wounded in the left thigh." It may be that wounds were interpreted as omens based on their location.

The final phrase could be about being rescued by a horse rather than gelding it. That the first reference to the calling pheasant is favorable and the subsequent ones are not does not argue against this as the line texts may well have been composed as a collection of pheasant omens, not a narrative sequence. The identical phrase also occurs in 59.1.

36.3 As previously mentioned, in hierarchical societies to be leaderless, that is without a powerful backer, is a situation of extreme vulnerability. Hence gaining a leader would make oneself and one's family more secure. This phrase has also been translated as gaining, in the sense of capturing, someone of high rank.

The final phrase likely represents a diviner's declining to advise about illness. Diviners not infrequently state that they cannot get information about a specific question. A modern example is the words spoken by Madame Sosostris' famous clairvoyant line from T. S. Eliot's *The Wasteland* in which she claims to be forbidden to see what is on one of her wicked pack of cards. To not to be able to see everything likely increases the credibility of the diviner or allows sensitive questions to be avoided.

36.4 Here the pheasant is a game animal. Wilhelm-Baynes' translation shows the inherent difficulty of his literary style of translation:

He penetrates the left side of the belly.
One gets at the very heart of the darkening of the light ... (141)

The second phrase at first glance seems to mean something but on closer reading says nothing intelligible. In the era of the Western cliché of the inscrutable Orient, this might have passed, but now it unnecessarily exacerbates the *I Ching*'s reputation for obscurity. There is nothing mysterious or profound about shooting a pheasant with bow and arrow.

36.5 In contrast to the previous line, here the pheasant is an augury. Note that being an auspicious augury does not protect an animal against being eaten.

Rutt notes that *Jizi* was a righteous minister of the last [evil] Shang king. *Jizi* frequently remonstrated against the evil ruler, yet somehow survived and went into voluntary exile after the Zhou conquest (Rutt: 330). There are surprisingly few such uses of proper names in the *Zhouyi*, though some may not have been recognized. This is odd since many of the phrases must have been extracted from actual divinations.

36.6 *Ming* in context here must mean "bright," even though the line as a whole is about the flight of the pheasant. It is tempting to interpret this as an augury meaning being successful at first, then failing.

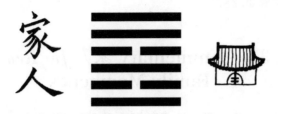

37. 家人 *Jia Ren* Family Members (The Family; The Clan)

The Judgment:

37.0 Beneficial for a woman to divine.
利女貞.

The Line Texts:

37.1 The household is gated.
Regret is gone.
初九閑有家. 悔亡.

37.2 Nothing goes forward.
Inside for women's work, divination auspicious.
六二无攸遂. 在中饋, 吉.

37.3 In the household, regretting harsh scolding is auspicious.
Wives and sons giggling—ends in regret.
九三家人, 嗃悔厲吉.
婦子嘻嘻—終吝.

37.4 For wealthy families, greatly auspicious.
六四富家, 大.

37.5 The king goes to his household.
Do not worry, auspicious.
九五王假有家. 勿恤, 吉.

37.6 Holding captives who tremble as if in awe. Ends auspiciously.
上九有孚威如. 終吉.

37. Commentary 家人 *Jia Ren* Family Members

Jiaren 家人 refers to the members of the family or household, sometimes including servants. All lines except 37.6 are concerned with domestic matters, mostly of ordinary families but also of the king.

37.0 One of the *Zhouyi*'s infrequent references to women (*nü* 女 appears only nine times), this suggests that women, too, perform divination with the *Changes*. However, it could equally mean, "Divination favorable for a woman." Read either way, it indicates that divination was not exclusively for men. Chinese decorum tended to keep women from the public eye—though probably less so in early China. This decorum extended even to many canonical texts. For example, Confucius mentions women only once in the *Lunyu*. In the *Zhouyi*, most mentions of women are about marriages. The 左傳, *Zuozhuan*, nominally a commentary on the *Chunqiu* (*Spring and Autumn Annals*), as well as much later vernacular literature, contain abundant references to women, not infrequently erotic, and often derogatory. Women are particularly blamed for stirring up discord, as with the wife of the evil last Shang king. Lady Macbeth is, after all, an archetypal, if not historically accurate, figure.

37.2 The second phrase of this line refers to women's domestic work. While the Western Zhou was hardly a time of opportunity for most women, we must remember that in an era with none of the conveniences we take for granted, division of labor within families was essential for survival and such tasks as preparing food, making clothing and caring for children would have absorbed most of the waking hours for wives and concubines, even in affluent households with servants.

37.3 This line is particularly interesting because it seems to condemn excessive strictness in the household—unexpected in an authoritarian society. Given that the most senior man had almost unlimited power over the others in the household, in many families the women and children must have been in a nearly constant state of fear. There is not much gentleness in the *Zhouyi*, so it is reassuring that Western Zhou life was not always one of unrelenting harshness. Nonetheless, there is no indication that the leniency mentioned here extends to the captives in 37.6.

The second phrase, in context with the first, might be saying that women and children should not be too silly acting. However, in the *Zhouyi*, giggling or laughing seem usually to be indications of anxiety. So this might be nervous giggling, with the male authority figure regretting that he has terrified the women and children.

37.4 That being wealthy is auspicious seems self-evident, but wealthy families could be destroyed, especially by malicious allegations of witchcraft or fomenting rebellion (Liang Cai).

37.5 The king heading home would suggest a state of relative security in the country. *Wu xu* 勿恤 also occurs in 35.5.

37.6 The likely significance of the first phrase is that they are trembling in awe at the might of the Zhou. Obviously the auspicious ending is not for the terrified captives. Once again we find no expression of compassion for the human sacrificial victims.

Yin Xu (Anyang), where the Shang-inscribed oracle bones were found, contains remains of thousands of sacrificial victims—identifiable as such because the skulls are separated from the bodies. Unfortunately, the notion that innocents need to be killed for the benefit of society is still present in the modern world. Examples are Stalin's death camps, the 35 million deaths in the Chinese "Great Leap Forward," and the Khmer Rouge extermination of the literate. Pol Pot, the perpetrator of this latter atrocity, has been quoted as saying after his show trial and house arrest, "If it were not for me, there would be no Cambodia."

Minford translates 37.6 last line as:

Captives are terrified.
Auspicious conclusion.

He interprets this as,

> Captives are being taken on as household slaves (and therefore
> part of the family. At first terrified and defiant, but ultimately
> they submit and all is well. (2014: 662)

This puts a much better face on this and similar passages than do
Kunst, Rutt, Field and myself. Given that mass sacrifice is verified
by archaeology, Minford's benign version seems unlikely. Although
Minford is a deservedly renowned translator, his Western Zhou
reconstruction seems not to have removed all traces of the book of
wisdom reading of the *Changes*.

38. 睽 *Kui* Opposition (Opposition)

The Judgment:

38.0 For small matters, auspicious.
小事,吉.

The Line Texts:

38.1 Regret goes away.
Losing one's horse, do not pursue it. Naturally, it will return.
Glimpsing a disfigured person, there will be no blame.
初九悔亡. 喪馬勿逐. 自, 復. 見惡人无咎.

38.2 Encountering a lord in a back alley, will not be blamed.
九二遇主于巷, 无咎.

38.3 Seeing a cart hauled by its ox.
Its man, heaven even cut off his nose.
Though without a beginning, it has an end.
六三見輿曳其牛掣. 其人天且劓. 无初, 有終

38.4 Separated and orphaned, first falls in with a conscripted laborer.
Handing over captives, harshly, but not blameworthy.
九四睽孤. 遇元夫. 交孚, 厲, 无咎.

38.5 Regret is gone.
Their ancestors gnaw the diced meat.
In going, how can there be blame?
六五悔亡. 厥宗噬膚. 往何咎?

38.6 Opposed and orphaned, sees a pig with mud on its back.
Ghosts carried in a cart.
First, draw his bow; after, sets down the bow.
Not bandits, but a marriage match.
When going, if caught in the rain, then auspicious.
上九睽孤, 見豕負塗. 載鬼一車. 先張之弧; 後說之弧. 匪寇婚媾.往
遇雨則,吉.

38. Commentary 睽 *Kui* Opposition

The tag character appears only in 38.4 and 38.6. It can mean
separated as well as opposed.

38.0 A standard divinatory phrase.

38.1 The theme of not having to search for what has been lost is
a recurrent one in the *Zhouyi*. Seeing a deformed person would be
assumed to be bad luck but we are reassured that it will not be so
in relation to this circumstance. In a well-known anecdote, a son
with a clubfoot is denied permission to carry out the rituals for
ancestors as he is not a complete human being. Such superstitions
further hindered the lives of people with physical abnormalities by
causing them to be shunned as bringing bad luck. This prejudice
has only partly been overcome. Some years ago I witnessed this in
Cambodia when our guide told us not to give money to beggars
who had lost legs from land mines. Some, she told us, even owned
motorbikes, as if they were somehow at fault themselves for having
mutilated bodies. Such attitudes are suppressed in the developed
countries, but sometimes persist.

Rutt makes the interesting suggestion that the lost horse may
be a constellation that will reappear as the earth rotates (331).
There are many such elements in the *Zhouyi* that could well
refer to astronomical events, but so far as I am aware, Chinese

commentarial traditions have not given much attention to this mode of exegesis. Cosmology was greatly elaborated during the Han Dynasty, but tended toward virtual, calculating star positions rather than actually observing them.

Yin-yang and wu xing (five phrases) cycles served as metaphysical models for all natural and human phenomena. While this cosmology was added to the I Ching rather than being intrinsic to it, it contributed to the influence of the I Ching, even into the modern era. Joseph Needham blamed the Changes for being a major factor inhibiting the development of science in China (Redmond and Hon: 158–70).

Rutt points out that several possible astrological references in the line texts such as "heavenly horse," or "man leading an ox," are also names of asterisms. Since these play little role in the later Confucian received tradition of interpretation, they seem to hint at an alternate, perhaps esoteric, tradition of reading the Changes. If so, it would have been read on two levels, one in which the texts refer to matters of daily life, including omens, and the other as references to astrology. However, I have not found a systematic reading based on the calendrical and astronomical meanings of characters. This is an aspect of the Changes that could reward more study. I have pointed out some astronomical references but generally translated based on the more concrete meanings. Pankenier is the most comprehensive consideration of early Chinese astrology in English and includes a discussion of astronomical phenomena (2013: 44–90 et passim). Astrology is beginning to receive scholarly study as central to the thought of the ancient world, only now overcoming dismissal as superstition unworthy of serious consideration.

38.2 This line is somewhat obscure. Perhaps it means: when one meets a superior out of sight of others, one is less likely to be blamed for omitting correct ritual courtesies.

38.3 As I have translated, the second phrase means, "not only has fate made him an ox-cart driver, it has even caused him to have his nose cut off." Mutilating punishments were standard for all sorts of offenses. These included tattooing on the face, cutting off the nose, cutting off the feet, and castration. Such people were almost certainly socially shunned. There is little record of how these unfortunates managed to survive. Often physical punishments were remitted upon payment of a fine. Thus the affluent were usually spared. In a notorious episode of the Han Dynasty, the founder of Chinese historical writing, Sima Qian (d. 86 BCE), was castrated— his friends refused to lend him the money to prevent the castration. This punishment not only prevented sexual pleasure, it induced further shame as making it impossible to carry out the filial duty of fathering children.

Here *tian* means heaven as arbitrary fate; the implication is that the oxcart driver lost his nose because of bad luck rather than misconduct on his part. Chinese attitudes toward fate were mixed. In the later classics, notably the *Dao De Jing* and the *Lunyu*, Heaven is an impersonal entity that regulates the cosmos. Humans frequently violate the Way of Heaven; this causes personal disasters and social disruption. For this reason, even minor ritual errors can have serious consequences. Confucius often spoke of heaven but famously declined to discuss anomalies, along with spirits and feats of strength. This reticence was one factor that led Leibniz, Voltaire, and other Enlightenment *philosophes* interested in China to imagine it as a totally rational society. Not only the Chinese but medieval Western philosophers kept the rational and the supernatural in separate mental compartments, as indeed many people do today.

The last phrase may be a proverb about human life, meaning either that although one does not know when one's troubles began, they will come to an end. Or perhaps more philosophically, that we do not know our birth but do know we will die.

38.4 This is the sort of line text that makes the *Zhouyi* seem so confusing. It is an odd mixture of elements that seem unrelated. The obscurity dissipates somewhat once one realizes that it refers to a solitary person seeing a forced laborer, or perhaps that being solitary, he has no choice but to join with this person. This could be an omen, as in 4.3. This might be calamitous but if the final prognosis applies to this phrase, blame will be avoided. Indeed, an important function of *Zhouyi* divination seems to have been to help the inquirer avert the ill consequences of such an omen. The second phrase has no evident relation to the first, unless the laborer is assigned to guarding captives, but one would expect a soldier to be given this responsibility.

The variety of proposed emendations and translations of *yu* is unusually extensive, even for the *Zhouyi*. These are summarized by Rutt (31). Another example is emendation of 孤 *gu*, orphan, to 狐 *hu*, fox (Rutt: 210, 261, 331. See also Kunst: 314f.; Field 2015: 170f.). They speculate that this may have been a reference to Sirius, the Dog Star. While this speculation is plausible, the meaning as orphan is supported by the child radical 子 *zi* being one of its components.

While the mode of thought that assumes chance sightings may portend disaster is foreign to us, traces survive in familiar superstitions such as a black cat crossing one's path. What is revealed in this, as in many other passages in the *Zhouyi*, is the extreme fearfulness induced by supernatural beliefs. This is brought out well by Constance Cook who describes the extreme apprehension of a middle-level government official afflicted with an incurable disease, who has traveled frequently, possibly incurring the enmity of the local spirits he had not known how to propitiate.

38.5 Obviously the ancestors cannot actually bite the meat. The biting is not literal and the offering was likely later consumed by those offering the sacrifice. *Fu* 膚 meat can also have the implication of human flesh. Cannibalism may well have been part of some human sacrifices, but most historical texts gloss over this gruesome possibility and scholars have tended to avoid it also.

38.6 This line repeats the initial two words of 38.4. One is alone and beset and sees a mud-covered pig—this being the usual state of pigs penned on farms. Being alone was likely an unusual situation in traditional China—and even now as anyone who has traveled in the Chinese countryside is well aware. The phrase probably reflects the anxiety of being alone and unprotected. The pig might be an omen that the orphan will find something to eat, perhaps by stealing the pig. In traditional China, as in the West until relatively recently, there were many homeless wanderers begging or making a living as herb-sellers, story-tellers, diviners, and other ways, not all honest.

The remainder of this line text is a jumble of seemingly unrelated omens. Rutt shows that the ghostly cart, pig, and archer are likely astrological references (332). Nonetheless, as I have already noted, such were probably read on at least two levels, as natural omens and as celestial ones.

The third phrase seems to be a proverb, somewhat akin to the supposed maxim of the American Wild West, "Shoot first and ask questions later." Rutt suggests the reference to bandits is about mock bride-stealing. Alternatively, a wedding ceremony might also be a common target for robbers, as wealth would be on display. If *fei* 匪 is taken as "bandits" rather than "not," the line becomes the opposite to how I have rendered it: "Bandits invade the wedding." The Fuyang manuscript has *fei* written as 非, making "not" the more likely reading (160). However, with homophonic characters, it is often impossible to resolve ambiguity with certainty.

In contrast to modern urban life, in agricultural societies rain was always welcome.

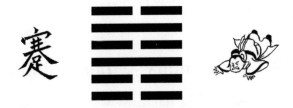

39. 蹇 *Jian* Stumbling (Obstruction)

The Judgment:

39.0 Beneficial in the west and south.
Not beneficial in the east and north.
Beneficial to see the important person.
Divination auspicious.
利西南. 不利東北. 利見大人.貞吉.

The Line Texts:

39.1 Going forth stumbling, on arrival, praised.
初六往蹇, 來譽.

39.2 The king's ministers—stumbling, stumbling, not bowing intentionally.
六二王臣蹇蹇. 匪躬之故.

39.3 Going forth stumbling, on arrival turning back.
[Divination about illness—will not die.]
九三往蹇, 來反. [卜病不死.]

39.4 Going forth stumbling, arrive one after another.
六四往蹇, 來連.

39.5 With big stumbles, friends arrive.
九五大蹇, 朋來.

39.6 Going forth stumbling; arrival greatly auspicious.
Beneficial to see the important person.
上六往蹇; 來碩吉. 利見大人.

39. Commentary 蹇 *Jian* Stumbling

This word could also be translated as "limping" or "crippled."
Though absent in the judgment, the tag character is repeated in
each of the line texts, giving this hexagram an unusual degree of
thematic unity. Contrary to the usual denigration of any sort of
handicap in the *Zhouyi*, in this hexagram those who stumble seem
to end up favorably. The divinatory significance of this is quite
clear—struggling with a task ultimately pays off.

39.0 The directions could also be translated as southwest and
northeast but early Chinese texts usually refer to the four cardinal
directions. Associations of directions with favorable or unfavorable
prognoses are usual in Chinese divinations. Years ago, I myself
received a warning from a palm reader in a Gaoxiong night market
to avoid traveling to the south and west. I did so anyway and
became severely ill. This has not made me a believer in palmistry
but did serve to fix the episode in my memory.

The usual translation of *da ren* 大人 as with Wilhelm-Baynes
is, "great man." Because this sounds both snobbish and sexist to
contemporary readers, I have used important person. This is not to
gloss over the fact that traditional China was rigidly hierarchical
and subordinated women. However, as elsewhere I see no reason
to add gender when it is not in the original.

39.1 This seems to mean that one is praised for coming despite
the effort indicated by stumbling. In his translation of the slightly
different Mawangdui version, Shaughnessy has, "Going afoot,
coming in a cart" (76f.). This is consistent with the received version
in suggesting that the going is difficult but the return is better,
rather than lameness being miraculously cured.

39.2 It would seem that bowing before the king would be
intentional, so this likely refers to awkward body posture.

39.3 The Fuyang manuscript has an additional phrase, 卜病不死 *bu bing bu si*, "Divining about sickness: they will not die ..." (Shaughnessy 2014: 262). There are only a few such additional phrases in the excavated manuscripts. It seems best to resist the temptation to conjecture if such phrases were lost in the received text or added to a later one.

39.4 and 39.5 These lines seem to suggest some sort of mutual help. Given the arrival of guests, this might be a social occasion resulting in drunkenness.

39.6 Another phrase with the same theme.

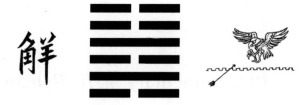

40. 解 *Jie*: Release (Deliverance)

The Judgment:

40.0 Beneficial in the west and south.
If there is no place to set out to, their coming back is auspicious.
For having someplace to go, early is auspicious.
利西南. 无所往, 其來復吉. 有攸往, 夙吉.

The Line Texts:

40.1 There will be no blame.
无咎.

40.2 In the field catch three foxes and find a bronze arrow, divination auspicious.
九二田獲三狐得黃矢, 貞: 吉.

40.3 Carrying [possessions] on one's back while riding in a cart attracts the arrival of bandits.
Divination: regret.
六三負且乘致寇至. 貞吝.

40.4 Release their thumbs with the arrival of friends of the captives.
九四解而拇朋至斯孚.

40.5 The nobleman is safe, having been released, auspicious.
Holding captive the petty people.
六五君子維有解,吉. 有孚于小人.

40.6 Using an arrow, the duke shoots a falcon high above the city wall, bagging it.
Nothing not beneficial.
上六公用射隼于高墉之上獲之. 无不利.

40 Commentary 解 *Jie* Release

While 40.4 and 40.5 include the tag character, there is no general theme related to releasing. Hacker suggests that the tag refers back to that for 39, for which he translated the character as "obstruction" (54). However, with some exceptions, such as hexagrams 1 and 2 and 63 and 64, the tags mostly seem unrelated to the line texts, though later literati commentators found ways to read the tags so that they seemed to fit the hexagram figure and the line texts.

Most of the line texts are about hunting or the disposition of captives. The tag 解 can mean releasing, but also separating or cutting. Thus 40.5 could mean cutting the captives, rather than releasing them. Given the rather grim fate of captives in the *Zhouyi*, the former is plausibly the early meaning but I have chosen to grant amnesty to these captives by choosing to translate as "releasing."

40.0 The final phrase sounds like a proverb, though a rather obvious one.

40.2 *Hu* 狐 clearly means "fox" here. Likely finding an arrowhead was lucky and a bronze one would have had significant monetary value. At one time in the United States, finding stone Native American arrowheads was considered lucky. They were still passed around frequently when I was a child, though I was unable to judge their authenticity.

40.3 The first phrase sounds like a proverb, "If you let your possessions be too visible, robbers are likely to come."

40.4 The first phrase is obscure, but might mean releasing bound captives, or releasing a bowstring, presumably to shoot the captives. Alternatively, Rutt suggests, it could refer to cutting off the thumbs of captives (334f.). The Fuyang and Mawangdui manuscripts shed no light on this passage.

40.5 As I have translated this obscure passage, the high-ranking person is released but those of low rank are kept prisoner.

40.6 Success in hunting was important for the powerful to maintain their aura.

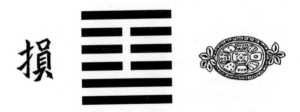

41. 損 *Sun* Decrease (Decrease)

The Judgment:

41.0 Holding captives. Begins auspiciously. Nothing blameworthy can be divined.
Beneficial if having to go somewhere.
What is the use for a two-handled *gui*? It can be used for making offerings.
有孚.元吉. 无咎可貞. 利有攸往. 曷之用二簋? 可用享。

The Line Texts:

41.1 Finish the matter, will not be blamed.
Pouring wine diminishes it.
初九已事遄往, 无咎. 酌損之.

41.2 Beneficial to divine—for a campaign, ominous.
Neither decreasing nor increasing.
九二利貞—征凶. 弗損益之.

41.3 If three people walk, then lose one person.
If one person walks, then obtains a companion.
六三人行, 則損一人. 一人行, 則得其友.

41.4 To those diminished by illness, quickly send some joy.
There will be no blame.
六四損其疾, 使遄有喜. 无咎.

41.5 Perhaps advantageous—ten cowry shells for a tortoise.
Must not resist or disobey.
Begins auspiciously.
六五或益之—十朋之龜. 弗克違. 元吉.

41.6 Neither decreasing nor increasing.
Nothing blameworthy. Divination auspicious.
Beneficial if having somewhere to go.
Obtain a servant without a family.
上九弗損益之. 无咎; 貞吉. 利有攸往. 得臣无家.

41. Commentary 損 *Sun* Decrease

Sun occurs in all the line texts except 41.5. The sorts of decrease however are quite different, so the basis of inclusion of the line texts is the character, rather than a common theme. Lines 41.2 and 41.6 both include the set phrase, "neither decreasing nor increasing."

41.0 A *gui* is a round bowl for holding grain known from the Shang Dynasty. When used for offerings it would presumably be bronze, but early examples are pottery.

41.1 The first phrase has often been translated as meaning that a sacrifice should be performed quickly (Shaughnessy: 293; Kunst: 320f.; Rutt: 264). This is plausible, but my own view is that as often as the *Zhouyi* refers to sacrifice, that does not mean that any incomplete phrase should be interpreted as being about sacrifice. This might be a terse proverb to the effect that finishing a task averts blame.

The final phrase seems to be a proverb to the effect, "If you pour your wine, you will have less left." When it is offered to the spirits, one has less left for oneself, perhaps a wry comment on the cost of sacrifice, which consumed a quite significant portion of the resources of many early cultures.

41.2 As noted previously *zhen g* 征 can mean a military campaign as well as a long journey. As both would be dangerous, neither would have been undertaken without divination. As often in the *Zhouyi*, context is too slight to determine the correct meaning with any certainty.

"Neither decreasing nor increasing," is a set phrase, something like English, "Neither here not there," or French, "*Comme ci, comme ça.*" It remains a common phrase in modern Chinese.

41.3 On its face, this is a rather odd phrase, given that walking in a group of three does not predispose to losing one, nor does a solitary person necessarily gain a friend. It might be a numerological prognostication—under the circumstances divined about, it would be better to walk alone than in a group of three. There is a somewhat similar phrase in the *Lunyu*, that when three walk together one will be the teacher, meaning that people should always be learning from each other. It is a familiar phrase in modern Chinese. Alternatively, the phrase in the *Zhouyi* might be an ancient version of the proverb, "Two's company but three's a crowd." That is, three are likely to quarrel, while being by oneself invites others to befriend you.

41.4 This is a straightforward suggestion that could be uttered today, "If someone is ill, cheer him or her up." Such references to being kind to others are infrequent in the *Zhouyi*. Norman Cousins, editor of the once prestigious *Saturday Review*, was widely hailed as an innovator when he published a book claiming to have cured his illness (probably a form of arthritis) by reading humorous books to make himself laugh. The idea that happiness is good for health is an ancient one.

41.5 This is usually translated as meaning that ten cowry shells are traded for a tortoise shell. At least to me this does not seem like a good deal. Most oracle bones are ox scapulae rather than tortoise plastrons because the latter were rare and expensive—at times the tortoise population became severely depleted because of use for plastromancy, and perhaps for longevity soup as well. It seems that the owner of the tortoise shell could not refuse the offer, presumably because the exchange was with the king or another powerful person. Later Chinese history has numerous examples of emperors who "borrowed" items, such as valuable calligraphy or paintings. These were, of course, never returned.

41.6 A servant with a family would mean more hands to do the work, but also more mouths to feed.

42. 益 *Yi* Advantage (Increase)

The Judgment:

42.0 Beneficial if having to go somewhere.
Beneficial to ford the great river.
利有攸往. 利涉大川.

The Line Texts:

42.1 Beneficial to act in major undertakings.
Begins auspiciously, nothing blameworthy.
初九利用為大作. 元吉, 无咎.

42.2 Perhaps advantageous—ten cowry shells for a tortoise.
Cannot overcome or avoid.
Long-lasting auspicious divination.
The king uses for an offering to *Di* (the high god), auspicious.
六二或益之十朋之龜. 弗克違. 永貞吉. 王用享于帝,吉.

42.3 Advantageously used for an ominous affair.
Nothing blameworthy.
Hold the captives in the center while marching.
Report to the duke using a jade tablet.
六三益之用凶事. 无咎. 有孚中行. 告公用圭.

42.4 March in the center, and report to the duke obediently.
Beneficial, serving to move the capital city.
六四中行, 告公從. 利為依遷國.

42.5 Holding captives, kind-heartedly. Do not put to questioning.
Begins auspiciously.
Holding captives kindly, shows our power.
九五有孚惠心. 勿問. 元吉. 有孚惠我德.

42.6 Nothing advantageous, perhaps attacked, be resolute of heart.
Do not persist when ominous.
上九莫益之. 或擊之立心. 勿恆凶.

42. Commentary 益 *Yi* Advantage

Wilhelm-Baynes translate the tag as Increase to make it an antonym
of 41 Decrease, but this is an approximation, not strictly correct.
No doubt this was done because the hexagrams are inversions of
each other. In the Mawangdui version, the two hexagrams are not
juxtaposed; 41 and 42 are 12 and 64 respectively, though the tags
are the same.

42.0 The first two lines are set phrase prognostications, whose
metaphorical meanings are straightforward. Favorable to see the
great person reminds us that approaching someone powerful at
the wrong time can be hazardous and with a despotic ruler, even
fatal. Even now, when asking for a favor, most are conscious of
the mood of boss, parent, even spouse. Favorable to cross the
wide river is a metaphor for any difficult or potentially hazardous
undertaking, as well as for present day international travel. (As an
example, I did a divination demonstration as part of a program
on the *I Ching* and obtained the negative of this—not favorable to
cross the great water. It turned out that the inquirer's fiancé wanted
her to move to China but she did not want to. I do not know what
she finally decided but in this simple example we can see how this
sort of general statement can resonate with the inquirer. I make
no claims of supernatural talent but find such demonstrations
useful to show what the experience of divination with the *Changes*
is like.)

42.2 The first phrase repeats 41.5. The final phrase refers to *Di* 帝
or *Shangdi* 上帝, a deity who was worshipped in the Shang; this

practice carried over into the Zhou, but is not referred to elsewhere in the *Zhouyi*. Missionaries of some denominations, trying to find an analogue of monotheism in Chinese religion, claimed that *Di* actually referred to the Judeo-Christian creator God. This was used to claim that ancient China had Christian-like religious ideas that had degenerated into polytheism. We know relatively little about worship of *Shangdi*, but there is no basis for assuming monotheism in early China. *Tian* 天, Heaven, came to replace *Shangdi* in the Zhou and later. Both were transcendent, impersonal entities.

42.3 and 42.4 Walking in the center probably had ritual significance. Presumably what was reported to the duke was the capture of prisoners or their sacrifice.

Capitals were moved in the Shang and many times in later Chinese history.

42.5 It is unusual for the *Zhouyi* to recommend being compassionate to captives. I have taken this line text to mean that one can be kind to captives, and still use them to display one's power. However, it is not certain that compassion to captives is here recommended. Indeed, *de* here could mean potency as a result of carrying out the sacrifice, which might involve removal and display of the hearts. Despite the harshness of Western Zhou life as represented in the *Changes*, we should not conclude that the era was entirely without compassion.

Though human sacrifice did not cease with the defeat of the Shang, it did gradually diminish. Tracing the history of this gruesome practice is difficult as most texts refer to blood sacrifice tangentially if at all.

42.6 This seems to be advice that when circumstances are unfavorable, one should be strong, but abstain from doing what is hazardous. For quite different readings see Kunst (323) and Rutt (265, 324) who take it to be a reference to a ritual to fix one's luck. This is plausible, but unprovable. Hence I have stayed with what seems to me to be the literal meaning.

43. 夬 *Guai* Determination (Breakthrough; Resoluteness)

The Judgment:

43.0 Displayed in the king's courtyard, the captives wail at this harshness.
Get out the word in one's own county that it is not beneficial to go to battle.
Beneficial if having to go somewhere.
揚于王庭, 孚號有厲. 告自邑不利即戎. 利有攸往.

The Line Texts:

43.1 Sturdily forward on foot, yet going is unbearable, becoming shameful.
初九壯于前趾, 往不勝為咎.

43.2 Alarmed by wailing. Nothing but night-time military actions.
Do not worry.
九二惕號. 莫夜有戎. 勿恤.

43.3 Sturdy cheekbones—will be ominous.
The upright person very determinedly walks alone, though caught in the rain.
If drenched, irritated but nothing blameworthy.
九三壯于頄—有凶. 君子夬夬獨行, 遇雨. 若濡,有慍无咎.

43.4 The buttocks have no skin; he walks with difficulty.
Leading a sheep, but regrets that it runs away.
Words are heard, but not believed.
九四臀无膚; 其行次且. 牽羊悔亡. 聞言不信.

43.5 A wild goat very determinedly runs through the middle. There
will be no blame.
九五莧陸夬夬中行, 无咎.

43.6 There is no wailing—ends ominously.
上六无號—終有凶.

43. Commentary 夬 *Guai* Determination

Resoluteness seems too abstract a character trait for the Western
Zhou, hence I have substituted "determination." The tag can,
though with some strain, be applied to all the lines except 43.6.

43.0 This consists of a standard reference to captives, followed by
a line of advice and a prognostication.

43.1 One of many references to traveling by foot. There have been
two ways to translate this first line. Kunst, Rutt, and Shaughnessy
(201) translate to the effect that the foot is injured, consistent
with the second phrase. The first phrase, however, seems to mean
stepping forward vigorously, as rendered by Wilhelm-Baynes. Read
either way, the overall meaning clearly indicates a problem with
walking.

43.2 Night-time military actions would be worrisome unless
one's own side is defeating an enemy whose soldiers are the ones
wailing. The last phrase might mean not to have pity rather than
not be disturbed or anxious. It could be read differently by different
readers.

43.3 "Sturdy cheekbones—will be ominous." Some have taken
this as meaning injury to the cheekbone. Although Wang Bi took
this phrase to be a visual reference to the top *yin* line (Lynn: 407),

it must instead have been yet another reference to divination by physiognomy. In such systems facial features have a prognostic whose significance can be deciphered by those learned in their interpretations. Similar systems exist in many cultures. The basis for associating specific features to good and bad fortune is rarely self-evident. China has many systems of divining from body attributes, including breast shape. Folk practices of this sort undoubtedly existed in the Western Zhou but most have left no written record. The notion that high cheekbones are dangerous persists in present-day China, supposedly because they are knife-like.

The rest of this line text seems to be a statement about character. The upright person walks through the rain and, though naturally irritated, does nothing shameful. As with later Confucian ethics, virtue is here described as how the upright behave, rather than as abstract principles.

43.4 The lack of skin on the buttocks might be due to a beating or an abrasion, such as would occur with sliding down a hill. Or perhaps it is a simile: walking as if no skin on his backside. Rutt relates this to sacrificial victims—perhaps they were beaten before being beheaded.

I chose to let the sheep run away as without doubt they were being led to sacrifice. However, it could be that leading the sheep was a gesture of humility, as recounted in the *Zuozhuan* (Rutt: 335f.).

Words heard but not believed has the sound of a set phrase and describes a situation as common today as it likely was in the Bronze Age.

43.5 This and the preceding line almost certainly refer to sacrificial animals escaping. The final phrase means the person responsible for the escape will not be blamed.

43.6 Rutt notes that Gao Heng proposed that 无 *wu* was a homophone for "dog," whose howling would have been a bad omen. However, 號 *hao* wailing commonly appears in phrases describing captives about to be sacrificed. The screaming of victims was, at least in some circumstances, necessary for the efficacy of the sacrifice. Hence lack of wailing would be ominous.

44. 姤 *Gou* Meeting (Coming to Meet)

The Judgment:

44.0 Though the woman is robust, do not choose this woman.
女壯, 勿用取女.

The Line Texts:

44.1 Tied to a bronze spindle, divination auspicious.
If having to go somewhere, ominous observation.
A weak pig can be captured as it paces back and forth.
初六繫于金柅, 貞吉. 有攸往, 見凶. 羸豕孚蹢躅.

44.2 The sack holds fish.
Nothing blameworthy, but not beneficial for guests.
九二包有魚. 无咎, 不利賓.

44.3 His buttocks have no skin. He walks with difficulty, harshly.
No great blame.
九三臀无膚, 其行次且, 厲. 无大咎.

44.4 The sack holds no fish. Get up! It's ominous!
九四包无魚. 起! 凶.

44.5 Use purple willow to wrap the melon.
Hold in the mouth the jade seal that has fallen from the sky.
九五以杞包瓜. 含章有隕自天.

44.6 They meet with horns.
Shame, not blame.
上九姤其角. 吝, 无咎.

44. Commentary 姤 *Gou* Meeting

Gou 姤 can refer to "meeting" in the usual sense but also to sexual intercourse. With the notable exception of hexagram 18 *Gu*, the *Zhouyi* contains few obvious references to sexual acts, in contrast to the *Shijing* 诗经 and *Chu Ci* 楚辞 (*Songs of Chu* or *Songs of the South*.) The line texts contain nothing sexual. The buttocks in 44.3 without skin have no conceivable erotic implication.

44.0 This may be the most misunderstood line in the entire *I Ching*, having been translated as meaning that *because* the woman is strong, she should not be taken as a wife (or concubine, or servant), implying that a woman who is not suitably submissive is to be avoided. Several notable translators have perpetuated this mistranslation (Legge: 187; Wilhelm-Baynes: 171; Whincup: 148). As I have explained at length elsewhere (Redmond and Hon 2014: 82f.) the Chinese phrase simply says "the woman is strong, do not choose her." In traditional China, life expectancy for women was only into the mid-twenties and death in childbirth was frequent, making health a major factor in suitability for marriage. In addition, food preparation and housework were physically challenging, making robust or strong women desirable as members of the household. Thus the line means not to choose her, *even though* she is strong.

The disapproval of feminine strength was added by later commentators, notably Wang Bi, who projected his own misogyny onto the *Zhouyi* (Lynn: 410f.).Wilhelm-Baynes followed this tradition by rendering the line as "The maiden is powerful. One should not marry such a maiden" (171).This was also read into the hexagram figure, which consists of one *yin* line at the base with the other five being *yang* lines, as if the female principle is furtively sneaking back. While the *Zhouyi* can hardly be claimed to advocate female equality, any misogyny supposedly found in it was the creation of later interpreters (see Redmond and Hon 2014: 72–91).

44.1 The first phrase probably refers to a tied-up animal. The next phrase refers to seeing a bad omen while traveling. Omens were not simply warnings: they could cause the bad luck they implied. The pacing of the pig may indicate agitation. Farm animals often can tell they are about to be slaughtered by the sounds of other animals and the smell of blood.

44.2 A bag with fish. It would seem that there is nothing wrong with the fish but that they are not of adequate quality to serve guests.

44.3 This reprises 43.4.

44.4 It is not surprising that picking up a bag with fish is lucky while picking up one without fish is not. Fish symbolize abundance, so this line is akin to, "The cupboard was bare" in English.

44.5 The second phrase has been translated in quite diverse ways. I believe mine makes the most sense, but as so often with the *Zhouyi*, that a translation makes sense does not prove it is correct. In any case, the line clearly refers to ritual use of jade.

44.6 This likely refers to rams butting each other, but is perhaps a *double entendre* also meaning sexual intercourse. If so, the final phrase means that it was shameful but that they get away with it.

45. 萃 *Cui* Assembling
(Gathering Together; Massing)

The Judgment:

45.0 For the offering, the king uses the ancestral temple.
Beneficial to see the important person.
Offering for a beneficial divination, using a large animal is auspicious.
Favorable if having to go somewhere.
亨王假有廟. 利見大人. 亨利貞, 用大牲吉. 利有攸往.

The Line Texts:

45.1 Holding of captives has not ended. Now disorderly, then assembled.
Wailing when grabbed by a hand, then tittering.
Do not sorrow, going will not be blamed.
初六有孚不終. 乃亂乃萃. 若號一握為笑. 勿恤, 往无咎.

45.2 Drawn out auspiciousness.
Nothing blameworthy.
Thus beneficial to use captives for the *Yue* summer sacrifice.
六二引吉. 无咎. 孚乃利用禴.

45.3 Assembling, lamenting.
Not beneficial to go somewhere.
No blame, but slight shame.
六三萃如嗟如. 无攸利. 无咎, 小吝.

45.4 Greatly auspicious; nothing blameworthy.
九四大吉; 无咎.

45.5 Assembled into position. Nothing blameworthy.
Brigands captured.
Begin the divination for the long term—regret is gone.
九五萃有位; 无咎. 匪孚. 元永貞—悔亡.

45.6 Sighing, lamenting, moaning, tears and snuffling.
There will be no blame.
上六齎咨涕洟. 无咎.

45. Commentary 萃 *Cui* Assembling

As most of this hexagram is about sacrifice, the tag could refer to
people gathering for this event. Field substitutes the homophone
瘁 *cui* meaning suffer (2015), which he suggests is supported by
the Mawangdui tag being 卒 *zu* finish or die (Shaughnessy 1997:
122f.). Suffering certainly describes the content of this hexagram,
with its wretched captives about to be sacrificed.

45.0 This describes the offering of a large animal, presumably an
ox, in sacrifice by or for the king. The most important way a ruler
provided for the well-being of his subjects was by correct ritual
performance. This was also required for credibility and thus for
maintenance of power. The Zhou overthrow of the Shang was
justified not only because of King Zhou Xin's cruelty, but also
because he did not carry out the rituals properly (Redmond and
Hon: 57–62). Ritual remains relevant to effective government.
To pick an instance not long before the present writing, President
Obama was widely criticized on social media for an official
appearance at which he wore a tan suit rather than a dark one. We
still expect ritual correctness from those in government, but the
rules are unwritten.

45.1 I have translated 勿恤 *wu xu* as "do not sorrow" rather than
"do not pity" as I do not find much evidence of the latter emotion
in the *Zhouyi*. Yet my translation here of "no sorrow," still leaves

the possibility of some sympathy while observing a sacrifice. No doubt pity was not the proper emotion at such occasions, yet we should not assume it was not felt, simply because it was not mentioned. Wailing and tittering seems to be a stock description of the vocalizations of victims about to be sacrificed. Alternatively, it could be the victims wailing and the captors laughing, but we have very little mention of captors' feelings about the killing. Laughter is possible however as taunting has been common at public executions.

45.2 *Yin* 引 is based on a pictograph of a bow and means drawn out. The *Yue* summer sacrifice is also mentioned in 46.2 and 63.5 (Rutt: 337). This phrase is an explicit statement of the belief that killing captives is beneficial for the state. Given the many lines recommending sacrifices, one wonders if there were ever situations for which they were not recommended, or when a particular form of sacrifice would not be welcomed by the presumed recipient. Given that Confucian exegesis of the *Changes* censored references to sacrifice, there was awareness on some level that it was wrong. No doubt this is why the practice was gradually abandoned, but how this came about we do not know. We have no record of anything like the modern-day activism against the death penalty. Public protests in early times were mainly due to famine or other hardships. It was high officials who were able to influence king or emperor.

45.4 "Greatly auspicious, nothing blameworthy." Phrases like this seem redundant but can be simply emphatic or, more likely, a divination akin to a spell, in effect "May everything be greatly auspicious and incur no blame to make the prognostication come true."

45.5 *Fei* 匪 here makes most sense as brigand. A less likely alternative would be, "not blameworthy that there are no captives."

45.6 This is a particularly vivid description of the misery of those about to be sacrificed. In such instances it is hard to imagine "there will be no blame" being anything other than a charm to avert blame. Even if they believed that sacrifice was necessary, bystanders at such events must have felt intense emotional agitation

and worry that their turn might come. Fear-averting procedures are
major components of magical systems: verbal formulae, talismans
(carried or eaten), amulets, relics, images of protective deities and
the like.

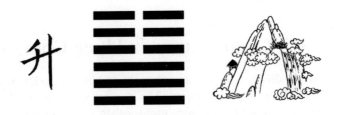

46. 升 *Sheng* Going Up
(Pushing Upward)

The Judgment:

46.0 Begin the offering.
Useful to see the important person.
Do not worry, for the southern campaign, auspicious.
元亨. 用見大人. 勿恤, 南征吉.

The Line Texts:

46.1 Truly goes up, greatly auspicious.
初六允升, 大吉.

46.2 Captives are beneficial to use for *Yue* sacrifice.
Nothing blameworthy.
孚乃利用禴. 无咎.

46.3 Going up to the empty city.
九三升虛邑.

46.4 The king carries out an offering at Qi Mountain. Auspicious;
there will be no blame.
六四王用亨于岐山. 吉, 无咎.

46.5 Divination auspicious for going up steps.
六五貞吉升階.

46.6 Going up in the dark, it is beneficial not to stop to divine.
上六冥升, 利于不息之貞.

46. Commentary 升 *Sheng* Going Up

The tag simply means rising. The tag is related to the line texts as all but 46.2 are about going up. The chapter would be easily applied to responding to divinatory inquiries since going up is a virtually daily activity. In itself, this chapter is banal. Decisions about going up steps do not seem momentous, even in an enchanted world.

46.0 Do not worry is a recurring set phrase. Seeing an important person, undertaking a journey, marching against an enemy would all be anxious undertakings. A positive prognosis and a spell to bring about a positive outcome would be frequently useful.

46.3 This might be a reference to 空城計 the "empty fortress or city stratagem," number 32 of the well-known *Thirty-six Stratagems*. In this maneuver, those in the besieged city act deceptively calm, misleading the enemy to suspect a trap. If the line is an allusion to this stratagem, we need not assume that the *Zhouyi* compiler knew the specific text, or that it even existed in written form at the time, simply that the phrase was in use. However, the *Thirty-six Stratagems* seems a more advanced text than the *Zhouyi* as it offers specific tactical advice rather than simple prognostications of auspicious or ominous.

46.4 In context, "there will be no blame" has the implication that the ritual was properly performed.

46.6 This sounds like a proverb—when in a potentially hazardous place, keep moving. It suggests postponing divination when in exigent circumstances, and that in urgent circumstances even divination is best postponed. This is of interest because it indicates that even in the enchanted Western Zhou, common sense could prevail over supernatural beliefs.

47. 困 *Kun* Obstruction
(Oppression; Exhaustion)

The Judgment:

47.0 Make offering, the divination for the important person is auspicious.
Nothing blameworthy.
There is talk, but not trusted.
亨, 貞大人吉. 无咎. 有言不信.

The Line Texts:

47.1 Buttocks obstructed by stumps and trees while entering into a deep and secluded valley.
Then three years no face-to-face meeting.
初六臀困于株木, 入于幽谷. 三歲不覿.

47.2 Obstructed from food and drink.
A vermillion ceremonial garment with seal arrives from a beneficial direction—is to be used for offering a sacrifice.
Going on an expedition,—ominous, but not blameworthy.
九二困于酒食. 朱紱方來利—用享祀. 征—凶, 征凶无咎.

47.3 Obstructed by rocks, grasp at brambles.
Entering into his house, he does not see his wife, ominous.
六三困于石, 據于蒺藜. 入于其宮, 不見其妻, 凶.

47.4 Coming, slowly, slowly. Obstructed in his bronze chariot. Regrets have ended.
九四來徐徐. 困于金車. 吝有終.

47.5 Cutting off the nose and feet is obstructed by one wearing vermillion, then calmly makes his statement.
Beneficial to use for sacrificing to ancestors.
九五劓刖. 困于赤紱, 乃徐有說. 利用祭祀.

47.6 Obstructed by creeping vines, worried and unsteady
Says: moving regretted, has repented—expedition auspicious.
上六困于葛藟, 臲卼. 曰動悔有悔, 征吉.

47. Commentary 困 *Kun* Obstruction

The theme of obstruction is carried out in all the line texts, which share the general theme of facing oppressive circumstances that interfere with one's activities. The references to rocks and brambles were likely proverbial ways of referring to difficulties, equivalent to our, "Between a rock and a hard place." The image would be particularly meaningful during a time when traveling was often along footpaths or narrow dirt roads that would often have been overgrown.

47.0 This repeats by now familiar stock phrases. Words not being trusted is the same phrase as 43.4, but which I have translated slightly differently as, "there are words but not believed."

47.1 Instead of *tun* 臀 (buttocks), the Mawangdui silk manuscript has a homophone 脣 *chun*, meaning lips or labia (Shaughnessy 1996: 310). Given that the received text refers to buttocks and a deep valley, there is almost certainly an erotic implication here. It could plausibly refer to sexual intercourse in a wooded area—no doubt a common place for such encounters, given the general lack of privacy. "Three years" could refer to an interval of reclusion, perhaps because of a political falling-out or the mourning period for parents. Given the sexual reference, separation from the loved one seems equally plausible—this being a universal poetic theme.

47.2 No food or drink might be a period of required fasting.
Zhu fu 朱紱 is a garment for ritual use for sacrifice performed in a specific direction (Rutt: 228f.). Directionality of sacrifice may have been based on belief as to where the ancestor or deity was thought to be located.

47.3 Obstructed by rocks—grasp at brambles.
This seems to be a proverb, that when prevented from accomplishing something, choose another way, however unpleasant—the lesser evil in effect. Not seeing his wife is likely an omen of bad luck rather than a reference to a marriage problem. However, given the oppressiveness of many women's lives, it could be that she has run away. No doubt many women of households did flee oppressive circumstances but many would likely be forced to return, not having any means to survive on their own.

47.4 A bronze-covered chariot would have been a sign of great wealth. It is tempting to take this as a proverb to the effect that even the wealthy can be blocked from their goals.

47.5 The vermillion ceremonial garment was previously mentioned in 47.2 I have taken it to be a metonymy for an official. My translation to the effect that the official stops the mutilating punishment is perhaps wishful thinking on my part.

47.6 The first phrase shares with 47.1 and 47.3 the theme of being hindered by vegetation and terrain. *Yue* 曰 appears also in 26.3. There is much speculation about its meaning (Bernardo 2012: 259f.). Of interest, this is the character throughout the *Lunyu* that introduces utterances by Confucius: "*Zi yue*," the Master said. However, there is no notion of an authoritative speaker or "master" in the *Zhouyi*, though the phrase is found in the *Ten Wing*-like appendices of the Mawangdui *I Ching* and in many other Chinese classics (Shaughnessy 1996: 126 *et passim*).

48. 井 *Jing* The Well (The Well)

The Judgment:

48.0 Can change the city; cannot change the well.
There is no loss; there is no gain.
Coming and going, to and from the well.
The well is almost dried up; when they arrive does not have a well-rope and its jar is worn out. Ominous.
改邑; 不改井. 无喪无得. 往來井. 井汔至亦未繘. 羸其瓶. 凶.

The Line Texts:

48.1 The well is muddy, not drinkable.
By the old well there are no birds and beasts.
初六井泥, 不食. 舊井无禽.

48.2 The well in the valley—shooting carp with arrows.
The earthenware jar is worn out and drips.
九二井谷射鮒. 甕敝漏.

48.3 The well has been drained. It cannot serve for drinking; our hearts are saddened.
Can be used to draw water.
The luminous king moreover grants his favor.
九三井渫不食。為我心惻。可用汲。王明。並受其福.

48.4 The well is lined with bricks. There will be no blame.
六四井甃. 无咎.

48.5 The well is cold, a frigid spring for drinking.
九五井冽, 寒泉食.

48.6 To draw from the well, it must not be covered.
Holding captives, begins auspiciously.
上六井收勿幕. 有孚元吉.

48. Commentary 井 *Jing* The Well

Since water is essential to life, wells were of great importance. The abundance and purity of their water would have been of great concern. The line texts of this chapter are various statements about wells.

48.0 This is a proverb, still in use among Chinese in somewhat different form, "Depart your village, leave your well," implying leaving one's village is to leave the source of one's life. Here in the *Zhouyi*, it seems also to refer to the fact that a city, which is entirely a human construction, can be moved almost anywhere, but a well cannot, as it depends on finding the water table. Consequently, availability of water would have been a major prerequisite for locating towns.

Here the set phrase of no loss; no gain seems to have a specific concrete reference—the level of water in a well remains constant, no matter how much is drawn out.

Yi 亦 is also the eighth earthly branch, associated with early afternoon and with the sheep in the so-called animal zodiac, but does not seem to have these meanings in context. Such references to time would have been apparent to diviners, but we do not know what role they played in the divination. Considerable work has been done regarding later Chinese hemerology, the branch of divination intended to determine timing of events (Kalinowski 2003: 213–99).

48.1 Wells must often have been contaminated with animal and human feces that would have been washed in by rain, bringing bacteria and parasite larvae. Though there was no germ theory of disease, it would have been known that bad water was dangerous.

Animals deserting a well could mean that it was dried up or grossly contaminated so as to make the water unpotable. While disease would have spread rapidly when a contaminated well was used by an entire village, tainted water would not necessarily have been recognized as the cause. Muddy water need not be infected and infected water can be perfectly clear.

48.2 Shooting fish in a well seems odd. Perhaps the well was used to keep the fish alive until it was time to cook them. The Mawangdui silk manuscript has different characters meaning "worn out fish trap" (Shaughnessy 1997: 299 n.8).This suggests that the fish were shot because the trap was not working.

48.3 Literally 明 *ming* means luminous or bright. In context it likely praises the ritual power of the king and the power of his favor. Given that royal rituals were essential to maintaining society, perhaps here the king was expected to use his supernatural charisma to improve the condition of the well or to locate another.

48.4 Water in a brick-lined well would presumably be less likely to be muddy. The formula, "there will be no blame" might mean that the earth spirits were not disturbed by the construction of the brick lining.

48.5 The well water is pleasant to drink.

48.6 This possibly refers to sacrificing captives so the well would provide enough water. In many agricultural societies, human sacrifice was considered necessary to maintain the earth's bounty.

49. 革 *Ge* Tanning Leather (Revolution; Moulting)

The Judgment:

49.0 On a *si* day, sacrifice captives.
Begin with an offering, beneficial to divine.
Regrets go away.
巳日乃孚. 元亨利貞. 悔亡.

The Line Texts:

49.1 Tie up using the tanned hide of a yellow cow.
初九鞏用黃牛之革.

49.2 On a *si* (sacrifice) day, then tanned hide.
For an expedition, auspicious, nothing blameworthy.
六二巳日乃革之. 征吉, 无咎.

49.3 For an expedition, ominous, divination harsh.
Binding with leather, speak three times while approaching the captives.
九三征凶貞厲。革言三就有孚.

49.4 Regret goes away.
Holding captives.
Changing orders, auspicious.
九四悔亡. 有孚. 改命吉.

49.5 The great person undergoes a tiger change.
Before, prognosticates about the captives.
九五大人虎變. 未占有孚.

49.6 The upright person undergoes a leopard change.
The petty person changes his face.
For an expedition, ominous.
For a home, divination auspicious.
上六君子豹變. 小人革面. 征凶. 居貞吉.

49. Commentary 革 *Ge* Tanning Leather

The tag for this hexagram is usually translated into English as "Revolution" (Hacker 1993: 56; Whincup: 162; Wilhelm-Baynes: 189). This is problematic on several grounds. First, the early meaning of the phrase was definitely tanning leather, and by analogy, change, because the tanning process transforms raw animal skin into leather. The Mawangdui manuscript has 勒 *le* specifically meaning "bridle," obviously related to the early meaning of "leather" (Shaughnessy 1997: 129, 311).

Most important, considering the eventual canonical status of the *Changes*, no ruler would endorse a divinatory system that might recommend his overthrow. Nor would the Confucians whose power, and even survival, depended on their being trusted by the emperor. In the Confucian ideology, there was no place for rebellion; if their admonitions to the emperor went unheeded, they were to withdraw from government, not rebel against it. As Confucius said of the sage:

> When the Way prevails in the world; he appears; when the Way is lacking, he retires. (*Lunyu* 8.13, in Watson 2007: 56)

This ideology did not, of course, prevent rebellions, but Confucianism did not provide their ideological justification. They might of course decide that a new regime had the mandate of heaven in order to be employed by it.

49.0 As usual, events begin with a human sacrifice. Somehow it has been determined that this should be done on a *si* day, the sixth of the earthly branches used in the sixty-day calendrical system. That this is followed by the standard four-character invocation raises the question of how often *Zhouyi* divinations were preceded by such sacrifices. It seems unlikely to have been the routine practice because the classic lent itself to getting quick answers without a major effort. Nor do we have any textual evidence for sacrifices as part of *Zhouyi* procedures. Such is not mentioned in the *Zuozhuan Changes* divination anecdotes.

49.1 and 49.2 This must mean that the prisoners are to be bound with tanned hide.

49.3 The second phrase likely refers to a ritual recitation to precede the sacrifice.

49.5 and 49.6 The phrases "tiger change" and "leopard change" have baffled many readers. Note that the word for change here is not the hexagram tag 革 *ge*, nor 易 *yi* as in *Zhouyi* or *I Ching*, but an entirely different word 變 *bian*. This can refer to a transformation, particularly the seasonal change of an animal's coat. Tiger change and leopard change make sense if regarded as shamanic. Men in high positions could enhance their charisma by shamanic activities involving imitating animals. In context here, this means the important person and upright person would take on the mythical attributes of the tiger and leopard, though we are not told what these attributes are. Some have translated the phrases as referring to wearing the hides of the animals. This is possible, especially given that many phrases in this hexagram refer to animal skins, but still leaves the significance obscure. Shamanism was widely practiced in early China and later, though despised by many Confucians. Their official disapproval did not necessarily mean that they did not occasionally avail themselves of the services of shamans. Zhu Xi 朱熹 (1130–1200) for example, the main progenitor of the Neo-Confucian orthodoxy that lasted until the fall of the Qing, had high regard for shamanism (Sukhu 2012: 76 *et passim*).

49.6 That the petty person only changes his face seems to be saying that the upright person (or prince) can make a basic change in himself, while the unimportant one can only change his facial expression. The implication is similar to the modern phrase, "two-faced."

50. 鼎 *Ding* The Bronze Cauldron (Cauldron)

The Judgment:

50.0 Begin with an auspicious offering.
元吉亨.

The Line Texts:

50.1 The cauldron topples over—beneficial for releasing the bad.
To obtain a concubine for her son. Not blameworthy.
初六鼎顛趾—利出否. 得妾以其子. 无咎.

50.2 The cauldron has been filled.
Our foes having fallen ill, they cannot approach us. Auspicious.
九二鼎有實. 我仇有疾, 不我能即. 吉.

50.3 Cauldron ears with leather straps for carrying.
Though crammed with fat meat of the pheasant, it is not eaten.
In the area the rain is diminished—regretted, but ends auspiciously.
九三鼎耳革其行. 塞雉膏不食. 方雨虧—悔, 終吉.

50.4 The cauldron's leg breaks, overturning the duke's stew. His
severe punishment—executed inside. Ominous.
九四鼎折足, 覆公餗. 其形渥, 凶.

50.5 A yellow cauldron, hooked by its bronze ears. Divination beneficial.

六五鼎黃耳金鉉. 貞利.

50.6 Cauldron lifted with jade hooks. Greatly auspicious. Nothing not beneficial.

上九鼎玉鉉. 大吉. 无不利.

50. Commentary 鼎 *Ding* The Bronze Cauldron

A *ding* 鼎 is a three-legged ancient bronze vessel, shaped like the picture above. The basic shape has great aesthetic appeal and had many subsequent imitations, particularly during the Song Dynasty. So many of these vessels were made that they are to be found in virtually any museum with a Chinese collection. They were used for ritual food preparations and often had inscriptions commemorating an important event, such as enfeoffment of a noble. (Regarding inscriptions, see Shaughnessy [1991]. For some beautifully photographed examples, see National Palace Museum [2001].)

The character 鼎, which is identical in the Mawangdui manuscript, is pictographic and the hexagram itself can also be imagined to resemble the bronze vessel with the divided line at the base representing the legs and the divided line at position 5, the handles. One can infer that this hexagram was selected to represent the *ding* theme, but we actually have no direct evidence of how each hexagram came to be associated with specific sets of texts.

50.0 A variant invocation; presumably the offering is to be made with the *ding*.

50.1 This may be based on the notion that minor mishaps can avert worse bad luck.

Qie 妾, which I have translated as concubine, in the oracle bone inscriptions can refer to a female sacrificial victim. In contrast to these centuries-earlier texts, the *Zhouyi* does not specify the gender of victims except for the horse in 2.0. Most are

孚 *fu*, captives—presumably male soldiers of a defeated enemy. Usually, though not always, victims were selected from outside the sacrificers' own tribe or society. Women and children were also sacrificed, but our knowledge of the details of human sacrifice is largely based on archaeology rather than textual evidence, so we know little about how victims were selected. There is no indication of sacrifice of women and children in the *Zhouyi*.

Here and in the only other use of the character, in 33.3, the meaning is clearly servant or concubine. A common reason for taking an additional wife was failure of the first to produce a son. This was virtually always assumed to be the fault of the woman. With no knowledge of the physiology of reproduction, other than the need for fertilization by the male, explanations were arbitrary, curses being a frequent supposed reason for barrenness.

Examples of following-in-death, that is wives, servants, and others being buried with the deceased, are known as late as the Ming Dynasty. The episode of Iphigenia in the *Iliad* is a well-known literary example of human sacrifice, and tells us that such was not necessarily a happy occasion for anyone involved; rather it was thought necessary. Only recently have scholars of early culture been willing to give this practice due attention. For a useful survey, see Bremmer (2007).

50.2 我 *wo*, the first person pronoun, appears only eleven times in the *Zhouyi*. More often, as in modern Chinese, subjects of sentences were understood rather than stated. Chinese pronouns do not have different forms to distinguish between singular and plural. In this case where there is a military implication, the foes have been soldiers in the opposing army, so the plural fits better.

50.3 This line text has attracted very diverse interpretations, though its meaning seems to be clear enough. Pheasants have been hunted throughout Chinese history to the present day. That the fatty meat is not eaten is likely a negative omen, much like the animal not bleeding when stabbed. High fat content was considered desirable in meat until quite recently. Diminished rain, like the pheasant fat not eaten, suggests a state of scarcity.

50.4 This line recounts a disturbing anecdote, one often expurgated in both Confucian exegesis and Western language translations. The setting is a ritual meal during which one of the three legs of the ding tripod breaks, spilling the duke's meal on him. Wilhelm-Baynes translate, "The prince's meal is spilled. / And his person is soiled." Kunst, based on careful analysis of possible character variants, takes 形 *xing* to mean execution or other severe punishment and translates 形渥 *xing wo* as, "execution in chamber" (433–5). This is yet another instance of the arbitrary violence of early China. Given the great importance placed on proper ritual observance for the well-being of the ruler and the country as a whole, any error could be regarded as a serious breach. An alternative explanation is that the spilling was a pretext for the duke to rid himself of an enemy, as described in another famous anecdote in which a general is executed for being late to a meeting with the king. Kunst further notes that to be executed privately rather than in the marketplace was a "privilege" of nobility. This can be likened to the "right" of English nobility to be beheaded in the Tower of London, rather than publicly hanged like common thieves.

50.5 and 50.6 The cauldron would have been placed over a fire and so would be too hot to be grasped by its handles. Instead a special hook was used, or a rod passed through the handles on both sides. The cauldron is yellow, the original color of bronze before it develops the patina that we see on museum pieces.

51. 震 *Zhen* Thunder
(The Arousing; Shock, Thunder)

The Judgment:

51.0 Make offering. Thunder comes—frightening, frightening.
Laughing, chattering, ha ha ha.
Thunder shocks for a hundred *li*.
No spooning of the sacrificial wine.
亨. 震來, 虩虩. 笑言啞啞. 震驚百里. 不比鬯.

The Line Texts:

51.1 初九震來—虩, 虩. 後笑言啞啞.吉.
Thunder comes—terrifying, terrifying.
Afterwards, laughing, chattering, ha, ha, ha. Auspicious.

51.2 Thunder comes, harshly.
Many thousands of cowry shells for the funeral.
Ascend nine times to the burial mound.
Do not pursue, in seven days will be obtained.
六二震來, 厲. 億喪貝, 躋于九陵. 勿逐,七日得.

51.3 Thunder, frightening, frightening. Thunder, but in walking,
there will be no error.
六三震蘇蘇.震行无眚.

51.4 Thunder, then mud.
九四震遂泥.

51.5 Thunder, coming and going for a purpose.
No loss in having to attend to affairs.
六五震, 往來意. 无喪有事.

51.6 Thunder, trembling, trembling.
Look around, panicky, panicky.
For an expedition ominous.
Thunders not at oneself personally, at one's neighbor. There will
be no blame.
A marriage agreement is spoken about.
上六震, 索,索. 視矍矍. 征凶. 震不于其躬,于其鄰. 无咎. 婚媾有言.

51. Commentary 震 *Zhen* Thunder

Zhen 震 is the title of the trigram that is doubled up to form this
hexagram.

It is usually taken to mean thunder, though it can denote other
startling or shocking events, such as earthquakes. This hexagram
has an unusual number of repeated characters. Thunder is the first
word in each line text. In lines 51.0, 51.1, 51.3, and 51.6, thunder
is followed by one or two sets of doubled-up terms, all expressing
the alarm the thunder evokes. The repetition is for emphasis,
but also mimics the repetitive claps of thunder. Unique to this
hexagram are the emphatic expressions of emotion. Most emotion
mentioned in the *Zhouyi* is unhappy. Thunder, however, is not
truly harmful and so the tone here is basically silly; one wonders if
it derived from a mnemonic to teach vocabulary to children. It may
also be a collection of thunder-derived omens.

The tag in the Mawangdui text is *chen* 辰 (Shaughnessy 1997:
300). This is the lower component of the character in the received
version, so perhaps simply an abbreviation. *Chen* also refers to the
third month of the solar year when agricultural labor begins, to the
fifth earthly branch, 7 to 9 a.m., and to asterisms associated with
this season. Such may have been part of the now forgotten esoteric
hemerological system that I have postulated.

51.0 The laughter may be nervousness or, as Rutt suggests, a positive sign in that thunder was thought to induce ease in childbirth (343). However, even in a polygamous household, childbirth would have been infrequent and there is no direct reference to it here. The thunder is auspicious in 51.1, harmless in 51.3, but harmful in 51.5, indicating that as an omen it would be interpreted differently in different circumstances. A *li*, or "Chinese mile" is generally held to be about one-third of a Western mile, but the exact length varied over time. A hundred *li* in such statements is taken to be an approximation—"a long way."

Not spooning the wine might be to avoid spilling it if startled, or a ritual taboo against offering wine during a thunderstorm.

51.1 Here again, laughing is associated with fear, but seemingly in relief when it is realized that the loud noise is only harmless thunder. The final word of this line text is "auspicious," which seems paradoxical. Possibly the thunder is auspicious because of the relief when it is realized to be harmless. However, as so many times in the *Zhouyi*, the meanings of omens are counter-intuitive. Why this should be so is not entirely clear, except that the human brain is hard-wired to think in terms of opposites. Nor should we ignore the obvious fact that diviners, then as now, had to present their findings so as to please their clients. Giving a powerful person a bad reading could be hazardous to the health of the savant doing the divination.

51.2 *Bei* 貝 cowry shells were used as money. I have translated *yi* 億 as many thousands. Literally it meant 100,000, later 100 million, but such numbers simply meant a very large quantity. Finding, let alone carrying, so many shells is not plausible. *Sang* 喪 makes more sense as a funeral offering or payment for funeral expenses than something accidentally lost. The third phrase likely refers to climbing up a burial mound to offer the sacrifice, as in the Mawangdui version (Shaughnessy 1997: 87, 300). Rutt suggests that "nine" means "all" in this context, or to a place name (343). I have speculated that the tomb was visited nine times. In any case, the line indicates a ritual observance.

The final phrase is a set one, referring to return in the usual seven days without the need to pursue, as in 38.1, which advises that one's horse will return of its own accord. It seems unlikely to refer back to the cowry shells.

51.6 In the final phrase 婚媾 *hungou* makes the most sense as referring to a marriage agreement. By themselves, these characters mean intercourse within marriage. Clouds and rain was a euphemism for sexual activity and this might be the reason this phrase was included in the Thunder hexagram. Mawangdui has a phrase translated as "confused slander" (Shaughnessy 1997: 25f., 300). Perhaps this was a later allusion to its sexual implication. That marriage agreement and intercourse use the same terms remind us that in ancient times the most important reason for marriage, though not the sole one, was having children. Here as with other sexual references in the *Changes*, the standard English translations evade the direct meanings. This may have been due not only to Confucian prudery but also to that of the early missionary translators. To be fair however, Richard Rutt, though at first an Anglican missionary to Korea and much later a Roman Catholic priest, was the most forthright about these implications.

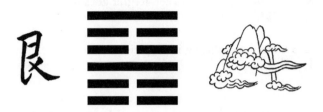

52. 艮 *Gen* Splitting
(Keeping Still, Mountain)

The Judgment:

52.0 Splitting its back, not getting into the body.
Goes walking in the courtyard, but does not see his men. Will not be blamed.
艮其背, 不獲其身. 行其庭不見其人. 无咎.

The Line Text:

52.1 Splitting the feet. There will be no blame. Long-term beneficial divination.
初六艮其趾. 无咎. 利永貞.

52.2 Splitting the calves.
Not lifting it up as usual.
Their hearts not at ease.
六二艮其腓. 不拯其隨. 其心不快.

52.3 Splitting the lower back. Breaking open the spine.
Harsh—the heart smokes.
九三艮其限. 列其夤厲. 熏心.

52.4 Splitting the trunk. There will be no blame.
六四艮其身. 无咎.

52.5 Splitting the jaws.
Words have the proper order. Regret goes away.
六五艮其輔. 言有序. 悔亡.

52.6 Complete splitting is auspicious.
上九敦艮吉.

52. Commentary 艮 *Gen* Splitting

This is an unusually interesting hexagram for what it reveals about the early *Zhouyi* in all its untidiness. In the received version and most commentaries *gen* 艮 is usually taken to mean mountain, based on the later meaning that was assigned to the doubled trigram that makes up the hexagram. Alternatively, it is translated as "keeping still," for which mountain is an obvious metaphor. Shaughnessy translates as, "stilling," based on the Mawangdui tag, the homophone *gen* 根 meaning root, consistent with being still (Shaughnessy 1997: 55; 2014: 274).

Both Kunst and Rutt, based on the suggestion of Gao Heng, translate *gen* as "cleaving" meaning cutting up a body. In context this is clearly correct. Wilhelm-Baynes and other translations that read it as stilling the specified body areas are strained at best, particularly in reference to the spine in 52.3. Other renderings include "at rest" (Legge: 219–21), "gnawing" (Waley: 134), and "tending" in the sense of tending to one's body (Minford 2014: 721).

As these are all learned translators, albeit with quite different viewpoints regarding the classic, a single correct meaning cannot be decided with certainty. Given that "mountain" was clearly not the early Western Zhou meaning, the other translations can be put into three categories: references to body regions, presumably of the person inquired for; splitting up a body, either as human sacrifice, or as butchering of an animal; or involuntary bodily movements, as such are known to have been taken as omens. However, the texts make no direct reference to twitches, birthmarks or other bodily signs that could be read as omens. Based on the above, the meaning as cutting up a body, probably animal, seems to me inescapable.

Butchering of animals would have been daily sights in farms; temple sacrifices and marketplace executions would have been familiar sights as well. I do, however, doubt Rutt's conclusion that the bodily disruption here is of a human. Other than his preoccupation with this practice, I see no evidence for a human rather than animal victim and the quotation from the *Odes* that he cites is about cutting up a bull, not a human (344). The thousands of skeletons of sacrificial victims discovered in excavations at Anyang (Yin Xu) and elsewhere are commonly decapitated and some are dismembered. None of the archaeological photographs I have seen show human spines that were split.

Since *gen* is contained in the judgment and repeated in each line text, how it is translated entirely determines the meanings of the rest of the texts. The sacrifice-related translations of Kunst and Rutt assume that *gen* is a homophone substitution for 墾 *ken* "cleave." This conjecture is strongly supported by the line texts that clearly refer to cutting up a body. Each act of splitting the body is followed by a prognostication.

This hexagram follows with more than usual consistency the bottom-to-top or foot-to-head organization pattern. Hexagram 23 "Flaying," does not carry out the anatomical correlation with the same consistency. Given that all the line texts begin with 艮 *gen* and are arranged in anatomical order, it seems likely that this chapter was composed as a unit, rather than as an assembly of diverse fragments.

52.0 This seems to mean that the splitting is not deep enough to get inside the body. Kunst translates 身 *shen* body as "womb," which is odd. In the past, this word was sometimes used of the interior of a woman's body but this English usage does not fit here (52).

That he does not see his men is similar to 47.3, referring to not seeing one's wife. Both are omens. The two phrases of this judgment do not seem to belong together.

52.2 Here the cutting seems to be part of a sacrifice but something has gone wrong so that the body is not held up for display, causing those in attendance to feel ill at ease.

52.3 "Smoking heart" has baffled most exegetes, who speculate the heart may have been smoked over a fire after removal. It seems to me that there is a more direct possibility. Because the inside of the body is hot, when cut open water vapor would be released and would be visible in cold air. The phrase then becomes an omen—if the heart smokes when removed, it indicates calamity.

52.4 That there will be no blame is the usual routine incantation and here suggests that proper ritual has been followed in dividing the body.

52.5 This advises that ritual incantations should be precise. That splitting of the jaw occurs with a phrase about speaking is possibly significant.

52.6 *Dun* 敦 here must mean complete—the butchering process is now finished and is pronounced to be auspicious.

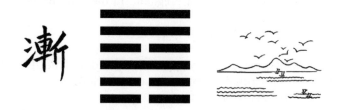

53. 漸 *Jian* Gradual Approach
(Development; Gradual Progress)

The Judgment:

53.0 The women return home. Auspicious. Beneficial divination.
女歸,吉. 利貞.

The Line Texts:

53.1 Wild geese gradually approach toward the riverbank.
For the small child, harsh.
Words without shame.
初六鴻漸于干. 小子厲. 有言無咎.

53.2 Wild geese gradually approach toward the boulders. Food and
drink—joy, joy, auspicious.
六二鴻漸于磐. 飲食衎衎, 吉.

53.3 Wild geese gradually approach toward the land.
The husband on campaign does not come back.
The wife, pregnant, does not give birth, calamitous.
Beneficial to repel the enemy.
九三鴻漸于陸. 夫征不復. 婦孕不育, 凶. 利禦寇.。

53.4 Wild geese gradually approach toward the trees; perhaps will
reach their branches. There will be no blame.
六四鴻漸于木; 或得其桷. 无咎.

53.5 Wild geese gradually approach toward the hill.
Wife after three years not pregnant. In the end nothing successful
or auspicious.
九五鴻漸于陵. 婦三歲不孕. 終莫之勝吉.

53.6 Wild geese gradually approach toward the land. Their feathers
can serve for ritual ceremonial use, auspicious.
上九鴻漸于陸. 羽可用為儀,吉.

53. Commentary 漸 *Jian*
Gradual Approach

Jian 漸 means gradual, but in context with the line texts it means
gradual approach. Like the preceding hexagram, this one has
thematic unity, all the line texts beginning with the phrase, "Wild
geese gradually approach ... ." Each time the geese approach a
specified place, but not in any specific geographic order. An oddity
in this hexagram is the association of geese returning with images
of sterility in 53.3 and 53.5.

53.0 Like the judgment in the received version, 24.0, this line
refers to women returning. In the Fuyang version it is specifically
servant women or concubines who return. The reference here is
probably also to servants (Shaughnessy 2014: 243; Redmond and
Hon 2014: 115).The judgment does not mention wild geese but is
parallel to the line texts in being about returning, presumably why
it was placed with this hexagram. *Gui* 歸 could also mean a woman
coming to her new husband's home, as is the case for the tag of the
next hexagram.

53.1 While migratory geese were often a symbol of autumn
melancholy, since they fly back in the spring they can just as easily
symbolize return. The use of this sort of natural imagery is very
similar to the *Shijing*. In the *Zhouyi*, however, they are clearly
auguries as they are followed with a phrase explaining what they
portend. Indeed, the line texts in the hexagram show a much more
consistent organizational pattern than most others: bird flight
direction; divinatory meaning; character of the augury—ominous,

auspicious, etc. For a more detailed discussion of this imagery see Rutt (345f.).

53.2 The geese are an omen promising a happy feast and may also have been its main dish.

53.3 The reference to the pregnant wife who does not give birth is less straightforward than it appears. That she is pregnant at all while the husband is away raises the possibility of adultery. Regarding not giving birth, a miscarriage or a stillborn would be obvious, at least to the other women in the family unit, though if early in pregnancy they would probably keep this from the father. Given that it is impossible to be pregnant indefinitely without giving birth, the significance of the line is symbolic, one of several images of sterility. This was a commonly expressed anxiety in early societies—that harvests would fail and no children be born. The husband not coming back from war is a similarly negative image—presumably he was killed.

53.3/53.4 Shaughnessy notes that wild geese can symbolize marital separation in the *Shijing* and suggests that this may be their meaning in these line texts (1983: 239–44). These various interpretations are alike in referring to separation and barrenness. The final phrase of 53.3 is one of many bits of military prognostication scattered through the *Zhouyi*; here it is another image of sterility, and loss.

53.5 Auspicious is placed as if it is the conclusion of the phrase, but in context it seems to be negated.

53.6 The final phrase reminds us that animals were thought of mainly in terms of their usefulness for humans. They were essential for food, warmth, and ritual.

54. 歸妹 *Gui Mei* Marrying Maiden (The Marrying Maiden)

The Judgment:

54.0 Expedition calamitous, nowhere favorable.

征凶, 无攸利.

The Line Texts:

54.1 Marrying the maiden with her younger sisters.
The lame can walk. Traveling is auspicious.

初九歸妹以娣. 跛能履. 征吉.

54.2 The blind in one eye can see.
Beneficial for an imprisoned person's divination.

九二眇能視. 利幽人之貞.

54.3 Marrying a maiden with concubines. Turns back, marries
with her younger sister.

三歸妹以如嬬 [須]. 反歸以娣.

54.4 The maiden arrives after the arranged time.
Later returns at a suitable time.

九四歸妹愆期. 遲歸有時.

54.5 Di Yi gave his daughter in marriage.
The lady's sleeves were inferior to those of her younger sister.
The moon was almost full in the distance, auspicious.

六五帝乙歸妹. 其君之袂. 不如其娣之袂良. 月幾望,吉.

54.6 The woman offers a basket; there is no fruit.
The official cuts a sheep, there is no blood.
There is nothing beneficial.
上六女承筐无實. 士刲羊, 无血. 无攸利.

54. Commentary 歸妹 *Gui Mei* Marrying Maiden

This is a famous hexagram and one of the most interesting because it refers to known historical events. It begins on a happy note with its mention of a wedding. As it proceeds however, as with real weddings, family relationships complicate matters.

The tag itself, 歸妹 *Gui Mei*, is ambiguous. Usually translated as The Marrying Maiden, it literally means "Returning Maiden." According to Shaughnessy (1983: 239–44; 1997: 94–5, 302) and Rutt (347–9), who provide detailed analyses of the historical references in the texts of this hexagram, "returning" was a conventional way of referring to a bride, because the groom would call for her at her family home and return with her. In some of the line texts, *gui* seems to refer to marriage, but in others it clearly means "returning." To add to the uncertainty, 妹 means a young woman or maiden, but can also mean "cousin," so it is possibly a consanguineous marriage. The latter seems to have been common among the aristocracy in early China, perhaps to prevent dilution of family wealth and power. It is now theoretically prohibited in the People's Republic of China. Because of the prevalence of polygamy, the existence of many half-brothers and half-sisters in a family, and many consanguineous marriages, family relationships were almost infinitely complex.

Shaughnessy notes that this is one of five hexagrams alluding to historically recognizable events and has parallels to events mentioned in the *Shijing* (*The Book of Songs*), roughly contemporaneous with the *Zhouyi* (1982: 240). Rutt provides a detailed discussion of the historical situation described (347–9). Although many efforts have been made to connect *Zhouyi* passages to actual Western Zhou historical events, few are sufficiently specific to be entirely convincing. We must ask why were there only a few such anecdotes, how were they chosen, and why were these specific ones placed in a divinatory text? One reason for inclusion may have to do with ritual impropriety, an obsession in early and later China. The importance placed on these is indicated by their making up a large part of the *Zuozhuan*, supposedly a commentary on events of the Spring and Autumn Period. The finer sleeves of the bridesmaid in 54.5 are likely mentioned because they represent ritual impropriety. To be blunt, we have here snippets of ancient gossip.

It is almost certain that there are many more allusions to historical events that were forgotten or are not recognizable because the text is a collection of fragments, complete description of events being rare. Other than suppression of some details for political reasons, it is not clear why the text seems so abbreviated, unless to save writing supplies and scribal labor.

54.0 The judgment consists of standard unfavorable prognostics. As is commonly the case in the *Zhouyi*, the judgment has no evident elation to the line texts that follow it. Instead of 征 *zheng*, meaning travel, or military expedition, for its tag, Mawangdui has 正 *zheng*, meaning upright. This is almost certainly a scribal variation, given that the characters look similar and are homophones. The Mawangdui version, translated by Shaughnessy as, "To be upright is inauspicious," is more interesting and certainly a common enough situation in Chinese history, in which those who told the truth to power might suffer horrible deaths.

54.1 This, taken together with 54.4 and 54.5, is one of the most commented upon of all *Zhouyi* texts. It is believed to refer to the marriage of the cousin of the next to last Shang King Diyi to King Wen, who was still Di Yi's vassal at the time. Rutt suggests that it was a "sororal" marriage, that is: King Wen married Di Yi's younger sisters at the same time. That the marriage was polygamous is clear, but there is some uncertainty as to whether the marrying maiden is a concubine or is a primary wife with her sisters or cousins becoming concubines.

For the complex arguments about the relation of this line to the historical events to which it is said to refer, see Shaughnessy (1983: 239–44) and Rutt (347–9). While it is of great interest to connect *Zhouyi* texts to historical events, as the centuries went by fewer readers would have been aware of these connections.

Wilhelm-Baynes' translation of these line texts shows no awareness of its relation to an historical event (Wilhelm-Baynes: 208–12, 663–8).

54.1 and 54.2 That the lame can walk and the blind see is a trope found elsewhere in literature. It can designate an impossible situation, or an anomaly—a cosmic transformation in which all human limitations are removed. In the context of this chapter these phrases do not have any evident relationship with those lines about marriage. As divinatory responses however, they can be read as saying that one can now move ahead as one's limitations have been removed—one can now see reality clearly and can move toward a goal. Alternatively, the anomalies can be a covert way to indicate that the events are contrary to the way of heaven.

Rather than meaning totally blind, 眇 *miao* can mean blind in one eye. Read this way, the line is a proverb to the effect that even those with impairments can still function, somewhat akin to, "In the land of the blind the one-eyed is king."

Wilhelm-Baynes interpret this line as:

> the situation of a girl married to a man who has disappointed her. Man and wife ought to work together like a pair of eyes. Here the girl is left behind in loneliness; the man of her choice either has become unfaithful or has died. But she does not lose her inner light of loyalty. Though the other eye is gone, she maintains her loyalty even in loneliness. (211)

This is an ingenious interpretation but erroneous in several ways. Most obviously, it is unlikely that the bride has chosen the man. Second, unlike modern monogamy, marriage in traditional China meant entering involuntarily into relationships with many relatives as well as other wives. Her husband might be the least of her problems. This reading is entirely suitable for present-day divination as it assumes contemporary patterns of family relationships but not those of early China.

54.3 In many editions, 嬬 *xu* meaning secondary wife as in the Mawangdui text replaces 須 *xu* meaning "wait" in the received text. The received version might be a homophone substitution, especially as it is an easier character to write. In context the line clearly refers to a secondary wife but her exact status is uncertain (Rutt: 348). A concubine was not a mistress or a prostitute but a legitimate member of the household. Bitterness and jealousy among plural wives is legendary.

A complicated system of terminology for familial relationships existed in traditional China. A standard reference provides eleven pages of fine print to enumerate all the possible terms for designating specific degrees of relationship (Instituts Ricci 2003: 405–15).

54.4 The suitable time would have been selected by divination. Since the bride did not arrive then, another auspicious time had to be determined for the wedding. This is no different now. (When I applied for an appointment to receive a marriage licence in Hong Kong, the auspicious dates were nearly all taken. But in accord with Chinese custom my fiancée was able to use her connections to get us a lucky date.)

54.5 Di Yi 帝乙 was the next to the last Shang emperor, while 帝 Di by itself refers to the supreme god. This phrase demonstrates that Shang material was incorporated into the *Zhouyi*, despite the book's association with the Zhou replacement of the Shang. It is almost certain that much else in the text was passed along from the Shang but with only a few exceptions it is impossible to date the line texts even approximately.

54.5 This is one of the most striking texts in the entire *Book of Changes*, in part because it demonstrates that upstaging the bride is nothing new. The character could refer to the bride's younger sister, or her sister-in-law, or a secondary bride. Whichever was meant, the line suggests that another woman was distracting attention from the bride. Female competition is particularly acute in patriarchal societies because a woman's fate depends entirely on her ability to attract and manipulate men. The finer sleeves may also have been an indication of higher social status than the bride. In early China, all ritual occasions had very detailed rules setting out what was allowable based on social rank and many other variables, including the season of the year. Given that the better dress is singled out for mention, it is plausible that this was a ritual error, which would have been inauspicious. For a variety of other interpretations, see Shaughnessy (1983: 239–44) and Rutt (349). In a well-known *Lunyu* passage referring to such sumptuary rules, Confucius comments unfavorably on an aristocrat having more musicians at a banquet than appropriate for his rank.

The reference to the moon, though poetic, is likely astrological. As so often, the prognostic seems contrary to other phrases in the same line text. Perhaps this was a routine expression of hope for good luck, or perhaps the marriage was auspicious despite the younger woman having better sleeves.

54.6 These are extremely ill omens for a wedding. The basket empty of fruit that is offered by the woman indicates she is unable to conceive. The failure of blood to flow from the sacrificial stabbing operates on two levels. On the human level, it seems to represent the man's inability to impregnate the woman. On the cosmic level, the failure of a sacrifice is potentially disastrous for society, which depended on the efficacy of the king's sacrifices— though his actual military might was obviously a major factor in maintaining rulership.

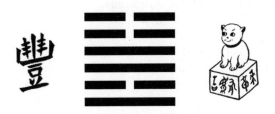

55. 豐 *Feng* Fullness
(Abundance; Fullness)

The Judgment:

55.0 The king advances to make offering. Do not worry, it is proper for midday.
亨王假之. 勿憂,宜日中.

The Line Texts:

55.1 Encountering the master's wife.
Even for the ten-day week, nothing blameworthy.
Going brings honor.
初九遇其配主. 雖旬,无咎. 往有尚.

55.2 Fully covered with their straw mats.
At midday, see the dipper.
Going results in doubts and indisposition.
Holding captives, letting them out is favorable. Auspicious.
六二豐其蔀. 日中見斗. 往得疑疾. 有孚發若. 吉.

55.3 Fully covered in the marshland. At midday sees dimly, breaks his right arm.
There will be no blame.
九三豐其沛. 日中見沫, 折其右肱. 无咎.

55.4 Fully covered with a straw mat. At midday, sees the dipper.
Meets his ordinary master, auspicious.
四豐其蔀. 日中見斗. 其夷主,吉.

55.5 Arrives with a seal.
Has celebration and praise, auspicious.
六五來章. 有慶譽,吉.

55.6 Fully covering their house is a straw mat.
Their family peers into the other's door.
All quiet—there is no one.
For three years, no one is seen, ominous.
上六豐其屋蔀. 其家闚其戶. 闃其无人. 三歲不覿, 凶.

55. Commentary 豐 *Feng* Fullness

Fullness is the usual translation of this tag. It occurs in 55.2, 55.3, 55.4, and 55.6, always in reference to being fully covered.

55.0 A routine mention of the king making an offering; here there is reassurance that it is ritually correct.

55.1 It is hard to translate this line into English without a sexual implication that is not implied in the Chinese. It seems to be just another omen. The second phrase is of a type that is frequent in oracle bone inscriptions: in the coming ten-day week there will be nothing harmful. This is as much an incantation as a prediction. Going bringing honor probably means that an official has successfully carried out a mission for the king, or is about to do so.

55.2 The referent of 蔀 *bu*, translated here as cover, is uncertain. It shields from the sun, but does not seem to be a hat. It could be a cover over a cart, though this is not stated directly. A straw pad to cover the head from the sun seems likely.

In rural Asia it is not unusual to see people walking along holding up an umbrella for sun protection.

The phrase 日中見斗 *ri zhong jian du* is repeated in 55.3 and 55.4. Several translations imply that the line means being able to see stars faintly by blocking the sun with a screen. This is optically impossible, unless during a total eclipse of the sun, as suggested by Rutt (349). Although Venus may be faintly visible just after dawn, neither it nor any other normal celestial object would be visible at midday. It is either a reference to a mythical celestial event, or an occurrence during an eclipse. Eclipses were frightening and memorable events in the ancient world. As an anomaly involving disruption of the natural order, an eclipse is akin to 53.1, "the lame can walk" and 53.2, "the blind can see." In Luke 3:5 (King James Version) a similar series of anomalies invokes the power of God:

> Every valley shall be filled, and every mountain and hill shall be brought low; and the crooked shall be made straight, and the rough ways shall be made smooth;

Anomalies are extreme deviations from normal natural processes. They could be signs that the emperor had lost the mandate of heaven, and therefore justify revolution. For this reason, anomalies engendered great anxiety. Indeed, Confucius himself refused to discuss "strange occurrences" (*Lunyu* 7.20, in Watson 2007: 50).

Kunst translates the third phrase of this line text as, "If you go, you will get the sickness of doubts" (349). This is more elegant than my rendering, but has a Christian or existentialist tone that could not have existed in the Western Zhou. Instead I have translated it as rare advice to liberate captives.

The character treated as "straw cover," can also refer to an "epact" a nineteen-year period when the phases of the moon recur on the same days of the month (Rutt: 248f.). Like other ancient cultures, the Chinese developed elaborate ideas connecting human life to astronomical events, explicated in great detail by Pankenier (2013), who also compares these to astrological theories in the ancient Middle East and Greece.

55.3 The final phrase is usually translated as "fractures." I have used "breaks" because precise diagnostic terms are anachronistic for ancient China. The arm could indeed be broken, or simply sprained or bruised. The Mawangdui version has the homophone 弓 *gong*, meaning a bow (weapon) (Shaughnessy 1997: 98f.) Nonetheless, as the right one is specified, it would seem to refer to the arm. This seems likely to be a fragment of a description of an

294 THE I CHING (BOOK OF CHANGES)

actual event. Less plausibly it might be a proverb to the effect that if your vision is poor, you might break your arm.

55.4 *Yizhu* 夷主 could also be calm or mild, foreign, vulgar, level-headed, wounded or several other things. All we are really told about the master is that meeting him is auspicious.

55.5 Here too, *zhang* 章 could have the meaning of the nineteen-year metonic lunar cycle. This could be part of my postulated hidden hemerological meanings.

55.6 This provides a vivid image: the house is in good condition, since the roof is in good condition, yet the house is deserted. It is a desolate image, but we do not know why the house is deserted. The family might have been exiled, or become destitute due to the father not returning home from war, or the family may have been imprisoned or executed. Such were common disasters that might befall a family, no matter how prosperous.

56. 旅 *Lu* The Traveler (The Wanderer)

The Judgment:

56.0 A small offering.
For travelers, the divination is auspicious.
小亨. 旅貞吉.

The Line Texts:

56.1 Travelers, their jades tinkling, tinkling.
Here they encounter calamity.
初六旅瑣瑣. 斯其所取災.

56.2 A traveler approaching his lodging holds his money close to the chest.
Obtains a servant boy, divines.
六二旅即次.懷其資. 得童僕貞.

56.3 The traveler, lodging set on fire, loses his servant boy.
Divination: harsh.
九三旅, 焚其次, 喪其童僕. 貞厲.

56.4 The traveler at the resting place.
Obtains his traveling expenses in spade coins.
Our hearts not at ease.
九四旅于處. 得其資斧. 我心不快.

56.5 Shooting a pheasant, one arrow kills it.
In the end, a commendatory decree.
六五射雉, 一矢亡. 終以譽命.

56.6 The bird tangles its nest.
The traveler first laughs, afterwards cries and wails.
Losing a cow in Yi, misfortune.
上九鳥焚其巢. 旅人先笑, 後號咷. 喪牛于易, 凶.

56. Commentary 旅 *Lu* Traveler

The tag was translated by Wilhelm-Baynes as the Wanderer. Traveler seems to fit better as the references in the texts here suggest someone with money, with the possible exception of 56.6. Also a traveler, unlike a wanderer, has a definite destination that he intends to visit for specific purposes. In ancient China this would usually have been on government business, but perhaps could also be visiting family or friends. Sightseeing was a common reason for travel in later China but we do not know when traveling for pleasure became usual.

A wanderer, on the other hand, is someone who is rootless, without fixed abode. While wandering often has romantic connotations today, this was not the case in pre-modern China. Later Chinese sources refer to all sorts of wanderers: diviners, shady Buddhist monks, musicians, story-tellers, itinerant healers, and a wide variety of fraudsters. Most would be wandering of necessity, not for pleasure.

56.0 The judgment is favorable for the traveler, though some of the line texts are not.

56.1 *Suo suo* 瑣瑣 "tinkling jade" is a single word in Chinese. Jades hanging from garments were indications of wealth and status. As now, displaying wealth could attract the unwelcome attention of bandits.

56.2 A proverb admonishing the traveler to be careful of his money, equally sound advice for our own time as well. Holding the money close to the chest is another ancient Chinese idiom close to a modern English one.

Use of boys as servants was common in China and is frequently depicted in Song Dynasty paintings.

56.3 Fires were common, buildings were usually wood; heat and light were provided by fire. Literally the phrase says that the traveler set the fire, but the rest of the text provides no basis for imputing such carelessness or maliciousness to the traveler, for whom it is clearly a disaster. A word seems to be missing here, perhaps 處 *chu*, which I have translated as "resting place," in 56.4. However, for alternate renderings in which the traveler sets the fire, see Kunst (350f.) and Rutt (279).

56.4 Early bronze coins were often molded in the shape of spades and knives. The former have been found in later Western Zhou tombs. That the word occurs following the phrase about being paid makes reference to coins plausible, if not certain. Use of 我 *wo*, the first person pronoun (which does not distinguish "I" from "we"), is infrequent in the *Zhouyi*, occurring only eleven times. The sudden change from third to first person makes this set phrase seem out of place here. "Heart not pleased" also appears in 52.2. One wonders if these were the additions of a different editor. As the work of Walter Ong, Eric Havelock, and others has shown, set phrases are often inserted in oral material to maintain meter or otherwise fill a gap, though unrelated in meaning.

56.5 This has been translated in opposite ways—the arrow hitting its mark and the arrow missing. Given the commendation in the next line, the former seems more likely. In 40.6 a hawk is shot by a prince. Hunting was the main enjoyment of the nobility—as in the feudal West—and killing the game enhanced the ruler's aura of potency.

56.6 A bird setting its nest on fire is a peculiar image. Accordingly I have substituted 棼 *fen* "to disorder wood or string" from the Mawangdui version (Shaughnessy 1997: 140f.). For an explanation based on reading *fen* as fire see Rutt (351).

The wailing could be due to loss of the cow, which would be an economic disaster for a subsistence farmer. References to wailing

and to alternating laughing and crying recur throughout the
Zhouyi, often about captives about to be sacrificed. It likely designates extreme emotional distress, here likely over the loss of the
cow in the final phrase. Losses of farm animals are frequent in the
Zhouyi, as they must have been in the life of the time. As elsewhere
in the *Zhouyi* text, 易 *yi* in the *Zhouyi* often refers to a place, not
to the title of the work, which must have been invented later.

57. 巽 *Xun* Kneeling (The Gentle; The Penetrating, Wind)

The Judgment:

57.0 Small offering.
Beneficial if having to go somewhere.
Beneficial to see an important person.
小亨. 利有攸往. 利見大人.

The Line Texts:

57.1 For advancing and retreating, for soldiers, beneficial divination.
初六進利退, 武人之貞.

57.2 Kneeling at the low platform. Employ record keepers and shamans in large numbers. Auspicious, there will be no blame.
九二巽在牀下. 用史巫紛若. 吉, 无咎.

57.3 Repeatedly kneeling in remorse.
九三頻巽吝.

57.4 Regret goes away.
In the field get three kinds of game.
六四悔亡. 田獲三品.

57.5 Divination auspicious, regret vanishes, nothing not beneficial.
Nothing begins but has an end.
From three days before a *geng* day to three days after *geng*,
auspicious.
九五貞吉, 悔亡. 无不利. 无初有終. 先庚三日; 後庚三日吉.

57.6 Kneeling at the low platform.
Below it is his lost spade money.
Divination ominous.
上九巽在牀. 下喪其資斧. 貞凶.

57. Commentary 巽 *Xun* Kneeling

The meaning of the tag is indeterminate. Wilhelm-Baynes' translation is based on the associations of the redoubled trigram,
correlated with wind and gentle. Since they were a much later
innovation, "gentle, penetrating, wind" cannot have been the
original meaning. The Mawangdui manuscript is damaged where
the tag would have been; Shaughnessy believes it was *suan* "to
calculate"; based on where this appears in the text (1997: 150f.,
317). Bernardo notes that the archaic form of the character has two
kneeling stick figures on the top (2012: 226). This is consistent with
food offering as used by Rutt (351). Kunst is similar. It is important
to note that while kneeling is a universal expression of submission,
it was also a usual way to sit, chairs appearing in China only with
the arrival of Buddhism in the Eastern Han Dynasty (Keightly
1999). Both food offering and kneeling are consistent with the
appearances of the tag character in lines 57.2, 57. 3, and 57. 6.

57.2 The first phrase refers to a ritual during which the participants
kneel before an altar. Gao Heng states that the phrase refers to
smearing with blood. While this unpleasant practice was indeed an
essential part of sacrifice, I do not see any reference to it in this line
or elsewhere in the line texts (Rutt: 351).

I have translated *shi* 史 as "record keepers" as this term
referred to a variety of officials responsible for maintaining texts,
which would include those related to ritual and divination. As
early as the Wu Ding oracle bone inscriptions we find the

Chinese pre-occupation with record keeping, much of which now seems about ephemera, including divination results. Shaughnessy's suggestion of *suan* "calculations" for the tag would be consistent with this reference to record keepers (150f., 317).

Wu 巫 "shamaness" originally referred to a female shaman, or spirit medium. Dancing was in China as elsewhere a major ritual and magical activity. As Confucian prudery advanced, shamans with official status were usually men, though female magical experts would continue to be consulted. For a recent consideration of shamanism in early China see Sukhu (2012).

57.5 "Nothing begins but has an end," is a proverb. See also 38.3. *Geng* 庚, is the seventh day of the ten-day week of the Chinese denary calendar, based on the ten "heavenly stems." For further details regarding this method of dating, see hexagram 18. Intervals or groups of three are extremely common in the *Zhouyi*, as also in 6.6 and 18.0. Numerical groups have been, and still are, pervasive in Chinese thought, undoubtedly originating as mnemonics in pre-literate times. Examples are *yin-yang*, heaven-earth-humanity, five tastes, five phases, five (or six) classics, four books, and many others. Buddhism similarly presents its fundamental doctrines as numerical lists—the three poisons, four noble truths, eightfold noble path, etc. Such made it possible in pre-literate times to retain abstract ideas.

57.6 This line refers back to the traveler's money that was lost in the preceding hexagram, 56.4. It is unusual for themes in a hexagram to continue in another one. Most likely, this phrase was simply misplaced from the preceding hexagram.

58. 兌 *Dui* Exchange (The Joyous; Lake)

The Judgment:

58.0 Make offering; beneficial to divine.
亨利; 貞.

The Line Texts:

58.1 Peace exchanged, auspicious.
初九和兌,吉.

58.2 Captives exchanged, auspicious.
Regret goes away.
九二孚兌.悔亡.

58.3 The exchange arrives, ominous.
六三來兌.凶.

58.4 The palaver is not cordial.
Being aided when ill brings happiness.
九四商兌未寧. 介疾有喜.

58.5 Captives flayed with harshness.
九五孚于剝有厲.

58.6 Drawn out exchange.
上六引兌.

58. Commentary 兌 *Dui* Exhange

Like the preceding hexagram, this is made up of a doubled trigram, which is the source of its name. While there is joy in some lines of this hexagram, 58.2 and 58.5 are decidedly grim to modern sensibility and 58.4 is at best ambiguous. Hence "exchange" fits the contexts better.

58.1 and 58.2 A peace agreement has been reached that includes the exchange of prisoners.

58.3 The exchange of captives would be a tense process as it brings the enemies in close proximity to each other.

58.4 Palaver, strictly defined, refers to a prolonged discussion and negotiation with tribal people in Africa. This seems appropriate for the clan-based society of the Western Zhou.

58.5 This is a particularly explicit reference to the cruelty inflicted upon captives, skinning being one of the most agonizing methods of killing. Why the means of killing is specified here and not elsewhere is not clear. Without denying the stereotypically fiendish nature of Chinese tortures, Western ones were equally cruel. It was only in the eighteenth century that these began to be eliminated. Sadly, penal reform is at best a work in progress. The guillotine, invented as a "humane" method of capital punishment, was only eliminated in 1977.

58.6 In oracle bone inscriptions, 引 *yin* can refer to a particular form of sacrifice, but this is not suggested in the context here. *Dui* 兌 was translated by Wilhelm-Baynes as "seductive joyousness"(226), based on the hexagram tag, but the early meaning in context is simply "exchange."

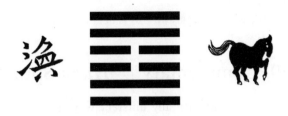

59. 渙 *Huan* Spurting
(Dispersion; Dissolution)

The Judgment:

59.0 For an offering, the king approaches into the ancestral temple.
Beneficial to cross the great river. Beneficial divination.
亨王假有廟. 利涉大. 利.

The Line Texts:

59.1 Use to geld a robust horse, auspicious.
初六用拯馬壯, 吉.

59.2 Spurts, bolts away with on the device.
Regret goes away.
九二渙, 奔其机悔亡.

59.3 Spurting onto their persons. No regret.
六三渙其躬, 无悔.

59.4 Spurting onto those assembled, greatly auspicious. Spurting
onto a knoll, not a smooth place as one would expect.
六四渙其羣, 元吉. 渙有丘, 匪夷所思.

59.5 Spraying sweat, it utters a great cry.
Sprays the king's residence, nothing blameworthy.
九五渙汗, 其大號. 渙王居,无咎.

59.6 Spurting its blood, sets out to get far away.
Nothing blameworthy.
上九渙其血, 去逖出. 无咎.

59. Commentary 渙 *Huan* Spurting

There are two fundamentally different ways to construe this tag character. The usual one has been as scattering, or dispersion. Given that 59.1 is unambiguously about castrating a stallion, the tag character has also been taken to mean spurting, referring to the horse's blood. I have followed Kunst (59f.) and Rutt (282, 352) in this. Shaughnessy, however, stays with the meaning of dispersal (1997: 160f.). In my view, dispersion fits only some of the line texts, while spurting makes sense in all. Spurting is unpleasantly vivid in reference to the horse gelding, but our (justified) phobia about being smeared with body fluids clearly had no precedent in early China.

59.0 The king and his temple also appear in 45.0.

59.1 "Geld" means to castrate a stallion, less often another large farm animal. This has been a common farm procedure to the present day. This meaning for 拯 *zheng* was suggested by Gao Heng and accepted by Kunst (356f.) and Rutt (282, 352). Although this reading is conjectural it fits the contexts and makes this hexagram one of the most vivid of the entire *Changes*.

59.2 This seems to refer to the knife or other device used to sever the scrotum and testicles.

59.3 and 59.4 As I have noted, since it was considered propitious to be smeared with sacrificial blood, this may have been true with geldings. Such procedures may well have been ritualized. Although the *Zhouyi* text does not state so explicitly, it is also plausible that the direction of the blood spurting was taken as an omen. The final phrase probably means that while the stallion was spurting blood it ran up a hill. The direction of its run may also have been an omen.

59.5. Kunst (1985: 356f.) and Rutt (1996: 282, 352) emend 汗 *han* "sweat" to 肝 *gan* "liver," as it is in the Mawangdui version (Shaughnessy 160f., 321). Removing the liver, usually of a sheep, for divination purposes (haruspicy) was pervasive in the ancient Middle East, Greece and Rome. However, this would have required killing the animal and thus is entirely inconsistent with castrating a horse to render him tame. Sweating seems correct—horses definitely do sweat and most of the line texts of this hexagram are about equine body fluids.

59.6 Once castrated, the horse would run away, blood still spurting from the fresh surgical wound, unrestrained by the farmhands whose main concern at this point would be to avoid being kicked.

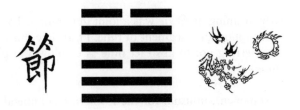

60. 節 *Jie* Time (Limitation)

The Judgment:

Offering in a bitter time; cannot divine.
亨苦節; 不可貞.

The Line Texts:

60.1 Not going out the door to the courtyard. Not blameworthy.
初九不出戶庭, 无咎.

60.2 Not going out the door into the courtyard. Ominous.
九二不出門庭, 凶.

60.3 Not time, thus sighing. Nothing blameworthy.
六三不節. 則嗟若. 无咎.

60.4 A calm time for make offering.
六四安節, 亨.

60.5 A pleasant time, auspicious.
Going brings approval.
九五甘節,吉. 往有尚.

60.6 A bitter time, divination ominous.
Regret vanishes.
上六苦節貞凶. 悔亡.

60. Commentary 節 *Jie* Time

The early meaning of 節 *Jie* was a joint in bamboo. This may have been a metaphor for a segment of time. I translate this character as "time," referring not to abstract time as employed in physics, but as an interval of time.

60.0 A statement, unusual for the *Zhouyi*, recommending *against* divining.

This hexagram is simply a grouping of prognostications and not of much interest. It does, however, clearly exemplify the *Zhouyi* notion of time as qualitative, that is as auspicious or inauspicious for specific activities. This is a pre-scientific notion of cause and effect in which the quality of the time determines, at least partially, the result. This notion of subjective time still exists in common locutions such as, "You called at a bad time"; "We had a good time at the party."

60.1 and 60.2. This pair of lines is reminiscent of the paired predictions on oracle bone inscriptions of the sort, "It will rain"; "It will not rain." The question is asked both ways, presumably for greater certainty in interpreting responses. This may be a remnant of the earliest divination systems, which were binary—giving only yes or no answers—as persists in coin tossing. These lines are not necessarily contradictory as only one of them would have been obtained by the selection procedure.

60.3 This line seems incomplete. The general meaning is "not the right time, so sighs," but what it is not the time for and why this would evoke sighs is not apparent.

60.4, 60.5 and 60.6 are simple divinatory responses.

61. 中孚 *Zhong Fu* Captives Within (Inner Truth)

The Judgment:

61.0 Suckling pigs and fishes, auspicious.
Beneficial to ford the great river. Beneficial to divine.
豚魚,吉. 利涉大川. 利貞.

The Line Texts:

61.1 To be prepared is auspicious; otherwise not at ease.
初九虞吉; 有他不燕.

61.2 Cranes calling from the shady riverbank; their young answer.
I have a good wine goblet; I will give to you generously.
九二鳴鶴在陰; 其子和之. 我有好爵; 吾與爾靡之.

61.3 Take the enemy!
Sometimes beating drums, sometimes stopping, sometimes sobbing,
sometimes singing.
六三得敵! 或鼓, 或罷, 或泣, 或歌.

61.4 The moon nearly full.
Horses run off.
There will be no blame.
六四月幾望. 馬匹亡. 无咎.

61.5 The captives as if twisted together. There will be no blame.
九五有孚攣如. 无咎.

61.6 The cock's call flies toward heaven. Divination ominous.
上九翰音登于天. 貞凶.

61. Commentary 中孚 *Zhong Fu*
Captives Within

This tag is yet another reference to captives. Oddly, although the character 孚 *fu* appears forty times in the *Zhouyi*, this is its only use as a tag. This is consistent with current scholarly opinion that considers the tags to have a different origin than the judgments and line texts. This would account for different vocabulary preferences. This two-character tag phrase seems to specify the location where the captives are held—inside, or surrounded by troops. Another possibility is that they were captured from the central position of the opposing army.

Wilhelm-Baynes' translation as "Inner Truth" is appealingly spiritual but not the early meaning. Here we can see the influence of Jungian depth psychology.

61.0 There has been much controversy about the meaning of "suckling pigs and fishes," but food has always been an auspicious symbol in China and so this likely refers to a banquet for an unknown occasion.

61.2 This is one of the best-known passages in the *Changes*, presumably because of its pleasant image of parental care (male as well as female cranes care for their young) and friendship. It is also the only appearance of 陰 *yin* in the entire *Zhouyi*. In emphasizing that the reference to the crane is gender-neutral, Pearson reminds us that *yin* had no gender correlation in the *Zhouyi* and that *yang* 陽 does not appear at all (22f., 223f.). In the Western Zhou these terms referred to light and shade, with none of the extensive correlations that developed later. For an excellent general monograph on *yin* and *yang* see R. R. Wang (2012) and for its place in the *Changes*, Pearson (2011).

61.3 This line lists some of the sounds of military activity. The final phrase is similar to other passages referring to alternating laughing and wailing, here perhaps the mingled joy of the victors and agony of the wounded and dying.

61.4 For Chinese notions regarding the effects of the moon on the human plane, see Pankenier (2014: 491–4).

61.5 This line could mean that since the captives were kept together, escape is unlikely, thus preventing the blame the guard would incur if they escaped. While the references to captives seem obsessive, repetition of this sort is characteristic of material that was originally orally recited and transmitted.

61.6 "The cock's cry flies to heaven," remains a stock phrase among Chinese, completed by, "while he himself stays on earth." Here it is an unfavorable omen. Bird cries in the *Shijing* are discussed by Rutt (353f.).

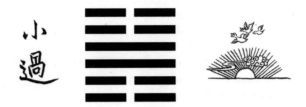

62. 小過 *Xian Guo* Small Mistake
(Preponderance of the Small)

The Judgment:

62.1 Make offering.
Divination can be beneficial for small matters; cannot for big matters.
Soaring birds leave behind their calls.
Not suitable to go up. Suitable to go down.
Greatly auspicious.
亨. 利貞可小事; 不可; 大事. 飛鳥遺之音. 不宜上. 宜下. 大吉.

The Line Texts:

62.1 Soaring birds, thus ominous.
初六飛鳥, 以凶.

62.2 Passes his grandparents; approaches his deceased mother.
Not reaching his prince, but encountering his minister.
Not blameworthy.
六二過其祖; 遇其妣. 不及其君, 遇其臣. 无咎.

62.3 Must not pass him. Be on guard, following, perhaps a killing.
Ominous.
九三弗過. 防之, 從或戕之. 凶.

62.4 There will be no blame. Must not pass by, but meet him.
Harsh going—must be on guard.
Do not utilize for long-term divination.
九四无咎. 弗過遇之. 往属一必戒. 勿用永貞.

62.5 Heavy clouds but no rain in our western outskirts.
The duke bags another while in a pit.
六五密雲不雨自我西郊. 公弋取彼在穴.

62.6 Not meeting but passing.
Soaring birds in the distance, ominous.
Truly called a calamitous mistake!
上六弗遇過之. 飛鳥離之, 凶. 是謂災眚!

62. Commentary 小過 *Xiao Guo*
Small Mistake

I have translated as Small Mistake to contrast with the tag of
hexagram 28, "Big Mistake," which uses the same character
過 *guo* for mistake. Both tags make sense as divinatory responses,
but have no specific content. It can be construed as related to the
judgment text stating that small matters are favored, but not large
ones. Wilhelm's translation of the tag is based on the diagram in
which weak or *yin* lines predominate. Others have translated *Xiao
Guo* as Small Passing, which fits the use of the character in the
line texts. I cannot find any way to put this into English in a way
that makes sense. Here I have deviated from my rule of translating
words identically throughout and have translated *guo* as "mistake"
in the tag and "passing" in the line texts.

62.0 This is one of the longest judgments. It consists of three of the
four words of the standard invocation, followed by stock phrases.

63.1 Partially repeats references to a fox getting its tail wet.

62.2 This line text embodies the obsession with people meeting
each other that is found throughout the *Zhouyi*. The first phrase
is about ritual behavior toward ancestors, for which there were

complex rules, possibly more complex than the rules for treating one's living relatives. Kunst translates as meeting the impersonators of the deceased forebears rather than visiting burial sites (362f.). In either case, there seems to be the implication that the behavior was not ritually correct, perhaps because a female relative is favored over a male one. Errors in treatment of ancestors could anger them, causing them to bring misfortune upon the living. The second phrase perhaps suggests that he should have met with his prince but met with his minister instead. Both phrases are about meeting, suggesting that virtual meetings with the dead and encounters with the living were considered alike.

62.3 and 62.4. The meaning here is uncertain. Ostensibly the lines refer to being in the vicinity of a killer and needing to be careful.

62.5 The Mawangdui manuscript has 茭 *jiao* meaning "pasture," instead of 郊, also *jiao*, often translated as "suburb." (Shaughnessy 1997: 92f., 302). I have rendered as "outskirts" because ancient cities had nothing like our modern, built-up suburbs. The duke seems to have been hiding in a pit just as duck hunters now conceal themselves behind a blind.

62.6 It is hard to make any connection between the phrases here.

63. 既濟 *Ji Ji* Already Across the River (After Completion)

The Judgment:

63.0 Make a small offering; beneficial to divine.
Begins auspiciously, ends chaotically.
亨小; 利貞. 初吉, 終亂.

The Line Texts:

63.1 Trailing a ribbon.
Dips its tail. There will be no blame.
初九曳其輪. 濡其尾. 无咎.

63.2 The wife loses her hair ornament.
Do not look for it—in seven days will be found.
六二婦喪其勿逐—七日得.

63.3 The high ancestor (King Wu Ding) defeated *Guizong*, the demon land, in the course of three years.
Petty people are not to be utilized.
九三高宗伐鬼方, 三年克之. 小人勿用.

63.4 Multicolored silk padded jacket to be prepared for winter days.
六四繻有衣袽冬日戒.

63.5 Eastern neighbors slaughter oxen.
Not like western neighbor's *Yue* (summer) ancestral sacrifice, that
truly obtains good fortune.
九五東鄰殺牛. 不如西鄰之禴祭, 實受其福.

63.6 Wetting one's head, danger.
上六濡其首, 厲.

63. Commentary 既濟 *Ji Ji* Across the River

The usual way to interpret the word 濟 *ji* is as a process completed.
I have translated it more literally as crossing or fording a river,
similar to Lynn's "Ferrying Complete." This makes it consistent
with the imagery of the *Zhouyi*, which is always natural, almost
never abstract. Metaphors are straightforward, as with crossing
a wide, possibly turbulent, river in an era of few bridges and no
tunnels.

The following hexagram, 64, the last in the received order, is
entitled *River Not Yet Crossed*, forming a complement to 63. In
later cosmological interpretations these two hexagrams were of
particular importance. Surprisingly, of the two, 63 is less auspicious than 64 because it represents stasis. All the lines are in
their "correct" positions—odd numbered positions are occupied
with solid (*yang*) lines and the even numbered ones with broken
(*yin*) lines. It might seem good to have all lines are in their proper
positions, but this was taken to mean being stuck in a situation
with no possible movement. In 64, all the lines occupy incorrect
positions, but this is highly dynamic. *Yin* and *yang* will move
toward their correct positions, creating the changes that animate
heaven, earth, and humanity. The contrast between activity and
inertia is fundamental, but other metaphysical meanings for the
two figures could just as easily be invented. The hexagrams did not
so much invent ideas as inspire them and provide a framework to
organize them.

Further evidence that this sort of abstract theorizing was not
present in the original composition is the Mawangdui order in
which hexagrams 63 and 64 are 22 and 54 respectively. Thus the

paired position of these two hexagrams was not inherent in the *Zhouyi*'s organization. This, of course, need not bother those who use the *Changes* for divination, or who find personal meaning in the *yin-yang* theory, but it does shed some light on the textual history.

63.0 "Will begin well but end badly," is a set phrase and a standard sort of divinatory advice because it will always come true—no matter how good things are at a particular moment there will be problems down the road.

63.1 Dipping the tail, another animal movement omen, presumably refers to the same fox as mentioned in 64.0. "Not blameworthy" is the meaning of the omen, not the implication for the animal. In the received text 輪 *lun* "wheel" is usually regarded as a homophone substitution for 綸 *lun* "cord" or "sash," the corresponding character in Mawangdui (Shaughnessy 1997: 80f., 298). Although neither makes a great deal of sense, having a cord stuck onto a fox's tail is more plausible than a wheel. Perhaps it was a tether and the fox escaped. For detailed discussion of other possibilities see Rutt (355–7).

63.2 Three thousand years ago losing things would have been common, as it is today, but may also have been regarded as an omen. In contrast to our time, in the *Zhouyi* most lost items seem to return of their own accord in seven days.

63.3. This is a reference to the defeat of Guifang by Wu Ding, referred to as the "high ancestor." Wu Ding (r. 1200–1181 BCE) is one of the best known of the Yin (late Shang) kings because the earliest oracle bones found near Anyang in 1899 were records of his divinations. His second wife, Fu Hao, whose intact tomb (sealed c. 1200 BCE) was excavated beginning in 1976, is a particularly interesting figure, having been a successful general. Whether she played a role in the defeat of Guifang is not mentioned. She was buried with 755 jade objects as well as many other burial goods, showing that the present popularity of luxury goods is nothing new. It is tempting to conjecture that it was her hair ornament that was lost in the preceding line, but there is no direct evidence (Rutt: 286, 358).

63.4 Silk stuffing is quite warm and continues to be used in China for comforters and winter coats. I have substituted the Mawangdui variant 冬 *dong* "winter" for the received version 終 *zhong* "end" (Shaughnessy 1997: 80f., 298).

63.5 As I have emphasized throughout, there was great anxiety that the details of the rituals would not please the ancestors or spirits because it was universally believed that the well-being of the king and society were dependent on their propitiation. One of the pretexts used to justify the Zhou overthrow of the Shang was the carelessness of the latter regarding the rites. Since the *Changes* was associated with the victorious Zhou, it was they who got to decide which method of sacrifice was the proper one. Rutt suggests that the Zhou method was to sacrifice humans, rather than animals, based on lines 45.5 and 46.2 (358). This contradicts the tradition that human sacrifice ceased with the Zhou conquest, but archaeological and textual evidence refutes this tradition (Redmond and Hon 2014: 47–9, 133–4). Human sacrifice persisted, but its practice did gradually wane during the Zhou.

63.6 Wetting the head is either an omen or the mistaken belief, similar to that of the West, that getting wet or chilled would cause disease. This belief is the basis of the common term of "cold" for upper respiratory infections. In many cultures the head is considered particularly vulnerable, as indicated in the nearly universal wearing of hats until recently. Because the body loses a substantial amount of heat through the head, and in the absence of central heating, the wearing of hats at all times during the cold seasons of the year would have been important for avoiding hypothermia. Outside in bitter cold temperatures, wetting the head would have caused considerable discomfort. The need to keep warm is obvious but it would have been much harder in the Bronze Age than in our own.

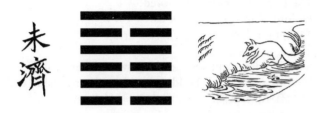

64. 未濟 *Wei Ji* River Not Yet Crossed (Before Completion)

The Judgment:

64.0 Make a small offering.
The fox, when nearly across the river wets its tail. Nothing is beneficial.
亨小. 狐, 汔濟, 濡其尾. 无攸利.

The Line Texts:

64.1 Wets its tail. Regret.
初六濡其尾. 吝.

64.2 Trailing a ribbon. Divination auspicious.
九二曳其輪. 貞吉.

64.3 Not yet across, for an expedition, ominous.
Beneficial to ford the great river.
六三未濟, 征, 凶. 利涉大川.

64.4 Divination auspicious, regret passes away.
Zhen used a military expedition against *Guifang*, the devil land.
In three years got his reward from the great country.
九四貞吉,悔亡. 震用伐鬼方. 三年有賞于大國.

64.5 Divination auspicious; there is nothing to regret.
The upright person is honored.
Holding captives, auspicious.
六五貞吉; 无悔. 君子之光. 有孚吉.

64.6 Holding captives; drinking wine. There will be no blame.
Wetting one's head. Holding captives, losing them, truly.
上九有孚; 于飲酒. 无咎. 濡其首. 有孚失是.

64. Commentary 未濟 *Wei Ji* River Not Yet Crossed

The incorporation of this hexagram into *yin-yang* metaphysics was discussed in the commentary on the previous hexagram. Several phrases that occur in hexagram 63 are repeated in 64, consistent with the two of them having been composed as a unit. This suggests, but does not prove, that the received order was original and that of Mawangdui a later corruption. A vast number of schemes have been proposed to "discover" the original order, ranging from plausible, to eccentric, to bizarre—one hesitates to add to these numerological fantasies. Finding the "real" sequences of the hexagrams is at best a diversion, akin to doing a crossword puzzle, but for some like Shao Yong or Father Joachim Bouvet, S.J. it became an obsession.

64.0 Here again the image of wetting is specified as happening to a fox.

64.3 A way to make sense of this seemingly contradictory prognostication would be that the army is vulnerable before getting across the river, but safe once on the far side. Tempting as it is to force separate phrases into coherence, with the *Zhouyi*, being too clever can be misleading. Here, I suspect that the compiler simply put the lines together because both are related to crossing a river.

64.4 According to Rutt, the second part of the text refers to the same military victory as 63.3. Zhen might be King Wu Ding, but several other possibilities have been suggested including the Duke of Zhou, to whom the composition of the line texts was later attributed. However, the predominant current scholarly consensus, which I share, is that the association of the King Wu, King Wen, and the Duke of Zhou with the *Changes* is entirely mythological. Certainly there is no unambiguous reference to any of these culture heroes in the *Zhouyi* texts. Attempts to establish the identity of the mysterious Zhen or identify other vague historical allusions are tendentious without adding anything to our understanding of the classic. However, for a contrary view, see Field (2015) and for further discussion on the candidates for Zhen, see Rutt (357–9).

64.5 Being of upright character is apparently compatible with sacrificing captives. The line probably refers to the celebration after a military victory, highlighted by the blood sacrifice.

64.6 The received text, that of the Shanghai Museum, and the Fuyang manuscript, all read 有孚 *you fu*, as elsewhere in the present translation, "holding captives," while Mawangdui reads 有復 *you fu*, "there is a return" (Shaughnessy: 144f., 316). If one considers the totality of contexts throughout the *Zhouyi*, *fu* clearly means captives. It is possible that it held the meaning of return in this specific phrase but is more likely a phonetic loan. There are many such variants but, as here, they do not fundamentally alter the meaning of the classic.

That the captives are lost seems inauspicious as the final phrase of the entire book, but because there is no evidence that the *Book of Changes* was conceived as a coherent work, there is no reason to place special significance on the ultimate line.

The final phrase, 失是 *shi shi*, was translated by Kunst (366f.) and Rutt (360) as losing a spoon. This is based on a presumed homophone substitution and assumes that losing a spoon would be an omen. To my mind there have been too many such speculative emendations in the modern history of *Changes*. They cannot be proven wrong but mere homophony does not seem to me sufficient reason to make up a phrase with no connection to the rest of the line. However, in terms of the basic understanding of the work, not much is at stake in these sort of speculations.

I would have been happy to be able to end my commentaries with a resounding conclusion, but such would be contrary to the very nature of the *Zhouyi*. To invert one of its recurrent motifs, the *Zhouyi* has a beginning but not an end. It began sometime in the Chinese Bronze Age as a means of coping with uncertainty. Uncertainty is still with us and so is the *Book of Changes*, now in daily use, worldwide, for the same purpose. Its end, if there will even be one, is nowhere in sight. The book has no end in another sense—it is an endless loop. Since the hexagram sequence is arbitrary, one can begin reading it anywhere and stop anywhere. When used for divination it will tell a new story every time. While the number of judgment and line texts is finite, the human ingenuity that interprets them is limitless. As a book of life, it reaches toward the infinite. It can be read in any order and, most importantly, can respond to any inquiry we can conceive of. As there is no end of uncertainty in life, there is no end to the use of the *Book of Changes*, indeed human life itself is a *Book of Changes*.

A final apology. In my translation and commentaries I have not done anything to gloss over the numerous unpleasantnesses in the ancient book. But since its Bronze Age origins, the long interpretive tradition has made the *Book of Changes* into a book of reflection and hope.

PART THREE

The quest for philosophy in the *Zhouyi*

6

What kind of book is the *Book of Changes*?

In China for thousands of years and in the West for a few centuries, the *Book of Changes* has been regarded as a work of utmost profundity. Its first Western admirers were intellectual luminaries— a French Jesuit missionary to China, Fr. Joachim Bouvet (d. 1732), and a German philosopher, Gottfried Leibniz (1646–1716), who was one of the inventors of the calculus.

Not all agreed that the *Book of Changes* is profound, or philosophical, or spiritual. With some notable exceptions, Protestant missionaries saw little value in the Chinese classics, which they regarded as an impediment to conversion to Christianity. More serious critiques were advanced by the Doubting Antiquity Movement, which initiated the reconstruction of the ancient meanings, the subject of the present work. Succinctly stated, the conclusion of the Doubting Antiquity Movement was that their reconstruction of the meanings of the earliest layer of the text, the *Zhouyi*, contained no philosophy or moral principles and was filled with barbaric practices. They pointed out that the philosophical ideas were much later additions. This analysis is not wrong, but it is incomplete. That the early text lacked philosophy does not by itself invalidate the ideas that were attached to it later. These later philosophical ideas deserve to be assessed on their own merits.

While the purpose of my translation has been to show the Western Zhou text without these later accretions, I do not do this to discredit the text, but rather to show how it began. I see two benefits to this approach. First, the *Zhouyi* is restored as an historical source for the life of the Western Zhou. It also gives us an opportunity to observe the not entirely prepossessing beginnings of Chinese philosophy.

We can start out from a strong statement of what I take to be a Christian critique, in the words of Richard Rutt:

> The only aspect of *I Ching* that can be properly called spiritual is communication with spirits, especially ancestral spirits, in order to discern future events (51).

This shows the indeterminacy of the concept of "spirituality." Without saying so directly, Rutt seems to feel that spirituality needs a supreme being. This is certainly true of the Religions of the Book, but it is not true of Buddhism and not true of the Daoist philosophy of Laozi. Rutt's perspective was that of a missionary and one suspects that for him, systems of thought unrelated to the Christian revelation were ultimately non-spiritual. To his great credit, this did not interfere with his scholarship on the *Zhouyi*, which was meticulous, nor did it prevent him from writing what is perhaps the best single book in English on the classic. He was a careful scholar, whose work, for me at least, is indispensable. When he moved from objective scholarship to judging the spirituality, or lack of it, in the classic, it would be unreasonable to expect him to set aside his Christian beliefs. This perspective is as legitimate as any other and he is open about it. What his view shows is the limitation of judging a supposedly spiritual text from the perspective of a different spiritual tradition. To do so makes it difficult to understand why it was so esteemed by Chinese literati and is now viewed as profound by those outside the Chinese tradition.

Rutt adds:

> If the *I Ching* has, in spite of itself, accrued a quasi-spiritual aura and been used for spiritual purposes, that is because its original meaning was forgotten. The resulting obscurity made it easy for the text to be used for many religions … its fascination lies in its availability as a vehicle for its readers' preoccupations. (51)

I agree with this statement, except spiritual texts are works in progress and, inevitably, new meanings supplant some of the older ones. To take an obvious modern example, Jung's idea of synchronicity was partly inspired by the *I Ching*, and is not any less meaningful because it is not present in the *I Ching* itself. Books teach us facts, but they also inspire us. Rutt does acknowledge some of the ways the *Changes* has been spiritualized by ways of thought external to it, particularly the psychology of Carl Jung. He was clearly ambivalent about the *Changes*, as I am, though in different ways. Given its complex history I do not see any way to feel otherwise.

My approach is dialectical. While I often express my disagreements with Rutt, as I mention at the beginning, it is only through his work that I came to whatever understanding I have of the classic. I believe Rutt had essential insights that made him able to identify critical issues with the *Zhouyi* that need to be addressed in any translation and commentary. Hence I have referred to him often, often agreeing, sometimes disagreeing. Rutt convinced me that there is little *direct* expression of spirituality, or wisdom, or philosophy, in the Western Zhou text. It was this however that prompted me to search for what is latent in the text that allowed it to become, at least in the minds of its exegetes, a work of both wisdom and philosophy.

While Rutt extensively discusses how the *Changes* was used for divination, he seems not to have practiced it himself. Thus he writes as a scholar, not as a practitioner. I believe this limits insight into the *Changes*. It is not that practicing divination will make one a believer, rather it enriches one's perspective on it. Like meditation and many other spiritual practices, divination is a physical and perceptual act. Whincup sums it up well. (223) When he consulted the *Changes* he often received good advice, but he decided it was better to make one's decisions oneself.

In contrast to simply listening to a lecture or reading—whether from print or screen—practicing divination with the *I Ching* is an active process, consisting of both mental and physical activity. While the mind controls most physical activity, sensation and movement in turn affect the mind. Traditionally, consulting the *I Ching* is done facing north as one would if conferring with a living sage. Incense is lit as a token offering, a few moments are taken to still the mind and concentrate the inquiry. Then a hexagram is selected, ideally with yarrow, alternatively with coins, beads or other methods. The selected passage is read, and if there are changing lines perhaps additional text is taken into consideration.

To conclude the session one thanks the oracle but continues to contemplate the response.

In the frenetic modern world these procedures are usually abbreviated, but it is still necessary to physically manipulate objects to select a hexagram, to open the book to the proper page, and to reflect on how the selected text bears on one's inquiry. That the text is selected without conscious choice is vital to the practice and one factor that distinguishes an *I Ching* consultation from dipping into a self-help book.

The spirituality of the *Book of Changes*, if there is any, requires the divination process to be fully experienced. The same can be true with other sorts of ethical and philosophical ideas. These may come to be understood as one reflects on their relevance to one's own life. Modern education tends to teach solely by lecture, book, and computer screen. In the past, practices were considered essential to philosophy. The ideas of Daoism were related to early use of breathing exercises (Michael 2015: xvi *et passim*). The central Buddhist idea of non-attachment is experienced during meditation.

I am not advocating any particular religious practices, nor taking a position on whether use of the *I Ching* benefits one's life, though many report benefit from such practices. Rather, my point is that study of the *Changes* solely as a text does not replicate its traditional use. This was true of Western classical philosophy as well. Pierre Hadot has argued convincingly that for the ancients, practice was integral to philosophizing:

> All schools denounced the risk taken by philosophers who imagine that philosophical discourse can be sufficient to itself without being in accord with the philosophical life ... they turn love of wisdom into love of words. (174)

I am not suggesting that the *Book of Changes* should not be studied as a text. After all, it is a book. Textual criticism and reconstruction are just as important as divination practice. Of the leading contemporary scholars, some admit to having tried divination with the *Changes*, others deny ever having done so. My only point is to recommend trying the *Changes* as a practice, not to find fault with those who do not use it as such.

Hadot's work is of great interest in taking us beyond the notion that practices, such as meditation, are part of Asian spirituality but are foreign to the West. I am not advocating any specific practice but want to make readers aware that simply understanding doctrines is not the same as experiencing them. The claims made for the spirituality of the *Changes* presume one also uses it for self-cultivation. This is true not only of the *Changes*, but of other scriptural texts. Put in another way, the spirituality of an inspirational text lies in how it improves the life of the believer or practitioner. I am not speaking of the Western Zhou use here. We have no actual evidence of how the *Changes* was used then, but it was almost certainly primarily for divination or for bringing good luck. The notion of self-cultivation is post-axial. While it is perhaps the central idea of Chinese philosophy (as it was with Socrates in a different way), we find no direct expression of it so early. However, many axial religious practices developed from pre-axial ones, holidays like Easter and Christmas being examples.

From divination to wisdom to philosophy

Some academic philosophers make a distinction between wisdom, insights on living a good life and coping with life's difficulties, and philosophy that goes deeper and analyzes the basic structure of reality, the nature of knowledge, the basis of right and wrong, the nature of being, etc. One way wisdom differs from philosophy is that it usually clarifies problems, while philosophy complicates them in order to stimulate us to think more deeply, as Socrates did with his dialogues. Not everyone appreciates being made to question their beliefs, as Socrates' tragic fate reminds us. Nor was he the only philosopher put to death for challenging the status quo.

There is a tendency to regard wisdom writings as on a lower level than philosophical ones. I do not take much interest in such hierarchies, instead expanding T. S. Eliot's famous dictum, that "art never improves, only its subject matter changes," to apply to philosophy as well. Who would declare Kant or Wittgenstein greater than Socrates or Aristotle? With literature and philosophy we see progression toward increasing complexity, but the later forms do not supplant the earlier ones. The early, seemingly simple, productions of the human intellect have their own special value that is not vitiated by later more sophisticated ones.

The *Zhouyi* is a record, though a limited one, of how Bronze Age humans made life decisions. While we are repelled by many of their decisions, such as to sacrifice captives, we should recognize that they were at least thinking about how they should live and act. If they used an incantation to ward off blame for killing innocent people, at least they sensed they needed a way to excuse it. Gradually, too gradually, this led to reductions in such cruel practices, a change not complete even in the world today.

So we must accept that at a literal level the *Zhouyi* is neither spiritually nor philosophically inspiring. Its interest comes from being a record of the early efforts of our remote ancestors to understand the strange cosmos in which we all find ourselves. The *Zhouyi* does contain bits of wisdom, as I shall detail below, but these are not systematic. We do not find general principles for living, as we do in the *Dao De Jing*. Unlike the *Lunyu*, which uses specific situations to advance general principles, in the *Zhouyi* the situations are simple metaphors for practical matters—is this a good time to see a powerful person, or cross a wide river, for example. When we do find more general ideas, it is in the form of proverbs, the earliest form of wisdom writing. The *Zhouyi* mainly provides answers to questions, "What do I do now?"

It is with the addition of the *Ten Wings*, particularly the *Dazhuan* or *Great Commentary*, that the *Changes* became an ethical, spiritual, and philosophical text in China. When this happened is uncertain. It may have been as early as the Spring and Autumn Period, or may not have reached final form until the Western Han Dynasty. Rutt notes correctly that it is the *Ten Wings*, particularly the *Dazhuan* or *Great Commentary* that brought philosophy and spirituality to the *Changes*, but completely dissociates these from the Western Zhou portion. Certainly, between the sensibility of the *Zhouyi* and that of the *Dazhuan* there is a wide gulf. However, this begs the question: why were the ideas recorded in the *Dazhuan* attached to the *Zhouyi*, rather than being left free-standing?

The *Dazhuan* contains many references to the *Zhouyi*, establishing that the authors of the commentary knew the early text well. It quotes many phrases from the line texts, including not only the famous ones such as the cranes calling to their young (61.2) and the overbearing dragon (1.6) but also rather banal ones, such as those about using white grass for mats (28.1) and not going out the door (60.1 and 2) (Lynn: 57–9). While some lines were likely known to some not otherwise familiar with the *Changes*, those latter two examples probably would not have been. Thus the author(s) of the *Dazhuan* were clearly quite familiar with the *Zhouyi* itself, although they added much lore not present in it.

As another example of the close relation of commentary to text, the *Dazhuan* begins where the *Changes* begins:

As Heaven is high and noble and Earth is low and humble, so it is the *Qian* and *Kun* are defined. (Lynn: 47)

To Confucius is attributed an exalted opinion of the *Changes*:

The Master [Confucius] said: "The *Changes*, how perfect it is! It was by means of the *Changes* that the sages exalted their virtues and broadened their undertakings. Wisdom made them exalted and ritual made them humble." (Lynn: 56)

That the *Changes* contained the wisdom of the ancient sages is clearly stated:

It is by means of the *Book of Changes* that the sages plumb the utmost profundity and dig into the very incipience (*ji*) of things. (Lynn: 63)

The most famous phrase in the *Dazhuan*, one that was echoed in Chinese writings through the ensuing centuries is:

When in ancient times [Fu Xi] ruled the world ... he looked upward and observed the images in heaven and looked downward and observed the models that the earth provided ... He thereupon made the eight trigrams in order to ... classify the myriad things in terms of their true, innate natures. (Lynn: 77)

This is a very expansive claim, that the ancient (mythical) sage-king observed the nature of heaven and earth and embodied them in the diagrams of the *Book of Changes*. While it is the trigrams rather than the texts that are referred to here, the *Zhouyi* makes no such claim for itself. It simply offers itself as a divination manual. Yet, to reiterate my basic point, while we cannot find a basis for such a grandiose conception in the *Zhouyi*, something about it seemed to later readers to have philosophical implications, "seeds" as I have termed them. While my identifications of these seeds are speculative, the association of the *Zhouyi* text as a whole with the development of Chinese philosophy is an undisputed historical fact. Restraint is necessary here, however, considering how much fantasy has been read into the *Book of Changes*.

I do not claim that those who added philosophy to the *Changes* did so entirely based on the Western Zhou text. Many of the ideas later associated with it, especially the dynamic interaction of *yin* and *yang*, were based almost entirely on the line patterns and had no precedent in the texts. Instead I suggest that the *Zhouyi* inspired philosophy rather than creating it.

The subjectivity of knowledge

Chinese philosophy sought patterns underlying the constant flux of the cosmos, but did not consider the world of experience to be a mere illusion. In a famous Daoist anecdote, Zhuangzi awakens from dreaming that he is a butterfly and then questions if it was him, Zhuangzi, dreaming of being a butterfly, or if he is really a butterfly dreaming it is Zhuangzi. As in his other famous anecdote regarding whether he can tell when fish are having a good time, these passages are about the subjectivity of knowledge. They force us to admit that what we assume is real is uncertain, but in a humorous rather than nihilistic sense. We all know we are not butterflies, but not how to prove it. With Confucianism, the nature of reality is never questioned; the concern of philosophy was the moral life.

The this-worldliness of Chinese culture was not absolute. The dead inhabited their own realm but it was not imagined in much detail until the arrival of Buddhism. Mind-journeys were part of philosophical Daoism, and as a religion it had an extremely elaborate pantheon. Yet the existence of the alternative realities did not imply that the normal world of these senses was merely an illusion, as Buddhism sometimes did.

Was pre-modern Chinese thought really philosophy?

It remains a debate among some Western philosophers as to whether Chinese thought can legitimately be termed philosophy. There is a related controversy as to whether Confucianism can be termed a religion. I mention these disputes, which I find unproductive, not to join in them, but simply to point out that the intellectual traditions of China are quite different from those referred to as philosophy in the West. The term philosophy in particular carries a value judgment as implying the highest levels of human thought. Thus stating that China did not have true philosophy holds the implication, sometimes explicitly stated, that its intellectual traditions are inferior to those of the ancient Greco-Roman world.

Ultimately, these are not questions about philosophy as an aspect of human thought; they are questions about definitions. As did philosophy in the West, that of China represented a people's attempts to understand existence on a deep level. To be sure, there was no Chinese Socrates, Aquinas, Kant, Wittgenstein, or Sartre, anymore than there was a Western Confucius, Mencius, Laozi, Zhuangzi, Shao Yong, or Zhu Xi. Would we think better of Chinese philosophy if it were more like what the West assigns to its own tradition? I would not; the very fact that it is different broadens our conception of what philosophy can be.

Chinese philosophy tends to represent abstractions in terms of concrete analogies. Heaven 天 *tian*, even though it represents higher unseen forces affecting human life, is also the sky as seen both day and night. Use of the visible to represent the abstract does not mean that the thought is stuck on the realm of the concrete. In regard to common criticism of analogy as an inferior form of argument, it can be pointed out that the fundamental idea of Platonism was the cave analogy in which we can only perceive the ideal in distorted form.

My reason for mentioning these issues is simply to forewarn the reader that what I will present as philosophy may not meet the expectations of those primarily familiar with the ancient Western philosophers. It may seem difficult to describe phrases about horses returning, or a bridesmaid having better sleeves than the bride, or human sacrifice, as philosophy—and indeed they are not. However, if the reader is patient, I will explain the relationship. The value of this exercise is the opportunity to observe the phase of human consciousness just when philosophy was about to appear.

The enchanted world of the Western Zhou

The cosmos of the *Zhouyi* is enchanted; causality is metaphysical and magical rather than empirical. According to the ideas of Friedrich Schiller and Max Weber the enchanted mental world is radically different from our own. All sorts of phenomena that seem random to us—meeting other people, bird flights, facial structure, animal movements—were experienced as messages relevant to a person's life. A walk through nature would be filled with omens that one would ignore at one's peril. In early Chinese poetry, what seems merely aesthetic to us often had symbolic or divinatory significance. Awareness that images often are omens is essential for understanding the *Zhouyi*. Descriptions that seem random: a piglet, an oreole's call—have meaning. The key to what these omens portend was lost long ago, yet we can understand why they were included once we realize that they were there because of their prognostic significance.

Most—but not all—early philosophers, including Socrates and Confucius, believed in divination. Despite their rationality they did not question the enchantment of the world. Cicero, in contrast, though an official augur—an interpreter of bird flight omens— was an early skeptic concerning the efficacy of divination (*De Divinatione*). The Chinese philosopher Xunzi was also a skeptic. As now, knowledge and practice of divination did not necessarily imply belief. In practice, augury was a source of political power as the augur could read his political goals into the bird flock patterns. Diviners in China would similarly interpret omens in ways that would benefit—or protect—themselves.

Metaphysical and cosmological concepts in the *Zhouyi*

Qualitative time

"Favorable if having to go someplace," "Beneficial to meet the important person," "Beneficial to ford the great river." These rather vague phrases actually tell us much about the mind of the Western Zhou. As Francois Jullien has expounded at length, a time has its own quality (1992: 5–16). In the *Zhouyi*, at a given moment some kinds of activities will succeed while others will fail or, even worse, bring blame from those in power. Times are subjective or psychological. This is also present in modern thought, but is attributed to a subjective response to factual circumstances, not to a quality of time itself. Yet we refer frequently to psychological time in such expressions as, "Have a nice day," "I'm not in the mood today," or, on telephoning someone, "Is this a good time for you to talk?" Or, as expressed to me by a prominent sinologist, whom I shall not name, regarding his gambling, "Sometimes you're just hot, you know?" Thus for humans, the actual experience of time is qualitative. Different activities are considered appropriate for different times of day. We have cereal or eggs for breakfast but not hot curry. Most Americans think of soup as a lunch or dinner food, but my wife, who is Chinese, has it for breakfast. The list could go on. Quantitative time does not replace psychological time; it supplements it.

Time intervals in the *Zhouyi* tend to be indefinite—three days and seven days mean approximately three or seven days. The *I Ching* advises as to whether an act is beneficial or not at the time of the inquiry, but rarely gives an exact time frame. This is consistent with time as experienced by agricultural societies which lived by sunrise and sunset and the changing seasons. Our need to be conscious of exact time so as to get to work, attend meetings, or catch planes, is a rather recent development. In using qualitative time, the *Zhouyi* contrasts with astrology; astronomical positions occur at exact times, predictable with sufficient knowledge. Later, Chinese divination methods became more specific about time. Examples are *bazi*, or eight-character divination, which is based on birth time and date, and *Tong Shu*, government-sponsored almanacs that state favorable days, even for such mundane matters as baths and haircuts.

The idea of favorable and unfavorable times is also present in the *Dao De Jing*:

Just as you breathe in and breathe out
Sometimes you're ahead and other times behind
Sometimes you're strong and other times weak
Sometimes you're with people and other times alone. (Star: 42)

Just as breathing is rhythmical, so are other aspects of human well-being. In this quotation from the *Dao De Jing*, this is stated as the inherent pattern of human life. The *Zhouyi* offers no general principle like this, but tells the inquirer when things are auspicious and when they are ominous for a specific activity. Time is qualitative and cyclical but the *Zhouyi* does not state these as general truths, as does the *Dao De Jing*. A related theme is action and withdrawal. The quality of the time determines when it is favorable to act and when it is better to avoid acting. In abstract terms this became an aspect part of the *yin-yang* duality.This alternation is fundamental to the Chinese conception of human life.

Contemporary Chinese politics also seems cyclical. The government sometimes tolerates mild dissent, but at other times suppresses it harshly. Similarly, its stance toward the United States alternates between an attitude of warm friendship and verbal hostility. Such is not unique to China, but perhaps only in China is it part of a philosophical tradition. It is best viewed not as inconsistency but as the alternation of the predominance of two basic forces.

Some *yin-yang* cycles are regular, such as the alternation of day and night, but others are not entirely predictable. Nonetheless it is invariable that once *yin* or *yang* reaches its peak, it starts to decline as the other rises. This notion of change is a distinct contrast to Western philosophy, which usually considers change as something that progresses irreversibly. Western philosophy has often felt that change needs to be explained, whereas in Chinese thought, change is simply the way things are.

Yin and *Yang*

This, the most famous concept associated with the *Book of Changes*, and one that has become part of world culture, is not actually found in the *Zhouyi*. *Yin* is mentioned once, in 61.2, where it refers to the shady south bank of a river and has no metaphysical implications. *Yang* does not appear at all.

Dualism is inherent in mental representations of experience: yes–no, dark–light, hot–cold, male–female, young–old, living–dead, and so on. Given this inherent tendency of the human mind to think in dualities, when the concepts of *yin* and *yang* became metaphysical it was an obvious step to symbolize them with the broken and solid lines of the *Zhouyi*. It has been suggested the two types of lines originally developed from a yes-or-no divination method akin to tossing a coin. Expanding the lines to sets of six allowed philosophical and cosmological meanings also to be represented by them.

While there was some understanding by the time of the Han that texts were historical entities, the sagely origin, and hence the validity, of the *Changes* was usually taken for granted. That all of the four elements of each chapter were related to each other was assumed, consistent with the supposed sagely origin. Thus it is only beginning in the twentieth century that the components were dissected from each other and analyzed separately.

Needham provides a useful summary of the nature of *yin* and *yang* and the correlative cosmology of which they are a part (1956: 273–91). His table of symbolic correlations is also quite useful (1956: 262f.).

The Way or *Dao* 道, which became the most fundamental term in Chinese metaphysics, appears only four times in the *Zhouyi* (9.1, 10.2, 17.4, and 24.0). With the possible exception of 10.2, which we can imagine is a metaphor, the word simply means path or road and has no metaphysical significance. A path is a natural metaphor for life but is extended in Chinese philosophy to refer to the workings of the cosmos and of the proper ways for humans to live within it. This concept is prominent in the *Dazhuan* but not in the *Zhouyi*.

Junzi and *da ren* versus *xiao ren*

The contrast between *junzi* 君子 or *da ren* 大人 and *xiao ren* 小人(upright or important people versus petty or small-minded ones) is used to suggest moral distinctions in the *Zhouyi*. The *xiao ren* or petty person is morally inferior and so can be dangerous to the cultivated person and to society as a whole. *Junzi* originally referred to a prince and *da ren* to someone of high rank. In early times, it was usual to equate social position with character and virtue. In English the word noble can refer to a virtuous character or hereditary high social position. This distinction between people of high or low character is funda- mental to Chinese ethical thought, though it often sounds snobbish to Western readers. We find hints of moral distinctions in the *Zhouyi*—especially in the recurrent theme of avoiding blame—but most of the divinatory responses simply recommend what is auspicious. This has led some scholars, notably Richard Rutt, to declare the text to be amoral, advising what is in the inquirer's best interest rather than what is right. This criticism is not wrong, but somewhat unfair because we cannot take the lack of ethical language at this very early stage of human thought to imply there was no morality.

Are the hexagram figures philosophy?

As already mentioned, there is no evidence from the Western Zhou that the hexagram figures played any role in interpretation. Most scholarly opinion assumes that originally the hexagrams were simply a means for organizing the material and selecting the divinatory response. By the time of the Western Han, the diagrams had become the primary means of interpretation. This is not surprising as the texts themselves are rather recalcitrant, yet something had to be done to maintain the utility of the book that was believed to contain the wisdom of the ancient sages. Interpretation with diagrams is already present in the *Changes* anecdotes in the *Zuozhuan*. The earliest known conceptual discus- sions of the trigrams are in the *Dazhuan* and the *Shuogua* (*Explaining the Trigrams*), the eighth of the *Ten Wings*.

During the Han Dynasty, interpretation by means of the diagrams became a distinct school, known as 象數 *Xiangshu* or Images and Numbers. In the Song Dynasty this reached further elaboration, particularly in the speculative philosophy of Shao Yong. (Two of the many modern examples of how elaborate analysis of hexagram patterns can become are the works of R. S. Cook and Yang Li.)

Wang Bi (226–49) reasserted the importance of the texts in what became known as the 義理 *Yili* or Meanings and Principles School, though this still made use of the diagrams.

Both modes of interpretation are in use today. Most casual readers focus on the texts, usually in the Wilhelm-Baynes version. Much of Wilhelm's explanations are actually based on the diagrams, though this would not be apparent to the casual reader—who in any case might not care. Difficult as the texts are, direct interpretation from line patterns is far from self-evident. On the other hand, anything can be projected onto them. Divination from the texts must have some relation to them for the sake of credibility.

Much confusion has been created by the assumption that all four components are closely related thematically. This is true only for a few chapters. The exceptions are minor. The hexagrams for Lower Jaw and Cauldron do resemble the objects they refer to. Hexagram 5 has references to wetness in the texts and contains the trigram for water. Such relationships are not systematic, however. A few hexagrams have thematic unity, for example 59 Spurting, about the castration of a stallion, or the nervous chattering induced by thunder in 51. On the other hand, why Oreole, the tag of 30, is connected to fire, the association of the hexagram, or weeping, as in 30.5 is not apparent. However, when we recognize the texts of hexagram 30 as a miscellaneous collection they make sense separately.

Wilhelm-Baynes' attempt to make sense of the tag and associated judgment, "What is dark clings to what is bright and so enhances the brightness of the latter," makes metaphysical nonsense of a text that is clear, if banal. It is the attempt to make it profound that makes it obscure. Now, I will admit that the Wilhelm-Baynes rendering is more interesting that mine, "Beneficial to divine; make offering. For breeding cows, auspicious." Unfortunately, the actual text has nothing to do with dark paradoxically enhancing bright.

That the diagrams came to be the basis of much exegesis should not surprise us. Diagrams have always been a means of representing the sacred. Certain geometric shapes strike the human mind as having meaning. Obvious examples include crosses of several configurations, constellation patterns, mandalas, or the circle within a square symbolizing heaven and earth, later the basis of the *luopan* or geomantic compass. The most influential modern writer on symbolism, Carl G. Jung—who was also the most influential Western interpreter of the *I Ching*—explained symbols as elements of what he called the "collective unconscious." That is to say, they somehow resonate with built-in mental structures related to cognitive processing mechanisms. The brain tends to reduce complex visual phenomena to simpler geometric representations. Given the sensation of numenousness that many feel when looking at hexagram arrays, they suggest esoteric meanings and we can understand why, in a pre-scientific era, they were thought to represent all the phenomena of nature.

Modern analytic philosophy would not find any philosophy in the hexagram figures. Yet they did serve as a systematic way of representing the situations of human life. Symbolic logic is quite unlike the hexagrams, yet both are ways of manipulating symbols to elucidate reality. Needham may have been right when he said that the very explanatory power of the system inhibited the development of science in China. However, I would modify this hypothesis to blame not the ancient system, but the social conservatism that sought truth by looking back to antiquity rather than considering other models of reality.

Sagehood, incipience, and human flourishing

As already discussed, time in the *Zhouyi* is qualitative, with each time having a particular nature in which some things can be accomplished while others cannot. Many of the repeated terms and phrases of the *Zhouyi* refer to the quality of time: auspicious, beneficial, without blame, harsh, ominous, to name a few. Chinese thought analyzes time phenomenologically. While the time of physics is regular and objective, the human experience of time is not. Waiting on line feels long, watching an exciting film is short.

The nature of the sage is to recognize incipience, in effect to be aware of the quality of a given time and thus act properly in every situation, knowing in advance how it will proceed. Thus he (the usual gender for sages) would instinctively be in accord with heaven at each moment. This ability, along with breathing exercises and herb ingestion, resulted in great longevity, extending even to centuries, though in historical times there were no more sages. One of the Eight Immortals was female, but this myth is relatively late. Regarding any notion of female sagehood, we have little documentation. Transcendence was implicit in the concept of the sage, but its effect was to enhance the sage's ability to enhance social order. This is expressed in the *Lunyu* as the Master saying: "Of those who ruled through inaction, surely Shun was one. What did he do? Dedicating himself to courtesy, he faced directly south and that was all" (*Lunyu* 15.2, in Watson 106).

Somehow the sage knows just how to set an example to cause others to assume their proper social role.

Traditionally the sage either did not need the *I Ching*, or he could understand its responses from looking at the hexagrams alone without the aid of the text. There is an implicit epistemology here that is recurrent in Chinese philosophy—the highest form of knowledge is intuitive or innate, as indicated in the famous first line of the *Dao De Jing*, "The Dao that can be expressed in words is not the unchanging Dao." While the sage either understands the *Zhouyi* from the diagrams alone, or does not need it at all, those who are not sages can avail themselves of the wisdom of the *Changes* via the diagrams and the texts that supposedly clarify them, though in actuality are mostly unrelated. There is an epistemological theory here: that some have a special ability to perceive deep meanings not apparent through the senses alone. It was left indefinite whether this ability is supernatural or a normal, though rare, human talent. Sagehood can be regarded as an ideal, perhaps not fully attainable in actuality, but approachable by self-cultivation. Notions of sagehood and personal development have a long history in China (Keenan). The *I Ching* has always been closely associated with the notion of the sage. Though early divination assumed that answers came from spirits, ancestors, or other supernatural entities, commentators on the *I Ching* consultation tended simply to avoid supernatural references.

Divination can provide practical advice, but also advises about esoteric matters. While esotericism is not considered respectable in academic analytic philosophy, humans have always wanted this sort of knowledge, and divination has been a common method of seeking to attain it. China developed many techniques for assessing special knowledge and developed a rich trove of literature about the supernatural (Santangelo). The earliest known example of communicating with the other world is the oracle bone inscriptions (earliest c. 14 BCE). The *I Ching* is the only written method that had literary respectability, although shamanism was praised by Zhu Xi, the Song Dynasty founder of neo-Confucianism. The epistemology of divination, if I can be permitted such a notion, is by its nature assumed rather than proven. With spirit mediums it was a particular being who responded. In the case of the *I Ching* the source was impersonal. This is in a way a philosophical advance in that it moves away from personalizing all natural forces and phenomena.

The concept referred to here as "incipience" is also philosophically respectable—it embodies the idea that one must look beyond what is immediately apparent to make proper decisions, that there are deeper truths under the surface of phenomena. In Chinese thought these truths, unlike those of the Platonists, are not of essences or numena, but about proper ordering of personal and social life. The very existence of the *Book of Changes* implies that hidden factors affecting people's lives can be understood, even by the non-sage.

When a hexagram and line text are selected by a random method to answer an inquiry, the question arises as to whether this assumes magical beliefs. The answer is not as obvious as it might seem. With correlative cosmology, in which all events in the cosmos are interconnected, divination represents a sort of sampling of the state of things and is not necessarily magical. It may assume forms of interactions that science has not discovered, but conceivably might someday. If, however, it is assumed that spirits guide the reply, then the supernatural is involved. My point here is that whether divination somehow works or not, belief in it can be irrational, but is not inherently so. Divination is not based on empirical science (though astrology depends upon scientific knowledge of planet movements) but, like science, it assumes that the world is knowable and can be figured out by the human mind. (For a consideration of different ways—both supernatural and psychological—that divination might work, see Redmond and Hon: 19–36.) Though seemingly self-evident now, the notion that we can understand the world better by seeking to know things not immediately available to the senses seems to have been absolutely essential for the development of civilization. It is the beginning of religion, philosophy, and science.

To appreciate the role of the *Zhouyi* or other divination systems in ancient life, it is important to be aware of the positive functions it served. To state the obvious, there were no self-help books and no psychologists, no physical therapists to help with mobility problems, no financial advisors—and almost no wealth in the form of money. In a hierarchical society, asking others for advice is awkward if they are not of similar status. Though it is far from being a work of psychology, use of the *Zhouyi* was one of few ways to help with decision-making, and so can be considered as a means of nourishing life. (For a contemporary perspective on the concept of nourishing life, see Farquhar and Zhang 2012.) Those who use divination commonly feel helped by it. While divination can lead to bad decisions, most of us are quite capable of making bad decisions on our own.

Change, truth, and happiness

As the title, *Book of Changes* implies, Chinese metaphysics is about processes, not fixed essences. In this it differs fundamentally from Plato, Neo-Platonism and much Western thought that seeks constancy behind changing appearances. In Chinese thought, there were deeper truths that might be realized, but no conception of a split between phenomena and numena, no Kantian notion of the unknowability of ultimate reality. Nor do we find anything like the analytical approach of Aristotle with his types of causality. In contrast to Buddhism and other Indian philosophies, native Chinese philosophy did not conceive of human existence in a negative way, comparable to the Buddhist doctrine that life is suffering (*dukkha*) because of impermanence (*anicca*). These concepts did enter China with Buddhism in the Eastern Han, but they were not present before that. While change is the nature of things, the *Book of Changes* can aid in accommodating it. While pre-Buddhist Chinese thought does not equate change or impermanence with suffering, neither does it hold the view of American popular psychology that change is always good, as exemplified by the title of a recent book by Dr. Wayne W. Dyer: *Change Your Thoughts—Change Your Life: Living the Wisdom of the Tao.* (Also available as an unabridged eight CD set). Dr. Dyer tells us that he spent *an entire year* studying the *Dao De Jing.* I have spent more than thirty years, but when it comes to ancient texts, it seems I am a slow learner.

Certainly the Chinese did not rate their classics by degree of optimism or pessimism, yet it is interesting to consider them from this perspective. The *Ten Wings* and particularly the *Dazhuan* are rather more optimistic than the *Zhouyi.* The *Dazhuan* provides a positive outlook on life, encourages virtue, and tends to skip over violence, never recommending sacrificing captives, for example. However, it has nothing like the forced optimism of modern self-help books. The Chinese attitude toward change is more realistic and neutral: sometimes your plans will succeed; at other times they will not. Life is constant change; one copes by learning to accord with Heaven or the *Dao* with the aid of the *I Ching.*

Meaning change as the rise of conscience

The most dramatic of all recent discoveries of the early meanings of the *Zhouyi* is that 孚 *fu*, which was taken to mean "trust" or "sincerity" in the received meanings, actually meant captives who were being held for sacrifice. Human sacrifice turns out to have been a major subject of the *Zhouyi.* These meanings are distinguished orthographically in later Chinese. The person radical, 人 *ren*, was added to the early character to make it specific for *fu* prisoner 俘, while the early form of 孚 *fu* became specific for trust or sincerity. The recognition that *fu* was not a virtue, but was in fact something quite terrible, made the traditional view of the *Changes* as a guide to morality and wisdom no longer tenable. This, and the other moralistic readings of the *Changes* that had inspired readers for so many centuries, turned out to be absent from the Western Zhou texts entirely.

Confucius famously remarked, "I no longer dream of the Duke of Zhou," meaning that he had somehow lost his sense of connection with this supposed paragon of virtue. After the work of the Doubting Antiquity Movement, it would be confusing to dream of the Duke of Zhou. His role is writing the line texts of the *Zhouyi* was shown to be myth, as was King Wu's authorship of the judgments. (The roles attributed to the two culture heroes varied.) Fu Xi was relegated to myth. Even the foundational myth of the legitimacy of the imperial government—the Zhou conquest of Shang as a triumph of virtue—was no longer plausible (Redmond and Hon: 60f.). Despite its clear refutation, the appealing mythic account is still taught in China and widely believed.

Many admirers of the *Changes* have resisted the new understanding that resulted from the work of the Doubting Antiquity Movement; even more simply ignore it. A vocal opponent of "context criticism" of the *Changes* is Bradford Hatcher (2009: I. 16–49 *et passim*). His criticisms are too detailed for fair consideration here, but basically he objects to replacing the received meanings with reconstructed ones, *fu* being a prominent example. Hatcher makes a valid point that the extreme polysemy of the Chinese language makes it often impossible to determine which meaning was intended. This reminds us that there remain many uncertainties regarding the early meanings, but it does not change the fact that these were radically different from the later Confucianized ones. *Fu* in particular fits all its contexts as captives, while there is no evidence for concepts like trust and sincerity in the Western Zhou. A variety of theories have been advanced as to how *fu* came to mean trust, though none are convincing. This is often the case with changes in meaning in any language. Paradoxically, the removal—or cover-up—of references to human sacrifice indicates a rising awareness that this practice was wrong, a major ethical advance. We would like to know how this radical change in consciousness occurred—from human sacrifice being beneficial to society, to its being wrong. Unfortunately, the old texts are silent on such matters.

With scriptural texts, there are often multiple interpretive traditions, and from the point of view of religious history, all have some validity. That the early meanings were different does not mean the later ones were wrong, though it takes away ancientness as the basis of their supposed authority. Critical scholarship should not, in my opinion, try to negate the inspiration that believers find in the *I Ching* (or the Bible, or the *Heart* or *Lotus* sutras, or any other scriptural text). That the inspiration resides as much in tradition as in literal meanings does not invalidate it. Like many, I sometimes find spiritual meaning in the Wilhelm-Baynes *I Ching* despite (or because of) its bearing scant resemblance to the Western Zhou meanings.

An idea of the wide range of ways of construing the *Book of Changes* is apparent from perusing the annotated bibliography of Hacker, Moore, and Patsco (2002) and the *I Ching Handbook* by Hacker (1993) Also of interest in this regard are works in English by Chinese practitioners, such as those of Wei Tat and Chung Wu. Perusal of these various works will give a good sense of the extraordinary range of ideas that have been associated with this single 3,000-year-old book. Finally, as one continues to study the *Changes*, there is no reason to prematurely confine oneself to one of the many viewpoints about the book.

To point out what should be common sense, when using the *I Ching* for divination or any other sort of practice, prudence is to be exercised in deciding whether to follow any advice seemingly provided by the classic. Personally, I find divination fascinating as an aspect of human consciousness, though as to anything supernatural in the process I remain agnostic, if only because I like to leave the door open on mystery. Despite my preference for the scholarly approach, I think that without the diversity of points of view, 易學 *Yi xue,* study of the *Changes* would be far less interesting.

Did the *Changes* inhibit the development of science in China?

Joseph Needham regarded the correlative cosmology of traditional China as a major factor that kept China from developing systematic science. This British historian of science was preoccupied with the paradox that China had made many technological and scientific discoveries—ceramic manufacture superior to any in the West and smallpox vaccination, are two examples—yet did not develop an empirically-based science. Needham's theory was that the *yin-yang* and *wu xing* cosmology provided such convenient explanations for all phenomena that they took away the incentive to study the cosmos empirically. While this idea is plausible, it is problematic in assuming that China *should* have developed science.

Furthermore, speculating on why something did not happen in history is questionable. A further difficulty with Needham's theory is that metaphysical theories in the West, such as those of Aristotle or the four humors, did not ultimately prevent science from developing in the West. Yet his theory is a useful reminder for our own time's nostalgia for enchantment, that metaphysics and the supernatural, however emotionally satisfying their explanations, do not lead to useful real-world outcomes.

7

Philosophy in the *Zhouyi*

Between the quite mundane Western Zhou text and the well-developed philosophy of the *Dazhuan* we have no intermediate historical sources. While explicitly philosophical statements are not found in the *Zhouyi*, I believe we can identify passages in which philosophy was latent. These passages hint at reflections about human life that go beyond the simple concrete imagery, or suggest some degree of ethical awareness. I do not want to exaggerate this point. I do not think most of the philosophy later associated with the *Changes* was somehow hidden in the Western Zhou text. Rather, as with *yin* and *yang*, I believe much of the later philosophy arose from multiple sources, of which the *Zhouyi* was one.

Confucianism invented its own history but projected it back onto the ancient classics, not only the *Zhouyi* but also the *Shijing* and *Spring and Autumn Annals*. Its mythology went mostly unquestioned until the Doubting Antiquity Movement. The Confucian meanings are not self-evident; if one did not already know them from commentaries, one could not guess what they were. Yet there must have been some relation between the original classics and their later orthodox readings.

In the following, I suggest that some material in the *Zhouyi* may have been suggestive of philosophical ideas. I think of these as seeds, or perhaps even sprouts, struggling to rise up through the soil of pre-axiality. While I admit to starting out with an idea of what I hoped to find, I have tried to be self-disciplined in staying close to the texts, as I have translated them. I cannot claim that my findings rise to the level of certainty, but I believe they are suggestive.

Cosmology and religion

Heaven and earth: Coming together and separating

Hexagrams 11 and 12 have been particularly important in *I Ching* philosophy. The standard philosophical meanings of these hexagrams were derived entirely from the two possible arrangements for the trigrams designated as heaven and earth. Heaven in Chinese philosophy was what established the proper order of things. In hexagram 11 heaven rises up and earth descends, so the human level moves to accord with the cosmic level. On the other hand, in hexagram 12, heaven floats up away from earth, which sinks down. Thus hexagram 11 is the ideal state of affairs, while hexagram 12 represented the separation of earth and humanity from heaven. Thus the two hexagrams were convenient representations of the two overall states of society: living in accord with heaven's way, or contrary to it. This interpretation fits Chinese cosmology neatly. It is arbitrary, however. The two diagrams could just as easily be interpreted in the opposite way. In hexagram 12 the trigram positions could be considered normal—heaven is above earth. By this logic, in hexagram 11, earth above heaven, the cosmos would be disordered. I am not implying that the traditional interpretation is wrong, simply that it is not the only meaning that could be imagined for the figures.

This contrast between hexagrams 11 and 12 fits with Chinese socio-political theory. For Confucius the way of heaven was being followed, or it was not. The *Dao* was in the world, or it was not.

Heaven in Chinese philosophy was what established the proper order of things. If the will of heaven was followed by everyone from the emperor on down, there would be peace and prosperity. While the emperor had near-absolute power, ritual errors could raise suspicion that he was not suited to be ruler—expressed not in terms of competence, but as losing the mandate of heaven. As we saw in the *Zhouyi*, even failure to shoot game could cause his potency to be questioned. That the king or emperor was in effect appointed by heaven was a powerful argument for his legitimacy, but lacked objective basis. Since heaven showed its pleasure or displeasure by natural phenomena—good harvests indicated heaven's satisfaction, anomalies its displeasure, and so on. Since the ruler had no actual control over such, the mandate of heaven could often be challenged. In practical terms, the mandate was usually assumed after military conquest.

Chinese writings on government constantly express anxiety that in their own time people were not following the way of heaven. Impropriety on the human level caused disruption on the cosmic level.

The importance of this hexagram pairing is an example of the great importance Chinese thought places on proper position, whether in soldiers preparing for battle, guests sitting at a banquet, direction for travel, and other activities such as sacrifice, even facing the right direction—north—to consult the *I Ching*. Likely one reason for the persistence of the hexagrams is that they seem almost custom-made to represent a hierarchical society. In traditional China, hierarchy went beyond social rank; all sorts of situations had rules for correct ordering. The king's legitimacy was in part dependent upon his fidelity to ritual, which required the correct positioning with respect to heaven.

We do not find anything like a political theory in the *Zhouyi*, except that the diagrams and line texts themselves are hierarchical and seem to prescribe a rigid social structure. It is not that higher line positions are necessarily better, but that lines, and therefore people, should be in their proper position.

This makes it paradoxical that the *Changes*, though entirely orthodox in China, became an icon of the egalitarian Western counter-culture of the 1960s. Its use, besides being fashionable, was an act of resistance against the dominant scientific worldview, though not a very serious one, as its use did not mean giving up the benefits of technology.

The sixties was not the only time divination has been used to serve for protest or resistance. Because divination can carry supernatural authority, yet be made to serve any agenda, in the hands of charismatic figures it can be a way to justify disorder and revolt.

Before we completely disparage the authoritarian governmental system of pre-modern China, we should mention its usual apologetic—that it held China together for over two millennia, an enormous country with many different languages and ethnicities. Control was never complete, as expressed in the proverb "Heaven is high above and the emperor is far away." One of the best-known lines in Chinese literature is that which opens *The Romance of Three Kingdoms*, "The empire once united, must divide; once divided, must unite." China has continued to unite, while Europe became fragmented after the fall of the Roman Empire and remains so today. This is not to say that the Chinese system of government is better than Western ones, or that it should serve as a model for other countries, as has been recently proposed, simply that it succeeded in maintaining itself. Hard as it is for those of us fortunate enough to live in a democratic society to sympathize with autocracy, China did have an effective philosophy of social order and the *Book of Changes* played a part in it.

What jawbones can tell us

Hexagram 27 begins with the enigmatic judgment:

Divination auspicious according to observation of the jaw.

Following this, we are admonished:

Leave at home your numinous tortoise.

The words of the judgment make grammatical sense but are otherwise baffling. When one realizes that they are about divination based on movements of the mandible, the lower jaw, they become understandable, even if far-fetched. Divination methods, such as physiognomy, based on the body, were pervasive in the ancient world. They could be based on bodily locations, markings such as moles, sensations, or involuntary movements. Another example is 31.2, "sensation in one's calf, ominous."

Odd as these methods seem, they are based on the as-above-so-below cosmology, also referred to as macro-microcosmic equivalence. All parts of the cosmos are conceived to be interconnected so that what happens in any part is also present in all the other parts. The body is a microcosm of the cosmos. In recent decades it has become fashionable to argue that modern quantum physics was anticipated in China 3,000 years ago (Capra). Despite its appeal to many in the West and in China, this idea is not correct.

Chinese cosmology did not lead to any advances in science or technology, nor is the macro-micro-equivalence verifiable in any objective way. Physics sees distant interactions in the universe but not equivalence. To give a simplistic example, watching the jaw movements of family members or guests cannot tell us anything about the structure of distant galaxies—or even relatively close objects like the moon. It may, like other methods of divination, stimulate our intuition, but it cannot reveal remote events.

Physiognomy has been popular at times in the West, most recently as phrenology: reading a person's character by feeling the shape of his or her head. This was the invention of Franz Joseph Gall, in 1796. It is not inherently illogical to hypothesize that the skull could be shaped by the underlying brain. In fact, the skull's size is determined by brain growth, but not its surface shape. The bumps palpated by the phrenologists bore no actual relationship to character traits. Phrenology mainly served as a parlor game.

While phrenology enthusiasts in the nineteenth century should have known better, in their practice there is something akin to the scientific attitude in physiognomy—searching for anatomical correlates of individual differences in brain functioning. This is like the scientific attitude in searching for relationships amongst phenomena that led to philosophy, and much later to science. What was lacking was any sense of empirical validation. Ideas about the significance of facial features were imagined but never tested.

Another aspect of divination that anticipates philosophy is the notion of expertise, that some people know more about a subject than others because they have studied it intensively and, presumably, gotten better at it. Diviners are experts of a sort, though amateurs too can do it. One could argue cynically that the expertise of diviners lies in bilking their clients, and this is certainly often the case. Yet there is no reason to doubt that many were—and are—sincere in their practice. Confucius, for example, was modest about his divinatory abilities, stating that he was accurate about two thirds of the time.

I am not claiming that divination or correlative cosmology led directly to science, rather that they are examples of people looking for patterns in phenomena. The clearest example is astrology, now despised by astronomers but acknowledged to be the origin of systematic observation of celestial events. This does not negate Needham's view that metaphysics seems to explain phenomena and thus inhibits more open-minded inquiry. This was certainly true in medicine. Ancient diagnostic methods, including those of China and Greece, were essentially divination. This is still true of Chinese tongue and pulse diagnosis, though fans of Chinese medicine imagine they somehow reveal disordered physiology. Nonetheless, the most skilled pulse diagnostician cannot discover what a cardiac echo will quickly reveal. Pulse analysis did not lead to cardiology. On the other hand, ancient diagnostic methods were the precursors of physical diagnosis.

It is important not to go too far in finding philosophical or scientific thought in the ancient world. Causality in pre-scientific cultures was conceived quite differently from scientific causality, and even today supernatural beliefs persist today in many parts of the world. Fortunately curiosity seems to be hard-wired into our brains, otherwise culture and civilization could not have come to be. However, curiosity needed the addition of empiricism to lead to science.

A time of sterility

Line 54.6 is one of the most striking images in the *Zhouyi* and illustrates vividly the nature of correlative thought:

> The woman offers a basket; there is no fruit.
> The official cuts a sheep, there is no blood.
> There is nothing beneficial.

The images depict impotence, sterility, and ritual inefficacy. The implication is that the sterility is somehow the fault of the man and woman. While expressed in terms that may seem superstitious, underlying these concrete images is a notion of the universe as vulnerable to the actions of humanity. Fear that humans will harm the earth persists today in the ecological movement, particularly its concern with climate change. The human actions that could disrupt the cosmic order, which the ancients feared, of course differed radically from those of modern ecology, yet they embodied a recognition that the environment is vulnerable to human behavior. The responses to such omens were ritual rather than ecological. They did not limit forest clearance—necessary for the spread of cultivation—nor over-hunting, which was a problem with tortoises and other species. But there were rules for the maintenance of harmony between humans and the cosmos with recognition that violations of them, particularly by the king, could result in harm, or anomalies such as crop failure, drought, and earthquakes. Humans have had a sense of their actions harming the earth much longer than is usually imagined. What was missing until recently was the scientific knowledge to identify environmental harm and propose solutions. This represents a seismic shift in consciousness, long after the axial age, in which technical measures replace ritual as the means for enhancing human flourishing. The extent to which technology is good or bad is an issue beyond the scope of this book. My point is that our concern for the environment is ancient; while knowledge of effective ways to protect it is recent.

Ethics

The changing meanings of the first line of the *Zhouyi*, 元亨利貞 *yuan, heng, li, zhen,* can be used to illustrate the development of Chinese philosophical thought. In the Western Zhou they were simply an invocation. As I have translated:

Begin with an offering for beneficial divination.

Later this phrase was read as an itemization of good character traits. Wilhelm-Baynes translate as:

THE CREATIVE works sublime success,
Furthering through perseverance. (4)

Lynn translates as:

Qian consists of fundamentality [*yuan*], prevalence [*heng*], fitness [*li*], and constancy [*zhen*]. (1994: 129 *et passim*)

These later meanings, although vague, are about virtue or character traits and have no evident relation to the ritual incantation of the *Zhouyi*, raising once again the question of how the new meanings

360 THE I CHING (BOOK OF CHANGES)

came to be. Given that the book owed its prestige to its connection
with the supposedly virtuous Zhou Dynasty, the first words would
have been assumed to be particularly profound, and hence taken to
refer to human ethical ideals as part of the Confucian program to
make the ancient classics advance their interests. These men (their
ideology included confinement of women to the household) were
of the 士 *shi* class that justified its claim to fitness for office based
on a knowledge of these very classics, which they in effect rewrote.
Thus the superior suitability for office that the Confucians claimed
for themselves was intertwined with the authority of the classics.

Chinese ethical thought to the present day has always been situational. There is no Chinese equivalent of the Ten Commandments.
There were, however, many rules for the minutiae of daily life,
and also awareness that ethical decisions must be made in very
diverse circumstances. Men who were examplars of paradigmatic
virtue, such as the Duke of Zhou or Confucius, were particularly
prominent in ethical thought—the truly virtuous person would
always know the right course in any situation. Chinese ethical
writing expresses high ideals of character, so much so that Leibniz
and other Europeans who knew of China only through translations
of its classics imagined the country to be an ethical utopia. Thus
yuan, heng, li, zhen are meant to inspire virtue, not to explain
specific virtues. As such they were about being virtuous rather than
about virtues. We will see how this functioned in the anecdote of
Lady Mu Jiang, to be discussed below.

The line texts of *Qian* have an unusual degree of thematic
consistency. The dragon image appears in all the lines, except 1.3,
but here the upright person is implicitly compared to a dragon. As
one moves upward in reading the lines they show progression in
two ways—higher physical location and progressively later stages
of a process.

Traditionally this was the most important hexagram, as it represents pure *yang*, the creative principle. The early Jesuit missionaries
claimed that the dragon was a reference to the creator God, vainly
hoping that this analogy to Genesis would facilitate conversion of
the Chinese. Wang Bi's commentary on the supposed references to
creation were quite different from Christian ones:

The myriad things are provided their beginnings by it, and as
such, it controls heaven.

Yet continued reading shows that the lines are clearly based on Chinese mythology:

> When it is the moment for it, ride one of the six dragons to drive through the sky. (Lynn: 129)

The six dragons here are, of course, the line texts of this hexagram. While nothing in the Western Zhou text explains the symbolic meaning of the dragons, they obviously represent energy and so naturally became correlated with *yang*, making *Qian*, with all solid lines, maximum *yang*. The line texts describe this energy transforming from potential to active when the dragon, first hidden in the depths, rises higher and higher. While dragons are obviously phallic, this aspect does not play a significant role in the *Zhouyi* or later commentaries. Rather, the shape of a dragon is thought to have been inspired by lightning and came to be commonly depicted in stormy skies or turbulent waters. It is important to recognize that the associations with *yang* are far more extensive than just masculinity, as *yin* associations go beyond femininity. The Western notion that *yang* and *yin* are equal is not entirely correct; *yin* has many negative associations, including old age, the criminal underworld and the realm of the dead.

Because the texts for *Qian* are more structured than is the case for most of the other hexagrams, it has been suggested that it is a later addition. As I have pointed out with regard to many proposed emendations of the *Changes*, the only evidence for this one is negative. There is no evidence to refute it. Recent research indicates that the dragons originally represented positions of constellations, suggesting that the texts were not originally *yang* correlations.

While the diagram and the texts of *Qian* all fit with *yang*, with *Kun*, the second hexagram and the one associated with *yin*, there is little relationship of the tag or diagrams with the texts. It was an obvious step to correlate it with maximum *yin*, but the only basis for this was the hexagram. There are no other obvious *yin* correlations. Although the judgment text refers to a mare, in context she is not a symbol of femininity but the choice of an animal for a blood sacrifice. Significantly, in the Mawangdui silk manuscript this hexagram is not paired with 1 as 2, but is 33. Thus the *yin-yang* associations of these two hexagrams were not inherent in the *Zhouyi*, but once the *yin-yang* cosmology was applied to the *Zhouyi*, *Kun* would be the necessary choice for *yin*.

In conclusion, the simple dualism represented by the solid and broken lines easily permitted the more philosophical dualism of *yin* and *yang* to be superimposed on them. The trigrams and hexagrams could serve as visual models of the complex combinations of the two forces that were thought to make up all phenomena. Without dismissing Needham's judgment of the adverse effects of this metaphysics on Chinese intellectual development, it was an extremely successful system in giving Chinese a way to think about their universe. Simply put, the *yin* and *yang* metaphysics helped make sense of the world.

For a more detailed exposition of the moral and cosmological ideas that developed around the *Zhouyi*, see my colleague Tze-ke Hon's chapters in our *Teaching the I Ching (Book of Changes)* (2015: 140–80).

Was early China monotheistic?

Here is line 42.2:

> Perhaps advantageous—ten cowry shells for a tortoise.
> Cannot overcome or avoid.
> Long-lasting auspicious divination.
> The king uses for an offering to *Di* (the high god), auspicious.

I will begin by considering the mention of *Di* 帝, the translation of which has been highly controversial. In the Shang Dynasty it referred to a spirit to whom sacrifices were offered. Perhaps the most accurate translation for early usage is "Great Ancestor." Sometimes the term was *Shangdi* 上帝, or high ancestor/spirit. During the Zhou, *Di* 帝 was replaced by *tian* 天 heaven. This would not have been a radical change, as the character *shang* probably referred to the god being in the sky, where gods tend to reside. Politics may have been involved as well, since deities had regional or clan affiliations.

Other commonly-used English translations were often based on inaccurate implications of monotheism. The question of whether

Shangdi could be considered to refer to the Christian creator God was acrimoniously debated by missionaries in China and their organizations back home. Both Catholics and Protestants wanted to find some form of monotheism in Chinese belief systems, not only to aid the conversion of Chinese but also to maintain credibility for their own faith in the Christian revelation as universal. Other missionaries felt the Chinese religions were entirely heathen and any comparison to Christianity was impious. They were correct to the extent that arguments for an early but forgotten monotheism or creator god in China are entirely unpersuasive.

Di was never the creator god, nor the proclaimer of a moral code, analogous to the Ten Commandments. Chinese moral thinking is not based on a declaration from God propagated by a prophet such as Moses, Jesus, or Mohammed. The source of moral knowledge is not a single authority, but mythical sages, culture heroes, or real-life philosophical writers, such as Confucius. The ancient Chinese worried about angering spirits, especially their ancestors, but this was mostly a matter of mourning behavior and sacrifice, not personal morality. Heaven, however, would react to improper behavior, particularly by the king or emperor, and particularly regarding excessive sexual indulgence.

Study and self-cultivation were the key to moral development in ancient China. The *I Ching* had become an important resource for this purpose as early as the *Zuozhuan* anecdotes. Whether it was seen as an ethical guide in the Western Zhou is doubtful, though it clearly was by the time of the *Zuozhuan*. The *I Ching* facilitated personal morality, not by lists of rules but by stimulating self-examination, as we find in the anecdote of Lady Mu Jiang. In contrast to the religions of the book, Chinese classics did not describe specific law-givers, instead, morality was based on the collective wisdom of (hypothetical) ancient sages. In practice this situational ethical system was problematic because right and wrong could be whatever those in power decided it was. Qing Dynasty legal codes, in listing various offences, state the final one as, "doing what should not be done." Thus anything offending someone in power could be a crime. My personal conclusion from what I know about early Chinese ethical and legal thought is that it provides a valuable way for developing one's own morality, but does not lend itself to a government of laws rather than of men or women. Nor does it provide much provision for protecting the weak from the powerful.

Returning to the role of *Di* or *Shangdi*, because China had no law-giver equivalent to Yahweh (Jehovah), this was sometimes taken to support a prejudice that Chinese had no morality. It is true that no Chinese deity has attributes comparable to those of Yahweh. They are more akin to those of Greek mythology in that they were not primarily paragons or judges of morality but beings who would interfere with humans and needed to be propitiated. This could include human sacrifice, as with Iphigenia in the Iliad. In China moral teaching came to be attributed to philosophers rather than religious figures. The cult of Mao Zedong and the *Little Red Book* suggested by Lin Biao in some ways continued this tradition of humans becoming sages and definitive sources of morality, though this comparison is unfair to Confucius, Laozi, Mengzi, and many others.

Supernatural beings were everywhere in ancient and later China. They bred as prolifically as Marquis Kang's horses (35.0), but did not resemble the monotheistic God of Western Abrahamic faiths singly or collectively. There was nothing comparable to the first commandment; the various gods were usually not jealous of the others. Some became more than local, such as Guanyin, the Buddhist Goddess of Compassion. Confucius and Laozi were deified. Another is the ghost-catcher or demon-queller 鍾馗 Zhong Kui. His mythology originated in the Tang Dynasty; we have little record of Western Zhou mythology. According to legend, Zhong Kui came first in the imperial examinations but because he was deformed he was stripped of his title, leading him to commit suicide. He ended up in hell, but because of his righteousness he took on the mission of controlling the evil denizens of hell. A famous painting shows his marriage procession of a variety of comical-looking demons. Zhong Kui is one of many figures who died wrongful deaths and were then deified. General Guan, a hero of the *Romance of Three Kingdoms* (*San Guo*), is another. The main role such deities play in the Chinese spiritual imagination is as protectors or bringers of good fortune in the form of money and children. Catholic saints have similar roles in the folk beliefs of many Catholics. Zhong Kui was a subject of humorous illustrations and mostly employed for scary fun, akin to Halloween or the Chinese Hungry Ghost Festival. These figures are all supernatural but do not have any elaborate theology or philosophy attached to them.

The point I am trying to make here is that Chinese philosophy, except for that of Buddhism, although overlapping with religion in ideas and practices, is not much based on deities and spirits. For most Chinese their relationship to deities is little more than creating altars at home or place of business and making offerings of fruit and incense. Daoism and Buddhism were philosophical as well as practical, but the philosophy was of interest only to a few.

The non-theism of Confucius and the *I Ching*

The seemingly non-theistic character of Confucianism made it very attractive to Westerners of the Enlightenment who were dissatisfied with the theistic and institutional nature of the established religions. It is true that Confucianism is non-theistic, but its earlier admirers did not realize that the actual Confucians had a rich variety of other gods. The *I Ching*, at least as depicted in the *Zuozhuan*, and later, was also non-theistic, though not atheistic, and this no doubt was a great part of its attractiveness for many of its admirers, from Leibniz to Wilhelm, to Jung, to sixties counter-culture. This same non-theism resulted in antagonism, particularly on the part of the missionaries such as McClatchie, Legge, and Rutt. (Why these men worked so hard for so many years to accurately translate one of the world's most difficult non-Christian classics is a great literary mystery, so far unsolved.)

The *I Ching* did not require any specific religious or supernatural beliefs on the part of the user, nor was it incompatible with any. One could believe its practice enhanced one's personal spirituality without contradicting one's other beliefs or values. The exception would be religions that consider it trafficking with the devil, but this is more a matter of religious authority than doctrine.

Given that in the Western Zhou religious beliefs were completely embedded within the rest of culture, the *Zhouyi* would not have been discordant with any other practices. While this ancient society cannot by any stretch of the imagination be termed secular, relationships with deities were mostly what Ong termed as "bribery." This is not spiritual in the contemporary use of the word. As soon as we have evidence of self-conscious spirituality in China, that is, with axialization, the *I Ching* became part of it. There were deities but they mainly served to meet the human need for myth and ritual.

The great figures of Confucianism, Daoism, and Buddhism were all human, and all died natural deaths.

Rutt's view, that what became the *Book of Changes* was not spiritual in the Western Zhou, is not entirely wrong. Spiritual meanings were superimposed on it later, though it did not, however, advocate specific religious dogmas or practices and was arguably more philosophical than religious.

Human relationships

Teacher and students

Tag 4, "neophytes," suggests students or beginners, as does Wilhelm-Baynes' translation as "youthful folly." Rare for the *Zhouyi*, the judgment is a first person statement and seems to be a teacher or other mature person expressing dislike of being asked the same question repeatedly:

> I do not ask the neophytes; the neophytes ask me.
> The initial yarrow divination informs, but to repeat several times is disrespectful.
> When disrespected, it does not inform.
> 亨. 匪我求童蒙; 童蒙求我.
> 初筮告, 再三瀆. 瀆則不告.

Here we have, 3,000 years ago, a teacher interacting with students. (The passage was also construed as asking the *Changes* the same question repeatedly.) The oracle was to be treated with the respect due a sage. It would be going too far to claim this as analogous to the Platonic dialogues, which were written at least three centuries after the *Zhouyi*, by which time philosophy had blossomed in both Greece and China. What we do find is that there was discussion of ideas as early as the Western Zhou, presumably between teachers and students. One can imagine that the subject being taught was the *Zhouyi*. Any teacher recognizes the tensions inherent in the student-teacher relationship. Debate is essential for the development of philosophy. Indeed, early philosophical texts including the Theravada sutras, the Questions of King Milinda, the Platonic dialogues, and the *Lunyu* are records of conversations. This example is as close as we get to a depiction of discussions in the Western Zhou. Details of human interactions are not often described in the *Zhouyi*.

Actual divination is usually in the form of a dialogue—a question is asked, the diviner replies, the inquirer is likely to have comments or further questions, and the diviner may modify the prediction in response. Sadly, we have few records of these interactions and those that we have are from centuries later than the Western Zhou.

Walter Ong emphasizes that early discussions were agonistic, by which he means verbally combative:

> Socrates taught by attacking, relentlessly, like a bull ...
> Oral modes of storing and retrieving knowledge are formulaic in design and tend to be agonistic in operation. (2002: 480)

The formulaic nature of the *Zhouyi* is apparent throughout, but this judgment text gives a hint of what was likely the agonistic nature of serious dialogue. The next line, 4.1, is startling to those used to current thinking on education:

> If the neophytes speak out loud—it is beneficial to use physical punishment. Use scolding to restrain them from shame.

Ong points out that for most of history, when teaching outside of the home was only for boys, physical punishment was considered necessary for education, particularly in the teaching of Latin which, "normally entailed physical punishment, often very severe ..." and he quotes George Orwell, who thought it was impossible to teach Latin without physical punishment. Ong also notes that in Renaissance iconography the schoolmaster is often depicted carrying a bundle of switches (2002: 485). Coincidentally, the Chinese character for father, 父 *fu*, is supposedly two crossed belts as would be used to discipline sons. Thus in these lines we have a representation of two aspects of education, harsh discussion and severe discipline, likely similar in Ancient China and Ancient Greece. Why the harshness and severity were thought necessary, I have no theory to propose, but will point out that the notion of "nurturing" students is quite recent.

Affection

The image of the crane calling to its young in 61.2 is one of the most famous and appealing in the *Book of Changes*. It is also the only line in which the character 陰 *yin* appears. No doubt this was another bird-call omen, but given the subsequent line about sharing the goblet, there is an atmosphere of warm conviviality, something not prominent in the *Zhouyi*. There is also an ethical undertone—appreciation of nurturing as a value in human life. As generally the case in the *Zhouyi*, this is not expressed in descriptive prose but through an image from the natural world. This line somewhat softens the rather harsh attitude of hexagram 4.1.

Ethics

Self-examination with the *Zhouyi*

The most interesting early example of an exchange between diviner and inquirer is the anecdote of Lady Mu Jiang in the *Zuozhuan*, in which the noblewoman, placed under house arrest for stirring up political unrest, performs a divination to determine if she will ever be released. She casts the yarrow sticks and obtains 52 *Gen*, changing to 17 *Sui*. The divination is based on the judgment line of *Sui*, which is in my translation:

> 17.0 Begin with an offering, beneficial to divine.
> There will be no blame.
> 元亨利貞. 无咎.

The diviner, no doubt wanting to please his client, interprets the opening formula, *yuan, heng, li, zhen*, as, "goodness ... sum of all excellence ... harmony of all that is right ..." He goes on to predict, "Your ladyship will get out soon."

The lady replies to the contrary:

> I am a woman involved in disorder ... I am not benevolent, so *yuan* does not apply to me. I have not stabilized the dynasty, so

heng does not apply to me. I have acted against my own good, so *li* does not apply to me. I have descended into intrigue, so *zhen* does not apply to me.

She goes on:

Sui means no trouble, but only for a person with these four virtues. I have none of them ... . I shall not get out. (*Zuozhuan*, trans. Rutt: 187f.)

It has been suggested that whoever composed Lady Mu Jiang's self-critical statement, it was not the allegedly wicked lady herself. Certainly the language is far more sophisticated than that of the *Spring and Autumn Annals* on which the *Zuozhuan* is supposedly a commentary. Let us set aside the question of whether such a dialogue could actually have taken place during the spring and autumn period and accept the consensus that it was a retelling added in the Warring States or Early Han. (The extent to which speeches recorded in early Chinese classics were transcriptions of what was actually said is the subject of a well-known sinological controversy between David Shaberg and Yuri Pines.)

The Mu Jiang anecdote is very informative on several levels. First, a woman is an active participant in the divination, casting the yarrow herself. Second, she clearly has a more profound understanding of the *I Ching* than the diviner, presumably male, indicating that women, at least high-born ones, could be learned in the classics. Confident of her knowledge, Lady Mu Jiang does not hesitate to authoritatively challenge the diviner's reading. The episode is of interest on a philosophical level as well, as it is the earliest example we have of the *Changes* being used for self-analysis. It does not matter whether the real Lady Mu Jiang composed this self-criticism, or was aware of her faults, or even knew the *Zhouyi* because it shows what was believed about the *Zhouyi*. Lady Mu Jiang's rejection of the diviner's flattering reading embodies the *Changes* ideology that the oracle would not give accurate answers to those who are dishonest or insincere. She receives a line that is a list of virtues, yet recognizes that she is unworthy, confessing that she has none of the virtues and therefore the positive prognosis does not apply to her, indeed that she does not deserve to be released from her punishment.

This expresses ethical philosophy in a way characteristic of Chinese thought—as anecdotes about individuals who are examples of high or low morals. It also contains another important point, that humans are capable of moral development. Lady Mu Jiang comes to recognize her failings and that her punishment is the result of her own actions. Further characteristic of Confucian thought is that her moral insight is possible because of her study of a classic.

In his famous Foreword to the Wilhelm-Baynes *I Ching*, Carl Jung declared:

> The *I Ching* insists upon self-knowledge throughout. The method by which this is to be achieved is open to every kind of misuse, and is therefore not for the frivolous-minded and immature; nor is it for intellectualists and rationalists. It is appropriate only for thoughtful and reflective people who like to think about what they do and what happens to them. (xxxiii)

He then issues a disclaimer that he cannot reconcile use of the *I Ching* with scientific rationalism.

Let us set aside the question of how a psychologist writing 3,000 years after the *Zhouyi* can have anything to tell us about it, besides the facile dismissal of "intellectualists and rationalists." His warning that the *Changes* is for "those who like to think about what they do and what happens to them," applies not only to ourselves but to Chinese at least as far back as the Spring and Autumn Period, and perhaps even to the Western Zhou. Whatever its limitations—and they are many, not least the later-suppressed acceptance of human sacrifice—the *Changes* was and is a way of looking deeper into reality and thus is at root served as a philosophical work. It can also serve, as it did for Carl Jung, to restore a bit of enchantment to the modern world.

Many who use the *Book of Changes*, or other divination methods, do not trouble themselves as to whether it is rational, because they think of it simply as a way to find fresh ways of thinking about a challenging situation—to "think outside the box," to use a contemporary set phrase. These ideas can be about simple practical matters, or ethical dilemmas, or the nature of the cosmos, or anything else. Bibliomancy can be performed with many texts, not simply the *I Ching*. A common practice in the past was to open a Bible at random and find a phrase to illuminate one's situation.

To return to the simple example I gave previously of an *I Ching* reading I did for a young woman who was considering a marriage that would require her to move to China. The selected line stated, "Not beneficial to cross the great water." When I told her this, she acknowledged that she was actually reluctant to make this move. I do not know what she finally decided, but I think that the divinatory response was helpful in encouraging her to examine her misgivings about this crucial life decision. This is the proper use of divination—considering what it has to say, rather than automatically following it.

Respectful intention

Line 30.1, "Treading unevenly but respectfully, he has no blame," seems banal, but contains an important principle of ethical reasoning. As I have emphasized throughout, ancient Chinese rules for comportment were elaborate. Violating them was a serious matter, as it could be seen as disrespecting the ruler, or deviating from the way of heaven. In this line, we find one of the most fundamental ethical concepts: intent. The improper gait is excused because there was no intention to be disrespectful. Obvious as this may seem to us, it represents an early example of ethical thinking. Confucius also considered intent. Although he advised, "If it is contrary to ritual, don't do it" (*Lunyu* 12.1, in Watson: 80) he also said, "When a person comes to you in good faith, give him credit for the good faith" (*Lunyu* 7.28, in Watson: 51). While Confucius felt adherence to ritual was essential both for the individual and society, he often voiced his disapproval of insincerity and ostentation:

> Although one may have talents as admirable as those of the Duke of Zhou, if he employs them in an arrogant manner … whatever other qualities he has are not worth a look! (*Lunyu* 8.1, in Watson: 55)

What we would consider mere etiquette, in China was considered ethical necessity, given the metaphysics in which all events potentially affected all other events. There was great anxiety that improper ritual behavior would result in social disorder, even in as trivial a matter as using the wrong sauce for a particular dish. While this extreme formality is out of favor in the modern West, particularly America, we must not let ourselves forget that proper behavior towards others is the glue that holds societies together.

Another line in this hexagram, 30.3, refers to mourning behavior in eras that were themselves ancient by the time of the Western Zhou. Drumming on an earthenware jar, or singing, are here regarded as sincere expressions of mourning, in contrast to the elaborate and wasteful mortuary practices of the affluent. The very ancient expressed their grief modestly, with a song. As in much Chinese philosophical writings, high antiquity was imagined as a time of simple lives and instinctive morality. Both lines described situations in which someone might be blamed—walking seemingly casually, or mourning informally. In both, sincerity averts blame.

Averting blame

The frequency of prognostications about blame and regret indicates that these were matters of great anxiety. In hexagram 32, the line texts 2 and 3 are about shame or regret. These terms are among the most frequent in the *Zhouyi*. *Jiu* 咎 which I have translated as "blame" appears ninety-nine times. *Hui* 悔 "regret" appears thirty-two times. *Lin* 吝 "shame" appears twenty times. Most often the phrases in which these words occur are not direct ethical propositions, but rather warnings that a specific action will incur blame, regret or shame—or reassurance that it will not. The frequency of these words indicates a rigid morality, yet blame can still be averted by what seem to be magical incantations rather than contrition.

A frequent Western criticism of Chinese culture, though less often encountered now, is that China is a shame culture rather than a guilt culture; that is, morality is based on fear of public embarrassment rather than an inner sense of right and wrong. The *Zhouyi* seems to support this theory by use of the terms noted above. However, it must be kept in mind that guilt is a mental state and the *Zhouyi* rarely has anything to say about mental states or feelings. The shame theory has been criticized, rightly in my opinion, on the ground that shame is not an inferior form of morality but one essential to regulation of social behavior. All of us avoid behaviors because of the effect they might have on others' opinions of us. The shame theory ignores the obvious fact that feeling shame does not preclude feeling guilt. In Christianity, guilt is encouraged because salvation requires recognition of one's own sinfulness. In traditional China, a sense of almost unlimited obligation to both living and dead was the most fundamental moral principle. Guilt was most common regarding failure to adequately fulfill filial obligations. Feeling guilty, commonly for not doing enough for one's parents, also made one feel virtuous. People can be shamed when what they did was not morally wrong. This has become common on the Internet, but throughout history has been a powerful means of social control. This is especially in the small communities of rural China, where all behavior is visible to the entire community. People can feel unnecessary guilt as well. The notion that Chinese felt shame but not guilt is simply prejudicial.

Caught in the rain

The upright person very determinedly walks alone, though caught in the rain.

> If drenched has irritation, but nothing blameworthy.
> 九三 壯于┌ -- 有凶. 君子夬夬獨行, 遇雨. 若濡,有慍无咎.

This statement, 43.3, is about character. While irritation at such things as being caught in the rain is natural, the person of good character does not express frustration. Self-control is fundamental to the Confucian outlook; it is part of learning to be fully humane. The *Zhouyi* phrase also contains subtle encouragement—if you do not get too upset when soaked in the rain, then you are a better person. This is an important aspect of moral instruction—for most people, feeling one is a good person is psychologically rewarding. Many statements in Chinese ethical philosophy, such as those about how the *junzi* acts, have the subtext saying that the reader can be a *junzi* if he follows the principle advocated. Unfortunately, this can lend itself to helping treacherous people pretend to be good.

Observing our lives: Going forward and retreating

The line texts of hexagram 20 all refer to looking over one's surroundings, but end with different prognoses. The prognoses are unusually consistent for the *Zhouyi*, and all are favorable except for the second phrase of 20.1. Careful observing is a beneficial activity. This notion of observing life has been a consistent one in Chinese thought, culminating in the Song philosopher Zhu Xi's idea of *dao xue*, or study of the *dao*. Observation in Chinese philosophy was a somewhat different concept from that of natural science. It was not only objective observation of what the senses revealed, but also reflection on it. For working out the significance of what was observed, the *I Ching* was a valuable aid.

Both Confucian and Daoist philosophy emphasized self-knowledge, but in Confucianism this was about one's own righteousness and how one could properly fulfill social obligations. In Daoism, self-knowledge was more about one's own mind. Withdrawal from society and imaginary mind journeys were recommended by Laozi and Zhuangzi. With Buddhism, particularly Chan Buddhism, one was to question everything one experienced.

The *Zhouyi* does not express such sophisticated forms of inquiry. But it does express the importance of observing and interpreting one's surroundings. Line 20.3, "Observing our lives going forward and retreating," is particularly interesting as it suggests a deeper reflection on human life than simply asking whether to act or not. Furthermore, the nature of the *Zhouyi* itself implies a deeper reality that can be accessed through use of the book for divination.

Also of interest, 20.2 refers to women as participants in the divinatory process. There are relatively few references to women but none express the misogyny later attached to the *Changes*, notably by Wang Bi. I have discussed references to women in the *Zhouyi* in more detail elsewhere (Redmond and Hon: 72–92).

In later use, reflection stimulated by the *I Ching* could range far from the texts. In his work on Chinese hermeneutics, Ming Dong Gu comments:

> In Chinese history there have been a few scholars who have intuitively appreciated the open nature of the book.

Gu goes on to quote the Song philosopher Cheng Yi (1033–1107):

> If one sticks to one thing, then the three hundred eighty-four
> lines would only represent three hundred eighty-four things.
> That would be the end of it all.
> [...]
> When one uses it in observing people and conducting affairs, he
> will find it fitting for everything. (Gu: 101)

While the *Zhouyi* does not define itself expansively, in its own way,
particularly in hexagram 20, it suggests the value of examining
phenomena, even including bird calls, which somehow led to
speculative thought such as that of Cheng Yi just quoted.

Government

An imperial divination

Kidder Smith retells an episode regarding the Kangxi emperor
康熙帝 (1654–1722) (Smith: 14). Having fasted to end a drought,
he had the *I Ching* cast for him, obtaining hexagram 43. He
interpreted the tag character (which I have translated as "determination" but which can also mean "cut off") as prognosticating
that the drought, "... would end only after some of the great had
been humbled ..." There is no explicit textual basis for this reading.
However the hexagram, with its solitary broken line in the top
place, could be interpreted as meaning weakness at high level,
or that the weak are over-reaching. The emperor then removed
officials of a rival faction, all "members of Grand Secretary
Mingju's clique."

Smith states that here the *I Ching* was used to provide, "... super-
human sanction for politically difficult acts" (12). We have no such
detailed description of political use of the *Changes* in the Western
Zhou, though there are some in the *Zuozhuan*, for example in
excluding a possible successor to the throne (Rutt: 193f.). Doubtless
the supernatural authority of the *Changes* was used on many other
occasions to justify pre-existing agendas. Control of omen interpretation was a powerful means of maintaining and exercising power.

I have known something like this to happen on a personal level. I was trying to convince a colleague to present a paper at a session with me. He consulted the Wilhelm-Baynes *I Ching* and obtained hexagram 64, *Before Completion*. I took this to mean he had something to complete, namely the paper for presentation; he read it as meaning he was not ready to present the paper.

I give these two examples to show how the *Changes* can provide excuses for doing what one wanted to do—or not do—anyway. I have no reason to doubt that what might be called manipulation by *I Ching* was widely used even in the Western Zhou.

Marxism in the *Zhouyi*?

Line 35.3, *Zhong yun* 眾允, could be translated as "masses approve," to give it a Marxist flavor. Marxist readings of ancient texts were prevalent in Mao's China, at least in those intervals when it was permissible to read the classics at all. Accordingly, I see no reason to add anything further to this anachronistic exegetic mode. (For discussion of the *Book of Changes* under Mao, see Redmond and Hon: 185–91.) Rather than imagining that the *Zhouyi* anticipated Marx, I regard this line as indicating some concern in the Western Zhou of the overall welfare of the common people, something not prominent in the *Zhouyi*. By the time of Confucius and Laozi, however, there are many references to the responsibility of rulers to benefit the people. This brief text of the Western Zhou suggests that the welfare of the masses was considered then, though it had not yet developed into a philosophy of government.

Conclusion: The river crossed, or not yet?

Hexagrams 63 and 64 came to be considered among the most philosophical by Chinese and Western practitioners alike, because within the *yin-yang* system they represent archetypal situations of stagnation and dynamic change respectively. As usual, the *Zhouyi* expresses this contrast in concrete terms rather than abstract ones. Potential energy becoming active is described with the dragon imagery of hexagram 1, *Qian*. Hexagram 48.0 describes a situation of stasis by reference to an everyday activity, "There is no loss; there is no gain. Coming and going, to and from the well." Many other phrases refer to the natural alteration of activity and inactivity that are inherent in human life—day/night, sleep/wake, work/rest, happy/sad, hungry/full, arousal/release, and so on. The dark-light cycle, the most fundamental of all, is less prominent in modern life, yet change, cyclical and otherwise, remains fundamental.

Yin and *yang* provide imagery for change, but do not actually explain it. Yet such should not be simply dismissed as the metaphysics of a pre-scientific culture, because imagery and metaphor are fundamental ways the mind functions. I could say I have worked like a dog to complete this book, a simile—though an inaccurate one as all the dogs I have owned have been lazy. To remove the simile I could say I have worked hard, but "hard" is also a metaphor based on sensory qualities of objects. I give these examples to point out that *yin* and *yang* are not always metaphysical, but often simply convenient ways to describe the processes that govern our lives.

Hexagrams 63 and 64 stand out because they are inverses of each other in two ways. First, they are the two possible ways of having broken and solid alternate. Second, they have rotational symmetry—when rotated top to bottom each turns into the other. This made them natural for representing the basic principle that *yin* and *yang* transform into each other. The properties of the diagram seem to confirm the metaphysics they represent. Such numerological or geometric traits fascinate a certain cognitive temperament—not mine I must admit. For those of us who do not see a profound secret in such patterns, they are still of interest in their use as philosophical symbols.

The tags of these two hexagrams, in my translation, *Already Across the River* and *River Not Yet Crossed* indicate completion and non-completion and so do correlate with the later-added metaphysical meanings. Wilhelm-Baynes' *Before Completion* and *After Completion* are more concise but take away the concrete imagery characteristic of the Western Zhou text. Both contain references to a fox crossing a river, so this concrete image could be the origin of the tags.

The tags of these two adjacent hexagrams are consistent with my theory that the Chinese pre-occupation with cyclical change is implicit in the *Zhouyi*, even though it had not yet developed into the more abstract *yin-yang* doctrine. I suspect that most of the philosophical additions to the *Zhouyi* were opportunistic— later editors searched for elements to which their metaphysical ideas could be attached. Plausibly, lines in the *Zhouyi* inspired metaphysical ideas as well.

On the one hand, the *Zhouyi* offers no abstract formulation of stasis alternating with change, on the other, this recurring cycle is implicit throughout the entire work. Thus the *Zhouyi* dealt with the most fundamental characteristic of existence, though not expressing this in philosophical language. The numinous-appearing hexagrams, able to transform into each other by multiple pathways, seemed to embody the mysterious nature of change. The various phrases associated with them were about *specific* changes: what would happen, whether it was beneficial or ominous, whether you would be blamed for it, what to do about it. Thus the omens, proverbs, set phrases, prognostications, emotionally intense events, and events depicted, were the concrete manifestations of the hidden forces—*yin* and *yang*—revealed by the hexagrams. We do not know what those who added the metaphysics to the *Zhouyi* thought of what they were doing, but this is clearly the underlying principle.

While I have emphasized the interpretation of 63 as stasis and 64 as activity, a slightly different view was entertained by some traditional *I Ching* scholars. As Wilhelm explained hexagram 63:

For it is just when perfect equilibrium has been reached that any movement may cause order to revert to disorder (244).

Regarding 64, he wrote:

This hexagram indicates a time when the transition from disorder to order is not yet completed. The conditions are difficult. The task is great and full of responsibility. It is nothing less than that of leading the world out of confusion back to order. (248f.)

This is perhaps meant as an echo of the already quoted famous first line of the *Romance of Three Kingdoms* (*San Guo*):

The empire, once divided must unite; once united must divide.

Despite the slightly different interpretation of the two final hexagrams, Wilhelm's reading is still about stasis and change, order and disorder.

Some final thoughts on the philosophy of change

Heraclitus proclaimed that one can never step in the same river twice, thus introducing the paradox of constancy and change. Plato's cave myth attempts to explain the paradox of constancy and change, a preoccupation of the Greeks, but not the Chinese. Confucius famously referred to a river endlessly flowing, but did not ask himself whether it was still the same river.

Chinese thought did not consider change as good or bad in itself, but instead focused their attention on understanding it. The *I Ching* does not explain change, but reveals underlying patterns to help us prepare for it and accommodate to it. The cosmology of *yin-yang* and five phases do not explain change but offer a refined metaphysical description of it, one that is subjective rather than scientific.

River Not Yet Crossed is a fitting phrase with which to conclude this chapter. How the *Book of Changes* is read will continue to change, as it has for 3,000 years. With respect to scholarship on the classic, despite thousands of studies, there remain rivers not yet crossed. For me one of the most intriguing of the remaining mysteries is how the *Zhouyi* became the *I Ching* and also, even more basic, how the *Zhouyi* came to be in the first place. In this book I have proposed my own hypothesis, but much remains uncertain.

A *lacuna* in *I Ching* scholarship has been the tendency to focus either on the received, that is, Confucianized meanings, that were dominant from the *Zuozhuan* onward, or on the reconstructed Western Zhou meanings. Few scholars have worked on both. It is as if they are different works. Yet without the *Zhouyi* there would have been no *Ten Wings*, no Wang Bi commentaries, and no Zhu Xi or Shao Yong commentaries either. And no Wilhelm-Baynes translation and no Carl Jung "Foreword." Somehow, the Western Zhou text that now seems so peculiar grew into the classic that inspired China's greatest thinkers and is now a world classic. I have offered some speculations on how this came to be, but these are at best a beginning.

Moving in the opposite direction, we need to try to better understand how the *Zhouyi* came to be put together in the first place. There has been extensive scholarship in the West on the nature of orally transmitted material and the traces it leaves in early writings. While this has been somewhat neglected by sinologists, I believe it can shed considerable light on the composition of the *Zhouyi*.

There is still more to be done on the excavated manuscripts and the anecdotes in the *Zuozhuan*. This should be facilitated by both now being published in accurate bilingual editions by renowned scholars (Shaughnessy 2014; Durrant et al. 2016).

Finally, I believe we need better accounts of what has made the *Changes* so spiritually inspiring for so long. Spirituality has long been suspect in the academy because of its subjective nature and its association with popular culture. Yet this is what most readers seek in classics. Jung's "Foreword" is a start. It explains some of the spiritual quality that has kept the work alive. Considering spiritual use does not mean ignoring or rejecting critical scholarship. Philology is a necessary beginning that opens doors to deeper secrets.

PART FOUR

Practical and theoretical aspects

8

Reading by topic

Reading the *Changes* as a conventional book, as most readers try to do, is bound to lead to frustration because it was never intended to be read as a narrative. Rather, it is a reference book, and was once even described by an early Western scholar as a dictionary. Its function was to find the correct divination result after selecting a hexagram by yarrow or other means.

A better way to get started reading the *Changes* is to pick a topic of interest and read related hexagrams, not necessarily in the received order. Here I provide a reading list of hexagrams organized by subject. In most cases, not all the lines in the hexagram are related to the topic listed here.

There are some duplications, because many hexagrams refer to multiple subjects. For a first time reading I suggest starting with my first category of interesting and important hexagrams. This will give a better sense of the work than reading in the standard order.

This is intended to help the reader get started. It is not meant as a concordance and does not list all references to the subjects listed. Some hexagrams are listed under more than one subject.

Interesting and important hexagrams: 1, 2, 4, 11, 12, 18, 27, 48, 49, 50 54, 56, 63, 64
Omens: 15, 31, 32, 33, 36, 38, 43, 51, 55, 60, 62, 64
Birds and beasts: 2, 3, 7, 8, 10, 36, 40, 49, 53, 56, 61
Dragons: 1, 2
Philosophy and metaphysics: 1, 2, 11, 12, 63, 64

Weddings, women, and family: 3, 4, 11, 18, 20, 31, 37, 44, 50, 53, 54, 55, 63
Agriculture: 23, 25, 26, 32, 33, 34, 35, 52, 59
Traveling: 38, 40, 56, 64
Warfare: 7, 13, 16, 34, 35, 57
Sacrifice and ritual: 2, 5, 9, 14, 17, 39, 42, 45, 47, 50, 59, 63
Wisdom: 4, 20, 34, 41, 48

9

How to consult the *I Ching*

As I have pointed out throughout this work, the *Book of Changes* was not a book to be read as we would read non-fiction, but most closely resembles a reference book, in effect a dictionary of divinatory responses. It is not alphabetical like a Western dictionary, but Chinese dictionaries cannot be alphabetical anyway. With divination, what is needed is a method of selecting the "correct" response. This means it is selected in a way the inquirer believes is credible. From the point of view of an agnostic or non-believer, it does not matter what response is selected, given that selection methods are generally random. One can browse the *I Ching* to find a passage that seems to apply to one's situation, but this does not replicate the experience of divination as practiced in the past. Nor is it as likely to provide a new perspective on one's concerns.

I suspect many people are reluctant to try divination because they fear giving way to superstition. Also, though they may not admit it, many are afraid of getting an unhappy prognostication. These fears are needless; divination by oneself is not addicting nor need it be taken so seriously as to create anxiety. Very few responses are inherently bad—there is usually a way to read them in a positive way. This is particularly important when doing a reading for someone else. When I do readings to demonstrate how the *I Ching* works, I always warn inquirers that they should not take the process too seriously, just as I do not. With this caution in mind, I suggest asking a serious question and pondering the response to see if it contains anything useful. This process need not be very time consuming. The *I Ching* gives concise responses, generally about the immediate situation. This contrasts with astrology, for example, which can provide detailed character analysis and long-term predictions. With the *Changes*, if one is unhappy with a response, one can always cast another hexagram; this is consistent with its underlying view of constant change. In contrast, with astrology one cannot pick another birth date. This makes *I Ching* divination inherently dynamic. This dynamism is part of the general optimism of Chinese culture, because change provides hope.

With any divination method, common sense always has priority, although in the past this was often not the case. If one uses the ancient *Zhouyi* for divination, of which more shortly, its recommendations about human sacrifice are obviously to be ignored, or taken metaphorically as a suggestion to make an offering, but a benign one. While I have emphasized the value of restoring the early meanings as a way of understanding ancient life, it also should be borne in mind that the Confucians replaced the unpleasant aspects of the *Zhouyi* with moralistic readings more than 2,000 years ago.

It is possible to quickly select a hexagram or line text and quickly read the response, all in less than ten minutes. However, the traditional method is more elaborate and meditative and this is what I suggest for experimentation. Traditionally there are four steps:

Proper frame of mind

As the book is conceived as a sage, the inquirer should sit at a table facing north, the traditional position of respect toward someone older, wiser, or more powerful. The *I Ching* and associated items such as coins or beads should be placed on the otherwise empty tabletop. One sits quietly and meditates briefly to induce a calm, open state of mind. In traditional China, consulting the *I Ching* was a devotional act, expressing profound respect for the sages and culture heroes of the past who created Chinese culture. Alternatively one can reflect on the *Dao*, the impersonal principle of cosmic order that sustains us all. *I Ching* consultation should be a spiritually affirmative act. In Chinese tradition the ritual included lighting incense. Alternatives would be placing a single fresh flower on the table to foster a feeling of harmony, or a personally meaningful object, such as a family picture.

Formulating the question

Chinese divinatory inquiries were generally in the form of, "What if I do such and such?" This might be paired with, "What if I do *not* do such and such?" To give an example, one would not ask, "Should I marry so-and-so?" but, "What will it be like if I marry so-and-so?" If appropriate, one asks the corollary question, "What if I do *not* marry so-and-so?" This dual mode of inquiry was in use more than 3,000 years ago as recorded on the King WuDing oracle bones. Sometimes a more general form was used, as with the Lady Mu Jiang anecdote, "What will happen regarding such and such situation?" My own practice is to ask the inquirer what area of life he or she is concerned about; there are less of these than one might think—romance, career, money, health. (The *I Ching* is no longer relied upon to predict rain or harvests.) In the imperial Chinese examination system, success was the number one question, for oneself or one's sons.

The reason that direct questions such as, "Should I marry so-and-so?" are not very productive is that the *I Ching* does not make decisions; these are up to the inquirer. Many report that *Changes* consultations have helped them identify implications of a decision, but did not tell them what to do. Lest I sound overly credulous about the *I Ching*, I would point out that this is exactly what a responsible therapist or other advisor would do. Although any sort of question can be asked, provided that it is asked sincerely; traditionally the *Changes* will respond to frivolous or repeated questions with a rebuke, as in 4.0. Also, traditionally, those who are corrupt, like Lady Mu Jiang, will not receive valid advice. This belief can be explained as maintaining the reputation of the *Changes* as morally infallible by allowing good prognoses for the undeserving or wicked to be set aside.

Hexagram and text selection

There are a great variety of methods for selecting the hexagram and specific line text. There are websites that will pick the text for you using a random number generator. To my mind, by taking away the human interaction, this method is pointless. Needless to say, it does not in any way replicate the experience of traditional Chinese use. The reflective state of mind is at least as important as the actual text selected. The various methods generate six lines, which in turn make up the hexagram. Each line will be broken (*yin*) or solid (*yang*), and fixed or moving. The moving line changes into its opposite, generating an additional hexagram. The most common principle is that if there are no moving lines, the judgment text is the divination response. If there is one moving line, that is the response to the inquiry. When there is more than one moving line then the new hexagram is the response, either the judgment text or the line texts that have changed.

I have provided a more detailed discussion of *I Ching* divination elsewhere (Redmond and Hon: 255–63). The clearest description of yarrow sorting is Whincup (216–31). Other useful discussions are those of Hacker (1993: 133–50) and Huang (175–8). Wilhelm-Baynes' explanation is overly concise and not very useful (721–4).

The ancient method of choosing a hexagram used a complex sorting procedure with fifty yarrow stalks. These sticks are available on line but the method is rather tedious for hurried modern lifestyles. The most widely used method is to use three coins. For reasons I shall explain shortly, I prefer a method using beads of four different colors.

What I believe is most important in imitating the traditional experience is replicating the probabilities of the ancient yarrow stick method. The procedure should result in some moving lines, but not an excessive number. Here is a table that compares odds of three methods.

	Yarrow	Beads	Coin
6 Changing *yin*	1 in 16	1 in 16	2 in 16
7 Fixed *yang*	5 in 16	5 in 16	6 in 16
8 Fixed *yin*	7 in 16	7 in 16	6 in 16
9 Changing *yang*	3 in 16	3 in 16	2 in 16

The first thing to notice here is that the probabilities are not identical—coins give more moving *yin* lines. The reason I find this problematic is not because of anything supernatural, but because changing lines result in more possibilities and therefore a less clear divination. Worst in this regard is a modern device consisting of six four-sided sticks, each side of which has one of the four kinds of lines. Casting these sticks is quick but results in about half the lines being moving. Of course, anyone is free to generate hexagrams by any method. There is even a way to do it using car license plate numbers, or any other sequence of digits. My suggestions are based on trying to replicate the traditional experience as closely as possible, 3,000 years later.

For those interested in *I Ching* consultation as a regular practice, unless he or she believes that a particular method has supernatural efficacy, it is simply a matter of preference. Asking advice is highly personal and so it is best to choose a method that feels comfortable. In explaining this I am not recommending regular *I Ching* consultation, but see no reason to discourage it either.

Yarrow stalk sorting

This is the method referred to in ancient sources. A bundle of fifty dried stems of the yarrow plant are repeatedly divided until the number of remaining sticks determines the kind of line. The process is repeated six times to generate the full hexagram and takes at least 20 minutes. We do not know how the sticks were manipulated originally, but at least two reconstructed methods are available. Most commonly referred to is that of Zhu Xi. He based this on his interpretation of *Dazhuan* 1.9, which refers to the process but without sufficient detail. A modern version is somewhat simpler and yields the numbers 6, 7, 8, and 9 directly. Most will find yarrow too tedious for regular use, but it is worth trying it a few times to gain a sense of the care Chinese put into consultation of the *Changes*.

The coin method

The coin method is the most widely used, though not the best. Three coins are used, preferably imitation Chinese cash coins. All three are tossed simultaneously for each line. Heads, or the side with fewer Chinese characters, count as *yin*, assigned the number 2, and tails are *yang*, assigned 3. The numbers are totaled to yield 6, 7, 8, or 9, which are the numbers that refer to each of the four line types. Each toss produces a line, so six are necessary. The first line obtained is the base, number 1, the last one is line 6.

Bead method (method of sixteen)

I prefer this method because it replicates the yarrow stick probabilities, but is much easier to perform. While almost as quick as the coin method it is more contemplative and does not result in as many moving lines.

One acquires sixteen beads as follows (the colors are arbitrary):

5 white or yellow for fixed *yang*
7 black for fixed *yin*
3 red for changing *yang*
1 blue for changing *yin*

Chinese cloisonné beads create the right ambiance. They are kept in a silk purse and taken out one at a time without looking. The line is recorded, the bead replaced in the purse, and the next one selected, until all lines have been determined. It is necessary to replace the bead so all are in the purse for each line selection.

Whether it is necessary to duplicate the probabilities of the ancient method is a matter of taste. The present author prefers to do so but many practitioners are content with the coin method.

The method of remainders

It is even possible to pick a hexagram from license plate numbers and other contemporary environmental annoyances, such as stock prices, airline flight numbers or arrival times, or any other random digits one encounters. The first number is then divided progressively by 8 until there is a remainder of the numbers 0, 1, 2, 3, 4, 5, 6, or 7. The 0 is counted as 8. One then counts around the *bagua* until the number is reached, which is the bottom trigram. The process is then repeated on another number for the upper trigram; this can be another from one's surroundings, or the date or time (Huang 2000: 175–8).

Other methods

Other than the physical manipulation, the major difference between methods is the number of changing lines obtained. The two sets of dice seen by the present author use different systems. One has two dice of eight sides each, upon which are embossed the characters for the trigrams. A third die has six sides and is used to decide which line is changing. In this method, the number of lines that change is decided by the inquirer. Another set has the usual six sides; each die has two fixed *yin* and *yang* lines and one changing line for each, giving a probability of 3/18 for each kind of changing line. Another system, using six sticks of four sides, has a very high 8/16 probability of a changing line. Too many changing lines, at least in the opinion of the present author, makes for confusion.

There is an extreme variety of other methods, including six-sided dice with trigrams, sticks, pendulums, dials, and numerological methods based on birth date. A rather obscure numerological passage in the *Dazhuan* 1.9 provides a pretext for many of these systems, otherwise without basis in the *I Ching*.

The most famous figure associated with the numerological approach is Shao Yong of the Song, who in turn influenced Zhu Xi, as discussed in Chapter 8. Numerological approaches interest mainly a very few who possess a certain sort of cognitive disposition that becomes entranced by number inter-relationships and finds spiritual meaning in them. These elaborate numerological methods are mere curiosities that diverge from the main received tradition and do not help us understand the *Zhouyi* as a text.

Interpreting the response

There are countless ways one can interpret hexagrams and their texts. How one interprets depends in part on the nature of one's interest. Some use the *Changes* only for casual divination and do not feel a need to know much about the traditional Chinese context. Those with a more serious interest will use divination to supplement their study of the place of the classic in Chinese intellectual history.

Divination is actually a skill. People who frequently patronize diviners, whether using *I Ching*, psychics (purely mental without any device), astrologers or Tarot readers, report that some diviners are much better than others. Some of this is clearly cold reading—throwing out suggestions and picking up on those to which the inquirer responds. While it is easy to deceive the gullible, as do spiritualist mediums who channel the deceased husbands of elderly widows, skilled readers are much more subtle.

In reading for oneself, keep in mind that interpretation is almost always metaphorical. This means free associating based on the line. As an example, consider line 47.3, "Entering into his house, he does not see his wife, ominous." Although this could be interpreted as his wife having left him, or even having died, such needlessly disturbing interpretations should be avoided. More appropriate possibilities could be that she has gone shopping, or that he does not adequately recognize her concerns or needs. If the inquirer is single, it might mean he is not thinking of marrying his present partner, or that he has not met anyone suitable. Genders can be switched as suitable for the situation.

Divination with the reconstructed early meanings of the *Zhouyi* would be a completely different experience to using a translation like that of Wilhelm-Baynes, which is based on the later Confucian moralistic meanings. With the present translation I suggest using it as the basis for a thought experiment, asking questions hypothetically as if one were living in the Western Zhou. I cannot imagine anyone would want to be transported back in time to that era. I have carried out this thought experiment frequently while doing this translation and found it humbling to realize how much easier our lives are than those of people who lived 3,000 years ago.

10

The challenges of translating the *Zhouyi*

To begin with a banality, the Chinese language is different. While it is not the purpose of this book to teach Chinese, knowledge of some aspects of the language will be both extremely helpful in understanding the *Zhouyi* in translation, and also, I hope, intrinsically interesting. Even for those with no intention of learning any Chinese, a sense of how the language works will improve one's appreciation of its writings.

In this chapter I provide additional details regarding textual criticism of the *Zhouyi* for those who, like me, are fascinated by the possibility of reconstructing the meanings of ancient texts.

Being optimistic about translation

It is a cliché that translation is impossible. This is expressed in a particularly pessimistic way by Nietzsche scholar, James L. Porter:

> Philology invents for itself an antiquity it can then go on to "discover."

And:

> The aim of philology, critically conceived, is not to substitute a more adequate picture of the ancients but to bring out inadequacies of the one we already have. (6)

These observations are not so much wrong as limited. Turning our inability to attain absolute certainty into a nihilistic conclusion that any text can mean anything—or nothing—is a self-defeating view peculiar to recent humanities scholarship. The hard sciences admit that knowledge is incomplete and work away patiently to fill in the gaps without fretting over the situation. The social sciences, which are less exact, also make their peace with uncertainty. After all, if everything were known, all of us knowledge workers would be out of jobs.

Philology is not exactly a hard science, but it is not completely soft, either. It works with precise data—texts in all their multiplicity—though interpretation is debated incessantly, frequently productively. What Porter describes is in fact the nature of the sciences. We form a hypothesis, test it, then modify it. Philology will never attain complete certainty about the meanings of ancient texts, just as astronomy will never discover the full details of distant galaxies. All we can do is work toward progressively more complete knowledge. Similarly, without a time machine, we will never fully experience what it was like to live in a remote time, but we can get some sense about it. No doubt any attempted reconstruction of ancient meanings, my own included, gets some of it wrong. Yet if we lose confidence in our ability to reconstruct humanity's past, we abandon our heritage. Some are willing to make this choice; I am not.

I suspect my background in medicine has affected my attitude. In medicine, one is faced with an urgent problem and while all too aware of what we do not know, we have to do something—waiting until knowledge is complete is not an option. We do not allow epistemological controversies to stop us from applying what we do know. I suggest that in philology, as with medicine, uncertainty should be reason for humility, not defeatism.

A less pessimistic way to approach translation is as an extended sequence of hard—but not impossible—choices. With the *Zhouyi*, nearly every word has multiple possible meanings, which in English are completely different words. I have chosen the meanings that seem most likely to me, in the context of the text and of what we know of Western Zhou life.

Effective translation requires, in my view, the ability to put oneself in the *imaginaire* of the time and place of the work. It is not only language that makes translation challenging. With the *Zhouyi* the translator must find a way to convey to the reader the nature of life in a time when banditry was rife, warfare almost continuous, human sacrifice performed as a social obligation, and individual autonomy was almost non-existent. Men of high rank were better off—but not entirely. While they could execute followers at whim, they might fall victims to those even more powerful. Regarding women's lives in this remote era, regrettably, we know very little. A few seem to have been able to make basic decisions about their lives, but most probably were subject to fathers, husbands, and more senior wives.

The study of divination is the study of human uncertainties. For moderns, divination is occasional and often just for entertainment, but in the ancient world it might be used for almost any decision regarding everyday matters such as travel, banquets, offerings, marriage, even when to have intercourse. Both translating and reading requires recognition of the extreme insecurity of ancient life. (Recognition does not mean excusing such cruelties as human sacrifice, mutilating punishment, or routine abuse of children and women. We cannot change the past but we can use it to be conscious of how easily human behavior can go awry.) We need to keep in mind that decisions that the *Zhouyi* was consulted about would have been made in conditions very different from those in the modern world. Daily life was fraught with innumerable hazards: brigands, warfare, crop failure, disease, death in childbirth, spiteful ancestors and spirits, and the imperative of conforming to complex ritual requirements. The resources for coping with such dangers were very limited compared to those available in the modern world. There were no weather forecasts, no sound medical diagnosis and no effective treatments. There was no aid for the destitute without family. To give an example from ordinary life, in the Wu Ding oracle bone inscriptions queries about toothache were frequent. What for us would be a simple, if unpleasant, trip to the dentist was a cause of long-term pain, often agonizing, with magic spells the only alternative to agonizing extraction without anesthesia. Thus much of daily life would have been fraught with dread. With this perspective, what now tends to be dismissed as superstition can be seen as one of the few resources against personal or public disaster. Modern translations of the *Book of Changes*, influenced by the New Age Movement, tend to put its prognostications in the language of personal growth, suitable for the dilemmas of easeful modern lives. For the denizens of the Chinese Bronze Age there was no such concept. Life was about basics, mainly survival.

With this in mind, we can recognize the intimate relationship between divination and emotion. Early Chinese texts do not often refer directly to emotion, but tend to tersely describe a situation and leave the reader to infer the emotion. Put differently, the *Zhouyi* is an assembly of images and, as with images generally, their impact is direct and only later, if at all, does abstract explanation arise. With the *Zhouyi*, interpretation would be left to the reader or listener during the course of the actual divination. In my view, translation should not add emotion words that are not in the text, and should leave the images consistent with the feelings that likely accompanied them. Although the *Zhouyi* only rarely mentions emotions, one should try to imagine the feelings of those involved in the situations described as a means to feel some connection with the lives of the ancients. Sometimes the emotions are directly apparent, as with the bride upstaged by her bridesmaid in 54.5. In 18, the references to parental sexual behavior affecting the child indicate anxiety about how parents affect the child, no less a cause of anxiety today, though our beliefs are different. The castration of the stallion in 54 must have stirred very intense emotion: the danger to those performing the deed, the soaking of the participants with blood, relief when it is over that the horse bolts away, and a sense of human power over the animal world. All these contrast with contemporary Western notions of animal rights, yet early civilization depended on exploitation of animals.

When making a divinatory inquiry, there is a mixture of hope and fear. The oracle may reassure by proposing the safest course of action in a risky situation, though in this it is hardly infallible. But there is the possibility of a bad prognostication, particularly that the inquirer might hear what no one wants to know, for example, the day of one's death. (In the Western renaissance diviners did make such predictions, with what psychological effect we do not know.)

Referring to translation as "resurrection," Tsai comments, "On the road to 'resurrection' there are difficulties and obstacles too numerous to count" (Tsai: 141–52).

I like this quote because it expresses these difficulties in supernatural terms, something that fits with the occult nature of the *Changes*. Resurrection is unnatural and more than a little scary.

A person brought back from the dead is dangerous and so is the *Zhouyi*—not only when used to prognosticate but also in reminding us of human sacrifice and practices that we would prefer not to think about, and that we wrongly imagine have vanished from the modern world. So engaging with the resurrected *Zhouyi* can produce anxious moments. It also induces anxiety in the translator. Though done in safe, comfortable settings, somehow struggling to restore to life a very ancient—and highly valued—literary work seems a high-stakes undertaking.

Text-critical controversies and early Chinese texts

Western textual criticism has developed primarily to distinguish the correct reading when there are multiple surviving versions ("witnesses") of a text. Theorizing about this began in antiquity and reached a considerable degree of sophistication; philology as a modern discipline developed in Germany during the nineteenth century. Much of that scholarship focused on the textual problems in editing of Greek New Testament texts, of which a very large number survive, created over several centuries. The stakes were high, given that from the perspective of a believer, the correct text was the actual word of God. The stakes are high too for the historian who wants to know what actually happened, or the literary critic who would like to understand how the variant versions are related to each other and how they originated. While all scholars are, or should be, concerned with accuracy, there are significant differences in approach. For the Biblical scholar the ideal would be a single correct reading. The historian, especially in the case of China, is interested in what the early texts tell us about life in the era they are studying. In this situation variants may be useful. Biblical criticism is split into two camps. Faith-based scholars want to restore authentic scripture—though now more likely to be accepting of uncertainties than was the case in the past—and in contrast, those who are skeptical of traditional beliefs, or regard religion as delusion, tend toward a debunking agenda, somewhat akin to the Chinese Doubting Antiquity Movement. A positive development is that modern scholars tend to accept the existence of variant versions rather than assuming a single correct "*urtext,*" and this limits quibbles over establishing a proposed single correct reading.

The study of texts has become somewhat fraught during the past half-century With the influence of continental "theory," and its tropes of the death of the author, difference, and deconstruction, philology came under attack. Close reading was eclipsed by a focus on power interests, following the lead of Michel Foucault. This movement in literary scholarship has had limited influence on the study of pre-modern Chinese texts. One reason is that with ancient texts, the very basic—and challenging—first step is to work out what the text actually says. Until this is done, social analysis is dubious at best. Simply put, philology is necessary for us to know our past. Another impetus for the revival of Chinese textual criticism is the need for such expertise in analyzing the numerous previously unknown works discovered in archaeological excavation. There are of course matters of national pride involved when any culture's classics are discussed, though this is not necessarily directly stated. (For a very different point of view regarding political aspects of textual scholarship, see Warren.)

The Doubting Antiquity Movement was invaluable in restoring the early meanings of the *Zhouyi*, yet, at least in my view, in their zeal to discredit the received meanings they introduced gratuitous obscurities. I have tried to apply a more temperate approach in the present translation.

The project to reconstruct the early meanings of the *Zhouyi* has itself stirred up yet another controversy. Most *I Ching* aficionados and practitioners simply ignored the Doubting Antiquity Movement critique, while some have vigorously disputed it. Bradford Hatcher, a self-taught sinologist, has published criticisms of New *Changes* Studies, which he refers to as "Context Criticism" (I: 16–42). (I have discussed his views in more detail in the chapter on philosophy.) The controversy about the Doubting Antiquity Movement is analogous to the split in Biblical criticism— the inevitable tension between believers, who are attached to the mythology of the *Changes* and read it for spiritual inspiration, and scholars whose work employs an evidence-based approach. Indeed, the same tension between believers and scholars exists for spiritual or religious texts generally. Diversity of approaches to difficult material is ultimately productive. Such controversies are by their nature not fully resolvable, and need not be. The simple solution is peaceful co-existence. Since my goal in the present work is historical reconstruction, I have not said much about *I Ching* as a practice. In part this is to restore balance—most English versions of the *Changes* are in the believer/practioner school. Some practitioners have quite interesting observations to offer regarding the *Changes*. It was, after all, intended not so much to be read as to be used. However, the practice of *I Ching*, ancient and modern, is a subject for another time.

Analogy and anomaly

Translating most modern works does not require much theoretical reflection. The translator develops a sense of the text and then works to decide the best equivalents in the target language. With ancient texts there are additional complexities, and some reflection on theoretical issues is necessary to produce a coherent version based on an as accurate a copy of the text as possible.

In China, textual criticism developed in two stages, which can be compared to the analogy and anomaly schools of Western antiquity, to be described shortly. First was the Evidentiary Scholarship movement of the late Qing Dynasty, foreshadowed in the Song (Elman 2001). This movement strived for accuracy but did not aim to refute tradition, hence it was not unlike the method of analogy. Later, as discussed previously, the more radical Doubting Antiquity Movement, advanced something akin to a hermeneutics of suspicion, resulting in a complete transformation of the received view of the ancient portion of the text. Many anomalous readings were introduced by assuming that characters in the received versions were actually homophones for other words. Indeed, they seem to have preferred meanings that did not fit the later Confucian orthodox readings. In English, the main exponents of this approach have been Richard Kunst, Edward Shaughnessy, and Richard Rutt. This movement has been extremely influential in the Western scholarly approach to the Chinese classics and continues to be applied in China, but has not supplanted the received tradition there. The Doubting Antiquity approach has less relevance to the work of such scholars as Richard John Lynn and Richard J. Smith, whose interests are mainly in later *I Ching* commentaries.

In the Classical West, there was a theoretical controversy about the proper way to establish authoritative editions of texts (Greetham: 296–302). The argument was between the followers of Aristotle, based in Alexandria, and the Stoics, based in Pergamon. The former held to analogy, which considered language to be based on regular patterns, while the latter, referred to as the "school of anomaly," emphasized irregularities. These terms applied not only to the proper way to establish correct texts, but also to their exegesis. The Alexandrian school held to the slogan, "Let scripture interpret scripture," a principle also referred to as, "The analogy of faith." In practice this meant emending to create a text in harmony with the editor's notion of the intended meaning. There is, of course, no ultimate escape from subjectivity in textual scholarship.

The method of analogy is not wrong—texts do have some degree of internal consistency in vocabulary, sentence structure and ideas; elements that do not fit the normal pattern need to be questioned. Those favoring anomaly, on the other hand, prefer to let variants stand and allow the text its irregularities and contradictions. (I am indebted to Professor Dai Lianbin's presentation at the Association of Asian Studies 2014 Conference for this way of categorizing different modes of textual criticism.) This approach has the advantage of preserving interesting oddities, but can overlook lacunae and later additions.

With the *Zhouyi*, neither approach can be applied rigidly. As I have emphasized, the ancient text is almost certainly a collection of fragments from different sources about which we know little. Thus anomalies could result from different sources or different editors— or scribal errors. On the other hand, many passages are ambiguous enough that we have no choice but to translate them to accord with the overall style of the work. Given that there is no final, objective criterion for determining which variant reading is correct, selection often comes down to that indefinable faculty referred to as "judgment." This was the conclusion of Johann Albrecht Bengel (1687–1752), one of the greatest of textual critics.

This brings us to "Bengel's rule," usually expressed as, "The more difficult reading is to be preferred." This rule was proposed in relation to New Testament Greek manuscripts and was based on the assumption that scribes would take it upon themselves to "clarify" obscure passages in scriptures they regarded as sacred. This assumption has in fact been refuted by statistical studies of New Testament manuscripts. I do occasionally hear Bengel's supposed rule quoted by sinologists, and suspect it is often tacitly applied. To the best of my knowledge there has been no formal study of its suitability for application to Chinese texts. In my opinion its use results in gratuitous obscuration.

It was actually Johann Jakob Griesbach (1745–1812) who put the rule into its now familiar, rather rigid formulation. What Bengel actually wrote is rather different:

> A reading, which does not allure by too great facility, but shines with its own native dignity of truth, is always to be preferred to those which may fairly be supposed to owe their origin to either the carelessness or the injudicious care of copyists (quoted in Marlowe).

Thus Bengel held, not that the least clear reading is invariably to be selected, but that too facile readings must be questioned—a quite different guideline. This point is important because in recent times critical examination of scriptural texts has often been intended to discredit them. This is true not only of Biblical scholarship, but also of the Doubting Antiquity Movement. The seminal figures of modern textual Western textual criticism, such as Bengel, saw their task differently, as trying to recover the exact revealed words that were the foundation of their faith. Philogists studying secular literary texts usually base their work on a deep respect for their authors and a belief that their exact words are of particular value. My own teacher, Fredson Bowers of the University of Virginia, was of this persuasion.

With texts such as the *Zhouyi*, the early meanings only reveal themselves with the aid of meticulous, rigorous examination. Almost any phrase can be read in a way that is difficult, so if the more difficult reading were always accepted, the text would be reduced to gibberish. While there is no end to the tension between analogy and anomaly, there can be a middle ground. To my mind, many of the existing translations of the *I Ching* fail to find this middle ground, either rewriting the text, as did Wilhelm-Baynes, or making it needlessly obscure, as did Richard Rutt. While both translations are of great value, neither is definitive, as indeed no version can be. My own goal has been to produce a translation based on the early meanings, but as easy to understand as possible —which led me to formulate my working principle that if the *Zhouyi* was understood 3,000 years ago it can be understood today.

Ambiguity

The great classicist Eric Havelock proposed that logic was invented in Greece because the Greek alphabet was the first to include vowels. These were (and still are) lacking in Hebrew and the other Semitic languages. Walter Ong went farther and proposed that the rise of logic in Greece was also due to the formal study of rhetoric, that is, use of language to convince (2002: 482). The basis for this seemingly chauvinistic theory is the fact that a fully alphabetic language has a lower level of ambiguity. Without entering into a debate about why something did not happen, it still must be pointed out that the Chinese language, particularly the ancient form, contains a much higher degree of ambiguity than modern European written languages. A major cause of this ambiguity is the extreme polysemy of Chinese. The modern language reduces this by using binomes (that is two characters rather than one to denote a word), but these are infrequent in the early language, making meanings much more context-dependent than is the case for English (Melzer: 49). A further problem is the lack of grammatical inflections due to the nature of the Chinese writing system. While there are many characters that serve as grammatical markers, they too are often ambiguous and are not much used in the *Zhouyi*. As a result there are no noun cases, no verb tenses, no designation of singular or plural. Pronouns are infrequent and ungendered. For the most part grammar is indicated by word order, but lack of punctuation in early and classical Chinese makes it often unclear where one sentence ends and another begins. Despite all this, Chinese communicate with each other as efficiently as do people of any other language and created one of the world's great literary and philosophical traditions.

The real difficulty that ambiguity poses for the translator is not that of finding the best English meaning. Rather it is the necessity of reducing multiple meanings to single ones. This is particularly problematic with very early Chinese.

Chad Hansen points out:

> What the translation paradigm ignores is that many alternative translation equivalents could make sense of each isolated sentence containing the term (8).

He further observes that English translations of Chinese texts tend to fix the meaning, giving the mistaken implication that there is one correct meaning, which it is the translator's task to recognize and represent in the target language. I would add that the assumption that all, or even most, readers in the original language would construe ambiguous passages identically is unlikely. It is entirely plausible, indeed probable, that early Chinese readers or listeners understood phrases in multiple ways. Thus meanings were multiple. Particularly in a text used for divination, multiple meanings would increase the apparent accuracy of its prognostications.

I think this problem is quite real, but not quite as bad as Hansen suggests. Often most of the possible meanings can be excluded by context. Others do not greatly affect the meaning and tone of the text. Finally, and most importantly, translators can and should alert readers to important ambiguities and disclose their assumptions about the text that determine how they translate. My key assumptions are: first, that the text was originally understandable and second, that it is about common matters of daily life and concrete rather than abstract, in other words, it is pre-axial. Furthermore, it seems unashamed of violence, though many translators have toned this down, and, finally, it does not seem to care about consistency.

Ambiguity is inherent in the *Zhouyi* and there is no definitive solution to the problems this poses in translating. To represent many possible meanings for the same character would result in unreadability. Nor should we, as one translator has, ask readers to turn back to a glossary to select the meanings they like best. Accordingly, I have included variant possible meanings when they seem particularly important, but not in all cases. I also point out to readers some instances in which my renderings diverge from those of other translators, acknowledging that both may be correct. Obviously, part of my reason for doing this is 无咎 *wu jiu*: to have no blame.

There is yet another source of uncertainty in reconstructing the early meanings of the words. This is frequency of scribal variation or homophone substation. The script was not standardized and scribes often wrote a different character of similar sound in place of the correct one. Such substitutions were frequent. The relative paucity of phonemes in the Chinese language results in a high frequency of homophones—words of different meanings that sound the same. To give an extreme example, in Schuessler's *Dictionary of Early Zhou Chinese*, characters pronounced *fu* have fifteen pages of definitions (if all four tones are included). English has relatively few such homophones. Words such as "there" and "their" or "weather" and "whether" are easily distinguished in context.

Deciphering homophone substitutions depends on reconstruction of the sounds of a language that has not been heard for more than two thousand years. While these reconstructions have been essential to recovering the Western Zhou meanings, they have also given philologists the opportunity to be overly creative in substituting improbable meanings for self-evident ones. A notable example is 4.0 蒙 *meng* translated by Wilhelm-Baynes as *Youthful Folly* and by me as the similar *Neophytes,* but emended by Waley to *Dodder,* a kind of weed. (I discuss this in more detail in my commentary to this hexagram.) Fortunately, phonetic reconstruction is moving toward consensus and scholars are more conservative about unsupported emendations. In China there is even a Trusting Antiquity Movement that is less willing to arbitrarily set aside received traditions.

Despite all these conundrums, it is possible to reconstruct the early texts with a reasonable degree of certainty, most of the time. As always, there are intense debates among scholars about details—this is part of the fun. Historical phonetic reconstruction is extremely complex and there are only a handful of scholars competent in this esoteric discipline. (For an up-to-date account, though not discussing the *Zhouyi,* see Baxter and Sargent.) The present translation could not have been made without the painstaking work of Chinese and Western philologists, on whose findings I have relied in identifying homophones. I have, however, made my own decisions about which meaning is most likely to be the correct one, based on my study of the text and its era.

My principles for this translation

Having itemized some of the challenges faced by the translator of ancient or classical Chinese, I will now describe some of my strategies responding to them. In stating them I am following the trend for full disclosure, believing that fairness to readers requires revealing one's assumptions.

First, I have tried to be as literal as possible not only with respect to meanings, but also the terseness and word order of the original. I have only altered these when necessary for comprehension. When the original itself is semantically awkward, I usually have not altered meaning for the sake of smoother flow. Some awkwardness is inevitable because the work is extremely terse and was composed from a collection of fragments. When necessary for clarity and ease of reading, I have sparingly added grammatical words regularly omitted in Chinese, such as pronouns, conjunctions, and definite and indefinite articles. I have only rarely added substantive words to the source text but instead have provided clarifications in the commentary. Fortunately, unlike some other ancient languages such as Sanskrit, there is no problem in separating words because each character stands for a single word. The characters are modular, made up of smaller characters, often with both semantic and phonetic elements, though these are of limited help in figuring out meaning and sound for a rare character.

I have chosen gender neutral words, except when the gender is apparent in context. While I do not doubt that such terms as 人 *ren*, person, or 君子 *junzi*, prince or upright person, almost always refer to males, I see no need to add grammatical male gender when it does not exist in the source text. While women unquestionably usually occupied a subordinate place, some clearly had agency as indicated in the oracle bone inscriptions and the *Zuozhuan*, among other texts. We need to know more about the place of women in bronze-age China and should not assume that autonomy was available solely to males. It would be particularly interesting to learn how exceptional women succeeded, such as Fu Hao, the second wife of King Wu Ding, who was able to become a powerful general.

Despite these good intentions, I have often been less literal than I hoped to be. I feel supported in this by the view of Michael Nylan:

translators ... should also feel free to disregard the original word order in Chinese, if doing so creates more readable English. Only pedantry prevents such rearrangements ... (2014)

However, I believe that the goal of more readable English can be attained without rewriting the Chinese text; an all too common practice.

An important part of translating the *Zhouyi*, rarely mentioned, is the addition of punctuation, of which there is none in the original. Though this narrows the possible meanings of the text—originally just strings of characters—it is essential to clarity. Most problematic, until commas or periods are added it is often unclear if a noun is the object of the preceding verb or the subject of the next.

Placement of a comma or period does often reduce the number of possible meanings, but it is necessary for modern readers, who do not have access to a traditionally educated teacher who has spent a lifetime studying that specific text. All punctuation represents the opinion of the translator as to the intended structure of phrases. I have tried to be judicious in the addition of punctuation, but much of the text would be incomprehensible without it. However, readers should be aware that punctuation is part of the translation. I have tried to limit punctuation to two sorts of situation: for smoother reading when placement is unambiguous, and when the meaning is completely obscure without it. Any reader is justified in imagining how meanings would change if commas, semicolons and periods were moved around in the line text.

I have made abundant use of dashes. These can be an author's best friend because they connect phrases without leaving open the exact nature of their relationship. I justify this by the nature of the original, which tends to leave it to the reader to figure out how phrases relate to each other—or if they do at all.

Another central issue in translation is how strict to be in translating source words consistently into the target language. My view, at least for the *Zhouyi*, is that translating the same word inconsistently conceals patterns of meaning that are important for full appreciation of the text. This is particularly important with prognostic words such as 利 *li* beneficial; 吉 *ji* auspicious; 吝 *lin* regret; 凶 *xiong* ominous; 无咎 *wu jiu* no blame; 君子 *junzi* upright person, etc. Prognostications may seem monotonous to us, but they

were of the greatest importance to early readers. Consistent translation is necessary to reveal the thought patterns that determined
the favorable and the ominous.

A contrary view is expressed by Lauren Pfister:

Representatives of both Protestant and French academic traditions in the first half of the nineteenth century tended to
standardize translations for key terms, leaving no room for
contextual nuance or connotative differences. This kind of error
Legge self-consciously avoided. (2001: 405f.)

The problem with this is that Legge, Wilhelm-Baynes and other
early translators lacked a historical conception of the text, resulting
in many of the "conceptual nuances" being the creations of the
translators themselves. Nor, as Legge's translation demonstrates,
does this approach necessarily result in clarity or readability. (The
notorious black magician and iconoclast Aleister Crowley cruelly
derided the Oxford Professor of Chinese as "Wood'n Legge,"
referring to his prose style.)

I have made a particular effort to avoid the use of words and
concepts that would have been anachronistic in the Western Zhou.
This is especially important with the psychological language that is
so embedded in modern English as to usually pass unnoticed. This
has predominated in writings on the *I Ching*, ever since Carl Jung's
1949 Foreword to the Wilhelm-Baynes translation. While I think
the great Swiss psychologist's Foreword is one of the best places to
start study of the *Changes*, it is only a start. Now that many more
of us in the West are familiar with Chinese culture and ideas, I feel
the time is ripe for a translation that tries to give a sense of how
the *Changes* was read in its own time. While I see nothing inherently wrong with translating the *Changes* in psychological terms
for those who find it helpful in their personal lives, I think those
who are curious about the work deserve to be able to read it on
its own terms.

In reading translations of diverse Chinese texts over the years,
and comparing them with their originals, I have the strong
impression that many translators modify them into what they wish
they said. I have done my best to avoid this. In fact, there is much
in the Western Zhou text that I strongly dislike, particularly the
frequent and unapologetic references to state-sponsored violence.

Another mistake I have tried to avoid is mixing up literal meanings with divinatory ones. Divinatory texts exist on at least two levels. One is what the text says directly, the other is how it is applied to the particular situations divined about. Given the persuasive power of divination, the *Book of Changes* was frequently used to serve political agendas, for example the politically expedient reading by the Kangxi Emperor (504). A divination from the *Book of Changes* can, of course, serve personal agendas as well, often as a reason for not doing something. Given its supernatural aura, it is hard to convince a believer that a prognostication is wrong.

My journey back in time to the Chinese Bronze Age has been a fascinating one for me, and I hope my translation will enable my readers to share this experience.

Notes on other translations

If I thought another translation of the *I Ching* was definitive, I would not have embarked on my own. In fact, given the ambiguity of the text, its 3,000 years of history, the many speculations that have been applied to it, there can be no single valid translation. Since some readers are likely to have encountered other translations, a brief schematization of their differences and limitations might be useful to those confused by the radically different English versions of the same word in Chinese. Indeed, it is not unusual that translations differ so much as to seem to be from different texts altogether.

I divide translations into three categories: sinologically sound, literary, and New Age. There is some overlap between these categories and within each there is considerable variety.

Many of the most important versions are the work of Westerners who are or were very knowledgeable about China, but who were not academic sinologists. These include the missionary translators: Canon Thomas McClatchie, James Legge, Richard Wilhelm, and Richard Rutt. Also important to mention is the psychiatrist and theorist of religion, Carl G. Jung. Though himself not a translator, it was his circle in Switzerland that inspired Wilhelm and Baynes. The *I Ching* continues to attract translators, such as myself, who hold no academic position in Chinese studies. Others include Greg Whincup, Cyrille Javary, author of the leading French translation,

Chung Wu, whose work is the most complete exposition of trigram interpretation in English, Kerson Huang, an MIT professor, Yale Law Professor Jack Balkin, and Hong Kong marketing expert Mun Kin Chok. Another translator with an interesting background is Alfred Huang, one-time professor at Shanghai University, who was "trained in secret by one of China's greatest *I Ching* masters." Those translators whose study of the *Changes* took place in China tend to have quite different ways of understanding the classic, and this difference has not received the attention it merits. As these examples show, the *I Ching* continues to possess a mystique that has attracted a strikingly diverse group of scholars.

The most important and sinologically sound translations are those of James Legge, Richard Kunst (unfortunately only available as an unpublished doctoral dissertation), Richard Rutt, Edward L. Shaughnessy (of the excavated manuscripts), and John Richard Lynn, whose work is based on the interpretations of Wang Bi (226–249 CE). Among other translations of interest are those of Greg Whincup and MIT professor Kerson Huang.

Within this group there is a fundamental distinction between those who worked to recreate the early Western Zhou meanings and those who worked within the later received tradition. In general, the early translators were scholars versed in classical Chinese who worked from rigorous principles, but did not question the late Qing Dynasty mode of exegesis. Richard Wilhelm, whose work fits in this group, was aided by his Chinese informant Lao Nai-hsuan (勞乃軒 Lao Naixuan), one of the last of the traditionally educated literati. James Legge's translation was also based on Chinese informants, but its ponderous diction makes it a hard slog. A translation more in line with current scholarly standards, though not based on the Western Zhou meanings, is that of Richard John Lynn, whose version is based on the commentary of Wang Bi (226–249 CE). Lynn's work is groundbreaking in that it is historical—he situates his translation within a specific time and interpretive school. This should be, in my opinion, the way of the future for translations of ancient texts—situating them within a specific commentarial tradition or lineage. Earlier translations such as those of Legge and Wilhelm-Baynes present it synchronically.

A second category consists of literary translations. These are based on sound knowledge of Chinese but translate more freely, based on what is to me a dubious assumption—that aesthetics takes precedence over accuracy. My own belief is that one should strive to translate both accurately and gracefully—what I hope I have achieved to some degree. Wilhelm-Baynes is of course, the pre-eminent literary translation but basically an adaptation, though an extremely influential one. Also in the category of literary translation is the recent one of John Minford. It contains much of interest but runs to over 800 pages, most of which are commentary. Wilhelm-Baynes had a similar problem, exacerbated by the unclear separation between different parts of the I Ching itself and their commentary. My personal approach to commentary is quite different—I strive to illuminate the meaning of the text but do so concisely enough so as not to overwhelm it.

Another sort of literary "translation" is that of David Hinton. This is actually a series of prose poems very loosely based on the Changes. One may or may not find it inspiring, but it is not the I Ching. Regrettably it makes the Changes more obscure in English than it is in Chinese. Such works are better regarded as imitations rather than translations—akin to Ezra Pound's Cathay, a major work of English poetry, but not of translation.

My third category is what I have termed New Age appropriations. These use the I Ching as a starting point for fashionable ideas, usually without actual basis in the Chinese classic. This category includes the work of Carol Anthony and Hanna Moog. Though serious devotees of the I Ching, they repetitiously insist that the Book of Changes is really about "overcoming the ego," a clichéd distortion of a Freudian concept with no basis in the Changes. Such work perpetuates a fallacy akin to the "all religions teach the same things" sort. By reducing the 3000-year-old classic to pop psychology they deprive the reader of the opportunity to encounter another way of thought.

The "wickedest man in the world" as the press dubbed Aleister Crowley (1875–1947) even produced a pseudo-translation in which he mapped the hexagram array on the Cabalistic Tree of Life. Even farther from the actual work are various I Chings intended to give advice on romance, on becoming an author or life coach and, perhaps oddest of all, the Toltec I Ching, whose authors were somehow privy to the spiritual insights of an extinct culture that left no writings. Common to these works seems to be using the prestige of the I Ching to add allure to commonplace ideas. (For more on the problem of English pseudo-translations see Redmond and Hon: 215–18.)

BIBLIOGRAPHY

Armstrong, Karen. 2007. *The Great Transformation: The Beginning of Our Religious Traditions*. New York: Knopf/Doubleday.

Arnason, Johann P. 2012. "Rehistoricizing the Axial Age." In Bellah and Joas, *The Axial Age and its Consequences*. Cambridge, MA and London: Belknap Press of Harvard University Press, 337–65.

Assman, Jan. 2012. "Cultural Memory and the Myth of the Axial Age." In Bellah and Joas, *The Axial Age and its Consequences*. Cambridge, MA and London: Belknap Press of Harvard University Press, 366–407.

Barnard, Noel. 1973. *The Ch'u Silk Manuscript: Translation and Commentary*. Canberra: Research School of Pacific Studies, Australian National University.

Barton, Tamsyn. 1994. *Ancient Astrology*. New York and London: Routledge.

Baxter, William H. and Laurent Sagart. 2014. *Old Chinese: A New Reconstruction*. Oxford: Oxford University Press.

Bellah, Robert N. and Hans Joas, eds. 2012. *The Axial Age and its Consequences*. Cambridge, MA and London: Belknap Press of Harvard University Press.

Blackmore, Susan. 1996. *In Search of the Light*. Amherst, NY: Prometheus Books.

Blackmore, Susan. 2004. *Consciousness: An Introduction*. New York: Oxford University Press.

Boltz, William G. 1994. *The Origin and Early Development of the Chinese Writing System*. Eisenbrauns: American Oriental Society.

Brady, Bernadette. 2014. *Cosmos, Chaosmos and Astrology: Rethinking the Nature of Astrology*. Ceredigion, Wales: Sophia Centre Press.

Bremmer, Jan N. 2007. *The Strange World of Human Sacrifice*. Leuven-Paris-Dudley: Peeters, 2007.

Capra, Fritjof. 1999. *The Tao of Physics: An Exploration of the Parallels Between Modern Physics and Eastern Mysticism*, 4th updated edn (35th Anniversary). Boston: Shambhala.

Cicero. *De Senectute, De Amicitia, De Divinatione*. With an English

Translation by William Armistead Falconer. 1923. Loeb Classical
Library 154. Cambridge, MA: Harvard University Press.

Cook, Constance. 2006. "From Bone to Bamboo: Number Sets and
Mortuary Ritual." *Journal of Oriental Studies* 41: 1–40.

Durrant, Stephen, Wai-yee Li, and David Shaberg. 2016. *Zuo Tradition/
Zuozhuan: Commentary on the Spring and Autumn Annals.* Seattle:
University of Washington Press.

Dyer, Dr. Wayne W. 2013. *Change Your Thoughts—Change Your Life:
Living the Wisdom of the Tao.* Carlsbad, CA: Hay House.

Eggert, Paul. 2013. "Apparatus, Text, Interface: How to Read a Printed
Critical Edition." In Neil Fraistat and Julia Flanders, *The Cambridge
Companion to Textual Scholarship,* 97–118.

Eliade, Mircea. 1976. *Occultism, Witchcraft, and Cultural Fashions:
Essays in Comparative Religion.* Chicago: University of Chicago
Press.

Elman, Benjamin A. 2001. *From Philosophy to Philology: Intellectual
and Social Aspects of Change in Late Imperial China,* 2nd edn. Los
Angeles: UCLA Asian Pacific Monograph Series.

Gardner, Daniel K. 1990. *Learning to be a Sage: Selections from the
Conversations of Master Chu, Arranged Topically.* University of
California Press.

Greetham, D. C. 1994. *Textual Scholarship: An Introduction.* New York
and London: Garland Publishing.

Gu, Ming Dong. 2005. *Chinese Theories of Reading and Writing: A
Route to Hermeneutics and Open Poetics.* Albany: State University of
New York Press.

Hacker, Edward. 1993. *The I Ching Handbook: A Practical Guide to
Logical and Personal Perspectives from the Ancient Chinese Book of
Change.* Brookline, MA: Paradigm Publications.

Hacker, Edward, Steve Moore and Lorraine Patsco. 2002. *I Ching: An
Annotated Bibliography.* New York and London: Routledge.

Hansen, Chad. 1992. *A Daoist Theory of Chinese Thought: A
Philosophical Interpretation.* Oxford and New York: Oxford
University Press.

Hatcher, Bradford. 2009. *The Book of Changes: Yijing Word by Word.*
2 Vol. Nucla, Colorado. (Print on demand and available online: www.
hermetica.info).

Henderson, John B. 1991. *Scripture, Canon, and Commentary: A
Comparison of Confucian and Western Exegesis.* Princeton: Princeton
University Press.

Hsu, Cho-yun. 1965. *Ancient China in Transition: An Analysis of Social
Mobility, 722–222 B.C.* Stanford: Stanford University Press.

Huang, Alfred. 1998. *The Complete I Ching: The Definitive Translation by the Taoist Master Alfred Huang*. Rochester, Vermont: Inner Traditions.

Instituts Ricci. 2003. *Aperçus de Civilization Chinois: Les Dossiers du Grand Ricci*. Paris and Taipei: Instituts Ricci–Desclee de Brouwer.

Jullien, Francois. 1992. "Yi King, Le Classique du Changement ou D'Un Logique de L'Immanence." In Philastre, Paul-Louis-Felix, *Le Yi king: Traduit du chinois*. Paris: Zulma.

Jullien, Francois. 1995. *The Propensity of Things: Toward a History of Efficacy in China*. New York: Zone Books.

Kalinowski, Marc. 2003. *Divination et Société dans la Chine Mediévale: Etude des Manuscripts de Dunhuang de la Bibliothèque Nationale de France et de la British Library*. Paris: Bibliothèque Nationale.

Keenan, Barry C. 2011. *Neo-Confucian Self-Cultivation*. Honolulu: University of Hawaii Press.

Keightley, David N. 1985. *Sources of Shang History: The Oracle-Bone Inscriptions of Bronze Age China*. Berkeley: University of California Press.

Keightley, David N. 1999. "At the Beginning: The Status of Women in Neolithic and Shang China." *Nan Nu: Men, Women and Gender in Early and Imperial China* 1 (1) (March): 1–63.

Keightly, David. 2014. *These Bones Shall Rise Again: Selected Writings on Early China*. Albany: State University of New York Press.

Knapp, Keith. 2005. *Selfless Offspring: Filial Children and Social Order in Medieval China*. Honolulu: University of Hawaii Press.

Kong, Y. C. 2010. *Huangdi Nei Jing: A Synopsis with Commentaries*. Hong Kong: The Chinese University Press.

Kroll, Paul W. 2014. *A Student's Dictionary of Classical and Medieval Chinese*. Leiden: Brill.

Kunst, Richard. 1985. *The Original Yijing: A Text, Phonetic Transcription, Translation, and Indexes, with Sample Glosses*. Ann Arbor: University Microfilms International.

Li, Shen 李申 and Guo Huo 郭彧. 2004. *Zhouyi Tushu Zonghui* 周易图书总汇 (*Collection of Diagrams of the Zhouyi*). Shanghai: Huadong Shifan Daxue Chubanshe.

Lianbin Dai. 2014. "Textual Collation and its Guiding Principles in Eighteenth-Century Evidential Scholarship: Illustrated with Lu Wenchao's (1717–1796) Work." Presented at Conference of Assocation for Asian Studies. Philadelphia, 30 March 2013.

Liang Cai. 2014. *Witchcraft and the Rise of the First Confucian Empire*. Albany: State University of New York Press.

Marlowe, Michael, ed., n.d. "Rules of Textual Criticism." Available online: http://www.bible-researcher.com/rules.html (accessed 2 May 2016).

Marshal, S. J. 2001. *The Mandate of Heaven: Hidden History in the I Ching*. New York: Columbia University Press.

Melzer, Arthur M. 2014. *Philosophy Between the Lines: The Lost History of Esoteric Writing*. Chicago: University of Chicago Press.

Michael, Thomas. 2015. *In the Shadows of the Dao: Laozi, the Sage, and the Daodejing*. Albany: State University of New York Press.

Minton, John. 2014. *I Ching: The Essential Translation of the Ancient Chinese Oracle and Book of Wisdom*. New York: Viking.

National Palace Museum, Taipei. 2001. 故宮西周金文录, *Gugong Xizhou Jin Wen Lu, Catalogue of the Western Chou Bronze Inscription in the National Palace Museum*.

Needham, Joseph. 1956. With the research assistance of Wang Ling. SCC Vol. 2 *History of Scientific Thought*. Cambridge: Cambridge University Press.

Nylan, Michael. 1993. *The Canon of Supreme Mystery by Yang Hsiung: A Translation of the T'ai Hsuan Ching*. Albany: State University of New York Press, 13.

Nylan, Michael. 2009. *The Riddle of the Bamboo Annals*. Taipei: Airiti Press.

Nylan, Michael. 2014. "Translating Texts in Chinese History and Philosophy." In Ming Dong Gu with Rainer Schulte, eds. *Translating China for Western Readers: Reflective, Critical, and Practical Essays*. Albany: State University of New York Press.

Ong, Walter J. 2002 [1982]. *Orality and Literacy: The Technologizing of the Word*. 30th Anniversary edn. With additional chapters by John Hartley. London and New York: Routledge.

Ong, Walter J. and Thomas J. Farrell. 2002. *An Ong Reader: Challenges for Further Inquiry*. New Jersey: Hampton Press.

Pankenier, David W. 2013. *Astrology and Cosmology in Early China: Conforming Earth to Heaven*. Cambridge: Cambridge University Press.

Pearson, Margaret J. 2011. *The Original I Ching: An Authentic Translation of the Book of Changes. Based on Recent Discoveries*. Tokyo, Rutland, and Singapore: Tuttle.

Pines, Yuri. 2002. *Foundations of Confucian Thought: Intellectual Life in the Chunqiu Period, 722–453 B.C.E.* Honolulu: University of Hawaii Press.

Santangelo, Paolo. 2013. In co-operation with Yan Beiwen. "Zibuyu, 'What the Master Would Not Discuss'". *According to Yuan Mei (1716–1798): A Collection of Supernatural Stories*. 2 vols. Leiden: Brill.

Sawyer, Ralph D. 2013. *Conquest and Domination in Early China: Rise and Demise of the Western Chou*. With the bibliographic collaboration of Mei-chun Lee Sawyer. Self published.

Schaberg, David. 2001. *A Patterned Past: Form and Thought in Early Chinese Historiography*. Cambridge: Harvard University East Asia Center.

Schuessler, Axel. 1987. A *Dictionary of Early Zhou Chinese*. Honolulu: University of Hawaii Press.

Schuessler, Axel. 2007. *ABC Etymological Dictionary of Old Chinese*. Honolulu: University of Hawaii Press.

Schuessler, Axel. 2009. *Minimal Old Chinese and Later Han Chinese: A Companion to Grammata Serica Recensa*. Honolulu: University of Hawaii Press.

Shaughnessy, Edward L. 1991. *Sources of Western Zhou History: Inscribed Bronze Vessels*. Berkeley: University of California Press.

Shaughnessy, Edward L. 1999. "Western Zhou History." In *The Cambridge History of Ancient China: From the Origins of Civilization to 221 B.C.*, Michael Lowe and Edward Shaughnessy, eds. Cambridge: Cambridge University Press, 292–351.

Smith, Kidder. 1993. "The Difficulty of the Yi Jing." *Chinese Literature: Essays, Articles, Reviews* 15: 1–15.

Spence, Jonathan D. 1985. *The Memory Palace of Matteo Ricci*. New York: Viking.

Star, Jonathan. 2001. *Tao Te Ching: The Definitive Edition. Lao Tzu. Translation and Commentary by Jonathan Star*. New York: Tarcher-Penguin.

Sukhu, Gopal. 2012. *The Shaman and the Heresiarch: A New Interpretation of the* Li Sao. Albany: State University of New York Press.

Taylor, Charles. "What was the Axial Revolution." In Bellah and Joas *The Axial Age and its Consequences*. Cambridge, MA and London: Belknap Press of Harvard University Press, 30–46.

Tsai, Frederick C. 2013. "The Name and Nature of Translation." In Lawrence Wang-chi Wong with the assistance of Stephanie Cheuk Wong, *Towards a History of Translating*, Vol. I. Hong Kong: Research Centre for Translation, Chinese University of Hong Kong.

Unschuld, Paul U. 2003. *Huang Di Nei Jing Su Wen: Nature, Knowledge, Imagery in an Ancient Chinese Medical Texts*. Berkeley: University of California Press.

Warren, Michelle. 2014. "The Politics of Textual Scholarship." In Neil Fraisant and Julia Flanders, eds. *The Cambridge Companion to Textual Scholarship*. Cambridge: Cambridge University Press.

Wilkinson, Endymion. 2013. *Chinese History: A New Manual*. Cambridge: Harvard University Asia Center.

Wu, Chung. 2003. *The Essentials of the Yi Jing: Translated, Annotated, and with an Introduction and Notes*. St. Paul: Paragon House.

Yang, Li. 1998. *Book of Changes and Traditional Chinese Medicine.* Beijing: Science and Technology Press.
Yates, Frances. 1966/96. *The Art of Memory.* London: Routledge and Kegan Paul.

INDEX

abstractions 337
Abundance *see Da you*
accidents 171
Adornment *see Bi* (Adornment)
Advantage *see Yi* (Advantage)
affection 368
agriculture 104, 105, 167, 188,
    383 see also *Da xu*
  animal skinning 158
  breeding 201
  human sacrifice 263
  time 339
Already Across the River *see Ji Ji*
ambiguity 402–5
analogy school 399, 400
ancestors 85, 316, 322
ancient texts 28–30 *see also*
    Chinese ancient texts;
    Chinese classical texts
animals 80, 188, 249, 283, 383,
    396 see also *Da xu*
  birds *see* birds
  boars 171
  butchering 278–9
  castration of stallion 306
  cows/bulls 166, 167, 171, 188,
    237
  dragons 67–70, 75, 360–1
  fish 159, 249, 263
  foxes 321, 324
  horses 72–3, 79, 171, 208,
    213, 306, 396
  leopards 267

  loss of 297–8
  mole crickets 209
  oxen 167, 237
  piglets/pigs 199–201, 225, 249
  rams 204, 205–6, 249
  rodents 128
  sheep 245, 307
  skins 158
  squirrels 209
  tail dipping 321, 324
  tigers 108, 109, 267
  tortoises 175, 237
  turtles 175
  venomous 140–1
Annals of the Spring and Autumn
    65–6
anomalies 293
anomaly school 399, 400
Anthony, Carol 59, 410
Anyang *see* Yin Xu site
Aristotle 36, 39, 400
Armstrong, Karen 37
arrowheads 151, 232
ars memorativa 32
Assembling *see Cui*
Assembling *see Tong Ren*
asterisms 68, 70, 75, 171, 223
astrology 16–17, 32, 46–7, 223,
    293
  moon, the 105
  Qian dragon sequence 68–70
  science 18, 357
  time 339

astronomy 120, 171, 222–3, 293, 339
auguries 170, 214, 338
Augustine, Saint 39
authorship 55–6
axialization 35–8

Bad see Fou
Balkin, Jack 409
bandits 79, 116, 124, 226
Baoshan 146, 167
Baynes, Cary F. 4
bead selection method 388, 390
beheading 190, 219, 279
belts 93
Bengel, Johann Albrecht 400
Bengel's rule 400–1
Bi (Adornment) 153
    commentary 154–5
Bi (Joining) 52, 99–100
    commentary 100–2
Bible, the 397, 400–1
bibliomancy 370 see also divination
Big Mistake see Da Guo
birds 114, 128–9, 132, 188, 383
    see also auguries
    cranes 312, 368
    geese 282–3
    orioles 117, 189 see also Lo
    pheasants 212–15, 271
Biting and Chewing see Shi ke
blame 69, 74, 101, 372–3
blindness 288
blood 89, 306
blood sacrifice 88–9 see also sacrifice
Bo (Flaying) 157
    commentary 158–9
boars 171
body fluids 89, 306–7
bones 174–5 see also Chinese oracle bones

cheekbones 244–5
fractured 293–4
jawbones 174–5, 177, 356–8
Book of Documents (Shangshu) 188
Book of Songs (Shijing) see Shijing
Bouvet, Joachim 154, 329
Bowers, Fredson 401
Brady, Bernadette 18
brain, the 344
breathing (in presence of emperor) 74
bricolage 30
bride abductions 79, 81, 154–5, 226
bronze 151, 236
Bronze Cauldron, The see Ding
Buddhism 34, 40, 146, 332, 374
    Jataka tales 213
    realities 336
    suffering 347
bulls 166, 171, 188
burials 74, 81

calendar see Chinese calendar
Calling Pheasant see Ming Yi
cannibalism 225
Cantos (Pound, Ezra) 58
capital punishment 304 see also decapitation
captives 92, 219–20, 232–3 see also Zhong Fu
    beheading 190
    compassion 241
    danger 205
    exchanging 304
    hunting 229
    losing 325
    physique 146
    prisoners 109, 185
    sacrifice 88, 113–14, 125, 136, 146, 219

skinning 304
soldiers 96
wailing 245, 253
Captives Within *see Zhong Fu*
cardinal directions 228
careers 21
castration 306
cauldrons 270, 272
Chan Buddhism 374 *see also* Buddhism
change 340, 347–8, 376–80
Change Your Thoughts—Change your Life: Living the Wisdom of the Tao (Dyer, Wayne W.) 348
character 120, 213, 245, 267–8, 373
    ethics 360
    rank 120, 128, 151, 181, 342
    sacrifice 325
charisma 32–4, 267
cheekbones 244–5
Cheng Yi 39, 375
Chi Ci (Songs of the South) 80
childbirth 275, 283
children 181
    as omens 146
    punishment 85–2
Chinese ancient texts 25–35
    oral material 28–30
    organization of 26–8
    physical nature of 25–6
    studying 398
Chinese calendar 46, 139, 162, 293
    auspicious dates 289
    dating 301
    hemerology 139, 262, 274, 294
    human sacrifice 267
Chinese characters 25–6, 51, 138, 174, 405
Chinese classical texts 5, 8, 10 *see also* Chinese ancient texts

Chinese "Great Leap Forward" 219
Chinese language 51–2, 271, 297, 402
Chinese numerology 139 *see also* numbers
Chinese oracle bones 12, 15–16, 175, 346 *see also* jawbones
    composition 237
    Shang oracle bones 27, 219
    Wu Ding oracle bones 12, 321, 395
Christianity 19, 154, 208, 241, 293, 329
    Biblical criticism 397
    guilt 373
    monotheism 363
    New Testament texts 397, 400–1
    saints 364
Chu Silk Manuscript 25
Chung Wu 350, 409
Chunqiu (Spring and Autumn Annals) 27, 369
Cicero, Marcus Tullius 170
    augury 338
    De Divinatione 16, 170
    divination 39
citation conventions 48–9
class *see* rank; society
classical texts 28 *see also* Chinese classical texts; Chinese ancient texts
clichés 29–30, 32
cogon grass 112–13, 116, 180
cognitive science 20
coin selection method 388, 390
coins 297
cold reading 21
coldness 322
commentaries 53–4
compassion 113–14, 241
compilation 55–7

comportment 189, 228, 371
composition 55–9
concubines 159, 270–1, 289
Confucianism 36, 353, 36, 365–6
    blood sacrifice 88
    filial piety 213
    government officials 213
    humility 129
    rebellion 266
    as religion 337
    self-knowledge 374
    sexual references 140
    violence 158
Confucius 3, 208, 348
    axialization 35, 36, 37–8
    death rites 81
    divination 39
    expertise 357
    intent 371
    Lunyu (*The Analects of
        Confucius*) see *Lunyu* (*The
        Analects of Confucius*)
    ritual 371
    women 218
consanguineous marriage 286
Cook, Constance 146, 225
Cook, R. S. 46
corruption 112
cosmology 19, 33–4, 223, 346,
    354–6
    physiognomy 356
    quantum physics 356–7
counter-culture (1960s) 355
Cousins, Norman 237
cowry shells 275
cows 166, 171, 188
cranes 312, 368
creation myths 360–1
Croesus, king of Lydia 163
Crowley, Aleister 410
crying 190
Cui (Assembling) 251–2
    commentary 252–4

cunning 205
Curry, Patrick 18

Da Guo (Big Mistake) 179–80
    commentary 180–2
da ren (important person) 342
Da xu (Large Livestock) 169–70
    commentary 170–1
Da you (Abundance) 123–4
    commentary 124–5
Da Zhuan (Great Strength) 203–4
    commentary 204–6
Dai, Lianbin 400
Dan, duke of Zhou 23, 24–5, 34,
    325, 348–9
dancing 114, 301
Dao (the Way) 16, 162, 341
Dao De Jing (*The Classic of the
    Way and Virtue*) 26, 57, 89,
    146, 345
    heaven 224
    principles for living 334
    time 340
Daoism 332, 336
    self–knowledge 374
dates, auspicious 289
dating 23–5, 176
*Daxiang, Greater Commentary
    on the Diagrams* 35–6
Dazhuan (*Xi Ci Great
    Commentary*) 34, 334–5,
    342, 348
de (virtue/obligation) 196–7
De Divinatione (Cicero, Marcus
    Tullius) 16
death 81, 97, 144, 189 *see also*
    mourning
    following-in death 271
    funerals 275
    necromancy 162
    suicide 176
decapitation 190, 219, 279
decisions 334, 347, 371, 387, 395

Decrease *see Sun*
deformity 222, 288
depth psychology 4–5
Determination *see Guai*
Di (the high god) 240–1, 289,
    362–3, 364
Di Yi, king of the Shang dynasty
    287, 289
diagrams 343–4 *see also*
    hexagrams
dialogue 39–41, 366–7
Diamond Sutra 25
Ding (The Bronze Cauldron) 174,
    269–70, 343
  commentary 270–2
directionality 73
directions 228
disembedding 37
disease 133, 167, 197 *see also Gu*
  illness 201
  water 262–3
Dispute see *Song*
distance 275
divination 15–22, 57–8, 166, 213,
    346–7, 392, 395
  astrology 16–17
  binary 310
  Christianity 19
  cold reading 21
  cosmology 19
  credibility 214
  definition 16
  dialogue 40–1, 367
  emotion 396
  epistemology 346
  esotericism 345–6
  expertise 357
  fraud 19
  hemerology 139
  inquiries 387, 396
  interpretation 392
  intuition 21
  military decisions 129

Mu Jiang, Lady 368–70
necromancy 162
orally transmitted material 33,
    34–5
philosophy 19, 39, 338
plastromancy 175
practicing 331–3, 371, 385–92
protest 355
psychism 21–2
psychology 19–22
randomness 20–1
science 17, 18, 20, 356–8
texts 370
time 339–40
tortoises 175
travel 73
turtles 175
universality of 15–19
women 218
yarrow 100, 113
yuan, heng, li, zhen phrase 49,
    64–6
divination manuals 13
divination systems 45, 46–7
divinatory texts 408
Doubting Antiquity Movement
    6–7, 329, 349, 398, 399
dragons 67–70, 75, 360–1, 383
dreams 152
drunkenness 229
dualism 341 *see also yin/yang*
Dui (Exchange) 303–4
  commentary 304
*Duke of Zhou's Manual of Dream
    Interpretation, The* 152
Dun (Piglet) 199–200
  commentary 200–1
Dyer, Wayne W.: *Change Your
    Thoughts—Change your
    Life: Living the Wisdom of
    the Tao* 348

Earth *see Kun* (Earth)

eating 170
eclipses 293
ecology 358–9
editing 55–6
education 85, 366–7
El Cid 97
Eliade, Mircea 17
Eliot, T. S. 333
   Wasteland, The 214
emotion 121, 163, 175, 193
   affection 368
   divination 396
   compassion 113–14, 241
   grief 189
   laughing 253, 275
   sacrifice 253–4
   shame 142, 196–7
   thunder 274
   weeping/wailing 190, 245,
      253, 297–8
enchanted worlds 18, 175, 338
Enduring *see Heng*
energy, *Qian* dragon sequence
   67–8, 361
environment, harming the 358–9
epistemology 345–6 *see also*
   knowledge
esotericism 345–6
ethics 65–6, 117, 245, 359–62,
   368–71
   intent 371–2
Evidentiary Scholarship
   movement 399
Exchange *see Dui*
executions 151, 190, 272
exegesis 41
expertise 357

family 383 *see also* children;
   marriage
   organization 105
   relationships 140, 141–2,
      180–1, 218–19, 289

Family Members *see Jia Ren*
fasting 259
fat 80
female roles 72–3 *see also* women
Feng (Fullness) 291–2
   commentary 292–4
fertility 52, 79–80, 104, 271
   sterility 283, 290, 358–9
festivals 154
feudal societies 73, 78, 125
   land 78, 132
Field, Stephen 24–5
   line texts 50
figurism 154
fire 188, 297
fish 159, 249, 263
Flaying see *Bo*
folk material 57
following-in death 271
food 80–1, 159, 200, 312 *see also*
   eating
   fasting 269
   meat 80, 116, 151, 225
   ritual 270, 272
   spoiled 138, 140
foreignness 101
fortune 117 *see also* misfortune
Fou (Bad) 115–16, 354
   commentary 116–17
Foucault, Michel 398
foxes 321, 324
Fu (Return) 161–2
   commentary 162–3
fu (trust/captives) 348, 349
Fu Hao, wife of King Wu Ding
   321, 405
Fu Xi 13, 23, 34, 349
Fullness *see Feng*
funerals 275

Gall, Franz Jospeh 357
Gao Heng 7, 101, 163, 188, 204
Gathering *see Tun*

Ge (Tanning Leather) 265–6
commentary 266–8
geese 282–3
Gen (Splitting) 56, 277–8, 368
commentary 278–80
gender 96, 228, 270–1, 405 *see
also* women
gifts 208
globality 37
gods 185, 362–5 see also *Di*
Going Up *see Sheng*
Gospels, the 28
Gou (Meeting) 247–8
commentary 248–9
government 375–9
government officials 112, 146,
205, 212–13
classics, the 360
garments 259
record keeping 300–1
grace 154
Gradual Approach *see Jian*
(Gradual Approach)
grammar 51, 271, 297, 402
Great *see Tai*
"Great Leap Forward" 219
Great Strength *see Da Zhuan*
Greek language 402
Griesbach, Johann Jakob 401
Gu, Ming Dong 374–5
Gu (Sickness from Sexual Excess)
137–8, 396
commentary 138–42
Gu Jiegang 7
Guai (Determination) 243–4, 373,
375
commentary 244–5
Guan (Observing) 145–6, 374, 375
commentary 146–7
Guan Yu, General 364
Guanyin, Bodhisattva 146
Guanyin, Goddess of Compassion
364

guests 147
Gui Mei (Marrying Maiden)
285–6, 358, 396
commentary 286–90
guilt 372–3

Hacker, Edward 44, 64, 350
I Ching Handbook 350
Hadot, Pierre 332–3
Han Yu 59
Hansen, Chad 403
happiness 237
Hatcher, Bradford 349, 398
Havelock, Eric 29, 30, 402
head, the 322
health 140–1 *see also* disease;
illness
fractured bones 293–4
Heart Sutra 10
heaven 171, 224, 337, 354–5
Heaven *see Qian* (Heaven)
hemerology 139, 262, 274, 294
Henderson, John B. 41
Heng (Enduring) 195–6, 372
commentary 196–7
heng (offering) 65, 85, 108
Heraclites 379
Hermes Trismegistus 13
Hexagram texts 48
hexagrams 10–11, 30–2, 33, 43,
44–6, 100 *see also under
individual names*
interpretation 343–4, 392
philosophy 342–4
selection 388–91
subjects 383–4
hierarchy 355
Hinton, David 410
history 23–5, 208, 286–8
homelessness 225
Homer 28
Iliad 271
homo sapiens

history 12
literacy 12
homophones 405
Hon Tze–ki 3
  Teaching the I Ching (*Book of Changes*) 362
horses 72–3, 79, 171, 208, 213, 306, 396
hosts 147
households 218–19
Hu Shi 7
Hua Yen 34
Huan (Spurting) 305–6, 343
  commentary 306–7
Huang, Alfred 409
Huang, Kerson 409
Huang Di Nei Jing Su Wen (*Yellow Emperor's Inner Classic of Medicine*) 141
human actions 358–9
human sacrifice 88–9, 104, 136, 184, 348, 349 *see also* sacrifice
  agriculture 263
  calendar 266–7
  compassion 113–14, 241
  gender 270–1
  splitting bodies 278–80
  victim suitability 146
  wailing 245
  Yin Xu site 219, 279
  Zhou, the 88, 322
Humble *see Qian* (Humble)
hunting 101, 197, 228, 233, 271, 297

I Ching (*Yijing*) (*Book of Changes*) 3–4 see also *Zhouyi*
  consulting 385–92
  dating 23–5, 176
  divination 16–18
  endings 326

interpretation 392
manuscripts 8–9, 185
Mawangdui manuscript 25, 44, 46, 64, 72, 259
meaning changes 348–50
moral development 363
practicing divination 331–2
reading 383–4
scholarship 379
variants 31
I Ching for Lovers 59
I Ching Handbook (Hacker, Edward) 350
identity 73
illness 201, 214, 322, 395 *see also* disease
incipience 68, 166, 344–5, 346
interpretation 392
intuition 21
invocations 49
Iphigenia 89, 271

jade 151, 249, 296
Jaspers, Karl 35
Jataka tales 213
Javary, Cyrille 408
jawbones 174–5, 177, 356–8
Ji Ji (Already Across the River) 319–20, 376, 377–9
  commentary 320–2
Jia Ren (Family Members) 217–18
  commentary 218–20
Jian (Gradual Approach) 281–2
  commentary 282–3
Jian (Stumbling) 227–8
  commentary 228–9
Jiantizi script 26
Jie (Release) 231–2
  commentary 232–3
Jie (Time) 309
  commentary 310
Jin (Progress) 57–8, 207–8, 376

commentary 208–9
jing 176
Jing (The Well) 261–2, 343, 377
  commentary 262–3
Jizi 214
Joining *see Bi* (Joining)
judgements, the 48, 205
Jung, Carl 4, 20, 22, 331, 380,
      407, 408
  self-knowledge 370
  symbols 344
junzi (cultivated/virtuous person)
      73, 342
Jupiter 120

Kaishu script 26
Kelber, Werner 32, 33, 34
Khmer Rouge 219
kneeling 300
Kneeling *see Xun*
knowledge 336, 345
Koch, Ulla Susanne 16
Kui (Opposition) 221–2
  commentary 222–6
Kun (Earth) 48, 67, 71–2, 3
      61–2
  commentary 72–5
Kun (Obstruction) 257–8, 392
  commentary 248–9
Kunst, Richard 6, 8, 65, 409

land 78, 132
language 402 *see also* dialogue
  grammar 51, 271, 297, 402
  homophones 405
  punctuation 51–2
Lao Nai-hsuan 4, 409
Laozi 35, 57, 364
Laozi 197, 208
  social criticism 159
Large Livestock *see Da xu*
laughing 253, 275
leaders 214

leather 266–7
legal codes 363
legal proceedings 92
Legge, James 49, 407, 408, 409
Leibniz, Gottfried 329
leisure 163
leopard change 267
Levi-Strauss, Claude 30
Li (Oreole) 187–8, 343, 371–2
  commentary 188–90
life decisions 334, 347, 371, 387,
      395
Lin (Wailing) 143–4
  commentary 144
Lin Biao: *Little Red Book* 364
line configuration 46–7
line texts 50
  interpretation 392
  selection 388–91
literacy 12, 27
literature 27, 356 *see also* Chinese
      ancient texts; Chinese
      classical texts
  charisma 33–4
  textual theory 397–9
  Yuan Me, tales of 175
Little Red Book (Lin Biao) 364
liver, removal of 307
logic 402
Lower Jaw *see Yi* (Lower Jaw)
Lu (The Traveler) 295–6
  commentary 296–8
Lu (Treading) 107–8
  commentary 108–9
Lunyu (*The Analects of
      Confucius*) 26, 40, 57, 259
  heaven 224
  morality 197
  petty people 146
  principles 334
  sagehood 345
  social criticism 159
Lynn, Richard John 8, 409

McClatchie, Canon Thomas 408
Mahayana Buddhism 146
Mao Zedong 57, 364
marriage 21, 79, 86, 116, 180–1
    see also Gui Mei
    bride abductions 79, 81,
        154–5, 226
    consanguineous marriage 286
    obedience 104
    polygamy 286, 287
    sexual intercourse 276
Marrying Maiden see Gui Mei
Marshal, S. J. 53
Marxism 57, 376
Mawangdui manuscript 25, 44,
        46, 259
    Kun (Earth)/Chuan (River or
        Flow) 72
    Qian (Heaven)/Jian (latch pin)
        64, 72
meat 80, 116, 151, 225
medicine 133, 197, 358 see also
        health
    happiness 237
Meeting see Gou
meetings 316–17
memory 32, 47
Mencius 88
Meng (Neophytes) 83–4, 366,
        367, 387, 404
    commentary 84–6
Mengzi 35
menstruation 176
method of sixteen 390
military, the 96–7, 120–1 see also
        war
    divination 129
    engagement 209, 244
    expeditions 205, 236–7, 324
Minford, John 219–20, 410
Ming Yi (Calling Pheasant)
        211–12
    commentary 212–15

misfortune 166 see also fortune
misogyny 73, 141–2, 248, 374
mistakes 180 see also Da Guo;
        Xian Guo
mole crickets 209
money 275, 296–7
monotheism 362–5
Moog, Hanna 59, 410
moon, the 105
Moore, Steve 350
morality 166–7, 213, 342, 348,
        363–4
    development 370
mourning 81, 182, 189, 372 see
        also Lin
Mu Jiang, Lady 368–70, 387
Mun Kin Chok 409
music 96
mutilation 192, 223–4

necromancy 162
Needham, Joseph 23, 30, 53, 223
    science 350–1
    yin/yang 341
neighborhoods 114
Neophytes see Meng
    commentary 84–6
New Testament texts 397, 400–1
nobility 272, 342 see also rank
non-theism 365–6
nostalgia 18
nourishing life concept 347
numbers 89, 139, 162, 237, 301
numerological methods 391
Numerous Pitfalls see Xi Kan
Nylan, Michael 405–6

Obama, Barack 252
obligation 196
observation 374–5
Observing see Guan
Obstruction see Kun
    (Obstruction)

offerings 49, 72, 185 *see also*
    heng; sacrifice
omens 152, 174, 249, 338, 383
Ong, Walter 29–30, 32–3, 34
    dialogue 39, 367
    education 367
    logic 402
Opposition *see Kui*
optimism 81, 348
oracle bones *see* Chinese oracles
    bones
oral cultures 29–30, 32
orally transmitted material 10,
    28–35 *see also* dialogue
    charisma 33–4
    dialogue and rhetoric 39–41
    set phrases 176
Oreole *see Li*
orioles 117, 189 *see also Li*
oxen 167, 237

palaver 304
Pankenier, David W. 223, 293
    asterisms 68, 75
    dragons 75
Partridge, John 39
Patsco, Lorraine 350
peace 74, 112
pessimism 348
Pfister, Lauren 407
pheasants 212–15, 271
philology 9, 380, 393–4, 397–8
philosophy 12, 329–30, 344–50,
    353, 376–80, 383
    affection 368
    blame 372–3
    change 379–80
    character 373
    Chinese thought 337–8
    Confucianism 353, 365–6
    cosmology and religion 354–6
    dialogue 39–41, 366–7
    divination 19, 39, 41

ethics 359–62, 368–71
    government 375–9
    hexagram figures 342–4
    jawbones 356–8
    monotheism 362–5
    non-theism 365–6
    observation 374–5
    respect 371–2
    self-analysis 369
    self-cultivation 333–4
    Socrates 333
    spirituality 330–3
    sterility 358–9
    subjectivity of knowledge 336
    wisdom 333–5
    Zhouyi 336
phrases 9–10, 50–3, 57–8, 237
    oral set phrases 176
    yuan, heng, li, zhen 49, 64–6
phrenology 357
physical abnormality 222, 288
physics 356–7
physiognomy 245
    cheekbones 244–5
    jawbones 174–5, 177, 356–8
Piglet *see Dun*
piglets/pigs 199–201, 225, 249
pits 184
plastromancy 175
Plato 36, 39, 366, 379
    Republic 30
poisoning 140–1, 151
Pol Pot 219
politics 112, 205, 340, 355–6,
    408 *see also* government
polygamy 286
Porter, James L. 393
post-axialization 35
pottery 101, 236
Pound, Ezra 58
    Cantos 58
power 354
    laws and 363

pre-axiality 38
pregnancy 283
Preparation *see Yu*
prisoners 109, 185 *see also*
    captives
prognostication 31–2, 58
    optimism 81
Progress *see Jin*
proverbs 147
psychism 21–2
psychology 4–5
    divination 19–22
    qualitative time 339–40
psychotherapy 17
punctuation 51–2, 406
punishment 85–6, 150–1, 152,
    223–4
    education 367
Pursuing *see Sui*

Qian (Heaven) 48, 49, 63–4,
    360–1
    commentary 64–70
    Qian dragon sequence 67–70,
        360–1, 377
    yuan, heng, li, zhen phrase 49,
        64–6
Qian (Humble) 127–8
    commentary 128–9
Qinshi Huangdi 13
qualitative time 339–40, 344
quantum physics 356–7
Questions of King Milinda 39

rain 104
Ramayana 28
rams 204, 205–6, 249
randomness 20–1
rank 120, 128, 151, 181, 342 *see
    also* royalty; society
    belts 93
    hierarchy 355
    nobility 272, 342

sumptuary rules 289–90
reality 336
rebellion 266, 355
record keeping 300–1
relationships
    family 140, 141–2, 180–1,
        218–19, 289
    teacher/student 366–7
Releas *see Jie* (Release)
religion 37, 330, 354–6 *see also*
    Buddhism; Christianity;
    divination
    Confucianism 337
    Daoism 332, 336, 374
    gods 185, 362–5 *see also Di*
    monotheism 362–5
    non-theism 365–6
    saints 364
    scripture 349–50
    spirituality 12, 330–3, 380
remainders selection method
    390–1
reproduction 79–80, 140, 271
Republic (Plato) 30
respect 371–2
resurrection 396–7
Return *see Fu*
rhetoric 39–41
Ricci, Matteo 154
ridgepoles 180, 181
ritual 75, 383 *see also* mourning;
    sacrifice
    ancestors 316–17, 322
    dancing 301
    death 81, 189, 271
    food 270, 272
    funeral 275
    garments 259, 287, 289–90
    government 252
    impropriety 287–8, 372
    kneeling 300
    offerings 49
    position 355

royalty 263
splitting bodies 278–80
River Not Yet Crossed *see Wei Ji*
rodents 128
Romance of Three Kingdoms, The
356, 364, 378
royalty 101
borrowing 237
power 354
ritual 263
runes 46
Rutt, Richard 6, 7, 8, 192, 330–1,
408, 409
dating 24
Kun (Earth) 72, 74
line texts 50
Qian (Heaven) 66, 68
sexual references 276
spirituality 330–1
tags 44

sacrifice 49, 72, 88–9, 104,
252–4, 383 *see also* human
sacrifice
animal 166
beheading 190
blood 306
cost of 236
emotion 253–4
meat 116, 151
modern world 219
pits 184
self-sacrifice 181–2
suffering 125
victim suitability 146
wailing 245, 253
Yin Xu site 219, 279
Zhou, the 322
sagehood 344–5 *see also* wisdom
saints 364
science 18, 20, 223, 344, 346,
350–1, 356–8
divination 357–8

physiognomy 357
quantum physics 356–7
Scorpio 171
scripts 25–6
scripture 349–50, 397, 400–1
second-order thinking 37
selection methods 389–91
self-analysis 369
self-cultivation 333–4, 363
self-examination 147, 368–71
self-knowledge 374
self-sacrifice 181–2
Sensation *see Xian*
servants 201, 238
set phrases 29–30
sexual references 72, 75, 80, 124,
248, 249, 258 *see also Gu*
clouds/rain 104, 276
Shakyamuni Buddha 36
shamanism 267, 301, 346
shame 142, 196–7, 372–3
Shang dynasty 289
Shang oracle bones 27, 219
Shangdi 240–1 *see also Di*
Shanghai Museum bamboo
manuscript 25
Shangshu (*Book of Documents*)
188
Shao Tuo 146, 167
Shao Yong 11, 39, 391
Shaughnessy, Edward 6, 8, 409
asterisms 68
dating 24
sheep 245, 307
Sheng (Going Up) 255–6
commentary 256
Shi (Troops) 95
commentary 96–7
Shi ke (Biting and Chewing) 51,
149–50
commentary 150–2
Shijing (*Book of Songs*) 80, 140,
188, 189

birds 212
emotion 193
oral material 28, 57
Shuogua (*Explaining the
     Trigrams*) 342
Sickness from Sexual Excess *see Gu*
silk stuffing 322
Sima Quan 27, 224
six line configuration 46–7
skinning 304
slavery 96 *see also* captives
Small Livestock *see Xiao Chu*
Small Mistake *see Xian Guo*
Smith, Kidder 375
society 159, 181, 224, 342, 354
     see also feudal societies;
     rank
  classics, the 360
  leaders 214
  welfare 209
Socrates 36, 39, 89, 333, 367
Song (Dispute) 91–2
  commentary 92–3
spirituality 12, 330–3, 380
Splitting *see Gen*
Spring and Autumn Annals
     (*Chunqiu*) 27, 369
Spurting *see Huan*
squirrels 209
Stalin, Joseph 219
stars 293
sterility 283, 290, 358–9
Stoics, the 400
structure 43
Stumbling *see Jian* (Stumbling)
students 366–7
subjectivity 336
Sui (Pursuing) 135–6, 368–9
  commentary 136
suicide 176
Sumerian cuneiform text 15
sumptuary rules 289–90 *see also*
     rank

sun
  protection 292
  viewing 293
Sun (Decrease) 235–6
  commentary 236–8
supernatural, the 175, 224–5,
     345–6, 364
Swift, Jonathan 39
synchronicity 20

tags 44
Tai (Great) 111–12, 354
  commentary 112–14
Tai Xuan Jing (*Canon of Supreme
     Mystery*) 31
Tanning Leather *see Ge*
Tarot 46
Taylor, Charles 36–7
teachers 366–7
Teaching the I Ching (*Book of
     Changes*) (Hon Tze-ki) 362
Ten Wings 3, 10–11, 53, 57, 348
     see also *Dazhuan*
  axialization 35, 38
  philosophy 334
  Shuogua (*Explaining the
       Trigrams*) 342
Terzani, Tiziano 18
texts, the 47
textual corruption 10
textual criticism 397–401
textual theory 398
Theravada Buddhism 40
Thirty-six Stratagems 256
Thunder *see Zhen*
Tian 241
tiger change 267
tigers 108, 109
time 310 *see also* incipience
  qualitative time 339–40, 344
Time *see Jie* (Time)
Toltec I Ching 59
Tong Ren (Assembling) 119–20

commentary 120–1
toothache 395
tortoises 175
torture 150–1, 304
transcendence 36, 345
translations 4–6, 11–12, 53, 348–9
  ambiguity 402–5
  anachronisms 407
  analogy school 399, 400–2
  anomaly school 399, 400–2
  axiality 38
  Bengel's rule 400–1
  Field, Stephen 24–5
  grammar 51, 271, 297
  homophones 405
  Legge, James 49, 407
  New Testament texts 397
  optimism 393–7
  principles 405–8
  punctuation 51–2, 406
  textual criticism 397–401
  Wilhelm-Baynes translation see
    Wilhelm-Baynes translation
translators 408–10
travel 108–9, 113, 167, 240, 384
    see also Lu (The Traveler)
  anxiety 73, 79, 109
  foot 108–9, 154, 244
  military expeditions 205,
    236–7
Traveler, The see Lu (The
  Traveler)
Treading see Lu (Treading)
treasures of life 188
trigrams 23
Troops see Shi
Trusting Antiquity Movement 404
Tun (Gathering) 77–8
  commentary 78–81
turtles 175

unconscious, the 344
Unexpected see Wu wang

violence 89, 150–1, 158, 192,
    272 see also punishment;
    sacrifice
  decapitation 190, 219, 279
  executions 151, 190, 272
  mutilation 192, 223–4
  skinning 304
  torture 150–1, 304
virtues 65–6, 245, 360

wailing 190, 245, 253, 297–8
Wailing see Lin
Waiting see Xu
Waley, Arthur 7, 84, 166, 192
wanderers 296
Wang Bi 39, 73, 75, 343, 409
  misogyny 141–2, 374
war 74, 112, 383 see also
    military, the
Wasteland, The (Eliot, T. S.) 214
water 262–3
Way, the see Dao
wealth 104, 124, 151, 219, 259
weddings 79, 116, 154–5, 383 see
    also Gui Mei; marriage
  bride abductions 79, 81,
    154–5, 226
  royal 114
weeping 190
Wei Ji (River Not Yet Crossed)
    323–4, 376, 377–9
  commentary 324–6
Wei Tat 350
welfare 209
Well, The see Jing
wells 262–3
Wen, emperor of Han 151
Wen, king of Zhou 23, 34, 97,
    287, 325
Western Zhou Dynasty 6, 21,
    338, 365
Whincup, Greg 8, 408, 409
Wilhelm, Helmut 4

Wilhelm, Richard 4, 7–8, 154, 378–9, 408, 409
Wilhelm-Baynes translation 4–5, 7–8, 44, 53, 410
  dragons 67
  hexagrams 343
  Kun (Earth) 72
  Qian (Heaven) 67, 69, 70
  Tun (Gathering) 78
wisdom 333–5, 383 *see also* sagehood
Wittgenstein, Ludwig 18–19
women 116, 146–7, 218–19, 259, 383 *see also Gui Mei*
  bride abductions 79, 81, 154–5, 226
  character 86
  choices 192–3
  competition 289
  compliance 72–3
  concubines 159, 270–1, 289
  divination 218
  domestic activities 176, 218
  fertility 52, 79–80, 271, 283
  Fu Hao, wife of King Wu Ding 321, 405
  generals 96, 405
  marriage 79, 181
  menstruation 176
  misogyny 73, 141–2, 248, 374
  Mu Jiang, Lady 368–70
  pregnancy 283
  returning 282
  robustness 248
  sagehood 345
  shamanism 301
  widows 182
work-life balance 213
wounds 213
Wu, king of the Zhou dynasty 97, 349
Wu Ding, king of the Shang dynasty 321, 324

Wu Ding oracle bones 12, 321, 395
wu jiu (blame averted) 69
Wu wang (Unexpected) 165–6
  commentary 166–7

Xi Jinping 112
Xi Kan (Numerous Pitfalls) 183–4
  commentary 184–5
Xian (Sensation) 56, 191–2
  commentary 192–3
Xian Guo (Small Mistake) 315–16
  commentary 316–17
Xiangshu (Images and Numbers) school 343
Xiao Chu (Small Livestock) 52, 103
  commentary 104–5
xiao ren (petty person) 342
Xu (Waiting) 87–8, 343
  commentary 88–9
Xun (Kneeling) 299–300
  commentary 300–1
Xunzi 35, 39

yang 68
yarrow 100, 113
yarrow sorting 388, 389
Yates, Frances 32
yellow 189
Yi (Advantage) 35–6, 239–40, 362
  commentary 240–1
Yi (Lower Jaw) 173–4, 356
  commentary 174–7
yili (Meanings and Principles School) 343
Yin Xu (Anyang) site 219, 279, 321
yin/yang 75, 189–90, 312, 320, 340–1
  change 376–7

equality 361
hexagrams 361–2
Yip, Mingmei 82
Yu (Preparation) 131–2
Yu the Great 213
yuan 65, 66
yuan, heng, li, zhen phrase 49,
    64–6, 359–60
Yuan Me, tales of 175

zhen 65, 66, 100
Zhen 324–5
Zhen (Thunder) 273–4, 343
    commentary 274–6
Zhong Fu (Captives Within)
    311–12, 368
    commentary 312–13
Zhong Kui 364
Zhou, Duke of 23, 24–5, 34, 325,
    348–9
Zhou, King Wen of 23, 34, 97,
    287
Zhou Dynasty, the 322, 360
Zhou Xin, king of the Shang
    dynasty 252
Zhouyi 3, 6 *see also under
    individual hexagram
    names*
    authorship 55–6
    axialization 38
    change 376–8
    citation conventions 48–9
    compilation 55–7, 380
    composition 55–9
    dating 23–5, 176
    dialogue 40
    divination 57–8
    enchanted world of 338
    endings 326

hexagrams 10–11, 30–2, 33,
    43, 44–6, 100
judgements, the 48
life decisions 334, 347
line texts 50
meaning 50–3, 348–50
obscurity 9–11
omens 338
orally transmitted material 10,
    30–3, 34–5, 380
organization 27, 30–2, 205
philosophy *see* philosophy
phrases 9–10, 50–3, 57–8
qualitative time 339–40, 344
reading 11–13
scripts 25–6
set phrases 29–30
six line configuration 46–7
structure 9, 43–53
tags 44
texts, the 47
textual corruption 10
wisdom 334
yuan, heng, li, zhen phrase 49,
    64–6, 359–60
Zhu Xi 39, 113, 147, 346, 374,
    389
Zhuangzi 35, 57, 150
    death ritual 189
    subjectivity of knowledge 336
Zhuangzi 26
    social criticism 159
Zuozhuan 24, 26, 40–1, 342, 380
    ethics 65
    language 369
    Mu Jiang, Lady 368
    ritual 287
    sexual references 138
    women 218